THINKING WITH ROUSSEAU

Although indisputably one of the most important thinkers in the Western intellectual tradition, Rousseau's actual place within that tradition, and the legacy of his thought, remains hotly disputed. *Thinking with Rousseau* reconsiders his contribution to this tradition through a series of essays exploring the relationship between Rousseau and another "Great Thinker." Ranging from "Rousseau and Machiavelli" to "Rousseau and Schmitt," this volume focuses on the kind of intricate work that intellectuals do when they read each other and grapple with one another's ideas. This approach is very helpful to explain how old ideas are transformed and/or transmitted and new ones are generated. Rousseau himself was a master at appropriating the ideas of others, while simultaneously subverting them, and as the essays in this volume vividly demonstrate, the resulting ambivalences and paradoxes in his thought were creatively mined by others.

PROFESSOR HELENA ROSENBLATT serves as executive officer of the Ph. D. program at the Graduate Center, City University of New York. She specializes in European intellectual history and is the author or editor of a number of titles including *Liberal Values: Benjamin Constant and the Politics of Religion* (Cambridge, 2008), and *Rousseau and Geneva: From the First Discourse to the Social Contract, 1749–1762* (Cambridge, 1997).

PAUL SCHWEIGERT earned an MA in History from the Graduate Center, City University of New York. He works as a data scientist in New York.

THINKING WITH ROUSSEAU

From Machiavelli to Schmitt

EDITED BY

HELENA ROSENBLATT
AND PAUL SCHWEIGERT

CAMBRIDGE
UNIVERSITY PRESS

CAMBRIDGE
UNIVERSITY PRESS

University Printing House, Cambridge CB2 8BS, United Kingdom

One Liberty Plaza, 20th Floor, New York, NY 10006, USA

477 Williamstown Road, Port Melbourne, VIC 3207, Australia

314-321, 3rd Floor, Plot 3, Splendor Forum, Jasola District Centre, New Delhi - 110025, India

79 Anson Road, #06-04/06, Singapore 079906

Cambridge University Press is part of the University of Cambridge.

It furthers the University's mission by disseminating knowledge in the pursuit of education, learning and research at the highest international levels of excellence.

www.cambridge.org
Information on this title: www.cambridge.org/9781107513594
DOI: 10.1017/9781316226490

© Helena Rosenblatt and Paul Schweigert 2017

First published 2017
First paperback edition 2020

A catalogue record for this publication is available from the British Library

Library of Congress Cataloging in Publication data
NAMES: Rosenblatt, Helena, 1961– editor.
TITLE: Thinking with Rousseau : from Machiavelli to Schmitt / Helena Rosenblatt and Paul Schweigert (eds.).
DESCRIPTION: New York : Cambridge University Press, 2017.
IDENTIFIERS: LCCN 2016056475 | ISBN 9781107105768
SUBJECTS: LCSH: Rousseau, Jean-Jacques, 1712–1778. | Philosophy – History. | Hermeneutics.
CLASSIFICATION: LCC B2137 .T45 2017 | DDC 194–dc23
LC record available at https://lccn.loc.gov/2016056475

ISBN 978-1-107-10576-8 Hardback
ISBN 978-1-107-51359-4 Paperback

Contents

v

Figures

Abbreviations

CC   *Correspondance complète de Jean-Jacques Rousseau*, ed. R. Leigh (Geneva, 1965–1991)

CW   *The Collected Writings of Rousseau*, eds. R. Masters and C. Kelly (Hanover, 1990–2010)

G1   *The Discourses and Other Early Political Writings*, ed. V. Gourevitch (Cambridge: Cambridge University Press, 1997)

G2   *The Social Contract and Other Later Political Writings*, ed. V. Gourevitch (Cambridge: Cambridge University Press, 1997)

PL   *Oeuvres complètes de Jean-Jacques Rousseau*, eds. B. Gagnebin and M. Raymond (Paris, 1959–1995)

Contributors

DAVID BATES, Professor, Rhetoric, University of California, Berkeley

AURELIAN CRAIUTU, Professor, Political Science, Indiana University

PIERRE FORCE, Professor, French and History, Columbia University

JONATHAN ISRAEL, Professor Emeritus, School of Historical Studies, Institute for Advanced Study

ANTHONY LA VOPA, Professor Emeritus, History, North Carolina State University

JAMES MILLER, Professor, Politics and Liberal Studies, New School for Social Research

HELENA ROSENBLATT, Professor, History and French, The Graduate Center, CUNY

PAUL SCHWEIGERT, Graduate Student, History, The Graduate Center, CUNY

JERROLD SEIGEL, Professor Emeritus, History, New York University

SUSAN SHELL, Professor, Political Science, Boston College

DAVID SORKIN, Professor, History, Yale University

JOANNA STALNAKER, Associate Professor, French, Columbia University

BARBARA TAYLOR, Professor, Humanities, Queen Mary University of London

RICHARD TUCK, Professor, Government, Harvard University

RICHARD VELKLEY, Professor, Philosophy, Tulane University

K. STEVEN VINCENT, Professor, History, North Carolina State University

MAURIZIO VIROLI, Professor Emeritus, Politics, Princeton University; Professor, Government, University of Texas (Austin); Professor, Political Communication, University of Italian Switzerland (Lugano)

J. KENT WRIGHT, Associate Professor, History, Arizona State University

Acknowledgments

The editors would like to take this opportunity to express their gratitude for the generous support and funding provided by Ambassador François Barras of the Consulate General of Switzerland in New York, and also by President William Kelly of the Graduate Center, CUNY, which made possible the conference for which most of the essays in this volume were initially prepared. We would also like to acknowledge the assistance of Gregory Zucker, who helped us launch this project. Finally, we would like to thank the editorial team at Cambridge University Press.

Introduction

Helena Rosenblatt and Paul Schweigert

Although indisputably one of the most important thinkers in the Western intellectual tradition, Rousseau's actual *place* in that tradition, and the legacy of his thought, remain hotly disputed. Was he the inventor of a radical form of democracy or was he, in fact, the progenitor of totalitarianism? Was he an individualist or a collectivist, a conservative or an apostle of revolution? The arguments on these questions show no signs of abating. And yet to a certain extent the discussion often remains on the level of generalities, where Rousseau's thought is broadly compared to a particular intellectual tradition ("republicanism," "liberalism," "socialism," "feminism," etc.) or examined with reference to a contested concept ("liberty," "the social contract," "the general will" or "modernity," etc.), with little attention to his often intricate and multidimensional relationship to individual thinkers.

The tercentenary of Rousseau's birth and the 250th anniversary of two of Rousseau's most influential writings, the *Social Contract* and the *Emile*, provided the perfect occasion to reconsider Rousseau's contributions to the Western intellectual tradition. On November 2–3, 2012, a conference was held on this topic at the Graduate Center of the City University of New York. A distinguished group of scholars presented papers, each one exploring the relationship of Rousseau to another great thinker, from "Rousseau and Machiavelli" to "Rousseau and Schmitt." This approach, privileging dialogue, comparison, and reception through the pairing of individual thinkers proved most illuminating. In the end, we reasoned, it is the closest we can get to hearing an actual conversation between the great thinkers. And focusing on the kind of complicated *work* that intellectuals do when they read each other and grapple with each other's ideas is very helpful for explaining how old ideas are transformed and/or transmitted while new ones are created. Rousseau himself was a master at appropriating the ideas of others, while simultaneously subverting them, and as the papers in this volume show, the resulting ambivalences and paradoxes in his thought were creatively mined by others. Taken together, the essays suggest that the Western intellectual tradition – with Rousseau as a central figure – is better seen as a series of conversations than a fixed canon of ideas.

The volume begins with Maurizio Viroli's essay comparing Machiavelli's republicanism to Rousseau's. Viroli finds a number of similarities as well as significant differences. This is particularly the case when it comes to the two men's views on religion. On the basis of notations found on the original version of the *Social Contract* located in the Bibliothèque publique et universitaire de Genève, Viroli shows that Rousseau was thinking about Machiavelli's *Discourses on Livy* precisely when he was writing his chapter on civil religion for the *Social Contract*. And yet despite his great admiration for Machiavelli, Rousseau's view of the nature and role of religion differed significantly from that of his Florentine predecessor. Viroli's interpretation allows him to suggest that Machiavelli's religious views were similar to those of the American founding fathers, while those of Rousseau may have influenced the French Jacobins. Viroli nevertheless thinks that the two views on religion might usefully be "harmonized."

Another one of Rousseau's important interlocutor was Montaigne. While Montaigne's *Essays* (1580) have often been seen as an influence on Rousseau (especially on the *Confessions*), James Miller reminds us that Rousseau initially had quite an ambivalent opinion of Montaigne and criticized him strongly. As Miller argues, the *Essays* and the *Confessions* were based on radically different premises and had different goals. Montaigne aimed to present an unbiased picture of himself, and thus came to accept that he had certain weaknesses and failings as a human being, while Rousseau used the *Confessions* to justify his own conduct and present himself as proof that man is naturally good. Miller shows that as Rousseau became more pessimistic about the possibility of living a life of public virtue, he also became more appreciative of Montaigne.

Scholars have generally seen Rousseau as profoundly anti-Hobbesian, but in his contribution to this volume Richard Tuck shows the many striking ways in which Rousseau's view of human nature, the social contract, democracy and representation are similar to Hobbes'. Both Rousseau and Hobbes identified the fundamental problem of human interaction as its competitive and unstable character. Both advanced a similar political solution to this problem, conveying an important status to democracy, rejecting the "double contract" theory, and drawing impor-tant distinctions between government and sovereignty. Despite the fact that Rousseau portrayed himself as a critic of Hobbes, Tuck's chapter shows that the famous Genevan was in many ways Hobbes' disciple.

In the fourth essay of this volume, J. Kent Wright examines Rousseau's intellectual allegiance to Montesquieu. The *Spirit of the Laws* (1748) stands at the center of their relationship, and was the subject of Rousseau's initial foray into politics when he was secretary to the Dupin family and later serving as the starting point for many of his political writings. While some scholars have seen Montesquieu and Rousseau as antithetical thinkers, an emerging scholarly consensus, analytically summarized by Wright, holds that the latter should better be seen as a "critical disciple" of the former. Agreeing with this general perspective, Wright interprets both thinkers as key contributors to the Atlantic republican tradition.

Although Rousseau's impact on eighteenth-century Germany has been studied, the crucial role played by Moses Mendelssohn (1729–1786) in the transmission and translation of Rousseau's ideas has been neglected. In the fifth chapter of this volume, David Sorkin examines Mendelssohn's life-long dialogue with Rousseau. As Sorkin shows, Rousseau's writings fired Mendelssohn's imagination, but this does not mean that Mendelssohn appropriated Rousseau's ideas uncritically. Rather, Mendelssohn assimilated many of Rousseau's moral concerns (such as the problems of luxury and human sociability) while evading or entirely recasting others.

In chapter six, Pierre Force takes up and develops ideas from an article he published in 1997, and a book published in 2003, that argued that Rousseau was an essential interlocutor for Smith, and that Smith in fact appropriated key elements of Rousseau's philosophy. Force summarizes the state of the scholarship on the question when his own work appeared, as well as the objections his own claims generated, before responding to his critics. In particular, Force argues that Smith borrowed from Rousseau's analysis of identification for his discussions of sympathy in the *Theory of Moral Sentiments* and from Rousseau's depiction of the development of commerce and agriculture in the *Wealth of Nations*.

Rousseau also had an influence on A.L. Thomas and his friend, Madame Necker, both of whom were prominent members of the Enlightenment although they are relatively little-known today. Anthony LaVopa's essay shows that Rousseau provided a language with which they could express their ambivalent feelings toward civilized sociability. Thomas and Necker hated *mondanité* while they also practiced it. In Rousseau's texts they found a voice with which to express a "spiritualized cult of male-female friend-ship." The writings of Thomas and Necker show, moreover, that Rousseau's ideas were partially assimilated and partially rejected, particularly when it comes to his provocative and disturbing statements about the ideal woman. Thomas suggested that it was by withdrawing into the solitude of the domestic sphere that women could engage in the serious work of authorship.

In chapter eight, Jonathan Israel sees the philosophical dispute that arose between Rousseau and the Baron d'Holbach as having especially important consequences during the French Revolution. Despite being on friendly terms initially, Rousseau eventually fell out with Holbach's circle (which included his friend Diderot). For Israel, this was more than a clash of personalities – the philosophies of Rousseau and Holbach were fundamentally incompatible, even though they made use of many related (if disputed) concepts, such as the general will. In particular, what divided the two men in Israel's eyes was Rousseau's emphasis on "the ordinary," personified in the person of Rousseau's lifelong companion, Thérèse Lavasseur. The divide between Rousseau and Holbach on this issue, Israel contends, was at the root of the conflicts during the radical phase of the French Revolution between the Montagnards and the Brissotins. For Israel, the philosophy of "the ordinary," as adapted by Robespierre, provided the ideological backbone of the Terror.

Although scholarship has tended to see Diderot, the radical materialist, and Rousseau, the sentimentalist, as diametrical opposites, Joanna Stalnaker's essay argues that there was an intellectual rapprochement between them during the last years of their lives. Although they never formally reconciled (or even saw each other), Stalnaker finds that each man was preoccupied with the same question in his final work: the failure of *philosophie* to provide an adequate account of man. In the end, both Rousseau and Diderot rejected the common eighteenth-century materialist convention that knowledge of man came solely from outside of the self. Instead, they believed that some account of the interiority of man was also necessary. Diderot came to this realization through his analysis of Helvétius's materialism, critiquing the author of *De l'homme* for reducing humanity to a series of animal impulses. In contrast, Rousseau approached the question by combining the anthropological accounts of his early writings with the autobiographical writings of his last years.

In chapter ten of this volume, Susan Shell's and Richard Velkley's contribution examines Rousseau's influence on Immanuel Kant. That Kant was a great admirer of Rousseau is widely known, but when it comes to influence scholars have tended to focus on Kant's indebtedness to Rousseau's notion of the general will in the *Social Contract*. By contrast, Shell and Velkley examine Kant's crucial insight, no doubt acquired from reading Rousseau, that although human evil is self-inflicted, reason is also self-correcting. Kant also borrowed from Rousseau the idea that the proper education of male and female could lead to a full development of human faculties and to a moral transformation of the species, and that the key to this transformation is the relation between the sexes.

Chapter eleven turns to another influential reader of Rousseau, namely the English writer Mary Wollstonecraft. While many, including Wollstonecraft herself, have criticized Rousseau for his depiction of women in the fifth book of the *Emile*, Barbara Taylor argues that Wollstonecraft nonetheless saw herself in some ways as a disciple of Rousseau. In particular, Wollstonecraft found in Rousseau a fellow "Solitary Walker," one who in an age that emphasized sociability shunned society in favor of solitude.

In chapter twelve, Aurelian Craiutu highlights the continued dialogue between Rousseau and Germaine de Staël throughout the latter's writings, as she evolved from a youthful infatuation with Rousseau in her *Letters on Rousseau*, to a sophisticated critic of his in her mature political thought. Craiutu emphasizes two reasons for this shift in Staël's perspective – the misappropriations of Rousseau during the Terror that highlighted some of the shortcomings in his thought, and the growing influence on de Staël of her father, Jaques Necker, and the thinkers known as the Coppet Group. In tracing the evolution of Staël's engagement with Rousseau, Craiutu shows how the principle of political moderation emerged for Staël as a key corrective to the errors of Rousseau's theory of the social contract and modern democracy.

K. Steven Vincent's contribution focuses on the anarchist/socialist thinker Pierre-Joseph Proudhon's assessment of Rousseau's works. While Proudhon was a frequent commenter on Rousseau, Vincent argues that there were substantial differences between them, specifically in their views of human nature, in their discussions of property relations, and in their overall political programs. Despite these differences, however, Vincent sees the two united by a common desire to correct the ills of modern society, albeit in ways that, for both thinkers, tended to emphasize their limited embrace of the deliberative elements of republican politics.

Jerrold Seigel's essay compares Rousseau and Marx as "theorists of human fulfillment," based on the observation that both were philosophical thinkers with a deep ambivalence about philosophy. Neither was an enemy of reason, even if Rousseau sometimes suggested he was, but both sought to embed their hopes in nonrational elements of human nature. Paradoxically, however, each one's program for doing this failed in some significant way, so that in the end both were fated to heighten the role of rational reflection in fulfilling human potential at the very points where they sought a way to diminish it.

In the final essay for the volume, David Bates compares the notion of the political in Schmitt's and Rousseau's thought. Bates identifies a number of similarities as well as some important differences. Although Schmitt read Rousseau attentively, Bates argues that he ultimately rejected Rousseau's concept of sovereignty and his related notion of the political. While Schmitt located the political in the so-called enemy-friend distinction, Rousseau grounded his in a rule of law meant to protect the freedom and equality of individuals. Noting that since 9/11 Schmitt's views have attracted much favorable attention in academic circles, Bates suggests that we have at least as much to learn from Rousseau.

CHAPTER I

Rousseau and Machiavelli: Two Interpretations of Republicanism

Maurizio Viroli

Despite his endorsement of a fair number of Machiavelli's ideas, Jean-Jacques Rousseau launched republican political theory on a path substantially different from that designed by Machiavelli two centuries earlier. Rousseau felt admiration and sympathy for the man and the writer. Yet, his conception of life, his ideas on the political and social effects of religion, and his aesthetic sensibility had little in common with those of the Florentine Secretary. Machiavelli's republicanism is much wiser than Rousseau's; but Rousseau appreciates the value of inward life better than Machiavelli. A theoretical question that I wish to raise here is whether Machiavelli's and Rousseau's moral and political perspectives can be harmonized in a broader conception of republicanism that remains centered on political life and yet recognizes that human life does not exhaust itself in the public square, in the sovereign assembly or the government cabinet.

I

The first issue I wish to discuss is when and where Rousseau read the works of Machiavelli. Which editions did he consult? Existing scholarship that I know of does not provide an answer to these questions. We know from a letter to Mr. Doutens of March 26, 1767, that he owned the *Florentine Histories* and the *Discourses on Livy* and he regarded them as highly valuable.[1] On the basis of this trace, I have examined almost all separate editions of the two works. I have also considered the possibility

---

Unless otherwise noted, all translations are by the author.

[1] "Si vous payez trop cher mes livres, Monsieur, je mets le trop sur votre conscience, car pour moi je n'en peux mais. Il y en a encore ici quelques-uns qui reviennent à la masse, entr'autres l'excellente Historia fiorentina, de Machiavel, ses discours sur Tite-Live, & le traité de Legibus romanis de Sigonius. Je prierai M. Davenport de vous les faire passer." Rousseau à V. Dutens, March 26, 1767, CC XXXII, p. 249.

that Rousseau read Machiavelli in his boyhood, in Geneva. Copies of Machiavelli's works – in particular the edition called "La Testina" – have been found in the small libraries of neighbors of the Rousseaus.[2] But Rousseau's direct citations in Italian from the *Discourses on Livy* and the *Florentine Histories* are too different from all the texts that I have examined. So far, my research has been unsuccessful.

Rousseau's earliest direct reference to Machiavelli is to be found in the *Political Economy* (1755), where he alludes to *The Prince* as a satire against tyranny: "the maxims of tyranny are inscribed all through the archives of history and in Machiavelli's satires. The others [the maxims of popular states] are found only in the writings of philosophers who dare to demand the rights of humanity."[3] In the *Social Contract* Rousseau lists Machiavelli among the radical opponents of monarchy and writes a line that has had a tremendous intellectual impact on republican political thought and action: "this is what Samuel so strongly pointed out to the Hebrews; and what Machiavelli showed with clarity. While pretending to give lessons to Kings, he gave great ones to the people. Machiavelli's *The Prince* is the book of republicans."[4]

Rousseau's interpretation continues and reinforces a tradition that goes back to Alberico Gentili, an Italian jurist educated at Perugia who fled to England and, in 1587, was appointed Regius Professor of Civil Law at Oxford. In his *De Legationibus*, issued in 1585, he wrote an eloquent eulogy of Machiavelli whom he praises as the author of the golden (*aureas*) observations on Livy, and as a man of unique prudence and learning. Those who have written against him, Gentili claims, have not understood Machiavelli's ideas at all, and have indeed slandered him. The truth is that Machiavelli was

> a strong supporter and enthusiast for democracy. [He] was born, educated and received public honors in a Republic. He was extremely hostile to tyranny. Therefore he did not help the tyrant; his intention was not to instruct the tyrant, but by making all his secrets clear and openly displaying the degree of wretchedness to the people [. . .] he excelled all other men in wisdom and while appearing to instruct the prince he was actually educating the people.[5]

---

[2] See my *Jean-Jacques Rousseau and the "Well-Ordered Society"* (Cambridge: Cambridge University Press, 1988), p. 168.

[3] J.-J. Rousseau, *Political Economy*, CW III, p. 145. I am not convinced by M. and B. Cottret's claim that "Rousseau cite Machiavel et Hobbes par audace et par défi, avec ce sens inné de la provocation qui chez lui n'est jamais gratuit"; M. and B. Cottret, *Jean Jacques Rousseau en son temps* (Paris: Perri, 2005), p. 291.

[4] Rousseau, *Social Contract*, CW IV, p. 177.

[5] A. Gentili, *De Legationibus* (London, 1585), Bk. III, Ch. 9.

Almost a century later, Spinoza resumed the interpretation of Machiavelli as a champion of liberty in his *Tractatus Theologico-Politicus*, published anonymously in 1670, probably in Hamburg. The opinions of that "wise man," wrote Spinoza, "seem to me particularly attractive in view of the well-known fact that he was an advocate of freedom [*pro libertate fuisse constat*], and also gave some very sound advice for preserving it."[6] After Spinoza, the idea of Machiavelli as a misunderstood republican was authoritatively endorsed by Pierre Bayle's *Dictionnaire*,[7] and by Diderot in the *Encyclopédie*: "it was the fault of his contemporaries if they misunderstood what he was getting at: they took a satire for a eulogy."[8] With evident, though implicit, reference to Rousseau's statement in the *Social Contract* the Italian poet Ugo Foscolo sketched in his *Sepolcri* (1807) the powerful image of Machiavelli:

> the great one
> who toughening the scepter of the Prince,
> strips him of laurels to reveal a brow
> bedewed with tears and dripping gouts of blood.
> (vv. 154–158)

As Foscolo's verses show, Rousseau's words on *The Prince* opened the pathway to nineteenth-century interpretations of Machiavelli as a champion of political liberty and Italian emancipation from foreign domination.[9]

In addition to the intellectual roots and the impact of Rousseau's words, it must be noted that in the *Social Contract* Rousseau cites Machiavelli's *Prince* along with the Book of Samuel from the Old Testament that contains the famous passage against monarchical rule that was the guiding light of many seventeenth- and eighteenth-century republican political writers.[10] Rousseau not only redeems Machiavelli from the charge of being a mentor of tyrants but also elevates him to the rank of the Old Testament prophets that had portrayed the evils not only of tyranny but of monarchy itself. It must also be noted that here Rousseau does not call Machiavelli's *Prince* a satire, as he had done in *Political Economy*. Instead,

---

[6] B. Spinoza, *The Political Works*, ed. A. Wernham (Oxford: Clarendon Press, 1958), p. 313.

[7] P. Bayle, "Machiavelli," *Dictionnaire historique et critique*, 2nd ed., 3 vols. (Rotterdam, 1702), note "o."

[8] "Machiavelisme," *Encyclopédie* (Neuchatel, 1765), IX, p. 793.

[9] I have examined this theme in my *Redeeming the Prince: The Meaning of Machiavelli's Masterpiece* (Princeton: Princeton University Press, 2013). See the excellent work of Anne Lübbers, *Alfieri, Foscolo und Manzoni als leser Machiavellis: Die Bedeutung der Literatur für das Risorgimento* (Würzburg: Königshausen u. Neumann, 2014).

[10] See E. Nelson, *The Hebrew Republic: Jewish Sources and the Transformation of European Political Thought* (Cambridge, MA: Harvard University Press, 2010).

he praises the *Prince* as an example of indirect or disguised teaching: "while pretending to give lessons to Kings, he gave great ones to the people."[11]

By the time he composed the *Social Contract*, Rousseau had incorporated within his own language the core of Machiavelli's republicanism, beginning with the principle that the foundations of the republic are the rule of law and the common good. Machiavelli had stressed over and over again that the rule of law must be the basic feature of a proper civil and political life. In the *Discourses on Livy*, for instance, he contrasts political life (*vivere politico*) with tyranny and defines the latter as authority unbound by laws (*autorità assoluta*). When laws are powerless, Machiavelli remarked, it is a sure sign that the republic is corrupt.[12] By rule of law, Machiavelli always means the rule of just laws, that is laws and statutes that aim at the common good. It is the law understood in this sense which is the foundation of true civil life and of the liberty of the citizens. As an anonymous speaker of the *Florentine Histories* eloquently explains, to enjoy a "free and civil life [*vero vivere libero e civile*]," Florence needs new laws and statutes that protect the common good and must replace "the laws, the statutes, and the civil orders that have been ordered 'not in accordance with free life' but by the ambition of that party which is in power."[13] In the *Discourses on Livy*, he stresses that when the Roman Republic became corrupt, "only the powerful proposed laws, not for the common liberty, but to augment their own power."[14] Rousseau masterfully puts Machiavelli's theory in a nutshell: "I therefore call every State ruled by laws a Republic, whatever the form of administration may be; for then alone the public interest governs and the commonwealth really exists. Every legitimate Government is republican."[15]

Rousseau also endorses Machiavelli's argument that republican liberty cannot survive without civic virtue. For Machiavelli, the republic must count on virtuous citizens who are "wholly devoted to the common good [*amando solo il bene comune*]" and are "in no way affected by private

---

[11] CW IV, p. 177.

[12] See *Discorsi sopra la prima deca di Tito Livio*, I.17; I am quoting from *Opere di Niccolò Machiavelli*, ed. C. Vivanti (Turin: Einaudi, 1997), hereafter *Opere*; *Discourses on Livy*, trans. H. Mansfield and N. Tarcov (Chicago: Chicago University Press, 1996), p. 159; and *Discorsi*, I.18; *Discourses on Livy*, p. 1600.

[13] "Perchè le leggi, gli statuti, gli ordini civili non secondo il viver libero, ma secondo l'ambizione di quella parte che è rimasta superiore, si sono in quella sempre ordinati e ordinano"; *Istorie Fiorentine*, in *Opere*, cit., III.5; *Florentine Historys*, trans. L. Banfield and H. Mansfield (Princeton: Princeton University Press, 1988), p. 110.

[14] "Solo i potenti proponevano leggi, non per la comune libertà ma per la potenza loro"; *Discorsi sopra la prima deca di Tito Livio*, I.18; *Discourses on Livy*, p. 162 (revised).

[15] *Social Contract*, CW IV, p. 153.

ambition [*e non risguarda in alcuna parte all'ambizione privata*]."[16] In addition to the virtue of the magistrates, republics demand the virtue of the whole citizenry, if corruption and tyranny are to be successfully repealed. The virtue Machiavelli praises is always joined with respect for the laws, for the constitution and for the magistrates entrusted with public powers. As long as the Roman Republic was incorrupt (*incorrotta*), he writes, the Roman people honorably kept its own place, obeyed the consuls and the dictators, when the public safety so required (*per la salute pubblica*), and resisted against powerful citizens, when they were attempting to destroy public liberty. The same is true also for his favorite example of virtuous citizenry in modern times, that is the German free cities. Their civic virtue, he remarks, consists in the fact that they "observe their laws" and do not permit anyone to "usurp them," and that they dutifully discharge their civic obligations, beginning with paying taxes in proportion to their income as determined by the city's magistrates.[17] The civic virtue which Machiavelli extolls is a virtue of everyday life which translates into an orderly fulfillment of civic obligations and law abidingness as well as expressing itself as military valor. The republic is not the embodiment of virtue, nor is it instituted to affirm and enhance virtue. Its main purpose is the defense of liberty, but it surely is a civil order which needs virtue.

Rousseau summarizes Machiavelli's teaching in a single sentence: "the fatherland cannot subsist without freedom, nor freedom without virtue, nor virtue without citizens."[18] While Montesquieu had defined political virtue as the spirit of democracy, Rousseau stresses that it must be the principle of any well-constituted state thereby emancipating civic virtue from the exclusive connection with a form of government that he considers to be too perfect for men, above all for modern men. As is well known, by democracy Rousseau means the democracy of the ancients – that is, a form of government in which the citizens are both members of the sovereign body and rulers; they pass and execute the laws. Since the concentration of both powers in the same hands offers numerous opportunities for corruption, a democratic executive can remain uncorrupt only if the citizen possesses a truly inhuman degree of virtue. "Such a perfect government," Rousseau concludes, "is not suited to men."[19]

---

[16] *Discorsi sopra la prima deca di Tito Livio*, III.22; *Discourses on Livy*, p. 469.
[17] *Discorsi sopra la prima deca di Tito Livio*, I.55; *Discourses on Livy*, pp. 244–245.
[18] *Political Economy*, CW III, p. 154. See also P. Manent, *Naissance de la politique moderne: Machiavel / Hobbes / Rousseau* (Paris: Payot, 1977), p. 136.
[19] *Social Contract*, CW IV, p. 174.

Unlike Machiavelli, however, Rousseau repeats in various instances that modern citizens do not consider the political virtue of the ancients as an example to imitate. They are neither willing nor capable of cultivating the "liberty of the ancients." As he writes in the *Letters Written from the Mountain*, they are tradesmen and craftsmen concerned with their particular interest, their work, their profit; they cannot and do not want to devote most of their time to politics; they are reluctant to involve themselves in public affairs because they find their activity and their family life more interesting and rewarding than participation in government, and because they know that politics is often dangerous and prejudicial to private interests. They can be civilized, peaceful, industrious and law-abiding citizens; they know what their rights are and are prepared to discharge their duties toward their community; they possess, at least in the best cases, the appropriate qualities for civil life: modesty, decency and gravity; they love the laws of their country and respect civic equality because they know that the laws and civic equality are the foundation of their personal security and prosperity. Liberty is for them "a means for acquiring without obstacle and for possessing in safety."[20]

Having acknowledged that the virtue of the ancients cannot be expected from modern citizens, Rousseau also remarks, and on this point he reconnects with Machiavelli, that the lack of civic virtue inevitably brings about the loss of individual liberty. For modern citizens to serve the common good is onerous, but disregard of their civic duties brings about servitude: "those who cannot bear work have only to seek rest in servitude."[21] The cause of the loss of liberty is not just a reluctance to participate in the legislative process or in government, but the habit of remaining silent and passive before the abuses committed by the government or by powerful citizens. If the citizens do not speak up and resist when the government imposes unfair taxes, manipulates electoral procedures, violates property rights, or denies fair trial, they put at stake their personal and political liberty. As soon as an injustice is perpetrated – no matter against whom – they must raise their voice and react promptly. If they do not realize that the public interest is also their personal interest, and do not defend the common liberty when there is still time, they will not be able to stop tyranny from destroying the republic.[22] Tyranny affirms itself in an oblique manner. It does not attack the public good

---

[20] *Letters Written from the Mountain*, CW IX, p. 293.   [21] Ibid.
[22] "Persuade everyone that the public interest is not that of anyone, and by that alone servitude is established; for when each will be under the yoke, where will common liberty be?" *Letters Written from the Moutain*, CW IX, p. 303.

directly, but erodes and weakens the citizens' belief that the republic is a good that they possess and enjoy in common. Not to resist the attacks on common liberty that take place when the liberty of a single citizen is oppressed is as wise as the behavior of that man who refused to get up out of his bed while his home was on fire because he said, "I am only a tenant."[23]

II

When he discusses the moral and political conditions that are necessary to institute and preserve a republican order, however, Rousseau's views are different from Machiavelli's. He takes inspiration from Machiavelli's considerations, but then he proceeds in a new direction. The best example is his considerations on civil religion in the *Geneva Manuscript*. The original manuscript, to be found in the Bibliothèque de Genève, shows a number of remarks *au verso* that Rousseau intended to add to what he had written on the corresponding page *au recto* of the chapter titled "On the Legislator". The most important, for my purpose, are the additions *au verso* of the folios 46–51, where Rousseau stresses the necessity of religion. Rousseau's remarks show evident traces of close reflections on the *Discourses on Livy*, Book I.11, as Rousseau himself reveals when he writes, in the final version of the *Social Contract*: "It is this sublime reason, which rises above the grasp of common men, whose decisions the legislator places in the mouth of the immortals in order to win over by divine authority those who cannot be moved by human prudence"; and in the footnote he adds: "Nor in fact, says Machiavelli, was there ever a legislator who, in introducing extraordinary laws to a people, did not have recourse to God, for otherwise they would not be accepted, since many benefits of which a prudent man is aware, are not so evident to reason [*raggioni* (sic)] that he can convince others of them."[24]

One of the central issues of the very same chapter in the *Discourses on Livy* that Rousseau has taken as his principal source is the oath:

> [W]hoever reviews infinite actions, both of the people of Rome all together and of many Romans by themselves, writes Machiavelli, will see that the citizens feared to break an oath much more than the laws, like those who esteemed the power of God more than that of men, as is seen manifestly by the examples of Scipio and of Manlius Torquatus. For after the defeat that Hannibal had given to the Romans at Cannae, many citizens gathered

[23] *Lettre à d'Alembert*, ed. L. Brunel (Paris: Hachette, 1922), p. 65.
[24] *Social Contract*, CW IV, p. 157.

together and, terrified for their fatherland, agreed to abandon Italy and move to Sicily. Hearing this, Scipio went to meet them and with naked steel in hand constrained them to swear they would not abandon the fatherland.

In his narration Livy emphasizes the terror that Scipio struck into the hearts of those citizens who wanted to abandon the fatherland: "Terrified, as though they were beholding the victorious Hannibal, they all take the oath, and deliver themselves to Scipio to be kept in custody."[25] Machiavelli stresses the strength of the oath in the face of extreme peril, when laws, and the love of the fatherland, strong though that was among the Romans, were no longer enough to win out over fear and to preserve the determination to defend liberty, even at the cost of one's life: "So those citizens whom the love of fatherland and its laws did not keep in Italy were kept there by an oath that they were forced to take."

From these pages of the *Discourses*, Rousseau proceeds to assert the need of a civil religion. The chapter "De la religion civile" in the *Geneva Manuscript* begins in fact with a statement – "as soon as men live in society, they must have a Religion that keeps them there" – which repeats almost verbatim Machiavelli's words: "he [Numa] turned to religion as a thing altogether necessary if one wants to maintain a civil life [*al tutto necessaria a volere mantenere una civiltà*]." After this endorsement of Machiavelli's thesis, however, Rousseau belittles the role of the oath and stresses that the republic must live in the hearts of the citizens: "I don't believe that this chapter contradicts what I said before concerning the limited usefulness of the oath in the contract of society, for there is a great difference between remaining faithful to a State solely because one has sworn to do so, or because one considers its institutions to be divine and indestructible".[26]

For Machiavelli religion is highly valuable because it instills in the citizens the fear of God. "As the observance of the divine cult is the cause of the greatness of republics," we read in *Discourses on Livy* I.11, "so disdain for it is the cause of their ruin. For where the fear of God fails, it must be either that the kingdom comes to ruin or that it is sustained by the fear of a prince, which supplies the defects of religion." Also in the *Art of War*, in a passage in which he stresses that soldiers and captains must have a sense of shame, if one wants to rely on a good army, Machiavelli does not assert that sincere beliefs are necessary to have the sense of shame; he speaks only of the practices of reverence and adoration.[27] For Rousseau religion is

---

[25] *Discorsi sopra la prima deca di Tito Livio*, I. 11.   [26] *Geneva Manuscript*, CW IV, pp. 104–105.
[27] Machiavelli, *Arte della Guerra*, in *Opere*, I, p. 687; *Machiavelli: The Chief Works and Others*, ed. A. Gilbert (Durham: Duke University Press, 1989), II, p. 723.

valuable in so far as it gives citizens a moral strength based on sincere beliefs on the existence of God, on the afterlife, on the punishment of the wicked and the reward of the just: "it is no less useful to be able to give the moral tie an internal force that reaches into the soul and is always independent of goods, of misfortunes, of life itself, and of all human events."[28] Consistently with his belief Rousseau prescribes the death penalty for citizens whose conduct shows that they do not actually *believe* the dogmas they have publicly declared to accept: "If someone who has publicly acknowledged these same dogmas behaves as though he does not believe them, he should be punished with death. He has committed the greatest of crimes: he lied before the law."[29]

Roman religion, Machiavelli had stressed, served "to command armies, to animate the plebs, to keep men good, to bring shame to the wicked." Rousseau appreciated the last two virtues of religion, but he was unmoved by the first two and had no admiration for the ferocity of ancient armies animated by the fear of national gods. Pagan religion, he writes:

> is bad in that, being based on error and falsehood, it deceives men, makes them credulous, superstitious, and drowns the true cult of divinity in empty ceremonial. It is bad, too, whenever it becomes exclusive and tyrannical and makes a people bloodthirsty and intolerant to the point where it lives only for murder and massacre, and believes it performs a holy act when killing whoever does not accept its Gods. This places such a people in a natural state of war with all others, which is very harmful to its own security.[30]

Machiavelli regarded expansion as one of the signs of political greatness. Rousseau admired republics that were happy with a small territory. He was proud of being a citizen of Geneva, a free city with no desire for conquest and protected by a fortunate location from fear of being invaded by powerful neighbors.[31]

Rousseau diverges from Machiavelli also in his judgment on Christian religion. In the *Discourses on Livy*, II.2, Machiavelli had written: "our religion has glorified humble and contemplative more than active men. It has then placed the highest good in humility, abjectness, and contempt of things human." If "our religion asks that you have strength in yourself, it wishes you to be capable more of suffering than of doing something strong." Christian religion therefore bears a heavy burden of responsibility for having rendered "the world weak," suffocated in modern individuals the love of republican liberty, and, therefore "given it in prey to criminal

---

[28] *Geneva Manuscript*, CW IV, p. 104.   [29] *Social Contract*, CW IV, p. 223.   [30] Ibid. p. 220.
[31] *Discourse on Inequality*, CW III, p. 5.

men, who can manage it securely, seeing that the collectivity of men, so as
to go to paradise, think more of enduring their beatings than of avenging
them." In the chapter on civil religion, of the *Social Contract*, Rousseau
fully endorses Machiavelli's analysis: "so far from binding the hearts of the
citizens to the State," Christian religion "has the effect of taking them away
from all earthly things. I know of nothing more contrary to the social
spirit." Christianity, Rousseau concludes, "preaches only servitude and
dependence. Its spirit is so favorable to tyranny that it always profits by
such a regime. True Christians are made to be slaves, and they know it and
do not much mind: this short life counts far too little in their eyes."

But Machiavelli had also written that the corrupting effects of Christian
religion were the consequence of the wrong interpretation of its principles
by popes and priests:

> and although the world appears to be made effeminate and heaven dis-
> armed, it arises without doubt more from the cowardice of the men who
> have interpreted our religion according to idleness and not according to
> virtue. For if they considered how it permits us the exaltation and defense of
> the fatherland, they would see that it wishes us to love and honor it and to
> prepare ourselves to be such that we can defend it.[32]

Harsh as it is, Machiavelli's indictment against Christian religion does not
exclude at all the possibility of a reform capable of resuscitating its original
spirit in support of republican liberty. Rousseau does not distinguish
between Christianity interpreted according to idleness and Christianity
interpreted according to virtue. For him that religion is inherently and
irredeemably hostile to true civic ethos. As a result, he does not envisage the
possibility of a new interpretation that would make Christian religion
a pillar of a good republican order. Instead, he prescribes the institution
of a new religion – *la religion civile* – with its dogmas, rituals and sanctions
imposed by the state: "There is, therefore, a purely civil profession of faith,
the articles of which are for the Sovereign to establish, not exactly as
Religious dogmas, but as sentiments of sociability without which it is
impossible to be a good Citizen or a faithful subject."[33]

The intellectual and political consequences of Rousseau's divergence
from Machiavelli's assessment of the social and political consequences of
Christian religion have been momentous in the history of republican
political ideas and republican political experiences. With the decisive
help of Montesquieu's *Spirit of the Laws*, Machiavelli's ideas helped the

---

[32] *Discorsi sopra la prima deca di Tito Livio*, II. 2.   [33] *Social Contract*, CW IV, p. 222.

birth of American civic religion. Montesquieu had in fact written, with clear reference to Machiavelli (whom he calls a "great man"), that "most of the ancients lived under governments that had virtue for their principle," and their religion imposed no conflict between duties to the fatherland and duties toward the gods.[34] In contrast with the ideas of Pierre Bayle, who claimed that Christianity is not suited to preserve a republic because it takes into consideration only the afterlife, Montesquieu claimed that:

> [true Christians] being infinitely enlightened with respect to the various duties of life, and having the warmest zeal to fulfil them, must be perfectly sensible of the rights of natural defense. The more they believe themselves indebted to religion, the more they would think due to their country. The principles of Christianity, deeply engraved on the heart, would be infinitely more powerful than the false honor of monarchies, than the humane virtues of republics, or the servile fear of despotic states.[35]

What is in contrast with the republican spirit, Montesquieu concludes, in full agreement with Machiavelli, is the Catholic religion, not the Christian religion, even less so the Protestant religion.[36] Similar considerations, with their strong Machiavellian flavor, abound in the writings and sermons of America's founding years. American patriots' common belief was – as Machiavelli had written – that a good republic needs a religion that instills love of the common good and that Christianity is the religion most apt to encourage civic ethos, if properly interpreted. Rousseau's theory of the civil religion encouraged instead the short-lived, and soon forgotten, Jacobin religion of the Supreme Being.[37]

III

A theme on which Rousseau manifestly follows in Machiavelli's footsteps is the assessment of the social basis of the republic. The Segretario had written in the *Discourses* that citizens do not appreciate the "*vivere libero*" for the same reasons: "without doubt, if one considers the end of the nobles and of the ignoble, one will see great desire to dominate in the former, and in the latter only desire not to be dominated; and, in consequence, a greater

---

[34] Montesquieu, *De l'esprit des lois*, VI.5 and IV.4, in *Œuvres complètes*, ed. R. Caillois (Paris: Gallimard, 1951).

[35] Ibid., XXIV.6.

[36] Ibid., XXIV.5. See also the entry *Christianisme* in the *Encyclopédie ou Dictionnaire Raisonné des Sciences des Arts et de Métiers*, facsimile ed. 1751–1780 (Stuttgart-Bad Cannstatt: Frommann, 1966), III, pp. 384–386.

[37] M. Viroli, *Machiavelli's God* (Princeton: Princeton University Press, 2010), pp. 11–26.

will to live free, being less able to hope to usurp it than are the great."[38]
The lower classes feel secure when they see that no one, including the
prince and the magistrates, is allowed to violate the laws. Rich and powerful citizens, on the contrary are possessed by the desire to unceasingly
augment their riches and their power. As a result, they are prone to
conspire to corrupt the republic and to become its masters. The most
reliable defenders of the republic are therefore the ordinary citizens. In the
Letters Written from the Mountain, Rousseau takes a similar stance:

> The Citizen only wants the Laws and the observation of the Laws. Each
> private individual in the people knows well that, if there are exceptions, they
> will not be in his favor. Thus all fear the exceptions, and the one who fears
> exceptions loves the Law. Among the Leaders it is a completely different
> thing: their very station is a station of preference, and they seek preferences
> everywhere. If they want Laws, it is not in order to obey them, it is in order
> to be their arbiters.[39]

Another central aspect of republican political theory on which Rousseau
departs from Machiavelli is the assessment of the effects of social conflicts.
In Book II, Chapter 3 of the *Social Contract*, to support his view that "there
should be no partial societies in the state," Rousseau cites in approbation
a passage from the *Florentine Histories* in which Machiavelli asserts that
"some divisions are harmful to the republic while others are helpful."
Machiavelli had prescribed that all citizens must have the right to propose
a law in the sovereign assembly and he welcomed open and even vigorous
discussion. As an example he cites the Roman Republic, where "a tribune,
or any other citizen whatever, could propose a law to the people, on which
every citizen was able to speak, either in favor or against, before it was
decided." It is a good thing, he comments, that "each one who intended
a good for the public could propose it; and it is good that each can speak his
opinion on it so that the people can then choose the best after each one has
been heard."[40] Upon closer reading, however, one notices that Rousseau
repudiates Machiavelli's wisdom. In the *Social Contract* IV.2, he writes:
"the long debates, dissentions and tumults betoken the ascendance of
private interests and the decline of the state," and Rome, that was tumul-
tuous even during the most glorious phases of its history, is to be
considered an exception "more apparent than real." A wise legislator,
Rousseau maintains, should prevent the degeneration of inevitable social

[38] Machiavelli, *Discorsi sopra la prima deca di Tito Livio*, I.5; *Discourses on Livy*, p. 18.
[39] *Letters Written from the Mountain*, CW IX, p. 301.
[40] Machiavelli, *Discorsi sopra la prima deca di Tito Livio*, I. 18; *Discourses on Livy*, p. 50.

conflicts into a conflict of sects and ensure that none of the social groups can gain so much power to the point of obtaining a *de facto* control of the republic.[41]

As is well known, one of the central ideas of Machiavelli's political thought is that of the founder. In Rousseau's works this idea is missing. The only concept, or myth, that can be compared to the Machiavellian founder is that of the "Legislator." Machiavelli's *"prudente ordinatore"* attempts to establish a *"republica ordinate bene"*; Rousseau's legislator attempts to transform a multitude of men into a well-regulated society. They both aim at the common good and the liberty of their people. Both have in mind the wisdom of the architect who surveys and tests the soil before designing the building on the basis of a good knowledge of the mores of their peoples. However, unlike Machiavelli's founder, who must endeavor to have all the power in his hands (*debbe ingegnarsi di avere l'autorità solo*) Rousseau's legislator has no political power at all. He is neither part of the magistrature nor of the sovereign body. He does not approve laws nor does he see that they are properly executed. His institutional role remains indeed mysterious.[42] A possible reason of Rousseau's tenuous interest in the founder is that he entrusts the foundation of the republican order to the normative artifice of the contract, not to the extraordinary virtue of a man. The social contract dispels the founder. With this move, Rousseau attenuates the political value of republican theory to reinforce its normative content in a way that opened the path for Kant's idea of the social contract as a pure idea of reason. Machiavelli's primary concern was how to resurrect republican political orders and ethos; Rousseau's was to show that the republican constitution, as he understood it, was the best possible way to harmonize justice and interest. "In this inquiry," he writes on the first page of the *Social Contract*, "I shall endeavor always to unite what right sanctions with what is prescribed by interest in order that justice and utility may in no case be divided." He hopes to prove that individuals may be persuaded to accept

---

[41] *Social Contract*, CW IV, pp. 147–148.

[42] "The legislator is an extraordinary man in the State in all respects. If he should be so by his genius, he is no less so by his functions. It is not magistracy, it is not sovereignty. This function, which constitutes the republic, does not enter into its constitution. It is a particular and superior activity that has nothing in common with human dominion. For if one who commands men should not command laws, one who commands laws should also not command men. Otherwise his laws, ministers of his passions, would often only perpetuate his injustices, and he could never avoid having private views alter the sanctity of his work." *Social Contract*, CW IV, p. 155. See R. Derathé's notes in PL III, pp. 1461–1462 and B. Gagnebin, "Le rôle du Legislateur dans les conceptions politiques de Rousseau," *Études sur le "Contrat social"* (Paris: Les Belles Lettres, 1964), pp. 277–290.

a republican order on the basis of self-interest properly understood. But who should found the new political institutions, and how, were not his preoccupations.

In addition to the founder, another theme dear to Machiavelli was the redeemer. *The Prince* ends with an exhortation to a redeemer of Italy.[43] In the preface to Book II of the *Discourses on Livy*, Machiavelli express the hope that someone "more loved by heaven [*più amato dal cielo*]" may accomplish the hard task of emancipating modern times from political corruption. In the *Discourse on Remodeling the State of Florence*, he writes an eloquent invocation to a reformer of the political orders of Florence:

> No man is so much exalted by any act of his as are those men who have with laws and with institutions remodeled republics and kingdoms; these are, after those who have been gods, the first to be praised. And because there have been few who have had opportunity to do it, and very few those who have understood how to do it, small is the number who have done it. And so much has this glory been esteemed by men seeking for nothing other than glory that when unable to form a republic in reality, they have done it in writing, as Aristotle, Plato, and many others, who have wished to show the world that if they have not founded a free government, as did Solon and Lycurgus, they have failed not through their ignorance but through their impotence for putting it into practice.[44]

The *Art of War* (1521) ends with the evocation of new political leaders capable of offering the kind of political advice that would help to resuscitate Italy from its present condition of corruption and servitude.[45] In the *Florentine Histories*, he expresses his hope that in Florence, "by the good fortune of a city there rises in it a wise, good and powerful citizen by whom laws are ordered by which these humors of the nobles and the men of the people are quieted or restrained so that they cannot do evil, then the city can be called free and the state be judged stable and firm."[46]

In Rousseau's works, no discussion of the redeemer and redemptive politics is to be found. To see Machiavelli's myth of the redeemer emerge in modern political thought we have to wait for Hegel's *Verfassung Deutschlands*, around 1803, which contains a long citation from the last chapter of *The Prince* and ends with the invocation of one of a new Theseus, one of Machiavelli's heroes, to unite and emancipate Germany. A possible reason why Rousseau did not focus on the redeemer and on

---

[43] See my *Redeeming The Prince*.
[44] Machiavelli, "Discursus florentinarum rerum," in *Opere*, I, p. 744; *Machiavelli: The Chief Works*, trans. A. Gilbert (Durham: Duke University Press, 1965), I, p. 114.
[45] Machiavelli, *Dell'arte della guerra*, VII, 7.   [46] Machiavelli, *Istorie fiorentine*, IV, 1.

redeeming politics is that he believed that moral and political corruption had so deeply and so extensively pervaded the mores of peoples of his times as to make the resurrection of republican liberty utterly unthinkable. Machiavelli had written that "having come to freedom, a corrupt people can with the greatest difficulty maintain itself free"; and that is difficult or indeed impossible "maintaining a republic in corrupt cities or of creating it anew." Rousseau has an even bleaker view: "free peoples, remember this maxim: Freedom can be acquired, but it can never be recovered." A corrupt people, he writes "must have a master and not a liberator."[47]

A relevant implication of Rousseau's silence on the issue of how to found, preserve and reform a republican political order is the absence of a detailed investigation into the necessity of resorting to extraordinary means, yet another a Machiavellian theme par excellence. Whereas Machiavelli, in the *Prince* had stressed that for a prince "it is much safer to be feared than to be loved, when one of the two must be lacking,"[48] Rousseau notes that history shows that the sovereign who enjoys the greatest authority is the one who has learnt to make himself loved by his people:

> Even ambition is better served by duty than by usurpation: when the people are convinced that rulers are laboring only for its happiness, its deference saves them the trouble of laboring to strengthen their power: and history shows us, in a thousand cases, that the authority of one who is beloved over those whom he loves is a hundred times more absolute than all the tyranny of usurpers.

In the same text he remarks that "We find in history a thousand examples of pusillanimous or ambitious rulers, who were ruined by their slackness or their pride; not one who suffered for having been strictly just."[49] Instead of following Machiavelli, Rousseau espouses the classical Ciceronian view:

> And we recently discovered, if it was not known before, that no amount of power can withstand the hatred of the many. The death of this tyrant [Julius Caesar] whose yoke the state endured under the constraint of armed force and whom it still obeys more humbly than ever, though he is dead, illustrate the deadly effects of popular hatred; and the same lesson is taught by the similar fate of all other despots, of whom practically no one has ever escaped

---

[47] *Social Contract*, CW IV, p. 158.
[48] Machiavelli, *Il Principe*, in *Opere*, I., p. 163; Machiavelli, *The Prince*, trans. P. Bondanella (Oxford: Oxford University Press, 2005), p. 58.
[49] *Political Economy*, CW III, p. 150.

such death. For fear is but a poor safeguard of lasting power; while affection, on the other hand, may be trusted to keep it safe for ever.[50]

Rousseau regards political action as either a corrupt and corrupting activity, or, in an ideal well-ordered society, as a blameless practice. Machiavelli's admonition that a good man who wants to found, or redeem or reform a political order must be prepared to enter into evil is not part of Rousseau's political theory.

IV

While he was revising Machiavelli's republican theory, Rousseau put on paper a strong eulogy of Niccolò Machiavelli:

> Machiavelli was a decent man and a good citizen; but being attached to the Medici household, he was forced, during the oppression of his fatherland, to disguise his love of freedom. The choice of his execrable Hero is in itself enough to make manifest his hidden invention; and the contrast between the maxims of his Book *The Prince* and those of his *Discourses on Titus Livy* and of his *History of Florence* shows that this profound political thinker has had only superficial or corrupt Readers until now. The Court of Rome has severely forbidden his book. I can well believe it; it is the court that he most clearly depicts.[51]

The text is a fragment that comes from a manuscript preserved in the Bibliothèque Universitaire et Publique de Neuchâtel. I have examined it and I think that Rousseau wrote it between December 1766 and January 1767. Two considerations induce me to this conclusion. The first is the position of the folio that contains the note between a letter to Lord Nuncham of December 24, 1766 and the draft of a letter of January 1767. The second consideration is the strong anti-Voltaire content of that note. The preface to the *Anti-Machiavelli* published under the name of Frederik II King of Prussia, but written in fact by Voltaire, contains a very harsh assault against Machiavelli.[52] In 1766, in London, Voltaire had published a violent

---

[50] Cicero, *De Officiis*, II., 23–24.
[51] I am referring to the note that was added to the 1782 edition of the *Contrat social*: CW IV, p. 177. Rousseau distinguished "Machiavelism" and Machiavelli's true teaching. In a letter to Lenieps dated December 4, 1758, he wrote with regard to Frederik II: "I am unable to esteem or have any sympathy for a man without principles, who tramples underfoot all the human rights, who does not believe in virtue, but sees it as a delusion fit only for fools and who begins his Machiavelism by refuting Machiavelli." PL I, p. 1567, n4.
[52] "I venture to undertake the Defence of Humanity against this Monster, who would destroy it, to oppose Reason and Justice to criminal Sophistry, and publish my Remarks on Machiavel's Prince, Chapter by Chapter, that the Antidote may be found immediately after the Poison"; Friedrick II,

attack against Rousseau.[53] By calling Machiavelli an honest man and a good citizen, Rousseau was explicitly confuting Voltaire's assertions and expressing his admirations, sympathy and affection for the man, not just for the writer.[54] He was praising Machiavelli for what he was and what he did, at least for what he believed Machiavelli was and did.

Rousseau recognized Machiavelli as a man who had beliefs and a life very similar to his own. Like Machiavelli, Rousseau came from a popular social milieu and was a republican hostile to tyrants and monarchs. The most relevant common intellectual and moral ground between Machiavelli and Rousseau was, however, patriotism. For the Florentine Segretario, love of country was love of the common good of the citizens which translates into acts of service and care for the republic, a passion which makes the individual's soul generous and strong. As such, it gives ordinary citizens the motivation to discharge everyday duties, and resist tyranny and corruption. It inspires the magistrates' and rulers' commitment to justice; sustains legislators' wisdom; gives redeemers and saviors the strength to restore liberty. For Machiavelli "common good" (*bene commune*) and "common fatherland" (*comune patria*) are equivalent expressions, opposed to "oneself" (*sè*) and "one's own lineage" (*la propria successione*) respectively.[55] Machiavelli not only endorses the conventional republican understanding of love of country as the passion which drives citizens to put the common good before personal and particular interests, but follows Roman political theorists in describing the conduct of those who labor to serve their country as the proper conduct of the *vir virtutis*. The deeds of kings, captains and lawgivers who have labored for their country (*per la patria loro affaticati*), he writes at the very outset of the *Discourses on Livy*, are "most virtuous" (*virtuosissime*).[56] He also equates fatherland (*patria*) with republic as opposed to principality and tyranny. In the *Discourses on Livy*, for instance, he distinguishes between conspiracies "against the fatherland"

King of Prussia, "Introduction," *Anti-Machiavel: or, an examination of Machiavel's Prince. With notes historical and political. Published by Mr. de Voltaire. Translated from the French* (London, 1741), p. vii.
[53] *Le docteur pansophe, ou lettre de Monsieur de Monsieur de Voltaire* (London, 1766).
[54] An honest man and a good citizen is exactly the kind of praise that Rousseau would have loved to receive from his fellow citizens: "Que si la Providence y avoit ajouté de plus une situation charmante, un climat tempéré, un pays fertile, & l'aspect le plus délicieux qui soit sous le Ciel, je n'aurois désiré, pour combler mon bonheur, que de jouir de tous ces biens dans le sein de cette heureuse Patrie, vivant paisiblement dans une douce société avec mes Concitoyens, exerçant envers eux & à leur exemple, l'humanité, l'amitié & toutes les vertus, & laissant après moi l'honorable mémoire d'un homme de bien & d'un honnête & vertueux Patriote."
[55] *Discorsi sopra la prima deca di Tito Livio*, I. 9.   [56] Ibid., Proem to Book I.

(*contro alla patria*) and conspiracies "against a prince" (*contro ad uno principe*).[57] As he clarifies toward the end of the chapter, to conspire against the fatherland does in fact mean to conspire against a republic in order to become prince or tyrant.

In all the examples he takes from Roman history, Machiavelli emphasizes that patriotism is a passion that makes them wise and virtuous. Because they can see beyond the boundaries of their family or of their social group, they act in the way that is most apt to secure their own and the republic's interest.[58] The title of Book III, Chapter 46 of the *Discourses on Livy* reads: "That a Good Citizen out of Love of his Country [*per amore della patria*] ought to ignore Personal Affronts." In his comment, Machiavelli remarks that Fabio Massimo Rulliano accepted the Senate's appeal to appoint as dictator a man who had offended him "moved by compassionate love of country" (*mosso da carità della patria*), even though he made it clear, by his silence and in other ways, that the nomination was for him very painful.[59] Machiavelli lived his life by these principles. In 1521, when he was in Carpi to discharge a quite inglorious mission on behalf of the Wool Guild of Florence, he had no hesitation to flatly explain to Francesco Guicciardini, at the time governor of the papal states of Modena and Reggio, that he took very seriously his duty, even if it was quite humbling for a man like him: "because never did I disappoint that republic whenever I was able to help her out – if not with deeds, then with words; if not with words, then with signs – I have no intention of disappointing her now."[60] In Machiavelli's case, these were not just mere proclamations. His life proves that love of country

[57] Ibid., III.6.
[58] Machiavelli eloquently describes these effects of patriotism in *Discorsi* III.8, where he comments upon Livy's account of the story of Manlius Capitolinus, who was sentenced to death by the Roman people because he caused tumults against the Senate and the laws of the fatherland (*leggi patrie*). What persuaded the Roman people to pass the severe verdict against a popular citizen was love of country: "with all of them love of country [*lo amore della patria*] weighted more than any other consideration."
[59] *Discorsi sopra la prima deca di Tito Livio*, III, 47.
[60] Machiavelli to F. Guicciardini, May 17, 1521, *Opere*, II, p. 372; *Machiavelli and His Friends: Their Personal Correspondence*, trans. J. Atkinson and D. Sices (Dekalb: Northern Illinois University Press, 1996), p. 336. Machiavelli expresses his love of the fatherland also in the opening of his *A Dialogue on Language* (*Discorso o dialogo intorno alla nostra lingua*), *Opere*, III, p. 261: "Whenever I have had an opportunity of honoring my country, even if this involved me in trouble and danger, I have done it willingly, for a man is under no greater obligation than to his country; he owes his very existence, and later, all the benefits that nature, and fortune offer him, to her. And the nobler one's country, the greater one's obligation. In fact he who shows himself by thought and deed an enemy of his country deserves the name of parricide, even if he has a legitimate grievance." *The Literary Works of Machiavelli: With Selections from the Private Correspondence*, trans. J. Hale (London: Oxford University Press, 1961), p. 175.

was for him a strong and lasting passion. He proudly proclaimed that his poverty was the evidence that when he was the Segretario, from 1498 to 1512, he served his fatherland with impeccable devotion, faith and honesty.[61] Even if Florence had been ungrateful and unjust to him, he never considered leaving it, not even when he was offered an excellent opportunity, in 1521, to move to Ragusa to be again at the service of the former Gonfalonier of the Republic, Pier Soderini.[62] He chose to stay in Florence even if all that his fatherland was offering him were very meager honors and poor jobs.[63]

Rousseau too eloquently proclaimed his patriotism. In the "Dedicatory Letter" in the *Discourse on Inequality* (1755), he had solemnly reaffirmed his attachment to the Republic of Geneva. He was already a *bourgeois* of Geneva by birth; he wanted to be it by choice. He had left his native city when he was a young boy. Geneva had also forced his father to leave; the laws of the Republic prevented Jean-Jacques from going back. Yet, he declares that he would choose Geneva as his *patria* and stresses that he loves Geneva because it is a good republic, at least in his imagination. I would love, he states, to live in a republic where "the sweet habit of seeing and knowing one another turned love of the Fatherland into love of the Citizens rather than love of the soil" and where the sovereign and the citizens "could have only one and the same interest" so that sovereign deliberations tend to promote the common happiness.[64] He loves Geneva, he asserts, because it is a republic in which the rule of law protects each citizens' liberty; "a happy and tranquil Republic, whose antiquity was in a way lost in the darkness of time, which had experienced only those attacks suited to display and strengthen courage and love of Fatherland"; a republic whose citizens "long accustomed to wise independence, were not only free but worthy of being so."[65] *Patrie* means for Rousseau a peaceful community in which one can live in "sweet society" with his fellow citizens, exhibiting toward them humanity and friendship, where one can hope to be remembered as "a good man and a decent and virtuous Patriot."[66]

Like Machiavelli's, Rousseau's patriotism is primarily a political love; a love that stems from gratitude for the liberty and the welfare that good government assures to all the citizens. To command the love of its citizens,

---

[61] Machiavelli to F. Vettori, December 10, 1513, *Opere*, II, p. 297.
[62] P. Soderini to Machiavelli, April 13, 1521, *Opere*, II, pp. 369–370.
[63] See Machiavelli's portrait of Francesco Valori as a citizen dedicated to the good of his fatherland in *Opere*, III, pp. 255–256.
[64] *Discourse on Inequality*, CW III, pp. 3–4.   [65] Ibid., p. 5.   [66] Ibid., p. 6.

Rousseau stresses, the *patrie* must love all and each of them equally. Her love too is political and expresses itself through a caring protection of the liberty and political rights of all citizens. By protecting their liberty the *patrie* makes the citizens feel secure; by recognizing their political rights, it makes them perceive their country as something that belongs to them: "Let the fatherland, then, be the common mother of the citizens; let the advantages they enjoy in their country endear it to them; let the government leave a large enough share of the public administration to them so that they feel at home; and let the laws be in their sight only guarantees of the common freedom."[67]

Rousseau, unlike Machiavelli, spent most of his life away from his fatherland Geneva, and, in 1764, he gave up his citizenship. As we learn from the letter he addressed on March 1, 1764, to Lieutenant Charles Pictet, what prompted his decision were the persecutions he suffered from Geneva's government. It was, he wrote, a painful decision, a definitive break. He was aware that, as a consequence of his decision, he would not have been able to see his fatherland again. Yet, he says that his pain is mild: he feels no love, no devotion, no attachment for his fatherland. Disillusion leaves no anger or resentment, just indifference and detachment. Geneva was still there, with its people, its history, its language, its institutions and laws. But it was no longer a free republic. Even if everything else was still in place, the corruption of the political relationship between the state and the citizen was sufficient to extinguish in Rousseau's heart his love for the *patrie*.[68] His choice, he says in the same letter, was the outcome of disillusion: after what she did to him, he could no longer continue to believe that he too had a *patrie* and that his *patrie* was the Republic of Geneva.

For Machiavelli, as we have seen, a good citizen must stay, forget ingratitude and offenses and continue to serve the common good as much as it is in his powers to do. In a letter written a few weeks before he died, he confessed to his friend Francesco Vettori "I love my country, more than my soul" and dedicated his last days to the cause of the emancipation of Italy. Rousseau, who had composed the most vibrant pages on the beauty of love of the fatherland, ended his life yearning for the heavenly fatherland, the "patrie des âmes justes," where the malignity of

---

[67] *Political Economy*, CW III, pp. 153–154.
[68] "Ce ne sont pas les murs, ni les hommes qui font la patrie, ce sont les lois, les moeurs, les coutumes, le gouvernement, la constitution, la manière d'être qui resulte de tout cela. La patrie est dans les rélations de l'état à ses membres; quand ces rélations changent ou s'aneantissent, la patrie s'évanouit," Rousseau to C. Pictet, CC XIX, p. 190.

human beings cannot enter.[69] Both Machiavelli and Rousseau regarded love of country as primarily a political love based on loyalty to the republican constitution and the republican way of life. But for Rousseau political life was not the whole life, not even the most important part of it. In the famous letter to Francesco Vettori of December 10, 1513, Machiavelli wrote that the true nourishment for his soul (*il cibo che solum è mio ed io nacqui per lui*) was politics, the grand politics of founders and redeemers. When he was meditating on political matters in the ideal company of the great men of antiquity who had become, through their virtue, immortal, he did find inward serenity. In their company, entirely transferred in them, Machiavelli was immune from life's anxieties, even from the fear of death. He was truly himself. No other life was for him more appealing.

Rousseau, in particular in his late autobiographical works, tells us that the proper and never-ending nourishment of his life, the only one that gave him a complete and perfect happiness was solitary meditation and introspection:

> Alone for the rest of my life – since I find consolation, hope, and peace only in myself – I no longer ought nor want to concern myself with anything but me. It is in this state that I again take up the sequel to the severe and sincere examination I formerly called my *Confessions*. I consecrate my last days to studying myself and to preparing in advance the account I will give of myself before long. Let me give myself up entirely to the sweetness of conversing with my soul, since that is the only thing men cannot take away from me.[70]

Completely detached from life, from all human beings, great men of antiquity included, Rousseau listens to the celestial voice of conscience, contemplates the natural order that reveals God's goodness and wisdom, enjoys the pleasure of pure existence, and thereby attains the inner calm that anticipates the peace of the afterlife.

For Machiavelli the greatest evils were tyranny and corruption; for Rousseau the greatest evil was society itself. All society was for him "a form of enslavement," as the late Judith Shklar wrote in her excellent *Men and Citizens*.[71] An enslavement to the tyranny of opinion, to the "fureur de se distinguer," to the immoderate search for honors and superiority that destroy human authenticity. Machiavelli never felt more authentic than when he was serving the republic or thinking and writing about politics.

---

[69] Rousseau to M. Moultou, August 1, 1763, CC XVII, p. 114.

[70] Rousseau, *Reveries*, CW VIII, p. 6.

[71] J. Shklar, *Men and Citizens: A Study of Rousseau's Social Theory* (Cambridge, MA: Harvard University Press, 1969).

When Machiavelli and Rousseau describe human beings' social and political behavior, their judgments are almost identical. However, Rousseau composed hundreds of pages to investigate and disclose his own heart and soul. Machiavelli very rarely, and reluctantly, examined and revealed his inner self; the idea of writing his *Confessions* never crossed his mind. As a true Florentine, he preferred to disguise his thoughts and feelings, or to cover them with jokes, gags, funny stories like the famous dream with which, we are told, he abandoned life.[72] With his praise of inward life as the only way to true happiness, Rousseau parts company with the intellectual trend that Civic Humanism had initiated in fourteenth-century Italy, of which Machiavelli was one of the most eminent champions.

Can Machiavelli's and Rousseau's perspectives be harmonized within a republican theory that centers on public life and yet recognizes the value of inner life, or, even better, that designs the former having in view above all the latter? I doubt it, but I believe that the attempt should be made. We need political life; but we also need to appreciate staying by ourselves and indulging in self-examination and introspection. A solitary or detached life must not be seen only as a refuge from the republic's corruption. It should be a permanent dimension of life to be cultivated in silence, if we want a truly humane polity.

---

[72] See the splendid pages of R. Ridolfi, *Vita di Niccolò Machiavelli* (Rome: A. Belardetti, 1954), Prefazione; Ridolfi, *The Life of Niccolò Machiavelli*, trans. C. Grayson (London: Routledge and Kegan Paul, 1963). On Machiavelli's dream see, G. Sasso, "Il celebrato sogno di Machiavelli," in *Machiavelli e gli antichi e altri saggi* (Milan: R. Ricciardi, 1988), III, pp. 211–300.

CHAPTER 2

Rousseau and Montaigne: From Enthusiasm to Equanimity

James Miller

It is well known that Rousseau "fleshes out and develops suggestions that Montaigne scatters throughout his *Essays*."[1] One thinks, for example, of the pictures of the noble savage in both authors; the attacks on pedantry; even the peculiarly rapturous autobiographical accounts of becoming unconscious (by falling off a horse, in Montaigne's case; by being bowled over by a big dog, in the incident evoked by Rousseau). So extensive are Rousseau's detailed debts to the *Essays* that in 1766, a critic published a pamphlet, *The Plagiarisms of J. J. Rousseau of Geneva*, which contained an entire chapter itemizing various ideas supposedly "stolen" from Montaigne.[2]

The broad similarities are, if anything, even more striking. Both men made an earnest effort to answer to the Delphic injunction "Know Thyself." Both approached philosophy as a way of life, and not just a set of propositions and theories.

Yet Rousseau notoriously criticized Montaigne when he came to write his *Confessions*, putting him "at the head of these falsely sincere people who want to deceive by speaking truthfully."[3]

Why was Rousseau so ambivalent about Montaigne?

With this question in mind, it will be good to recall, briefly, some of the contrasting conclusions that each man provisionally reached in the course of his philosophical quest.

***

For Montaigne, the search for wisdom had begun in a classically Stoic manner. A landed aristocrat who had served for several years as a counselor

---

[1] J. Starobinski, *Montaigne in Motion*, trans. A. Goldhammer (Chicago: University of Chicago Press, 1985), p. 251.

[2] J.-J. (Dom) Cajot, *Les Plagiats de M. J.J. R. de Genève sur l'éducation* (La Haye, 1766).

[3] Rousseau, original draft introduction to the *Confessions*, PL I, p. 1149. In general, see E. Silber, "Rousseau and Montaigne: The Evolution of a Literary Relationship" (PhD Dissertation: Columbia University, 1968).

to the Parliament at Bordeaux, Montaigne subsequently went into retirement at his family estate, where he was free to ponder perennial questions about human nature and to work on improving his character through study and introspection.

To this end, Montaigne in his reading and writing ranged widely, consulting contemporary historical chronicles, classical poetry, edifying ancient biographies (those of Plutarch above all), philosophical and theological treatises, even (to an unusual extent) his own personal experience, in order to weigh, and sometimes revise, his core beliefs. In his written record of this solitary quest, Montaigne asserts his candor, but he writes in an indirect, allusive, and often guarded style that is marked by contradictory assertions, non sequiturs, and paradoxical lines of apparent argument. Reading his *Essays*, it is hard, really, to know just what Montaigne actually believes. That makes his book quite different from, say, the *Moral Letters* of Seneca, in some ways a comparable work that Montaigne, like Rousseau, knew and admired.

Montaigne's *Essays* also differ sharply from the *Confessions* of Augustine, which provided Rousseau with a model for his own, much more immodest book of the same title. Unlike Augustine, or Rousseau in his *Confessions*, Montaigne makes no attempt to recollect the events of his life in sequence, or to create out of them a coherent narrative. He recounts no providential epiphanies. Instead, when he episodically, and rather erratically, focuses on himself, Montaigne's tone is generally wry.

In effect, he shows readers an author who is trying, and genially failing, to emulate either the stoic austerities of Seneca or the ascetic purity of Augustine, and who decides instead to describe himself as he really is. His deflationary self-portrait allows him to step outside the tradition of moral perfectionism that had linked the philosophical ideals of Socrates and Plato to those articulated by Seneca and Augustine. Implicitly rejecting the ideal of rational integrity exemplified by the character of Socrates – traditionally regarded as a paragon of perfect consistency in his beliefs and behavior – Montaigne suggests that the "fairest souls" are in fact inconstant, even inconsistent: that is, supple, flexible, and prepared to negotiate changing circumstances.[4]

He holds the changeability of human beliefs and behavior to be sometimes a blessing and not invariably a curse. He worried that an endless

---

[4] Michel de Montaigne, *Les Essais*, ed. P. Villey and V.-L. Saulnier, 3 vols. (Paris: Presses universitaires de France, 1965), III, p. 818.

quest for moral perfection, coupled with unyielding conviction in one's own righteousness, was a recipe for potentially murderous fanaticism. He thought it possible to "love virtue too much."[5] He took seriously one of Saint Paul's maxims: "Be not wiser than you should, but be soberly wise."[6] He understood that stubbornly aiming for a life of perfect virtue was potentially a recipe for constant guilt, and he was fortunate to have found for himself, in part through his introspective essays, an equable temperament, which enabled him to behold his failings and the follies of others with an enviable equanimity.

***

As everyone knows, equanimity was not Rousseau's strong suit. Unlike Montaigne, Rousseau wrote his major works in bursts of enthusiasm, provoked by an unwavering conviction, forged in a moment of vision, "that man is naturally good," and that it is society that makes men bad.[7] In his *Discourses*, Rousseau addressed readers as a visionary, a prophet, and a scourge, with passion, and with a monumental self-confidence that critics found self-righteous. Humility wasn't his style.

Whereas Montaigne shied away from offering himself as a model, Rousseau was generally unabashed about presenting himself as an exemplar – a good man in earnest pursuit of moral perfection, however buffeted by unfortunate external events that were beyond his control.

Montaigne had been able to compose himself in tranquil retreat, and to publish his autobiographical *Essays* to great acclaim. Rousseau by contrast felt compelled to justify himself in a series of autobiographical works written under great pressure, and posthumously published, in a desperate attempt to demonstrate beyond a reasonable doubt, before the court of posterity, that he was a good and innocent man, even though he had been forced into exile in 1763 after two of his books, *Emile* and *On the Social Contract*, had been censored, banned, and in some places burned as impious and seditious.

As Montaigne had in his *Essays*, Rousseau promised in all three of his autobiographical works to depict himself with candor. But unlike the former counselor, courtier and diplomat, the citizen of Geneva was prey to frenzied fits of self-justification – a susceptibility that became more pronounced over the course of writing his *Confessions*. There is a strident, sometimes belligerent aspect to his avowals of sincerity, as if he was a better

---

[5] Ibid., I, p. 197.   [6] Romans 12:3, cited in Ibid.
[7] Rousseau to M. de Malesherbes, 12 January 1762, PL I, p. 1136.

and more honest man than Montaigne, never mind most of his readers – and all of his enemies.

And Rousseau did have enemies. Some of them knew him well enough to know how to drive him crazy. In 1764, Voltaire, writing under a pseudonym, published an eight-page pamphlet attacking Rousseau for his hypocrisy, and describing how this supposed paladin of virtue had surreptitiously abandoned the children he had conceived out of wedlock at the door of a Parisian orphanage.

From the start, it was a primary burden of Rousseau's *Confessions* to address Voltaire's very public reproach, in part by putting this particular episode in a broader context. The key facts of his critics' indictment he conceded, though the circumstances, he argued, proved his good intentions. But try as he might, in his *Confessions*, and in the autobiographical writings that followed, Rousseau proved unable to lift this burden of guilt. The best he could do was insist that he had no regrets, and to claim at the end of his life that he had found "compensation for my sacrifice" in the insights he was able to elaborate about the raising of children in his books, wanly asserting that "it would assuredly be the most unbelievable thing in the world that *Héloïse* and *Émile* were the work of a man who did not love children."[8]

***

Rousseau's experience here sharply contrasts with that of Montaigne, who had managed with effort to achieve a measure of peace and tranquility through the relaxed ethos he was able to elaborate in his *Essays*. Confronted with Montaigne's apparent equanimity, it's no wonder that Rousseau sometimes felt jealous – and no surprise that he should sometimes express incredulity at the veracity of the self-portrait in the *Essays*.

Rousseau's acute sense of guilt may furthermore help explain the avowed certainty of Rousseau's fictive alter ego in *Emile*, the Savoyard Vicar. Perhaps because his conscience ultimately seemed to him a constant source of mortification, inwardly unwavering and relentless, Rousseau sometimes seemed to assume that it must similarly appear to everyone. In the teeth of all the evidence to the contrary that Montaigne had amassed in his *Essays*, and that Rousseau himself acknowledged elsewhere in his works, the Vicar solemnly asserts that "there is in the depths of our souls an innate principle

---

[8] Rousseau, *The Reveries of a Solitary Walker*, "Ninth Promenade," PL I, pp. 1087–1088. Cf. Rousseau, *Confessions*, PL I, p. 357: "By abandoning my children to public education for lack of power to bring them up myself; by destining them to become workers and peasants rather than adventurers and fortune hunters, I believed I was performing an action of a Citizen and father."

of justice and virtue ... and it is to this principle that I give the name *conscience*."[9]

Montaigne drew very different conclusions from his inward experience. Though he was no stranger to remorse, Montaigne famously doubted that human beings possessed anything like an innate principle of justice: "The laws of conscience, which we pretend to be derived from nature, proceed from custom .... Each man, holding in inward veneration the opinions and the behavior approved and accepted around him, cannot break loose from them without remorse, or apply himself to them without self-satisfaction .... [T]he common fancies that we find in repute around us, and infused into our soul by our fathers' seed, these seem to be the universal and natural ones. Whence it comes to pass, that whatever is off the hinges of custom, people believe to be off the hinges of reason; God knows how unreasonably, most of the time."[10]

***

In 1995, one of Rousseau's personal copies of Montaigne's *Essays* was auctioned at Christie's. The volume was one of only eighteen books in Rousseau's library at the time of his death. This edition of the *Essays* has marginal comments in Rousseau's hand on four pages. The most interesting of these comments both concern Montaigne's most controversial essay, his "Apology for Raymond Sebond." Circumstantial evidence strongly suggests that Rousseau wrote this and the other notes – and was rereading Montaigne – in 1757 or 1758, while he was working on *Emile*, and also breaking with Diderot, who had been the closest of his friends in Paris.[11]

The longest of Rousseau's notes was apparently jotted in haste, and consists of thirty-seven lines in pencil, concerning friendship, and also, in passing, remarks on the excellence of Rousseau's character.

Montaigne's adjacent text concerns neither friendship nor excellence of character, but monstrosities and the limits of human understanding: "There are species of men in certain places who have very little resemblance to our kind. And there are half-breed and ambiguous forms between human and brutish nature .... What of those who naturally changes into wolves, into mares, and then back into men? ... [H]ow many things there are within our knowledge which defy these fine rules that we have cut out and prescribed to nature! ... [T]o us, to go according to nature is only

---

[9] Rousseau, *Émile*, PL IV, p. 598.   [10] Montaigne, *Essais* I, pp. 115–116.
[11] See J. Starobinski, "Rousseau dans la marge de Montaigne: Cinq notes inédites," *Débat* 90 (1996): pp. 3–26.

to go according to our intelligence, as far as it can follow and as far as we can see; what is beyond is monstrous and disordered."[12]

That Rousseau was provoked by the substance of Montaigne's remarks is clear from the set of so-called *Moral Letters* he composed (but never sent) in these months, written in the didactic style of Seneca's letters, and addressed with platonic passion to Sophie d'Houdetot – the relevant passage reappears, virtually verbatim, a few years later in the Creed of a Savoyard Priest in *Emile*. Here Rousseau remarks that some philosophers "go to seek in the shadows some example that is obscure and known to themselves alone, as if all the inclinations of nature were annihilated by the depravity of some individuals and as soon as there are some monsters the human species is no longer anything." He goes on to admonish "the skeptic" directly: "Oh Montaigne, you who pride yourself for frankness and truth, be sincere and true, if a philosopher can be so, and tell me if there is some region on the earth where it is a crime to keep one's faith, to be clement, beneficent, and generous; in which the good man is contemptible and the scoundrel honored."[13]

The vehemence of this outburst implies a discomfort, both with Montaigne's fascination with biological anomalies, and also with Montaigne's equally palpable delight in detailing strange and disturbing customs.

Rousseau's second handwritten comment on Montaigne's "Apology for Raymond Sebond" is much shorter, and comes near the close of that long essay. It consists of a marginal phrase, written in ink: "*flux de choses.*" Things in flux.

In the adjacent text, Montaigne limns the transience of human existence: "[W]hat is beginning to be born never arrives at the perfection of being; inasmuch as this birth is never completed, and never stops as being at an end, but from the seed onward goes on ever changing and shifting from one thing into another . . . . [Y]esterday dies in today and today will die in tomorrow; and there is nothing that abides and is always the same."[14]

***

Montaigne here is quoting more or less directly from one of Plutarch's dialogues, on the riddle of the inscriptions on the temple at Delphi. Plutarch's text climaxes with an interpretation of the Delphic admonition

---

[12] Montaigne, *Essais* II, pp. 525–526. Cf. II, p. 713: "What we call monsters are not so to God, who sees in the immensity of his work the infinity of forms that he has comprised in it."

[13] Rousseau, "Moral Letters," PL IV, p. 1109. Cf. Rousseau, *Émile*, PL IV, pp. 598–599.

[14] Montaigne, *Essais* II, p. 602.

to "Know Thyself," understood "as a reminder to mortal man of his own nature and the weaknesses that beset him," not least the endless mutability of his mortal existence.[15]

Montaigne's paraphrase of Plutarch ends with a similar admonition, averring that a man "cannot raise himself above himself and humanity; for he can see only with his own eyes, and seize only with his own grasp."[16]

In his canonic works, from the *Discourses* to *Emile*, Rousseau had disagreed. Unlike most Catholics and Protestants, and unlike Montaigne as well, Rousseau had avowed that man "is naturally good." God had conferred free will upon men in order that they might become like unto Him by purging themselves of evil habits. In other words, a man *could*, with strenuous effort and a pure heart, "raise himself about himself."

Such was one message of Rousseau's *Moral Letters*, which he reiterated in *Emile*, where he made even more explicit the heretical view that human beings might achieve moral perfection independently, without God's grace – a heresy swiftly censured by the ecclesiastical authorities in both Catholic France and Protestant Geneva.

***

During his "period of effervescence," from 1749 until the appearance of the *Emile* and *On the Social Contract* over fifteen years later, Rousseau had tried to share his glad tidings about the natural goodness of the human being, offering himself as a living example of simple virtues, and inviting others to embark on a Promethean project, to rid mankind once and for all of the catastrophic institutions that had created universal slavery in place of universal freedom.

But as the years passed, and after his efforts to rebut accusations of hypocrisy through public readings of his draft of the *Confessions* failed to achieve the absolution he had evidently hoped for, Rousseau decided at last to withdraw from public affairs.

And in his final will and testament, *The Reveries of a Solitary Walker* that he left unfinished at his death, Rousseau reached some new conclusions.

He now acknowledged that anyone who endeavors to live a life of public virtue makes himself willy-nilly a hostage to fortune, to a host of external forces and factors that are well beyond the power of one man's will, or even a society's general will, when it is not strong, to control and direct toward a good end.

---

[15] Plutarch, "The E at Delphi," in *Moralia* (Cambridge, MA: Harvard University Press, 2014) V, p. 253.
[16] Montaigne, *Essais* II, p. 604.

At the same time, Rousseau's evaluation of Montaigne mellowed. According to one of his acquaintances, Rousseau at the end of his life avowed his admiration for "*ce premier philosophe français*" – this fundamental French philosopher. "What a man," his friend recalls Rousseau exclaiming: "Besides the directness, grace, and energy of his inimitable style, there are his broad views and, as he says, his extemporaneous spirit."[17]

The generosity of these sentiments is perhaps partially explained by Rousseau's own changing estimate of his capacity to live a life of perfect virtue. "Know Thyself," he now concedes, was "not as easy a maxim to follow as I had believed in my *Confessions*" – and that "to dare to profess great virtues" without the courage and strength needed in practice to live a life in true harmony with those great virtues "is to be arrogant and rash."[18]

Abjuring his prior vocation as a self-made moral exemplar comparable to Socrates, Rousseau feels able to celebrate in solitude the sheer "sentiment of existence," and to acknowledge, and even rejoice in, our transience and mutability – the fact that "everything is in continual flux."[19]

The final months of Rousseau's life were spent at a rural retreat twenty-five miles north of Paris, where Rousseau was content to botanize, and to record in writing his daydreams, and to recollect select episodes from his past in the pages of his *Reveries*. Transporting himself in his imagination, he was able to linger over those rare moments, fleeting yet sweet, that he had wished could last forever – even as he depicted his own passing thoughts. And by indulging in this manner a natural inclination for indolence, Rousseau was evidently able, at last, to achieve a measure of peace and tranquility.

Just like Montaigne.

[17] J. Dusaulx, *Des mes rapports avec J.J. Rousseau* (Paris, 1798), p. 100.
[18] Rousseau, *Reveries*, PL I, pp. 1024, 1039.   [19] Ibid., p. 1046.

CHAPTER 3

Rousseau and Hobbes: The Hobbesianism
of Rousseau

Richard Tuck

The importance of Hobbes for the Enlightenment has never seriously been doubted. But he has usually been thought of as someone who acted as a stimulating irritant for eighteenth-century writers by putting forward views which were antithetical to the moral theories most beloved of the period. Specialists on the Enlightenment, when they refer to Hobbes, casually say such things as "Hobbes believed that man is ruled by his passions, the most politically significant of which is fear."[1] Rousseau in particular is seen as profoundly anti-Hobbesian; as a representative utterance from an intelligent and influential reader (Alasdair Macintyre in his *A Short History of Ethics*) puts it, "Rousseau's view of the state of nature is quite unlike that of Hobbes. First, it is not presocial. Man's natural, unreflective impulses are not those of self-aggrandizement; natural man is moved by self-love, but self-love is not inconsistent with feelings of sympathy and compassion."[2] This view of Hobbes on the part of modern writers, it should be said, is not particularly distant from the view expressed by many people in the eighteenth century itself. Montesquieu, for example, remarked that "Hobbes gives men first the desire to subjugate one another, but this is not reasonable. The idea of empire and domination is so complex and depends on so many other ideas, that it would not be the one they would first have."[3] Rousseau himself said that Hobbes had concluded "that because man has no idea of goodness, he must be naturally wicked; that he is vicious because he does not know virtue."[4]

---

[1] M. Richter, *The Political Theory of Montesquieu* (Cambridge: Cambridge University Press, 1977), p. 38. The great exception to this was George Davy, in his Zaharoff Lecture of 1953 on "Thomas Hobbes et J.-J. Rousseau," and to some extent Robert Derathé.

[2] A. Macintyre, *A Short History of Ethics* (London: Routledge, 1966), p. 184.

[3] *The Spirit of the Laws*, ed. A. Cohler et al. (Cambridge: Cambridge University Press, 1989), p. 6.

[4] *Discourse on Inequality*, in *The Social Contract and Discourses*, trans. G. Cole, eds. J. Brumfitt and J. Hall (New York: Alfred A. Knopf, 1993), pp. 71–72.

The curious thing about this is that none of these accounts of Hobbes are correct, and, furthermore, that their falsehood is pretty obvious from a straightforward reading of Hobbes's texts. The Preface to *De Cive* (the work which was most accessible to a Continental audience in the eighteenth century) says plainly that his theory rests on a first principle

> well-known to all men by experience and which everyone admits, that men's natural Disposition is such that if they are not restrained by fear of a common power, they will distrust and fear each other, and each man rightly may, and necessarily will, look out for himself from his own resources . . . Some object that if we admit this principle, it follows directly not only that all Men are evil (which perhaps, though harsh, should be conceded, since it is clearly said in holy Scripture), but also (and this cannot be conceded without impiety) that they are evil by nature. However it does not follow from this Principle that men are evil by nature. For we cannot tell the good and the bad apart, hence even if there were fewer evil men than good men, good, decent people would still be saddled with the constant need to distrust, take precautions, anticipate, subdue, and protect themselves by all possible means.[5]

In other words, men are fundamentally self-protective, and only secondarily aggressive – it is the fear of an attack by a possible enemy which leads us to perform a preemptive strike on him, and not, strictly speaking, the desire to destroy him.

> Hobbes said the same in *De Cive* I.4:
> In the state of nature there is in all men a will to do harm, but not for the same reason or with equal culpability. One man practises the equality of nature, and allows others everything which he allows himself; this is the mark of a modest man, one who has a true estimate of his own capacities. Another, supposing himself superior to others, wants to be allowed everything, and demands more honor for himself than others have; that is the sign of an aggressive character. In his case, the will to do harm derives from conceit [*inane gloria*, what Hobbes elsewhere termed vainglory] and overvaluation of his strength. For the first man, it derives from the need to defend his property and liberty against the other.

But even the man with an "aggressive character" owes his aggression not to an innate disposition, but to his fear of other people: in the first part of the *Elements of Law* (available to eighteenth-century readers in English as *Humane Nature*, which first appeared in 1650, and in French in

---

[5] T. Hobbes, *On the Citizen*, eds. R. Tuck and M. Silverthorne (Cambridge: Cambridge University Press, 1998), pp. 11–12.

d'Holbach's translation, which appeared in 1772), Hobbes produced a systematic account of the passions as the "pleasure men have, or displeasure from the signs of honor or dishonor done to them," where "honor" is the conception that the man who is honored "hath the odds or excess of power above him that contendeth or compareth himself."[6] Glory in particular is the conception of our own power "above the power of him that contendeth with us," and vainglory is the "fiction (which also is imagination) of actions done by ourselves, which never were done."[7] So there is no such person, on Hobbes's account, as the man who is simply and spontaneously aggressive – even the destructive passions arise from measuring ourselves against other people in order to be confident of our own power over them, and consequently confident of our security from their attacks.

The prime source of the conflicts of the state of nature, for Hobbes, is thus epistemic in character: it is the differing judgments which people make about their own relative power, and about all other matters of importance to them. These judgments need not, strictly speaking, be driven by self-interest *at all*, since they may arise simply from the fact that there is no objective standard of truth. He put this very clearly in a passage at the end of the *Elements* (available in English in *De Corpore Politico* from 1650, and in French from 1652).

> In the state of nature, where every man is his own judge, and differeth from other concerning the names and appellations of things, and from those differences arise quarrels, and breach of peace; it was necessary there should be a common measure of all things that might fall in controversy; as for example: of what is to be called right, what good, what virtue, what much, what little, what *meum* and *tuum*, what a pound, what a quart, &c. For in these things private judgements may differ, and beget controversy. This common measure, some say, is right reason: with whom I should consent, if there were any such thing to be found or known in *rerum natura*. But commonly they that call for right reason to decide any controversy, do mean their own. But this is certain, seeing right reason is not existent, the reason of some man, or men, must supply the place thereof; and that man, or men, is he or they, that have the sovereign power. . .; and consequently the civil laws are to all subjects the measures of their actions, whereby to determine, whether they be right or wrong, profitable or unprofitable, virtuous or vicious; and by them the use and definition of all names not agreed upon, and tending to controversy, shall be established. As for example, upon the

---

[6] T. Hobbes, *The Elements of Law, Natural and Politic*, ed. F. Tönnies (London: Frank Cass & Co, 1969), pp. 34–35.
[7] Hobbes, *Elements of Law*, pp. 36–37.

occasion of some strange and deformed birth, it shall not be decided by
Aristotle, or the philosophers, whether the same be a man or no, but by the
laws.[8]

Hobbes's men are primarily fearful rather than aggressive creatures, who
are led into conflict by their differing judgments about what will protect
them. This can sometimes correspond to real conflicts over resources, but
in general Hobbes was loath to use this as an explanation of conflict – it
appears only last on the list of possible reasons in *De Cive*, after "vainglory"
and doctrinal conflict,[9] and Hobbes consistently argued that there was not
in fact any shortage of basic resources for all men, but merely a dispute over
their allocation. Moreover, men's fear of one another exists alongside an –
albeit minimal – sense of mutual respect. Hobbes explained the basis of the
"right of nature," the right to act on one's own judgment about what will
conduce to one's preservation, in something like the following terms in all
his works (this passage is from the *Elements of Law*): "it is not against reason
that a man doth all he can to preserve his own body and limbs, both from
death and pain. And that which is not against reason, men call RIGHT, or
jus, or blameless liberty of using our own natural power and ability."[10]
In other words, men respect in one another their intention to protect their
body, and will not *blame* anybody who does so. As I have argued
elsewhere,[11] this universal recognition by all men of the blamelessness of
self-preservation is the practical foundation for Hobbes's moral theory: his
confidence that his theory was of general applicability rested on his
confidence that all men displayed this fundamental moral agreement.
Clearly, mutual respect of this kind requires some degree of fellow-
feeling – men who call one another's "blameless liberty" a "right" are not
treating one another simply as material for exploitation. And given that the
first law of nature in all of Hobbes's writings is *seek peace*, not (for example)
seek power, and that peace (as he said repeatedly) involves respect for other
people, we are obliged to treat other human beings respectfully unless
doing so clearly endangers ourselves, as he said in *De Cive* III.13, making
clear the opposition between mutual respect and vanity.

> If then men are equal by nature, we must recognise their equality; if they are
> unequal, since they will struggle for power, *the pursuit of peace* requires *that
> they be regarded as equal*. And therefore the eighth precept of natural law is:

---

[8] Ibid., pp. 188–189.   [9] Hobbes, *On the Citizen*, pp. 4–6.   [10] Hobbes, *Elements of Law*, p. 71.
[11] See in particular my "Hobbes's Moral Philosophy," in *The Cambridge Companion to Hobbes*, ed.
    T. Sorell (Cambridge: Cambridge University Press, 1996), pp. 175–207.

everyone should be considered equal to everyone. Contrary to this law is
PRIDE.

If this is a correct reading of Hobbes, then, as I said at the beginning, it
poses an urgent question for the interpretation of Rousseau, since the
description I have given of Hobbes's fundamental ideas strikingly resem-
bles the normal description of Rousseau's. Furthermore, Rousseau's early
readers all saw the resemblance, particularly after they thought about
Rousseau's famous remark in the Preface to the *Second Discourse* that

> Contemplating the first and most simple operations of the human soul,
> I think I can perceive in it two principles prior to reason, one of them deeply
> interesting us in our welfare and preservation, and the other exciting
> a natural repugnance at seeing any other sensible being, and particularly
> any of our own species, suffer pain or death. It is from the agreement and
> combination which the understanding is in a position to establish between
> these two principles, without its being necessary to introduce that of
> sociability, that all the rules of natural right appear to me to be derived.[12]

Thus the aged Jesuit Louis Castel of Toulouse wrote in his *L'homme moral
opposé a l'homme physique de Monsieur R**** (1756) that

> One can believe that M. Rousseau has Hobbes fully in his sights, so that he
> can refute him in the parts of his system which are impious; but one cannot
> see that Hobbes's impiety fully revolts him. If he refutes it, it is in the process
> of competing with it or supplanting it. Hobbes is merely impious in that he
> presumes that man is capable of impiety. Having in himself neither virtues
> nor vices, no moral relationships and no awareness of duty, man cannot be
> thought of as impious, whatever he does, any more that can a brute beast or
> animal. Hobbes's man is a beast in his impiety; M. Rousseau's man is
> impious in his bestiality. He is not impious, but he is not pious either; he
> has no moral qualities.[13]

Castel's criticisms enjoyed a much longer life than most pamphlets of the
1750s, as they were reprinted in 1784 in the *Supplement* to the Geneva

---

[12] *The Social Contract and Discourses*, pp. 46–47.
[13] "On croiroit que M. Rousseau a beaucoup Hobbes en vue, pour le réfuter dans ce que son systême
a d'impie; on ne voit pourtant pas que li'impiété de Hobbes le révolte beaucoup; s'il la refute, c'est en
la courant, en l'effaçant. Hobbes n'est impie, qu'en ce qu'il suppose l'homme capable d'impiété.
L'homme n'ayant de soi ni vertus ni vices, ni relations morales, ni devoirs connus, ne sçauroit être
impie, quoi qu'il fasse, non plus que la bête brute & animale. L'homme de Hobbes est bête jusqu'à
l'impiété: celui de M. Rousseau est impie jusqu'à la bêtise. Il n'est pas impie, mais il n'est pas pieuse:
il n'est rien de moral …" [Louis Castel], *L'homme moral opposé a l'homme physique de Monsieur
R***. Lettre philosophique où l'on refute le Déisme du jour* (Toulouse, 1756), pp. 57–58. See also
pp. 202–204 on Rousseau as a Hobbist in religion (though it should be said that he also attacks Locke
in this context), and pp. 207ff on Rousseau as an Epicurean.

edition of Rousseau's works, and were thereby kept in full view of all the late eighteenth- and early nineteenth-century readers of Rousseau, including most importantly his German ones.

The same sense that Rousseau was only ambiguously a critic of Hobbes is found in another response to the Second Discourse from 1756, Jean de Castillon's *Discours sur l'origine de l'inégalité parmi les hommes*. Much of his book was devoted to documenting the claim that Rousseau had revived Epicureanism, but he was also explicit about the similarity to Hobbes. Rather perceptively, as we shall see, he observed that

> Rousseau has wished to find something different from that which the other philosophers have seen. But no sooner does his animated machine [*machine animée*] acquire a tincture of humanity, than it becomes at the same time a man of the kind which the philosophers whom he criticizes have devised. Rousseau's man is sociable like that of Grotius, since he has in pity [*la commisération*] all the social virtues, and is inclined to unite with [other men] given the needs which he has in various circumstances; and those circumstances manifest themselves as soon as he begins to think. His man is also evil like that of Hobbes. Vices accompany everything which can be associated with virtue; and while reason only forms slowly and is dependent on the situation, malevolence develops spontaneously and makes rapid progress ....[14]

The Catholic Theologian Hyacinth Sigismond Gerdil made a rather similar point. He observed that Rousseau "has pretended to exclude from the state of nature every cause of quarrel and dissension" by supposing that natural men lead a wholly solitary life and do not compare themselves with one another; but (he claimed) on Rousseau's own account they will compare themselves with animals, and acquire in the process exactly the self-consciousness and vanity which give rise to conflict. Rousseau's natural men, denied sociability, are thus essentially the same as Hobbes's, though the initial characterization of man in the two writers matched their different personalities: "they both equally stripped

---

[14] "Rousseau a voulu en trouver un différent de ceux qu'ont vus les autres philosophes. Mais à peine son machine animée prend une teinture d'humanité, qu'elle devient à la fois un homme tel que l'ont fait tous les philosophes qu'il critique. L'homme de Rousseau est sociable comme celui de Grotius, pusiqu'il a dans la commisération toutes les vertus sociales, & le penchant à s'unir avec eux dans le besoin qu'il en a dans quelques occasions: & ces occasions commencent à se presenter dès qu'il commence à penser. Il est méchant comme celui de Hobbes. Les vices accompagnent tout ce qui pouvoit s'associer avec la vertu: & pendant que la raison ne se forme que lentement & à la faveur des circonstances, la malignité se montre d'elle même & fait des progrès rapides ..." Jean de Castillon, *Discours sur l'origine de l'inégalité parmi les hommes* (Amsterdam, 1756), p. 129. See pp. vi, 20, 255–266 and 286–293 for Rousseau's Epicureanism.

man of his humanity; but Hobbes made of him a Tiger, Rousseau an Owl."[15]

When the *Social Contract* appeared, this too was often seen as Hobbist. For instance, the Dutch philosopher and jurist Eli Luzac, in his *Lettre d'un anonime à Monsieur J.J. Rousseau* (1766), seized on Rousseau's remark in Book I, Chapter 8 of the *Social Contract* that "the passage from the state of nature to the civil state produces a very remarkable change in man, by substituting justice for instinct in his conduct, and giving his actions the morality they had formerly lacked," and exclaimed that "to talk in this way is not only to outdo Hobbes, but to go beyond all the bounds of good sense."[16] And even some of Rousseau's former friends saw a resemblance to Hobbes in this work: thus the lengthy *Lettre d'un citoyen de Genève à un autre citoyen* of 1768, probably by the Genevan Jacob Vernet (an acute and not at all unsympathetic reader), expressly said of Rousseau that

> believing with *Hobbes* that men are born the enemies of one another, and that our worst enemies are our superiors, like him he remedies this by Despotism, though locating it in a different place. Whereas Hobbes gives arbitrary power to a Prince, Mr. Rousseau (who knows no middle ground) instead gives a similar power to the multitude.[17]

This widespread sense that Rousseau and Hobbes were fundamentally similar led Diderot, in his capacity as editor of and contributor to the *Encyclopédie*, to mount a counterattack. The most obvious evidence for this is Diderot's article on HOBBISME, which appeared in 1765 in Volume VIII of the *Encyclopédie* – that is, three years after the publication of *The Social Contract* and *Emile*, and ten years after the first responses to Rousseau's work, ten years in which the accusation that Rousseau was a Hobbist had been constantly made. Most of the article consists of a straightforward translation of the section on Hobbes in Brucker's *Historia Critica Philosophiae*, but at the end Diderot suddenly launched

---

[15] "Le P.G.B." [i.e. le Père Gerdil Barnabite, his religious order], *Discours philosophiques sur l'homme consideré relativement à l'état de nature, & à l'état de société* (Turin, 1769), pp. 61–62.

[16] "Vous dites que *le passage de l'état de nature, à l'état civil, substitue dans sa conduite la justice à l'instinct* &c. mais en parler commes vous faites, ce n'est pas seulement rencherir sur Hobbes, c'est passer toutes les bornes du bon sens." [Eli Luzac], *Lettre d'un anonime à Monsieur J.J. Rousseau* (Paris, 1766), p. 70. Luzac (1723–1796) was a commentator on Wolff as well as a writer on commerce, classical philology, etc. He was later to be a fierce opponent of the Batavian Republic.

[17] "Mr. Rousseau, qui croyant avec *Hobbes* que les hommes sont nés ennemis les uns des autres, & croyant de plus que nous n'avons pas de pires ennemis que nos supérieurs, y remédie comme lui par le Despotisme, mais en le plaçant differemment. Car au lieu que Hobbes donne le pouvoir arbitraire à un Prince, Mr. Rousseau qui ne connoit point les milieux, donne un semblable pouvoir à la multitude." *Lettre d'un citoyen de Genève à un autre citoyen* (Geneva, 1768), pp. 72–73.

into a completely unnecessary contrast between Rousseau and Hobbes, a contrast which would have been understood by all his readers as an attack on Rousseau's critics. Rousseau is in fact the only modern writer dealt with in the article, and his relationship to Hobbes was clearly uppermost in Diderot's mind at the time he was writing it (whenever that was – any date from 1755 would have been appropriate).[18]

> Beware of granting him [i.e. Hobbes] his first principles, if you do not wish to follow him completely where he is pleased to take you. The philosophy of M. Rousseau of Geneva is almost the inverse of that of Hobbes. The former believes that man is by nature good, the latter that he is evil. According to the philosopher of Geneva, the state of nature is a state of peace; according to the philosopher of Malmesbury, it is a state of war. It is the laws, and the creation of society, which have improved man, if one credits Hobbes; and it is those which have ruined him, if one credits M. Rousseau. The former was born in the midst of tumult and faction; the latter lives in polite society, among *savants*. Different times, different circumstances, different philosophies. M. Rousseau is eloquent and moving; Hobbes dry, austere, and vigorous. The latter saw the throne shaken, his citizens armed against one another, and his country drowned in blood, by the frenzies of presbyterian fanaticism, and he conceived an aversion to God, priest, and altar. The former saw men, conversant with all kinds of knowledge, who tore themselves apart, hated themselves and abandoned themselves to their passions, who were ambitious for esteem, for wealth, for dignities, and who lived in a fashion far removed from the enlightenment they had acquired; and he despised knowledge and the *savants*. Both of them were extremists.[19]

---

[18] Robert Wokler in his study of the question suggested a date for the writing of *Hobbisme* as early as 1751. But the Rousseau of the *First Discourse* was not regarded by the general public as a Hobbist in the way the Rousseau of the *Second Discourse* was, and it is unlikely that Diderot would have felt the need to dissociate the two in 1751. It would also follow that the verbal similarities between *Hobbisme* and the *Second Discourse* to which Wokler draws attention are more likely to be Diderot reading Rousseau than Rousseau reading Diderot. See R. Wokler, "The Influence of Diderot on the Political Theory of Rousseau: Two Aspects of a Relationship," *Studies on Voltaire and the Eighteenth Century* 132 (1975): pp. 101 n.108, 102 n.112.

[19] Gardez-vous de lui passer ses premiers principes, si vous ne voulez pas le suivre par-tout où il lui plaira de vous conduire. La philosophie de M. Rousseau de Genève, est presque l'inverse de celle de Hobbes. L'un croit l'homme de la nature bon, & l'autre le croit méchant. Selon le philosophe de Genève, l'état de nature est un état de paix; selon le philosophe de Malmesbury, c'est un état de guerre. Ce sont les lois & la formation de la société qui ont rendu l'homme meilleur, si l'on en croit Hobbes; & qui l'ont depravé, si l'on en croit M. Rousseau. L'un étoit né au milieu du tumulte & des factions; l'autre vivoit dans le monde, & parmi les savans. Autres tems, autres circonstances, autre philosophie. M. Rousseau est éloquent & pathétique; Hobbes sec, austere & vigoureux. Celui-ci voyoit le trône ébranlé, ses citoyens armés les uns contre les autres, & sa patrie inondée de sang par les fureurs du fanatisme presbytérien, & il avoit pris en aversion le dieu, le ministre & les autels. Celui-là voyoit des hommes versés dans toutes les connoissances, se déchirer, se haïr, se livrer à leurs passions, ambitionner la considération, la richesse, les dignités, & se conduire d'une maniere peu

But Diderot's attempt to separate Rousseau and Hobbes in this fashion had only a limited success; in Germany, particularly until well into the nineteenth century, it was customary to stress (and often to deplore) the similarity.

Were these early readers of Rousseau right, or was Diderot instead correct in emphasizing the difference between the two authors? The first thing to say is that while Rousseau may have shared the eighteenth-century misapprehension about Hobbes's belief in innate human violence, his actual theory as set out in the *Second Discourse* is indeed extremely close to Hobbes's *actual* beliefs. What has often misled readers is that Rousseau was concerned in part with a question to which Hobbes gave little thought: what would men be like if they had no interaction with other people? As I said at the beginning, Hobbes himself thought that the "multitude of passions" which led to conflict were the consequence of men measuring themselves against one another. It is true that this was not "society" for Hobbes, since for him a "society" had to be well-ordered and intentionally created; but Hobbes never supposed that in his state of nature men would be as isolated as they were in Rousseau's. Had he been asked how one would describe the character of men entirely cut off from one another, his answer would presumably have been very like Rousseau's, since such men would not yet have developed the passions which sprang from their "imagination" of one another's power. Instead, they would be governed by the two principles which were foundational to the state of nature, and continued into civil society as its basis, the right of self-preservation and the ban on unnecessary violence against other men.

One could put the similarity this way: Rousseau gave a psychological character to what in Hobbes were purely foundational principles of human interaction. What in Hobbes was a *right* of self-preservation became in Rousseau *amour de soi*, and what in Hobbes was a *duty* of mutual respect and abstention from unnecessary violence, in Rousseau became *pitié*.[20] And

---

conforme aux lumieres qu'ils avoient acquises, & il méprisa la science & les savans. Ils furent outrés tous les deux.

[20] Though one should say, once again, that Rousseau thought – or said that he thought – that Hobbes did not recognize such a duty: "There is another principle which has escaped Hobbes; which, having been bestowed upon mankind, to moderate, on certain occasions, the impetuosity of *amour-propre*, or, before its birth, the desire of self-preservation, tempers the ardour with which he pursues his own welfare, by an innate repugnance at seeing a fellow-creature suffer. I think I need not fear contradiction in holding man to be possessed of the only natural virtue which could not be denied by the most violent detractor of human virtue. I am speaking of compassion [*la pitié*]..." (*Discourse on Inequality*, in *The Social Contract and Discourses*, pp. 65–66).

the relationship between *amour de soi* and *pitié* was broadly similar to the relationship between the right of nature and the law of nature in Hobbes. Thus Rousseau said of *pitié* in the *Discourse* that

> instead of inculcating that sublime maxim of rational justice, Do to others as you would have them do to you, [it] inspires all men with that other maxim of natural goodness, much less perfect indeed, but perhaps more useful; Do good to yourself with as little evil as possible to others.[21]

And in his essay *L'État de Guerre*, without using the term *pitié*, he said something similar (incidentally making very clear that he was in effect psychologizing a moral principle)

> It is from the heart that natural law speaks to man more powerfully than all the precepts of the philosophers. It is from there that it cries out to him that he may not sacrifice the life of a fellow man except to save his own, and that even when he sees himself obliged to do so, he cannot but feel a sense of horror at the idea of killing in cold blood.[22]

So, the place to look for the equivalent of Hobbes's state of nature in the *Second Discourse* is not in the First Part, with its description of man "just as he must have come from the hands of nature," but in the Second Part, in which men begin to interact with one another (including when they begin to use language – something else Hobbes assumed is to be found in his state of nature). It is this level of interaction which for Rousseau precipitates conflict, driven by vanity or *amour propre* more than (say) conflict over scarce resources; indeed, in one striking passage in which he recapitulated the central notion of the *First Discourse*, he asserted that it was artistic rivalry and not economic necessity which led to the state of war. Once men

> accustomed themselves to assemble before their huts round a large tree; singing and dancing, the true offspring of love and leisure, became the amusement, or rather the occupation, of men and women thus assembled together with nothing else to do. Each one began to consider the rest, and to wish to be considered in turn; and thus a value came to be attached to public esteem. Whoever sang or danced best, whoever was the handsomest, the strongest, the most dexterous, or the most eloquent, came to be of most consideration; and this was the first step towards inequality, and at the same time towards vice. From these first distinctions arose on the one side vanity and contempt and on the other shame and envy: and the fermentation

---

[21] *The Social Contract and Discourses*, p. 76.
[22] G. Roosevelt, *Reading Rousseau in the Nuclear Age* (Philadelphia: Temple University Press, 1990), p. 189.

caused by these new leavens ended by producing combinations fatal to innocence and happiness.[23]

This concentration on aesthetic values rather than fundamental needs as the source of conflict would have appealed to Hobbes; it has considerable similarity to the wry account in Chapter One of *De Cive* of how when men

> meet for entertainment and fun, everyone usually takes most pleasure in the kind of funny incident from which (such is the nature of the ridiculous) he may come away with a better idea of himself in comparison with someone else's embarrassment or weakness. Even if this is sometimes harmless and inoffensive, it is still evident that their primary enjoyment is of their own glory and not of society.

If the fundamental problem of human interaction – its competitive and unstable character – was the same in both Hobbes and Rousseau, one might have expected the solution also to be the same in both cases. And yet here, in their accounts of politics, there seems to be the greatest divide between them: Rousseau is the first great theorist of democratic politics, and Hobbes is the most famous theorist of despotism. But one has to tread cautiously: while the specific solutions which each in the end endorsed are of course very different, in their general character they are in fact strikingly similar, something Rousseau signaled, in a way, when he said in a well-known letter to Mirabeau of 1767 that "I see no tolerable mean between the most austere Democracy, and the most perfect Hobbesianism." Hobbes's solution to the contestations of the state of nature was the cession by all men of their individual judgments about contentious issues to a sovereign whose judgment would stand in for each of theirs, and thereby produce an artificial agreement – what he termed "union" rather than "concord," where "concord" was merely the adventitious convergence of particular opinions. On one reading of Hobbes, this cession of judgment covered not simply external profession but *internal* commitment: we genuinely believe that the sovereign's determination of "just" and "unjust" etc. decides the meaning of the terms and therefore our own opinions about them. Indeed, the Preface to *De Cive* contains a remarkable and almost Nietzschean picture of the ideal civil society in which we have no inward dissent at all, through the elimination of the *damnosa hereditas* of Socratic philosophy. Once upon a time, he wrote, there had been an era of "peace . . . and a golden age, which did not end until Saturn was expelled and the doctrine

---

[23] *Discourse on Inequality*, in *The Social Contract and Discourses*, p. 90.

started up that one could take up arms against kings," and in which the "ancients" had

> preferred that the knowledge of Justice be wrapped up in fables rather than exposed to discussion. Before questions of that kind began to be debated, Princes did not lay claim to sovereign power, they simply exercised it. They did not defend their power by arguments but by punishing the wicked and defending the good. In return the citizens did not measure Justice by the comments of private men but by the laws of the commonwealth; and were kept at Peace not by discussions but by the power of Government. In fact, they revered sovereign power, whether it resided in a man or in an Assembly, as a kind of visible divinity.[24]

In comparing Rousseau and Hobbes, we always need to bear in mind this utopian strain in Hobbes, and the fact that Hobbes as much as Rousseau believed that in a well-founded commonwealth human nature itself will be transformed. Given that on Hobbes's account our passions, as I said earlier, are bound up with our sense of our own power or weakness compared with other people, then once men are in a world where there are no individual differences of power – for all men are equal in the face of the sovereign's power – many passions should simply fade away, and what will survive is that mutual respect and sense of equality which the natural law requires; what in *Leviathan* he termed "complaisance," which he described in the *Elements* as "that passion by which we strive mutually to accommodate each other."

Rousseau did not disagree with any of this. Like Hobbes, he too believed that law in a well-founded state is the moral authority which cannot be questioned, as he said in *Political Economy*, the *corps politique* is

> a corporate being possessed of a will; and this general will, which tends always to the preservation and welfare of the whole and every part, and is the source of the laws, constitutes for all the members of the State, in their relations to one another and to it, the rule of what is just or unjust: a truth which shows, by the way, how idly some writers have treated as theft the subtlety prescribed to children at Sparta for obtaining their frugal repasts, as if everything ordained by the law were not lawful.[25]

The remark about the Spartans is precisely the same as Hobbes' in *De Cive* VI.16, in the same context. And like Hobbes, he believed that the process of generalizing our particular interests in this way produces as a consequence a disposition toward equality and respect; this is the point of his remark in

---

[24] Hobbes, *On the Citizen*, p. 9.
[25] *Political Economy*, in *The Social Contract and Discourses*, p. 132.

Emile that "the more one generalizes this [particular] interest, the more it becomes equitable, and the love of mankind is nothing other than the love of justice."[26]

Hobbes' sovereign, representing the united wills of his or its citizens and thereby producing a single – we can perfectly well say, general – will, is a purely *procedural* device. There is a necessary arbitrariness about the sovereign's decisions, given what Hobbes thought about the absence of clear truth in contentious matters. So, the *content* of the decision does not reflect any underlying truth about the right thing for the society to do. Since the 1960s it has been common for interpreters of Rousseau to say, in sharp contrast to this, that the general will has some kind of objective status, and that the procedures Rousseau lays down for ascertaining it are to be understood as rather similar to a Condorcet jury decision, in which the procedure is justified as a means of approaching a correct answer, rather than, as in Hobbes, *constituting* the correct answer. On this view, the citizens when voting give their opinion about what would be the right thing to do, rather than what is in their individual interest, and the result is authoritative because it is likely to be true. Fully to deal with this issue in Rousseau would require more space than I have available in this paper, but I would say in particular that there is very little textual support for this interpretation. The main support for it comes from the well-known passage in Chapter 2 of Book IV of the *Social Contract* in which Rousseau discusses majoritarianism.

> When in the popular assembly a law is proposed, what the people is asked is not exactly whether it approves or rejects the proposal, but whether it is in conformity with the general will, which is their will. Each man, in giving his vote, states his opinion on that point; and the general will is found by counting votes. When therefore the opinion that is contrary to my own prevails, this proves neither more nor less than that I was mistaken, and that what I thought to be the general will was not so. If my particular opinion had carried the day I should have achieved the opposite of what was my will; and it is in that case that I should not have been free.
>
> This presupposes, indeed, that all the qualities of the general will still reside in the majority: when they cease to do so, whatever side a man may take, liberty is no longer possible.[27]

In addition, people who espouse this view sometimes point to the remarks with which Rousseau introduces the concept of the legislator:

[26] Rousseau, *Emile or On Education*, trans. A. Bloom (New York: Basic Books, 1979), p. 252.
[27] *The Social Contract and Discourses*, p. 275.

The individuals see the good they reject; the public wills the good it does not see. All stand equally in need of guidance. The former must be compelled to bring their wills into conformity with their reason; the latter must be taught to know what it wills. If that is done, public enlightenment leads to the union of understanding and will in the social body: the parts are made to work together, and the whole is raised to its highest power. This makes a legislator necessary.[28]

But neither of these passages seems to me to imply an "objectivist" view of the general will, and there is at least one other passage which fairly clearly rules it out. The second of the two passages I have just quoted, as I said, introduces the discussion of the legislator (II.7), and Rousseau is absolutely explicit in that chapter that

> he [. . .] who draws up the laws has, or should have, no right of legislation, and the people cannot, even if it wishes, deprive itself of this incommunicable right, because, according to the fundamental compact, only the general will can bind the individuals, and there can be no assurance that a particular will is in conformity with the general will, until it has been put to the free vote of the people.[29]

There is no suggestion in the chapter on the legislator that the general will is the "good" which "the public . . . does not see," and that the legislator has some special access to the things which are in the public interest and which he induces the people to will. Rather, Rousseau says that the legislator's task is to persuade citizens to form an effective state in the first place, in which each individual recognizes his own powerlessness in the face of the collective will. The legislator

> must, in a word, take away from man his own resources and give him instead new ones alien to him, and incapable of being made use of without the help of other men. The more completely these natural resources are annihilated, the greater and more lasting are those which he acquires, and the more stable and perfect the new institution; so that if each citizen is nothing and can do nothing without the rest, and the resources acquired by the whole are equal or superior to the aggregate of the resources of all the individuals, it may be said that legislation is at the highest point of perfection.[30]

The future *content* of the general will, will be given simply by the "free vote" of the citizens, and its generality will consist in its being accepted as wholly canonical for their life by each citizen. As Rousseau recognized,

---

[28] Ibid., p. 212.   [29] Ibid., p. 214.   [30] Ibid., p. 213.

accepting this is highly difficult, and it may require something like a great religious teacher to persuade men of their powerlessness.

As for the first passage I quoted, with its claim that my individual will is "mistaken" if I am outvoted, again that seems to have nothing to do with an objectivist view. As various people have pointed out, in it Rousseau appears to be wrestling with the puzzle which was expressed fifty years ago by Richard Wollheim: in a democracy, I seem to be committed to one outcome being best when I vote (say, the Labour Party to form a government) and another when the votes are counted, since as a democrat I am precommitted to willing what the majority wants. I don't myself think this is much of a "paradox," despite the title Wollheim gave it, but it is hard to see in Rousseau's remarks anything much more than a very vivid sense of the psychological oddity of majoritarianism.

The place where Rousseau makes clearest his view of the general will is, I think, Book II, Chapter 3.

> The general will is always upright and always tends to the public advantage; but it does not follow that the deliberations of the people always have the same rectitude. Our will is always for our own good, but we do not always see what that is; the people is never corrupted, but it is often deceived, and on such occasions only does it seem to will what is bad.
>
> There is often a great deal of difference between the will of all and the general will; the latter considers only the common interest, while the former takes private interest into account, and is no more than a sum of particular wills; but take away from these same wills the pluses and minuses that cancel one another, and the general will remains as the sum of the differences.
>
> If, when the people, being furnished with adequate information, held its deliberations, the citizens had no communication one with another, the grand total of the small differences would always give the general will, and the decision would always be good. But when intrigues arise, and partial associations are formed at the expense of the great association, the will of each of these associations becomes general in relation to its members, while it remains particular in relation to the State: it may then be said that there are no longer as many votes as there are men, but only as many as there are associations. The differences become less numerous and give a less general result. Lastly, when one of these associations is so great as to prevail over all the rest, the result is no longer a sum of small differences, but a single difference; in this case there is no longer a general will, and the opinion which prevails is purely particular.[31]

---

[31] Ibid., pp. 202–203.

Here we have all the key thoughts. First, it is clear from this that the general will is produced by a pure procedure. The "will of all" is what Hobbes would have called the wills of the *multitudo* – the separate private wills of the men and women who will after union comprise the *populus*. The general will is (as it always is in this tradition) the will of the *populus*. But the citizens do not have to abandon their individual private wills, based on whatever beliefs and commitments they may have: instead, they simply have to accept the overriding force of majoritarianism (for I take it that is what taking away "the pluses and minuses that cancel one another" means).[32] In a neglected passage from his *Considerations on the Government of Poland* Rousseau made this, I think, even clearer:

> the law, which is but the expression of the general will, is indeed the resultant of all the particular interests combined and in balance by virtue of their large number [*le résultat de tous les intérêts particuliers combinés et balancés par leur multitude*]. But corporate interests, because of their excessive weight, would upset the balance, and should not be included in it collectively. Each individual should have his vote, no [corporate] body whatsoever should have one.[33]

Rousseau is definite in these passages that the majority vote will only cease to be "good" when partial associations are formed, not when the citizens begin to think about their own interests rather than the common interest. Indeed, one could say that the opposite is the case: it is precisely because they are *not* thinking about their own interests, but instead have committed themselves to someone else's religious or political program, that the votes of the citizens cease to give rise to the general will. Rousseau's fear of partial association is the same as Hobbes', and like Hobbes' it finds expression above all in hostility to deliberation and public persuasion: the citizens (in this passage) must have "no communication one with another." In *Political Economy* he had argued the same, with greater specificity; there, he claimed that a democracy will never be unjust

> unless the people is seduced by private interests, which the credit or eloquence of some clever persons substitutes for those of the State: in which case the general will will be one thing, and the result of the public deliberation another. This is not contradicted by the case of the Athenian Democracy;

---

[32] The idea seems to be this. Suppose that 60 people vote "Yes" for a measure, and 40 vote "No." The "plus" votes of 40 out of the 60 are canceled by the 40 "minus" votes, leaving 20 "plus" votes. In an election between three or more candidates or proposals, the "sum of the differences" rather than merely "the difference" is relevant – Rousseau was of course writing before Borda pointed out (in 1781) the problems of this kind of vote, but that does not affect the general character of Rousseau's argument.

[33] G2, p. 206.

for Athens was in fact not a Democracy, but a very tyrannical Aristocracy, governed by philosophers and orators. Carefully determine what happens in every public deliberation, and it will be seen that the general will is always for the common good; but very often there is a secret division, a tacit confederacy, which, for particular ends, causes the natural disposition of the assembly to be set at naught. In such a case the body of society is really divided into other bodies, the members of which acquire a general will, which is good and just with respect to these new bodies, but unjust and bad with regard to the whole, from which each is thus dismembered.[34]

Like Hobbes, therefore, Rousseau believed that a procedure, without any corruption by partial associations, constituted the canon of good and evil for the citizens.[35] His procedure was, of course, a majority vote; but the curious thing (and something remarkably overlooked in Hobbes scholarship) is that exactly this is true of Hobbes also, at least the Hobbes of *De Cive* which was (as I said at the beginning) the work which was most widely read on the Continent. There, he said this:

---

[34] *The Social Contract and Discourses*, pp. 133–134.
[35] Rousseau stressed more than Hobbes had done the fact that the vote must be general *in form*, something to which he returned on many occasions; but it would be wrong to suppose that Hobbes had not shared even this idea. Hobbes certainly believed passionately in the general *application* of law – see his remark in *Leviathan* chapter 27 that:

> Of the Passions that most frequently are the causes of Crime, one, is Vain-glory, or a foolish over-rating of their own worth; as if difference of worth, were an effect of their wit, or riches, or bloud, or some other naturall quality, not depending on the Will of those that have the Soveraign Authority. From whence proceedeth a Presumption that the punishments ordained by the Lawes, and extended generally to all Subjects, ought not to be inflicted on them, with the same rigour they are inflicted on poore, obscure, and simple men, comprehended under the name of *Vulgar* (Hobbes, *Leviathan*, ed. R. Tuck [Cambridge: Cambridge University Press, 1996], p. 205).

And in the previous chapter he had observed that "all Lawes are generall Judgements, or Sentences of the Legislator; as also every particular Judgement, is a Law to him, whose case is Judged." (*Leviathan*, p. 197). But the most powerful statement in which he revealed his kinship with Rousseau was (as it happens) in a work which Rousseau is unlikely to have read – *Behemoth*. In this dialogue on the Civil War in England, the interlocutor ("B") asks the sage ("A"):

> Must tyrants [...] be obeyed in everything actively? Or is there nothing wherein a lawful King's command may be disobeyed? What if he should command me with my own hands to execute my father, in case he should be condemned to die by the law?
> A. This is a case that need not be put. We never have read nor heard of any King or tyrant so inhuman as to command it. If any did, we are to consider whether that command were one of his laws. For by disobeying Kings, we mean the disobeying of his laws, those his laws that were made before they were applied to any particular person; for the King, though as a father of children, and a master of domestic servants[,] command many things which bind those children and servants[,] yet he commands the people in general never but by a precedent law, and as a politic, not a natural person. And if such a command as you speak of were contrived into a general law (which never was, nor never will be), you were bound to obey it, unless you depart the kingdom after the publication of the law, and before the condemnation of your father (Hobbes, *Behemoth, or the Long Parliament*, ed. F. Tonnies [London, 1889], p. 51).

Let us now see what the founders do in the formation of each kind of commonwealth. When men have met to erect a commonwealth, they are, almost by the very fact that they have met, a *Democracy*. From the fact that they have gathered voluntarily, they are understood to be bound by the decisions made by agreement of the majority. And that is a *Democracy*, as long as the convention lasts, or is set to reconvene at certain times and places. For a convention whose will is the will of all the citizens has *sovereign power*. And because it is assumed that each man in this convention has the right to vote, it follows that it is a *Democracy*, by the definition given in the first article of this chapter [i.e. a democracy is "where *sovereign power* lies with an *Assembly* in which any citizen has the right to vote"].[36]

Majority voting, he made clear, was critical: "Two things ... constitute a *Democracy*, of which one (an uninterrupted schedule of meetings) constitutes a Δῆμος, and the other (which is majority voting) constitutes το κράτος or authority [*potestas*]."[37] It is true – and I will return to this presently – that this primeval democracy in Hobbes can then legitimately transfer its authority to an aristocracy or monarchy, whereas in Rousseau it cannot; but there can be no doubt that for Hobbes in *De Cive* democracy had a special status.[38]

This in turn is connected to an issue which is at the heart of Rousseau's political theory, his attack on the so-called "double contract" theory of writers such as Pufendorf and Burlamaqui, to which Helena Rosenblatt in particular has drawn our attention. The double contract theory was expressly an attack on Hobbes, for the Hobbesian account of the formation of civil society made it clear that there is only one moment of general agreement, when men in a state of nature all accept that their individual judgments will henceforward be replaced by the judgment of their sovereign. But Pufendorf denied this: what he said in his *De Iure Naturae et Gentium* of 1672 was that *two* contracts were necessary to form a fully developed civil society. The first was between the individuals "each with each in particular, to join into one lasting Society, and to concert the

---

[36] Hobbes, *On the Citizen*, p. 94.   [37] Ibid., p. 94.

[38] It might be thought that Hobbes had abandoned this position by the time he wrote *Leviathan*, and indeed there is only a slender trace of it in the later work, in the remark at the beginning of Chapter XVIII that "A *Common-wealth* is said to be *Instituted*, when a *Multitude* of men do Agree, and Covenant, *every one, with every one*, that to whatsoever *Man*, or *Assembly of Men*, shall be given by the major part, the *Right* to *Present* the Person of them all, ... every one, as well he that *Voted for it*, as he that *Voted against it*, shall *Authorise* all the Actions and Judgements, of that Man, or Assembly of men, in the same manner, as if they were his own ...." But one should not forget that he reprinted *De Cive* in 1668 as part of his *Opera*, with no emendation, so that he continued to regard it as an authoritative statement of his ideas.

Measures of their Welfare and Safety, by the publick Vote [*communi consilio ductuque*]."[39] The second was the covenant

> when the Person or Persons, upon whom the Sovereignty is conferred, shall be actually constituted; by which the Rulers, on the one hand, engage themselves to take care of the common Peace and Security, and the Subjects, on the other, to yield them faithful Obedience; in which, likewise, is included that Submission and Union of Wills, by which we conceive a State to be but *one Person*. And from this Covenant the State receives its final Completion and Perfection.[40]

This theory is of course peculiar, and it is no surprise that Rousseau pounced on it, for why is an agreement "to concert the Measures of their Welfare and Safety, by the publick Vote" not an agreement to create a Hobbesian sovereign? Indeed, plenty of people have supposed that the second contract in Pufendorf is more like the secondary agreement in Hobbes, whereby the initial democracy transfers its power to an oligarchy or monarch, than it is like the initial contract to form a civil society. Pufendorf himself was perfectly aware of this interpretation, and he expressly denied it. He conceded that

> [w]hen [. . .] a Number of free Persons assemble together, in order to enter upon a Covenant about uniting themselves in a civil Body, this preparative Assembly hath already some Appearance of a Democracy; properly in this Respect, that every Man hath the Privilege freely to deliver his Opinion concerning the common Affairs.

But it was not a true democracy, since

> he who dissents from the Vote of the Majority, shall not in the least be obliged by what they determine, till such time as, by means of a second Covenant, a popular Form shall be actually confirm'd and establish'd. Mr. Hobbes, for want of distinguishing these two Covenants, hath handled this Subject with great Confusion.

The identity of a civil society, for Pufendorf, was given by the first contract, and whatever a sovereign might do (in particular, whatever kind of union a sovereign might engineer with another people) this identity could not be lost. But the contract was an agreement simply to discuss and deliberate about their common life, not to make binding decisions. He gave a concrete illustration of the kind of debate he had in mind, in

---

[39] S. Pufendorf, *Of the Law of Nature and Nations*, trans. B. Kennett (London, 1729), p. 639.
[40] Ibid., p. 640.

that Account, which *Dionysius Halicarnassaeus* gives us of the first Settlement of the Monarchy in *Rome*. For here, first of all, a Number of Men flock together, with Design to fix themselves in a new State; in order to which Resolution a tacit Covenant, at least, must be supposed to have passed amongst them. After this, they deliberate about the Form of Government, and that, by Kings being preferred, they agree to invest *Romulus* with the sovereign Authority. And this holds too in the Case of an *Interregnum*, during which, the Society being held together only by the prime Compact, it is frequent to enter the Debate about the Frame and Model of the Commonwealth.[41]

What Pufendorf was doing, we might say, was trying to give an individualist or contractual substance to the idea of national identity, without submerging the nation in its sovereign, and without supposing that there was some kind of real or higher identity to the nation; he wished to retain the idea of a "people" without conceding that it must be able to act collectively through democratic institutions if it was to have a collective identity. (It should be said that a goal of this kind has haunted Western political thought ever since.)

So Pufendorf's double contract theory was in large part driven by his fear of ascribing a power of democratic collective action to a people, and he entirely understood that such a power was central to the Hobbesian model. Equally, when Rousseau turned against the double contract, saying scornfully "There is only one contract in the State, and that is the act of association, which in itself excludes the existence of a second. It is impossible to conceive of any public contract that would not be a violation of the first,"[42] he cannot have been unaware that in this respect as much as in his denial of natural sociability he was simply restating a view which had always been seen as Hobbesian, and attacked by the most influential writers of the previous hundred years for that very reason.

The same is true of another central feature of Rousseau's theory, his insistence that politics cannot be understood unless one made a sharp distinction between *sovereignty* and *government*.[43] While the roots of this distinction (as I show in a forthcoming book) lay in the writings of Jean Bodin, it too had been attacked by Pufendorf and his followers as specifically Hobbesian. This was because Hobbes provided in Chapter 7 of *De*

---

[41] Ibid., pp. 640–641.   [42] *Social Contract*, in *The Social Contract and Discourses*, p. 266.
[43] Strangely, in his Introduction to his 1914 edition of Rousseau's political writings, G. Cole, who was otherwise quite sensitive to the similarities between Hobbes and Rousseau, said bluntly that in this respect "Rousseau differentiates himself from Hobbes. For Hobbes, the Sovereign is identical with the government" – when the exact opposite is the case.

Cive an extensive and remarkable account of how a democracy could be considered a sleeping sovereign, awaking only on occasion to decide the allocation of governmental power and then falling asleep again, just as a monarch might hand power to his vizier before going to sleep, without ceasing to be the sovereign. Throughout his work Hobbes insisted (much to the puzzlement of some of his modern readers) that sovereignty does not involve *power*: an infant, an idiot and even – most astonishingly – a king in prison are all sovereign, despite their inability to issue commands. But Pufendorf immediately saw the implications of this idea:

> we utterly dislike the Assertion of Mr. *Hobbes*, which we meet with in his Book *De Cive*; [...] This Notion, if taken in the gross Sense in which it is deliver'd, we cannot but look upon as highly dangerous and prejudicial to all those limited Princes, who are ordain'd by the voluntary Donation of the People, and bound up to certain fundamental Laws. And the rather, because, as he hath taken the Liberty to call a King for Life a *temporary Monarch*, others may, with as much Reason, extend the Name to those who receive the Sovereignty, with the Privilege of transmitting it by Inheritance, yet so as to keep it within their own Line and Family. Besides, since Mr. *Hobbes* hath not determin'd how far he would stretch the Parallel which he useth, he may easily be intangled in a Train of very pernicious Consequences. For since Property, consider'd in itself, is a much more noble Right, than that of temporary Use; some Men may, on these Principles, conclude that the People are superior to the Prince, and have a Power of bringing him to Correction, in case he doth not govern, according to their Pleasure and Humour.[44]

In other words, in addition to arguing that democracy was conceptually distinctive and at the root of all politics, Hobbes (in Pufendorf's eyes) had provided an analysis of democratic sovereignty that allowed it to be detected behind many contemporary European monarchies, wherever there was (for example) the formality of an election, as there was in most of them.

So the analysis of democracy which Hobbes provided was virtually identical to Rousseau's, in that both of them were committed in principle to a sharp distinction between a democratic sovereign and the governmental structures which possessed day-to-day power. For Rousseau, a distinction of this kind was absolutely necessary to permit the reemergence of democracy in the modern world, since (as Istvan Hont stressed in his writing on Rousseau in the last years of his life), Rousseau was not

---

[44] Pufendorf, *Law of Nature and Nations*, pp. 704–705.

indulging in some idyll of ancient democracy. He was well aware of the
pressures of modernity, and the impossibility of putting modern government in the hands of citizens continuously meeting in assemblies; this is
particularly clear in the striking passage in the Ninth *Letter from the
Mountain* in which Rousseau said that even in a city the size of Geneva
ancient politics could not be revived.

> Ancient Peoples are no longer a model for modern ones; they are too alien to
> them in every respect [. . .] You are neither Romans, nor Spartans; you are
> not even Athenians. Leave aside these great names that do not suit you. You
> are Merchants, Artisans, Bourgeois, always occupied with their private
> interests, with their work, with their trafficking, with their gain; people
> for whom even liberty is only a means for acquiring without obstacle and for
> possessing in safety.
>
>   This situation demands maxims particular to you. Not being idle as
> ancient Peoples were, you cannot ceaselessly occupy yourselves with the
> Government as they did.

His solution to this was the distinction between sovereign and government
which Pufendorf had attacked (elsewhere labeling it "casuistry") and
which Hobbes had eloquently described; once again, it is hard to believe
that Rousseau was unaware of this lineage.

   The commonest response to this view of the resemblance between
Hobbes and Rousseau, when I have put it forward, has been that there is
nevertheless a key difference between them, in the area of *representation*.
Even scholars as sympathetic to the general case as Istvan Hont and
Michael Sonenscher have insisted that Hobbes was the great theorist of
representation, while Rousseau (in the words of Sonenscher) was "openly
critical of the idea of representation that was the cornerstone of Hobbes'
political theory."[45] Now, it is of course true that Rousseau denounced the
idea that the sovereign general will can be represented:

> Sovereignty, for the same reason as makes it inalienable, cannot be repre-
> sented; it lies essentially in the general will, and will does not admit of
> representation: it is either the same, or other; there is no intermediate
> possibility.[46]

But what he was addressing in this passage was representation by elected
deputies, as in England, and, as his remarks shortly afterwards about the
modern character of representation make clear, he was engaged here not

---

[45] E. Sieyès, *Political Writings*, ed. M. Sonenscher (Indianapolis: Hackett Pub. Co., 2003), p. xlvi.
[46] *Social Contract*, in *Social Contract and Discourses*, p. 263.

with Hobbes but with Montesquieu's chapter on the English constitution. Rousseau was not in fact at all critical of the idea of representation as used by Hobbes; there is no criticism in Rousseau of the fundamental Hobbesian thought that *individuals* are represented by the sovereign, that its will is taken to be their will, and that it is this (so to speak) collection of individual representations which makes the sovereign's will general in character. This is, as I have stressed, Rousseau's idea also, and is expressed in words with which Hobbes could not have disagreed: "Each of us puts his person and all his power in common under the supreme direction of the general will," and each person ceases to be "his own judge."[47]

What Rousseau profoundly disagreed with was the idea that a *sovereign*, once constituted, could be represented, and in particular that a sovereign people could be represented *in its sovereignty* through deputies; his rejection of this idea was simply part of his general rejection of the standard eighteenth-century view that a people could have an identity as a sovereign and autonomous body, but would be unable to act unless represented by an omnicompetent institution such as a King or a Parliament. The denial of representation is thus merely the correlate of the distinction between sovereign and government, for the essence of that distinction is that the government cannot represent the sovereign as sovereign. But it can act as the sovereign's agent in specific areas, and Rousseau had no problem with that – "in the exercise of the legislative power, the people cannot be represented; but in that of the executive power, which is only the force that is applied to give the law effect, it both can and should be represented," he said in Book III Chapter XV – though he immediately added, "we thus see that if we looked closely into the matter we should find that very few nations have any laws."[48] Again, Hobbes could not have disagreed with any of this; this after all was precisely his point in denying that an elective king was a sovereign. The moment at which a sovereign's agent represents a sovereign in the same sense that the sovereign represents the individual citizen – that is, that the will of the representative *fully comprehends* that of the represented person – is for Hobbes, as much as for Rousseau, a moment at which sovereignty has been transferred or usurped, and the vizier has become the king.

There is, however, one area where Rousseau unquestionably diverged from Hobbes, and it is the key difference between them. Rousseau, as we all know, did not believe that the sovereign legislature could transfer or

---

[47] Ibid., p. 191.   [48] Ibid., p. 264.

alienate its sovereignty to another person or assembly, and Hobbes did –
this after all was the basis of his own royalism, and why most readers of
Hobbes have taken his politics to be the antithesis of Rousseau's. But it is
fair to say that Rousseau spotted a genuine problem with Hobbes's
account. A democratic legislature in Hobbes has the full power to create
a new site of sovereignty for its citizens, for its decisions in all potentially
controversial matters are authoritative, and among those potentially
controversial matters is the location of sovereignty. So much is clear and
consistent. The problem arises from the fact that a democratic assembly,
for Hobbes, is itself an entity which has a single will and a determinate
institutional character, and that Hobbes treats it throughout his work as
strictly equivalent to a monarch. But no sovereign agent is entitled to
transfer its sovereignty to another: as Hobbes said in Chapter 30 of
Leviathan, "it is the Office of the Soveraign, to maintain those Rights
['the essentiall Rights of Sovereignty'] entire; and consequently against his
duty, First, to transferre to another, or to lay from himselfe any of them."[49]
Moreover, if an assembly dissolves itself, this is the equivalent of suicide in
a monarch, and no coherent account can be given of why it should choose
to do so. Hobbes may have had in mind the thought that a democratic
assembly might find its power being undermined by the "aristocracy of
orators"[50] who would hijack its discussions, and that eventually it would
have to transfer its powers to a monarch because it could no longer exercise
them effectively itself (as in the fall of the Roman Republic); but such
a failed sovereign assembly would no longer properly represent its citizens
already, before the moment of transfer. Rousseau, who certainly thought
that a democratic sovereign assembly would inevitably fail and be corrupted, interpreted this as the "death of the body politic,"[51] and on the face
of it this is more consistent with Hobbes's ideas than Hobbes's own claim
that a transfer could take place from a democracy to a monarchy. What
Rousseau's work revealed was that the underlying thrust of Hobbes's ideas,
remarkable as it may seem, was not toward absolutist government but

---

[49] Hobbes, *Leviathan*, p. 231.
[50] "A democracy, in effect, is no more than an aristocracy of orators, interrupted sometimes with the
temporary monarchy of one orator" (*Elements of Law*, pp. 120–121). This is of course virtually
identical to the remark by Rousseau in his *Political Economy* quoted above: "Athens was in fact not
a Democracy, but a very tyrannical Aristocracy, governed by philosophers and orators" (*Social
Contract and Discourses*, p. 134). This part of the *Elements* had been available in French since 1652, in
the form of *Le corps politique*; in French the passage reads "une Démocratie en effet n'est rien autre
chose qu'une Aristocratie de harangeurs, quelquefois aussi une Monarchie d'un seul Orateur."
[51] The title of Book III, Chapter 11 of the *Social Contract*; see *Social Contract and Discourses*, p. 257.

toward the modern theory of democratic sovereignty; though one should remember the acute comment of Jacob Vernet which I quoted earlier, that

> believing with *Hobbes* that men are born the enemies of one another, and that our worst enemies are our superiors, like him he remedies this by Despotism, though locating it in a different place. Whereas Hobbes gives arbitrary power to a Prince, Mr. Rousseau (who knows no middle ground) instead gives a similar power to the multitude.[52]

The last question to deal with on this subject is the hardest. As I have said, the similarities between much of Rousseau's theory and much of Hobbes' are striking, and acquire added force from the fact that they had been identified as ideas which were specifically Hobbes' in the work of the writers whom Rousseau most detested, such as Pufendorf. And yet on almost every occasion where Rousseau explicitly refers to Hobbes, it is in conventionally critical terms; the one exception, as is well known, is on the subject of civil religion, where Rousseau said that "the philosopher Hobbes alone . . . has dared to propose the reunion of the two heads of the eagle," i.e. church and state. One possibility is that by virtue of reacting strenuously against what he thought were the most distasteful features of the conventional theories of his time, he found himself necessarily, but to a degree unwittingly, recapitulating the ideas which those theories had been constructed to refute, and that may be all we need to say. But it is an unsatisfactory position to take up, both because the Hobbesian character of the ideas was so clearly signaled in those works, and because it is plain that Rousseau had read Hobbes quite closely – the various verbal echoes to which I have drawn attention illustrate that. I think that we are closer to the mark if we return to the fact from which I began this paper, the discrepancy between Hobbes' actual account of men as naturally timorous and not inherently violent, and the standard view to which much of the eighteenth century, including Rousseau, subscribed, that Hobbesian man is naturally bent on domination. Rousseau observed, in a well-known passage in the *First Discourse*, that

> Hobbes had seen clearly the defects of all the modern definitions of natural right: but the consequences which he deduces from his own show that he understands it in an equally false sense. In reasoning on the principles he lays

[52] "Mr. Rousseau, qui croyant avec *Hobbes* que les hommes sont nés ennemis les uns des autres, & croyant de plus que nous n'avons pas de pires ennemis que nos supérieurs, y remédie comme lui par le Despotisme, mais en le plaçant differemment. Car au lieu que Hobbes donne le pouvoir arbitraire à un Prince, Mr. Rousseau qui ne connoit point les milieux, donne un semblable pouvoir à la multitude." *Lettre d'un citoyen de Genève à un autre citoyen* (Geneva, 1768), pp. 72–73.

down, he ought to have said that the state of nature, being that in which the
care for our own preservation is the least prejudicial to that of others, was
consequently the best calculated to promote peace, and the most suitable for
mankind. He does say the exact opposite, in consequence of having impro-
perly admitted, as a part of savage man's care for self-preservation, the
gratification of a multitude of passions which are the work of society, and
have made laws necessary.

As we have seen, something like the correct conclusions from Hobbes'
principles which Rousseau drew were in fact the conclusions which
Hobbes himself had drawn. Rousseau, unwilling to repudiate the conventional view of Hobbes, thought that he had been able to go where in the
end Hobbes had not been able to go; but because they shared the same
premises, and more importantly shared the same kind of intuitive response
to the modern world, Rousseau almost found himself tracking Hobbes in
many more respects than he had, perhaps, realized.

CHAPTER 4

Rousseau and Montesquieu

J. Kent Wright

Among contemporaries with whom Rousseau had relationships of one kind or another, Montesquieu occupies a category all his own. The connection between the two was impersonal, confined to the printed page, and was thus without the intimacies and ruptures that are familiar from Rousseau's friendships with Diderot, Grimm, or Hume. However, Rousseau acquired a grasp of Montesquieu's writing that was probably without equal in his generation in breadth and depth, involving its own kind of intimacy. Hand in hand with this expertise went profound admiration. In Rousseau's works, references to Montesquieu are exceeded in number only by those to Grotius; unlike the latter, they are invariably respectful, with no trace of the sarcasm and mockery regularly meted out to the Dutchman. Yet admiration was no bar to disagreement with Montesquieu, on matters small and large. It was Rousseau himself who captured the chief point of divergence between the two most memorably. "The science of political right is yet to be born," he wrote in the Fifth Book of *Emile*, insisting that Grotius and Hobbes alike had failed utterly at the task. "The only modern in a position to create this great and useless science was the illustrious Montesquieu. But he was careful not to discuss the principles of political right. He was content to discuss the positive right of established governments, and nothing in the world is more different than these two studies."[1] Opinion has long been divided over the meaning of this characteristically Delphic statement. At one end of the spectrum, commentators from the Revolution onward have portrayed Rousseau and Montesquieu as antithetical figures, sitting on opposite sides of one divide or another – ancient vs. modern, conservative vs. radical, rationalist vs. empiricist, liberal vs. "totalitarian." For others, Montesquieu's survey of "positive right" and Rousseau's theory of "political right" were complementary rather than contradictory exercises: beneath the appearance of

---

[1] J.-J. Rousseau, *Emile, or, On Education*, trans. A. Bloom (New York: Basic Books, 1979), p. 458.

surface differences, the two thinkers shared a profound complicity. What few have doubted is the importance of the pairing for grasping the shape of modern political thought. As Christopher Kelly has recently remarked, the careers of Montesquieu and Rousseau "resemble the legs of a relay across the middle of the eighteenth century."[2] But exactly what kind of race were they running and toward what destination?

* * *

A meeting in passing between Rousseau and Montesquieu cannot be ruled out. Born only a generation apart, both resided in Paris for long stretches after 1745, and shared a skein of mutual acquaintances. Prominent among these were the wealthy tax farmer Claude Dupin and his wife Louise-Marie-Madeleine, inveterate intellectual dabblers who hosted a famous salon on the Île Saint-Louis. Rousseau met the latter, a renowned beauty, in 1743, their first encounter memorably described in the *Confessions*. He went on to work as secretary to Madame Dupin between 1746 and 1751. Montesquieu, who divided his time equally between Paris and La Brède during the final decade of his life, knew the Dupins, attended their salon, and may well have crossed paths there with their young employee. If so, neither he nor Rousseau left any mention of it; nor has any correspondence between them survived. What is certain, however, is that it was to the Dupins that Rousseau owed his initial engagement with Montesquieu's writing. For hardly was *The Spirit of the Laws* in print than Claude Dupin decided to write a critical response, aimed at Montesquieu's analysis of monarchy and his attack on tax farming in particular. Madame Dupin's secretary was duly set to work, closely studying not just the book itself, but a large number of Montesquieu's sources as well. The fruits of Rousseau's labors – hundreds of pages of *précis* and notes in his hand – remain unpublished, preserved in the Bibliothèque Municipale of Bordeaux.[3] They betray nothing of Rousseau's attitude toward the Dupins' project, the first expression of which was the two-volume *Réflexions sur quelques parties d'un livre intitulé "de l'Esprit des loix"* (1749). But the book's criticisms were sufficiently wounding to cause a permanent breach between the Dupins and Montesquieu himself, who sought, effectively, to have the work suppressed. Undeterred, Dupin pressed on, eventually publishing

[2] C. Kelly, "Rousseau and the Illustrious Montesquieu," in E. Grace and C. Kelly eds., *The Challenge of Rousseau* (Cambridge: Cambridge University Press, 2013), p. 19.
[3] See A. Sénéchal, "Jean-Jacques Rousseau, secrétaire de Madame Dupin d'après des documents inédits avec un inventaire des papiers Dupin dispersés en 1957 et 1958," in *Annales des la Société Jean-Jacques Rousseau* 36 (1963–65), pp. 173–288.

a more moderate but expanded version of the critique three years later. By this point, Madame Dupin had abandoned, unfinished, her own *Ouvrage sur les femmes*, on which Rousseau had labored for years as well, and which also took critical aim at *The Spirit of the Laws*.[4]

Whether they ever met or not, Montesquieu surely became aware of Rousseau's existence at some point. There is no copy of the *Discourse on the Sciences and the Arts* to be found in his libraries, at either Paris or La Brède. But its notoriety was such that Montesquieu could scarcely have failed to hear it spoken of – he was a close acquaintance with Stanisław Leszczyński, author of one of the major rejoinders to Rousseau. Moreover, in February 1752, Montesquieu received a letter from his friend Hénault, reporting on the imminent appearance of the revised edition of Dupin's *Réflexions*, and recording that Dupin had been aided in his work "by M. Rousseau of Geneva, as well as by others."[5] Whatever Montesquieu made of this news, the sole report of any comment on Rousseau is second-hand, coming years after his death. Late in 1764, shortly after receiving the invitation from Buttafoco to write on Corsica, Rousseau got a letter from his Swiss friend Vincent Capperonnier de Gauffecourt, encouraging him to take up the task: "I really hope that you work for the Corsicans. Only you can do it. M. le Président Montesquieu told me many times that you alone were capable of working on *The Spirit of the Laws*."[6] There is nothing implausible about the remark: Montesquieu might well have been acknowledging Rousseau's part in the Dupins' campaign against his book, while also paying tribute to the author of the *Discourse on the Sciences and the Arts*. But even if it could be verified – Robert Shackleton, among others, doubted that Gauffecourt ever met Montesquieu – it amounts to no more than a tantalizing *non sequitur*. Montesquieu's death early in 1755, five months before the publication of the *Discourse on Inequality*, ended any chance of a personal relationship between the two. Gauffecourt's report aside, all evidence comes from Rousseau's hand alone. There is no better introduction to its general tone than the letter he wrote to his compatriot Perdriau ten days after Montesquieu's death: "You will be saddened as I am by the death of the illustrious Montesquieu. All those who have a homeland and who love it will mourn this great man. He had no need of so long a life to become an

---

[4] The bulk of Madame Dupin's work on *Ouvrage sur les femmes*, including Rousseau's extensive notes, are now housed at the Harry Ransom Center, at the University of Texas at Austin.

[5] C. Hénault to Montesquieu (13 February 1752), in *Oeuvres complètes de Montesquieu*, ed. A. Masson (Paris: n.p., 1950–1955), III, p. 1421.

[6] J. Gauffecourt to Rousseau (9 December 1764, no. 3728), CC XXII, p. 204.

immortal; but he ought to have lived forever, to teach people their rights and their duties."[7] Here the same adjective figures as in the passage from *Emile*. As Christopher Kelly points out, Rousseau consistently made use of the word "*illustre*" to refer to fame that he believed was genuinely merited – its opposite number being the "celebrity" he ascribed to objects of scorn such as Voltaire or Grotius.[8]

If no reader of Rousseau's published works will doubt the depth of his intellectual allegiance to Montesquieu, modern scholarship has gradually revealed that the connection was far closer than was once supposed. First and foremost has been the recognition of how much the breakthrough of the *Discourse on the Sciences and the Arts* probably owed to the inspiration of *The Spirit of the Laws*. The timing was certainly right. In both the *Confessions* and the letter to Malesherbes of January 1762, describing the "illumination" on the way to Vincennes in greater detail, Rousseau portrayed the latter as a bolt from the blue, provoked by the Dijon Academy's prize question alone. But that bolt arrived, in October 1749, precisely when Rousseau had just completed his exhaustive study of *The Spirit of the Laws* for the Dupins. The textual evidence from the *Discourse* itself is circumstantial, but striking enough. Leo Strauss seems to have been the first to notice one of its chief exhibits. Early in the attack on "luxury" in Part II of the text, Rousseau encapsulated the *Discourse*'s founding contrast in memorable fashion: "The ancient politicians forever spoke of morals and virtue; ours speak only of commerce and of money. One will tell you that in a given land a man is worth the sum for which he would be sold in Algiers; another, pursuing this calculation, will find countries where a man is worth nothing, and others where he is worth less than nothing."[9] In a now-famous 1947 essay, "On the Intention of Rousseau," Strauss pointed out that Rousseau had here soldered together close paraphrases of two passages from *The Spirit of the Laws*: from Book III, Chapter 3: "The political men of Greece who lived under popular government recognized no other force to sustain it but virtue. Those of today speak to us only of manufacturing, commerce, finance, wealth, and even luxury"; and from Book XXIII, Chapter 17: "Sir William Petty has assumed in his calculations that a man in England is worth what he would be sold for in Algiers. This can be good only for England: there are

---

[7] Rousseau to J. Perdriau (20 February 1755, no. 277), CC III, p. 98. "I was in the country when he died," Rousseau continued, "and I am told that of all the men of letters with whom Paris teems, M. Diderot alone walked in the funeral cortège – fortunately, he was also the one whose presence would make the absence of the others less noticeable."
[8] Kelly, "Rousseau and the Illustrious Montesquieu," p. 33.   [9] *Discourse on Inequality*, G1, p. 18.

countries in which a man is worth nothing; there are some in which he is worth less than nothing."[10]

Strauss himself did not draw extensive conclusions, beyond noting a few other echoes of *The Spirit of the Laws* in the text and asserting that "it is not misleading to say that in the *Discourse* Rousseau starts by drawing the most extreme conclusions that a republican could draw from Montesquieu's analysis of republics."[11] But his surmise about Rousseau's debt to Montesquieu in the First Discourse has been amply vindicated by subsequent scholarship. By the mid-1960s, in the wake of the publication of the Pléiade edition of Rousseau's political writings, French scholars began to take notice of the same evidence, now considered in the light of his work for the Dupins, of which Strauss seems to have been unaware.[12] Today there is widespread acceptance of the notion that the origins of the *Discourse on the Sciences and the Arts* can be traced to ideas – skepticism about modern conceptions of historical "progress," in light of ancient "virtue" – that Rousseau first encountered in *The Spirit of the Laws* and then distilled into a considerably more pointed and polemical essence. Not only that, but this understanding of Rousseau's intellectual starting point has in turn made it possible to view virtually every stage in the evolution of his political thought, from 1749 down to the *Social Contract* and beyond, as the result of an uninterrupted dialogue with Montesquieu – such that Rousseau might well be considered, in Gabrielle Radica's apt phrase, a "critical disciple" of the author of *The Spirit of the Laws*.[13] It would be wrong to suggest that this view has swept all scholarly opinion before it – it counts for more in the Anglosphere than in France itself. But from that zone we now have not one but two recent accounts of this kind, each portraying Rousseau as the critical conductor of Montesquieu's thought to a revolutionary or post-revolutionary destination. Downstream from Strauss himself, there is Paul Rahe's *Soft Despotism, Democracy's Drift*, in which Rousseau serves as the relay between Montesquieu and Tocqueville.

---

[10] Montesquieu, *The Spirit of the Laws*, trans. and ed. A. Cohler et al. (Cambridge: Cambridge University Press, 1989), pp. 22–23, 439.

[11] L. Strauss, "On the Intention of Rousseau," in *Challenge of Rousseau*, pp. 125, 127. Strauss' essay, a review George Havens's critical edition of the First Discourse of a year earlier, was first published in *Social Research* 14 (1947): pp. 455–487.

[12] See A. Adam, "De quelques sources de Rousseau dans la littérature philosophique (1700–1750)," in *Jean-Jacques Rousseau et son oeuvre: problèmes et recherches* (Paris: Librairie C. Klincksieck, 1964), p. 127; and M. Launay, *Jean-Jacques Rousseau et son temps* (Paris: A.G. Nizet, 1969), pp. 93–103.

[13] G. Radica, "Rousseau, Jean-Jacques," online *Dictionnaire Montesquieu*, under the direction of C. Volpilhac-Auger, ENS de Lyon, septembre 2013. URL: http://dictionnaire-montesquieu.ens -lyon.fr/fr/article/1377669928/fr. This, and Jean Ehrard's "Le fils coupable," cited below, are by far the best introductions to the subject.

Michael Sonenscher had already adopted a similar position in his *Before the Deluge: Public Debt, Inequality, and the Intellectual Origins of the French Revolution*, in which Rousseau takes a prominent place in the "sequence of moves that, in a not particularly stylised way, can be said to have led from Montesquieu to Sieyès."[14]

We will return below to the wider conclusions drawn from these accounts. Here, it is enough to indicate the overlap in their understanding of the role that Montesquieu played in the development of Rousseau's thought. On this view, the Second and Third Discourses were very much like the First – works that can be seen as extended variations on themes introduced in *The Spirit of the Laws*, to which Rousseau gradually added original elements of his own. What Part One of the *Discourse on Inequality* offered, then, was a kind of reprise of Book I of *The Spirit of the Laws*, in which Montesquieu's critique of Hobbes's *hysteron proteron* was extended to the rest of the great seventeenth-century theorists of the state of nature: Grotius, Pufendorf, and Locke. At one with Montesquieu in rejecting both Hobbes and the theorists of "natural sociability," Rousseau also made a foundational move of his own at this point: he set aside Montesquieu's use of "fear" as first lever of social development, replacing it with "pity," which henceforth served as the linchpin of his philosophical anthropology. The stadial theory of Part Two of the Second Discourse – social stratification evolving via "revolutions" in modes of subsistence, then locked into place by ever more autocratic political states – is beyond anything in *The Spirit of the Laws* in specificity and detail. But neither is it discrepant in any way with Montesquieu's fleeting gestures at stadial history and the vague silhouette he offered of the course of history in the West, in its procession from ancient republics to modern monarchies. The main difference was simply Rousseau's focus on inequality which then figured centrally in the *Discourse on Political Economy*. Yet the inspiration of *The Spirit of the Laws* was, if anything, plainer still in the Third Discourse. For if the centerpiece of the first part of the text was Rousseau's defense of individual property rights as the foundation of all legitimate government, each of the three chief political developments of the theme in the second part owed a direct debt to Montesquieu: taxation – where Rousseau's arguments on behalf of proportionality are developed in dialogue, critical and approbative, with Montesquieu; the "general will" – whose first appearance in Rousseau's writing is all but certain to have been inspired

---

[14] M. Sonenscher, *Before the Deluge: Public Debt, Inequality, and the Intellectual Origins of the French Revolution* (Princeton: Princeton University Press, 2007), p. 19.

by its use in Book XI of *The Spirit of the Laws*; and finally, education – whose umbilical connection to "virtue," in Rousseau's eyes, looks like a straightforward application of Montesquieu's theory of republican education in Book V.[15]

From this angle, the three Discourses, taken together, indeed appear to be work of a "critical disciple" of Montesquieu. What then of the *Social Contract*? This returns us to the passage from *Emile*, for the *Social Contract* was precisely Rousseau's own effort to go beyond Montesquieu and set forth the "principles of political right" – the book's subtitle, of course. From the first page of the text, establishing political "legitimacy" as its central problematic, we are obviously in territory for which *The Spirit of the Laws* can have provided little inspiration or assistance to Rousseau. For his handling of the main topics of Books I and II of the *Social Contract* – social pact and political sovereignty – Rousseau plainly needed a model from the natural rights tradition itself, conventionally understood to be Hobbes.[16] Nor is it surprising, in light of his new understanding of "political right," that Rousseau should have now felt compelled to register serious disagreement with Montesquieu, beyond technicalities concerning taxation. His declaration in Book II, Chapter 6, that "Every legitimate Government is republican" already appears tacitly to have departed from the typology of *The Spirit of the Laws*. The divergence then becomes explicit indeed in Book III, whose topic is "government." Early on, there is Rousseau's complaint, in Chapter 4, that the author of *The Spirit of the Laws* had failed to grasp that "virtue" must be the principle of every legitimate government: "That is why a famous Author attributed virtue to Republics as their principle; for all these conditions could not subsist without virtue; but for want of drawing the necessary distinctions, this noble genius often lacked in precision, sometimes in clarity, and he failed to see that since Sovereign authority is everywhere the same, the same principle must obtain in every well-constituted State ..."[17] Eleven chapters later comes Rousseau's attack on "representation":

---

[15] For a pathbreaking recent analysis of the Third Discourse, see R. Hanley, "Political Economy and Individual Liberty," in *Challenge of Rousseau*, pp. 34–56.

[16] For the most incisive analysis of the evolution of rights theories, from the sixteenth to the eighteenth centuries, see J. Terrel, *Les Théories du pacte social: Droit natural, souveraineté et contrat de Bodin à Rousseau* (Paris: Éditions due Seuil, 2001); for a pithy recent statement of the central debt that Rousseau is assumed to have owed to Hobbes, see D. Wootton's "Introduction" to Rousseau, *The Basic Political Writings*, trans. D. Cress (Indianapolis: Hackett Pub. Co., 2011), pp. xxvi–xxvii.

[17] *Social Contract*, G2, pp. 91–92.

> Sovereignty cannot be represented for the same reason that it cannot be alienated; it consists essentially in the general will, and the will does not admit of being represented [...] The English people thinks it is free; it is greatly mistaken, it is free only during the election of Members of Parliament; as soon as they are elected, it is enslaved, it is nothing. The use it makes of its freedom during the brief moments it has it fully warrants its losing it [...] The idea of Representatives is modern: it comes to us from feudal Government, that iniquitous and absurd Government in which the human species is degraded, and the name of man dishonored.[18]

There is no mention of Montesquieu's name in Chapter 15 – but none was necessary, of course. Few readers have doubted the target of these famous lines. With them, Rousseau would appear not just to have declared his independence from Montesquieu, but to have adopted a diametrically opposed conception of political liberty. For surely we are faced here with mutually exclusive conceptions of freedom – in Isaiah Berlin's classic terms, Montesquieu defending the "negative liberty" secured by "checking and balancing" the power of the state, and Rousseau the "positive" liberty of participation in the formation of a "general will" unchecked in its exercise of power.

All the same, a long line of commentators, from Robert Derathé to the scholars cited above, warn us not to exaggerate the distance that had opened up between Montesquieu and Rousseau with the appearance of the latter's "science of political right." The fact that the conceptual center-piece of Rousseau's theory of popular sovereignty, the "general will," was originally a borrowing from *The Spirit of the Laws* says a good deal. It was in Book XI, Chapter 6 itself, introducing his notion of the "separation of powers," that Montesquieu described legislative power as "the general will of the state," and executive power as "the execution of that general will."[19] In refashioning the concept for his own purposes, Rousseau first assimilated the "general will" to sovereign authority *tout court* in the course of Book II. In the first chapter of Book III, he then introduced a distinction absent from *The Spirit of the Laws*, for obvious reasons, between "sovereignty" thus defined and "government" – identifying the former with legislative power, the latter with executive power alone. That done, in the ensuing analysis of the various forms of government, Rousseau actually followed very closely in the tracks laid down in *The Spirit of the Laws*. Montesquieu could be chastised for having failed to see that all legitimate government required "virtuous" subjects – but also warmly congratulated

---

[18] Ibid., p. 114.   [19] Montesquieu, *The Spirit of the Laws*, p. 158.

for grasping not just the necessary relations between the size of the populace and the appropriate form of its government, but also the relation of both to liberty: "Freedom, not being a fruit of every Clime, is not within the reach of every people. The more one meditates upon this principle established by Montesquieu, the more one senses its truth."[20] As for the critique of "representation" in Chapter 15, that of course applies to the representation of *sovereignty* alone. Without quite saying so, Rousseau clearly regarded representation in *government* as another thing entirely. After all, in Chapter 4, he had already declared direct democracy "unsuitable" to mankind, and in Chapter 5, described "electoral aristocracy" as the "best and most natural" form of government, not least for its tendency to maintain a proper separation of powers within its structure. Little surprise, then, that the echoes of *The Spirit of the Laws* should be as unmistakable as they are in Book IV of the *Social Contract*. Rousseau's analysis of the elaborate electoral machinery of the Roman Republic in Book IV owed much to the *Considerations on the Causes of the Greatness of the Romans and their Decline*; and the theory of "civil religion" that closes the *Social Contract* is to all intents and purposes identical to that of Montesquieu.

Despite appearances, then, not even in the *Social Contract* did Rousseau abandon his role as Montesquieu's "critical disciple." Derathé famously held that, had the former been able to complete the *Political Institutions*, it would have involved circling back closer still to *The Spirit of the Laws*.[21] In any case, Rousseau's dialogue with Montesquieu did not end with the *Social Contract*. Gabrielle Radica has recently shown how Rousseau developed a "substratum" of arguments about England in the latter work, less visible than the attack on "representation" – i.e., the analysis of "mixed government" in Book III, Chapter 6, the striking footnote praising "a little agitation" à la Machiavelli in Chapter 9 – for use in the *Letters Written from the Mountain*. There, where the English constitution is consistently held to be superior to that of Geneva, there are frequent appeals to the authority of Montesquieu.[22] On other occasions, Rousseau could revert to criticism, even while continuing to display a disciple's command of the master's writing. His final gesture in Montesquieu's direction came in the discussion of truth and fiction in the fourth episode of the *Reveries of the Solitary*

---

[20] *Social Contract*, G2, p. 100.
[21] See R. Derathé, *Jean-Jacques Rousseau et la science politique de son temps* (Paris: J. Vrin, 1970), pp. 52–62.
[22] G. Radica, "De Montesquieu à Rousseau: les Anglais sont-ils libres?" *Revue française des idées politiques* 35 (2012): pp. 159–169.

Walker. There, addressing "fictions which are entirely pointless, such as the majority of tales and novels," Rousseau had a *recherché* example ready to hand: "If there is, for example, some moral purpose in *The Temple of Cnidus*, it is obscured and undermined by the book's sensual and lascivious images. How did the author cover all that with a veneer of decency? He claimed that his work was the translation of a Greek manuscript in just such a way as to persuade his readers of the truth of his account. If that is not positively a lie, then I wish someone would tell me what lying is. However, has any ever taken it upon himself to treat the author's lie as a crime and to treat him as an impostor because of it?"[23] *The Temple of Cnidus* was a literary bagatelle among Montesquieu's works. But even there, Rousseau was alert to the difference between "is" and "ought."

***

If such, very roughly, is the evidence concerning Rousseau's relationship to Montesquieu, how should it be interpreted? There is no doubt that among ways of approaching the pairing, *contrast* has long prevailed over comparison, not to speak of acknowledging any kind of convergence between the two thinkers. The main reason for this is clear. From the Revolution onwards, the name and image of Rousseau were pressed into ever more extravagant ideological service, in ways that made it increasingly difficult to view him in intelligible relation to Montesquieu. As Kelly suggests in his essay on the First Discourse, the writing was already on the wall by 1791, in the distance between Burke's reverential treatment of Montesquieu in *An Appeal from the New to the Old Whigs* ("a genius not born in every country … with a Herculean robustness of mind … like the universal patriarch in Milton") and his savage commination against Rousseau ("We have had the great professor and founder of *the philosophy of vanity in England* … It is from this same deranged eccentric vanity that this, the insane *Socrates* of the national assembly, was impelled to publish a mad confession of his mad faults … Your assembly, knowing how much more powerful example is found than precept, have chosen this man [by his own account without a single virtue] for a model.").[24] The adoption of Rousseau as Jacobin mascot and his *panthéonisation* sealed the deal. A showpiece for classical liberalism, the notion of *la faute à Rousseau* was only confirmed by the ease with which he was subsequently enlisted as an ancestor of French socialism. As for the vicissitudes of Rousseau's

---

[23] Rousseau, *Reveries of the Solitary Walker*, trans. R. Goulbourne (Oxford: Oxford University Press, 2011), pp. 38–39.
[24] Kelly, "Rousseau and the Illustrious Montesquieu," pp. 19–20.

reputation in the twentieth century, we now have an incisive guide in Céline Spector's *Au prisme de Rousseau: usages politiques contemporains*, which highlights all the ways in which Rousseau's reputation became caught up, and mangled, in the great ideological battles that accompanied the careers of Communism and Fascism.[25] Mild approval within specific currents of Western Marxism – we will return to the case of Louis Althusser below – was more than balanced by furious assaults on Rousseau, not just from the far Right, but by the Cold War liberalism that commanded the heights of Western opinion after 1945. If the pioneers here were Austrian – Popper or Hayek depicting him as a "Platonist" or "constructivist" enemy of individual freedom – the definitive portrait of Rousseau as a "totalitarian" was the work of Anglo-American liberalism. The standouts in this regard were Jacob Talmon's *Origins of Totalitarian Democracy* and Isaiah Berlin's famous essay "Two Concepts of Liberty," which both assigned Rousseau a prominent role in the genealogy of twentieth-century collectivism, Nazi and Stalinist alike.

The textual warrant for these exercises rarely went beyond two or three citations from the *Social Contract*. But among their results was either to put discussion of the relationship between Rousseau and Montesquieu out of court altogether, or to confine it entirely to stark contrasts between them – the former's admiration for Spartan collectivism paving the way for every form of modern political terror, Jacobin, Communist, and Fascist, while the latter's celebration of English constitutionalism flowed directly into the modern liberal mainstream, etc. Not all of this writing was as crude as that. Berlin, for example, while treating Montesquieu as a paradigmatic "pluralist" and Rousseau as the quintessential modern "monist," remained an acute analyst of both thinkers – not least for declining to stage a direct confrontation between them. Moreover, with the ebbing away of Cold War passions, it became possible to approach contrasts between the two more coolly and creatively. A case in point is Norman Hampson's unjustly neglected *Will and Circumstance: Montesquieu, Rousseau, and the French Revolution* (1983). While not entirely avoiding the clichés – "Where Montesquieu, after some hesitation, had rejected antiquity in favor of the modern world, Rousseau remained wedded to a literal re-creation of Sparta"[26] – Hampson sought to ground the divergences between the two in a historical narrative, extending from the last years of the Old Regime to

---

[25] C. Spector, *Au Prisme de Rousseau: usages politiques contemporains* (Oxford: Voltaire Foundation, 2011).

[26] Hampson, *Will and Circumstance: Montesquieu, Rousseau, and the French Revolution* (Norman: University of Oklahoma Press, 1983), p. 50.

the Terror. Originally, a series of admirers, each destined to be major players in the Revolution (Mercier, Brissot, Marat, Robespierre, and Saint-Just), saw no chasm at all between Montesquieu and Rousseau – a conviction that survived through the first years of the Revolution. It was only the awful choices of the Year II, Hampson argues, that finally drove a firm wedge between them, in the view of these followers. More recent still is Paul Dubouchet's *De Montesquieu le moderne à Rousseau l'ancien: la démocratie et la république en question* (2001), the work of a political philosopher rather than an intellectual historian. Inspired by the legal philosopher Giovanni Lobrano, Dubouchet's compact study juxtaposes "two antagonistic models" of public law, "*the ancient or Roman model* [...]" theorized in the first instance by Cicero in his *Republic* before finding its fullest expression in the *Social Contract* of Rousseau," and the "*modern or Germano-English* model," which is "aristocratic *par excellence*" and which "found its first great systematization in the *Spirit of the Laws* of Montesquieu." The former model alone is authentically "republican," in its explicit embrace of popular sovereignty, and genuinely "democratic," for entrusting the protection of individual liberties to a popular "tribunate" rather than an oligarchic "balance" of powers.[27]

Treatments of Rousseau and Montesquieu by means of comparison and, especially, contrast, will probably always be with us. Far more interesting, however, has been the work of the scholars cited above, stressing the profound intellectual debt the former owed to the latter, and attempting to draw some wider conclusions about this complicity. Pride of place here belongs to the one very striking exception to the hostility shown to Rousseau by mainstream Western opinion, conservative and liberal alike, at the height of the Cold War. At the far right of the political spectrum, Strauss and his pupils have been generally immune to the temptation to treat Rousseau as a species of "totalitarian." For Strauss himself, Rousseau was the master-thinker of the "first crisis of modern natural right," whose proto-historicist critique of Hobbes and Locke paved the way for the second, even greater crossroads represented by Nietzsche. For followers such as Allan Bloom or Paul Rahe in the United States, or Pierre Manent in France, Rousseau remains the most thoughtful and acute of all critics of "bourgeois" modernity. Montesquieu, on the other hand, occupied a relatively marginal position in Strauss' work – though Strauss did insist

---

[27] As a quixotic intervention in contemporary politics, Dubouchet's book bears comparison with J. McCormick, *Machiavellian Democracy* (Cambridge: Cambridge University Press, 2011), which argues on behalf of amending the U.S. constitution by addition of a "tribunate," à la Machiavelli.

not just on the fundamental *modernity* of his outlook as well, but also on the specific character of his political choice: "*The Spirit of the Laws* reads as if it were nothing but the document of an incessant fight, an unresolved conflict, between two social and political ideals: the Roman republic, whose principle is virtue, and England, whose principle is liberty. But in fact Montesquieu decides eventually in favor of England."[28]

Still, it has taken some time, and the drawing of attention to the evidence of Rousseau's work for the Dupins, to develop an interpretation of the relations between the two thinkers from this standpoint. An initial step in this direction was taken by Bernard Yack – outside the Straussian perimeter proper, but close enough in spirit, and influenced by Strauss' essay – in his first book, *The Longing for Total Revolution*. In it, Yack set out to establish the "philosophical sources" of the longing in question, the yearning to overcome the "dehumanization" of mankind in modern society. The main part of the book traced the development of this desire from the "Kantian Left" down to its culmination in two great projects for "total revolution" on the Left and Right, those of Marx and Nietzsche. But the *first* modern thinker to express this kind of longing, Yack argues, was Rousseau, whose intoxicated appeal to "classical republicanism" was itself based on Montesquieu's infinitely more sober and ambivalent view of classical antiquity. Rousseau's "classical republicanism" was something very different from Pocock's "Atlantic republican tradition," which Yack dismissed as largely fictitious. For there is no question of Montesquieu's and especially Rousseau's modernity, the surest sign of which is its commitment to individualism: "Here is the great paradox of Rousseau's political thought: he demands the complete subordination of the individual *for the sake of the individual*, not to further the collectively shared goals that constitute the community. It is by pursuing the needs of the single individual that Rousseau comes to demand his total alienation to the general will of the community."[29]

Pierre Manent offered a similar interpretation of the relationship between Montesquieu and Rousseau, closer to Strauss in inspiration and focused more tightly on their respective conceptions of political "virtue," in the opening section of *La cité de l'homme* (1994). But by far the most worked-through interpretation from this camp comes in Paul Rahe's *Soft Despotism, Democracy's Drift*, which was published simultaneously with his

---

[28] L. Strauss, *What Is Political Philosophy?* (Chicago: University of Chicago Press, 1959), p. 164.
[29] B. Yack, *The Longing for Total Revolution: Philosophic Sources of Social Discontent from Rousseau to Marx and Nietzsche* (Berkeley: University of California Press, 1992), p. 63.

stand-alone study of Montesquieu.[30] For Rahe, as for Strauss, England was the pivot on which Montesquieu's mature work turned: "As Madison put it: 'The British Constitution was to Montesquieu, what Homer had been to the didactic poets.'"[31] But his admiration was not without reservations. Well aware of the flaws of the "modern republic," even at its best, Montesquieu erred on the side of caution in pursuing his deepest political hope, which was to "smooth the way for a gradual and unobtrusive transformation of the French monarchy in the direction taken by the English polity." For while his portrait of England was "uninspiring, to say the least," "the account he gave of early Rome in his *Considerations on the Romans* and that of the ancient Greek *polis* that he proffered in Part One of his *Spirit of Laws* excited profound admiration on the part of many of his readers, and it intensified in France and elsewhere the already existing, nascent enthusiasm for classical antiquity that he had evidently hoped to dispel."[32] In no one more so than the Dupins' secretary, of course. Montesquieu may have been prudent to a fault. But Rousseau, in Rahe's view, was a born "polemicist," who picked up and ran with the former's idealized depiction of the grandeur and glory of the classical city-state. It was the basis for his "indictment" of the Enlightenment in the First Discourse. In the Second, Rousseau's account of historical development was identical to that of Montesquieu, with one "great difference": "In his *Discourse on the Origin and Foundations of Inequality among Men*, Rousseau does what the former deliberately chose not to do: he spells out the process of social and political evolution in fine detail, and he indicates how from this account one might derive clear principles of political right."[33] Those principles were then set forth in the *Social Contract*, which sought a remedy for the "malady of sociability" in a conception of citizenship based, above all, on Montesquieu's depiction of the Roman republic in his *Considerations*. Rousseau's political project was no more successful than Montesquieu's, of course. As the *Reveries* would show, so profound a loneliness was no more curable by citizenship than it was by *Julie's* familial love or *Emile's* education. But the upshot for the relation between the two thinkers is evident – and worth quoting at length:

> What should by now be clear, however, is that Jean-Jacques Rousseau constructed his system within the framework of Montesquieu's political

[30] P. Rahe, *Montesquieu and the Logic of Liberty: War, Religion, Commerce, Climate, Terrain, Technology, Uneasiness of Mind, the Spirit of Political Vigilance, and the Foundations of the Modern Republic* (New Haven: Yale University Press, 2010).
[31] Rahe, *Soft Despotism, Democracy's Drift*, p. xiv.   [32] Ibid., pp. 65, 73.   [33] Ibid., p. 105.

science. It is also evident that the critique of bourgeois society that he shouted from the rooftops was a restatement of themes presented in a highly muted fashion in *The Spirit of Laws*. Rousseau was an archeologist of sorts. He unearthed and displayed to startling effect quite serious defects in commercial society that Montesquieu had clearly wished to indicate but without highlighting them or conferring on them undue stress . . . In every generation since, commercial society has had as its Doppelgänger a powerful, bohemian counter-culture grounded in a vulgarization of one or more aspects of the thinking of Rousseau. Every radical movement of both left and right, from Jacobinism at the time of the French Revolution through communism and fascism in the twentieth century to the anti-globalization movement, the environmental movement, and the Islamist jihad characteristic of our own time, has wittingly or unwittingly taken as its starting-point one or another variation on the powerful critique of bour-geois society first suggested in the *Discourse on the Sciences and the Arts*, first fully fleshed out in the *Discourse on the Origin and Foundation of Inequality among Men*, and then summarized again and again in Rousseau's works; and every such movement has served up as a remedy a program inspired in one fashion or another by the vision of revolutionary transformation and inte-gral community that Rousseau intimated in those works and projected most fully in the *Discourse on Political Economy* and *The Social Contract*.[34]

Rahe concludes: "The arguments that the citizen of Geneva disinterred from *The Spirit of Laws* and distilled, extended, refined, and supplemented are very much with us even today [. . .] If at times they appear to be the ravings of a profoundly tortured soul, they cannot be dismissed as such."[35]

Rahe's is far and away the most sweeping account of the relationship between Montesquieu and Rousseau, and its consequences for modern thought, currently on offer. Elsewhere, outside the Straussian orbit, there are only fragments, by comparison. However, as indicated above, after a curious delay Rousseau has attracted a good deal of attention from scholars associated with the Cambridge "school" in recent years. Helena Rosenblatt's study of Rousseau's relation to his Genevan milieu was the trailblazer – now bookended by Richard Whatmore's *Against War and Empire*.[36] In between came the two volumes by Michael Sonenscher, *Before the Deluge* and *Sans-Culottes: An Eighteenth-Century Emblem in the French Revolution*. As already noted, the first offered an account of Rousseau's debt to Montesquieu that bears comparison with that of Rahe. There are crucial

[34] Ibid., p. 138–140.   [35] Ibid., p. 140.
[36] H. Rosenblatt, *Jean-Jacques Rousseau and Geneva: From the First Discourse to the Social Contract, 1749–1762* (Cambridge: Cambridge University Press, 1997); R. Whatmore, *Against War and Empire: Geneva, Britain, and France in the Eighteenth Century* (New Haven: Yale University Press, 2012).

differences, however. Above all, Sonenscher's reading of the basic political message of *The Spirit of the Laws* is at odds with that of Strauss and Rahe. In his view, the peak of Montesquieu's admiration for England, reached with the *Considerations* on Rome, the unpublished *Reflections* on "universal monarchy," and the first draft of Chapter 6, Book 11 of *The Spirit of the Laws*, was merely a temporary stop on the way to his mature outlook. The political heart of *The Spirit of the Laws* was not its portrait of the English Constitution, but the unprecedented theory of *monarchy* that was the pivot of Montesquieu's typology itself. It was this conception of "Gothic" monarchy, whose foundation in a prepolitical social hierarchy made it possible, Montesquieu believed, to deal safely with contemporary levels of public debt, that was then reworked by a series of thinkers until it was transformed into what might look like its virtual opposite – Sieyès's theory of "representative government." On this reading, Rousseau – along with the Physiocrats, the Gournay circle, Mably, Helvétius – is just one of the figures whose "moves" made this transmogrification possible. Rousseau plays a far more central role in *Sans-Culottes*, as leading figure of the "skeptical" branch of the neo-Cynicism in which that idea, destined to become the most important of all revolutionary emblems, long incubated. In this account, however, any strong sense of Rousseau's debt to Montesquieu recedes into the background. Sonenscher acknowledges the importance of what he calls "the Rousseau-Montesquieu pairing" in the wider history of republican thought in France. Center stage in *Sans-Culottes* however, is a different duo, that of "Rousseau-Fénelon." We will have to wait for the sequel to get a fuller picture of Sonenscher's account of revolutionary republicanism as a whole. Here, he merely affirms that: "one of the points of this book is to suggest that there is actually nothing at all straightforward about republicanism."[37]

Sonenscher's reconstruction of a neo-Cynic tradition in eighteenth-century France is not the only work of its kind from scholars associated with Cambridge. The major recent case in point is Christopher Brooke's sweeping survey of neo-Stoicism in European political thought, *Philosophic Pride*, where the climax and end point is indeed Rousseau – but in which Montesquieu makes only a marginal appearance, alas.[38] More important for our purposes is Eric Nelson's *The Greek Tradition in Republican Thought*, a book that has attracted surprisingly little attention, given the

---

[37] M. Sonenscher, *Sans-Culottes: An Eighteenth-Century Emblem in the French Revolution* (Princeton: Princeton University Press, 2008), p. 406.
[38] C. Brooke, *Philosophic Pride: Stoicism and Political Thought from Lipsius to Rousseau* (Princeton: Princeton University Press, 2012).

provocation of its thesis. For Nelson proposes overturning all received notions of the shape of the history of republican thought, Cambridge and Straussian alike, by distinguishing sharply between "Greek" and "Roman" traditions. The former had no use for freedom as "non-dependence" in the Roman sense: the central token of Greek political thought was the notion of an egalitarian distribution, or at least regulation, of property for the good of the community as a whole, but especially its ruling elite – precisely what the Roman tradition anathematized as the dreaded "agrarian law." The contrast established, Nelson then follows the trajectory of "Greek" republicanism in European thought, in a narrative that largely tracks that of *The Machiavellian Moment* – Machiavelli to Harrington to Madison – though with two key differences. The story opens with an analysis of More's *Utopia*, presented as launching a modern, radically egalitarian strand of Platonism; and between the analysis of English and American thinkers, there fall two crucial chapters on writers in French – Montesquieu, Mably, and Rousseau. Nelson first traces Montesquieu's thinking about republics back to a set of "neo-Harringtonians" – Neville, Moyle, and Trenchard – as well as Leibniz and Shafesbury, arguing that the *Persian Letters*, the *Considerations* on Rome, and, above all, *The Spirit of the Laws* offered something like the distilled essence of the Greek tradition: "Montesquieu's republics were as Greek as they come."[39] Montesquieu's stylized portrait of the virtuous republics of antiquity became, in turn, the foundation on which still more radically egalitarian "classical republicanism" of Mably and Rousseau was founded. There the story ends, for our purposes, however. Nelson's next destination is not the French Revolution, as might have been expected from that windup, but the American. The upshot of this particular pairing of Montesquieu and Rousseau for republicanism in France is left suspended in the air – though presumably Nelson's judgment on its revolutionary incarnation would have been rather different from his verdict on the American: "There is indeed no sense in which the Greek tradition can serve as a foothold for the agenda of the contemporary Left in the prehistory of the Constitution."[40]

In fact, the political profile of Cambridge scholarship indeed tends to be resolutely centrist, ever suspicious of Straussian grand narratives, but at least as disdainful of what Sonenscher terms "the old master concepts of class and sovereignty." That raises the question: are there in fact any

---

[39] E. Nelson, *The Greek Tradition in Republican Thought* (Cambridge: Cambridge University Press, 2004), p. 176.
[40] Ibid., p. 233.

contributions regarding Rousseau and Montesquieu from the scholarly left, to match these from the right and center? There are, though they prove still more partial and disjointed than those coming from Cambridge. Marshall Berman's first book, *The Politics of Authenticity* (1970), traced the origins of a uniquely modern "radical individualism" – not very distant from Yack's conception – in the work of Montesquieu and Rousseau, but confined its attention to the *Persian Letters*, skipping over *The Spirit of the Laws* entirely.[41] Much more significant is the work of the one representative of Western Marxism to have devoted significant attention to the history of political philosophy. Louis Althusser's first published book, *Montesquieu: la politique et l'histoire* (1959) was a long study of *The Spirit of the Laws*, with two central themes. Montesquieu was, in many ways, the most important precursor to Marx himself, the role he ascribed to "principle" in the typology of governments anticipating the Marxist notion of a social totality "determined in the last instance" by one preponderant level within it. At the same time, Montesquieu remained a prisoner of the dominant ideological outlook of the time, as blind as anyone else to the fundamental social antagonism of the epoch – not the surface chafing between nobility and monarchy, in which he took the side of the former, but that between all social elites, including a still subordinate bourgeoisie, and the French *peasantry*. Seven years later, Althusser published a trenchant essay on the *Social Contract*, in which he analyzed the series of symptomatic "*décalages*" or "discrepancies" that marked the text: that of the social pact itself, which calls one of the parties to it into existence; that of the exchange of rights involved in the pact, which is simultaneously total and partial; that involving "particular" interests, at once the essence of the "general will" and the principal obstacles to it; and finally, the fundamental "discrepancy" between Rousseau's ideal polity and social reality – revealed in his equally impossible proposals for a "flight backward in economics" (schemes for agricultural autarky, such as those for Corsica or Poland) and a "flight forward in ideology" (on the *Social Contract*'s the theory of civil religion).[42] Althusser never published anything bringing these two thinkers together in a single optic. But a glance at the posthumous published notes for his courses in political philosophy and the philosophy of history at the Ecole Normale Supérieure between 1955 and 1972, as well as the later texts

---

[41] M. Berman, *The Politics of Authenticity: Radical Individualism and the Emergence of Modern Society* (London: Atheneum, 2009). For an amusing demonstration that extremes do not always meet, cf. Allan Bloom's indignant review in *The American Political Science Review* 68:3 (1974): pp. 1297–1299.

[42] English translations of the essays on Montesquieu and Rousseau were published together in L. Althusser, *Montesquieu, Rousseau, Marx*, trans. B. Brewster (London: Verso, 1972).

devoted to "la contingence de la nécessité" and "le materialisme de la rencontre," show how tantalizingly close Althusser was to such a synthesis.[43] In the latter, in particular, Montesquieu and Rousseau are together treated as the heirs to Machiavelli – pioneers, wholly out of step with the ideologists of their own epoch, of a nonhistoricist and nonteleological conception of historical change.

***

Such is the harvest of recent work on Rousseau's connections with Montesquieu – essentially, an emergent scholarly consensus that the textual evidence warrants considering the former a "critical disciple" of the latter to an extent not grasped before; a sweeping interpretation of their relations inspired by Strauss, arguing that Montesquieu's implicit criticisms of "bourgeois" modernity were rendered all too explicit by Rousseau, with explosive effects on modern politics and culture; more fragmentary or partial suggestions from scholars affiliated with Cambridge, focusing on a finer-grained capture of Montesquieu's and Rousseau's contributions to French republicanism, "classical" or otherwise; and, lastly, the silhouette of an unfinished Althusserian interpretation, mingling ideological critique of the two thinkers with an appreciation of their unique place in the development of modern philosophies of history. As the recent vintage of so much of this scholarship suggests, there is evidently a good deal still to be said on the subject. What might be attempted here, in conclusion, is to address three related questions, posed but not fully answered by the work summarized above. First, if it is true, as Strauss put it, that Rousseau drew "the most extreme conclusions that a republican could draw from Montesquieu's analysis of republics," where should we locate that analysis within the wider history of republican thought? Secondly, how should we characterize the conclusions that Rousseau drew from this analysis, "extreme" or otherwise – what specific contributions did Rousseau himself make to republicanism? Finally, how should we understand the particular pattern of convergence and divergence between the two thinkers – what kinds of explanation can be brought to bear upon what Sonenscher calls the "Rousseau-Montesquieu pairing"?

It will already be clear that the two main interpretative traditions at hand approach the history of republican thought in very different ways.

---

[43] For the first, see L. Althusser, *Politique et histoire, de Machiavel à Marx*, ed. F. Matheron (Paris: Éditions du Seuil, 2006); for the second, L. Althusser, *Ecrits philosophiques et politiques*, Tome I (Paris: Stock, 1994). For a superb analysis of this material, see K. Ohji, "Nécessité/Contingence: Rousseau et les Lumières selon Louis Althusser," *Lumières* 15 (2010), pp. 89–112.

Straussians, in particular, have been nothing if not critical when it comes to their opposite numbers from Cambridge. The discovery of "classical republicanism" or "civic humanism" at work in the epoch of the Renaissance, the reconstruction of a neo-Aristotelian "Atlantic republican tradition" connecting Machiavelli and Madison, or of a "neo-Roman" conception of liberty flourishing in seventeenth- and eighteenth-century Britain – all have been dismissed by followers of Strauss as chimerical enterprises based on a willful wishing away of the philosophical gulf separating "ancient" and "modern" republicanism. In *Soft Despotism, Democracy's Drift* Paul Rahe actually goes a step further. These confusions, he argues, can be traced to a fixation on Rousseau himself: Cambridge's leading scholars have all been engaged in an "ill-conceived attempt to read Rousseau's distinctive moral vision back into Machiavelli, the republican thought of the English interregnum, and English Whiggery more generally."[44] The charge might seem overblown – the culprits cited, joining Jacobins and Jihadis in the dock, are Pocock, Skinner, and Maurizio Viroli – but it is hard to deny it all justice. The Cambridge romance with republicanism may have owed a surreptitious debt to the Citizen of Geneva.[45] Still, there is an evident price to be paid for drawing so sharp a boundary between Rousseau and all previous republican thinkers. For it leaves all the key issues posed by Montesquieu's relation to Rousseau curiously underexplained. In line with Straussian tradition, Rahe treats Montesquieu as a thoroughly modern thinker, whose overriding political goal was to push France in the direction of "the peculiar species of commercial republicanism that had emerged in England in the course of the seventeenth century." If this is so, however, how did this supremely cautious and prudent writer *also* manage to enflame "in France and elsewhere the already existing nascent enthusiasm for classical antiquity that he evidently hoped to dispel"?[46] Despite the obvious importance of this moment – Rahe points ahead to Robespierre and Saint-Just as heirs to Montesquieu and Rousseau – we learn nothing more about this "nascent enthusiasm," nor about the reasons for Montesquieu's crucial contribution to intensifying it. As for Rousseau's own role in fanning the flames, this is ascribed entirely to psychological factors – "the ravings of a profoundly tortured soul" – that are themselves left largely unexamined, in terms of

---

[44] Rahe, *Soft Despotism, Democracy's Drift*, p. 310.
[45] Elsewhere, Rahe points, with equal plausibility, to Arendt and Habermas as influences on the Cambridge outlook: *Against Throne and Altar: Machiavelli and Political Theory under the English Republic* (Cambridge: Cambridge University Press, 2008), pp. 8, 182.
[46] Ibid., p. 9.

either biographical or political context. Finally, and ironically, Rahe's account plainly underestimates the novelty of Rousseau's most striking departure from all prior early-modern republican thinking: his recourse to natural rights theory in on the *Social Contract*.

No doubt Pocock and Skinner themselves will be of limited help in addressing these issues. France and French thinkers found no place in the former's "Atlantic republican tradition"; the names of Montesquieu and Rousseau never come up in Skinner's *Liberty Before Liberalism*. Among their followers, Michael Sonenscher stresses the novelty and importance of Montesquieu's political typology, but without setting it within a wider early modern context; while Eric Nelson confines his attention entirely to Montesquieu's role in prolonging an earlier "Greek" tradition. For help in answering the first of our questions, in particular, we need to turn instead to another critic of the Cambridge understanding of early modern republicanism. Though no Straussian himself, the English intellectual historian David Wootton has been second to none in excoriating both Pocock and Skinner for the anachronism of their conceptions of "civic humanism" or "neo-Romanism." Most pertinent to our concerns is an important essay entitled "The True Origins of Republicanism." In it, Wootton argues for the superiority of Franco Venturi's approach to republicanism, which tended to ignore the "classical" ornamentation that commanded the attention of the Cambridge School in order to focus on actually existing republics of the period: "By setting the question of the classical tradition to one side Venturi avoided an intellectual confusion which has bedeviled the discussion of republicanism ever since Montesquieu." What is the "confusion" in question? The fundamental problem, Wootton argues, is that the term "republic" in its modern sense had no equivalent at all in either classical Greek or Latin: *res publica*, in the latter, was plainly *not* understood as a form of government distinct from and opposed to monarchy, but was rather a generic term for all forms of the Roman state. That sense of the term persisted down through Bodin's *Six livres de la république* and well beyond. The remote origins of the modern concept could be traced to Renaissance Florence, where Scala could view a "republic" as distinct from a monarchy or an aristocracy, and Machiavelli could oppose "republics" and "principalities." But that usage long remained idiosyncratic, in all European languages. It was only in the course of the eighteenth century, Wootton concludes, when natural rights egalitarianism fused with growing hostility to monarchy, that the modern conception of the "republic" emerged once and for all.

Without using the term, what Wootton traces in "The True Origins of Republicanism" is the prehistory of what is often referred to today as "republican exclusivism" – the belief not just that republics and monarchies are antithetical forms of government, but that republics alone are legitimate. In his follow-up to *The Greek Tradition in Republican Thought*, *The Hebrew Republic*, Eric Nelson has argued that late-Renaissance rabbinic commentary, focused on Deuteronomy and 1 Samuel 8 above all, provided a crucial catalyst in this evolution, making possible the initial statements of republican exclusivism during the English Revolution – in the work of Milton, first and foremost.[47] Whatever shape we ascribe to this prehistory, however, there is no doubt where it comes to an end. The establishment of republican exclusivism as common currency in the political thought of the Atlantic world was the joint work of Montesquieu and Rousseau. That is the "relay" – to revert to Christopher Kelly's term – between the two that matters most. It was Montesquieu who performed most of the heavy lifting in the operation. Not only did the typology of governments set forth in *The Spirit of the Laws* establish a fundamental distinction between republic and monarchy, it also underscored their exclusivity by assigning "virtue," as animating principle, to the former alone. The ensuing uproar – the "*querelle The Spirit of the Laws*" that finally compelled Montesquieu to specify, in his forward to the 1757 edition, that by "virtue" he had meant "*political* virtue" alone – can be taken as a gauge of the scale of the earthquake caused by the typology. At the same time, Montesquieu also critically downgraded the notion of "mixed government," which had circulated widely in earlier republican thought, and indeed formed one of the key obstacles in the way of republican exclusivism. The term "mixed government" disappeared entirely from the text. What remained of its substance was assigned to what Montesquieu termed the "Gothic" estates-monarchies of the Renaissance, or repackaged in the amalgam of separation-of-powers and checks-and-balances theory in Montesquieu's analysis of the constitution of England, that "republic disguised as a monarchy." Undisguised, unchecked, and unbalanced, as it were, were republics, aristocratic or democratic, in their pure or "immoderate" state, as set forth in the typology.

By any measure, *The Spirit of the Laws* marked the founding moment in *modern* republican thought. As for Montesquieu's "critical disciple," Rousseau was, of course, a republican, as a matter of subjective political

---

[47] E. Nelson, *The Hebrew Republic: Jewish Sources and the Transformation of European Political Thought* (Cambridge, MA: Harvard University Press, 2010).

identity, in a way the former was not: "Every legitimate government is republican." But Rousseau also brought to his republicanism two specific features that took him beyond what he learned from *The Spirit of the Laws*. The first was his considerably heightened appeal to classical antiquity. What had been no more than faint nostalgia – or cool skepticism – in Montesquieu's writing was transformed into Rousseau's robust enthusiasm for Sparta and Rome and strenuous advocacy of ancient models for modern politics. Strangely enough, given its obvious importance, the topic is not one that can be said to have received the attention it deserves in recent scholarship. No feature of the political culture of eighteenth-century France is more salient than the cult of Greco-Roman antiquity that flourished – or resumed, since it had deep roots in the "*Querelle des anciens et des modernes*" of the preceding epoch – from mid-century down to its astonishing climax in the Revolution itself. This was far from Rousseau's work alone, of course. As we have seen, Paul Rahe acknowledges Montesquieu's own contribution to the "already existing nascent enthusiasm for classical antiquity" in France, but without accounting for its origins, progress, or amplitude, beyond Rousseau's own embrace of it. Yet we lack any recent study of the cult of classical antiquity in eighteenth-century and revolutionary France that is truly equal to the subject. This may only be a matter of time, given the growing amount of material available for such a synthesis. We noted above the important recent work on key aspects of this story, from scholars affiliated with Cambridge – Nelson's "Greek tradition," Sonenscher's neo-Cynics, and Brooke's neo-Stoics. To these we might add Luciano Guerci's much older, but still indispensable study of debates over Sparta and Athens in the course of the eighteenth century, and Marisa Linton's more recent *The Politics of Virtue in Eighteenth-Century France*, which establishes beyond dispute how crucial was Montesquieu's *politicization* of the idea of "virtue" for everything that followed. Badly needed, however, is not just a synoptic survey of this entire terrain, but one that takes the story to 1789 and beyond. In their time, thinkers as different as Hegel, Constant, and Marx regarded the cult of antiquity as central to understanding the course and meaning of the French Revolution. Today, the leading works on the subject remain Harold Parker's *The Cult of Antiquity and the French Revolutionaries*, published in 1937, and Claude Mossé's short essay of 1989, *L'Antiquité dans la Révolution française*, – the work of a classicist much indebted to Parker. In any case, there is little doubt that when the political uses of antiquity during the Enlightenment and French Revolution finally attract the attention they merit, the "Rousseau-Montesquieu pairing" will prove to be the hinge of the story. Among other things, this will make it possible to view Eric Nelson's "Greek tradition" in a very different light, furnishing his story with a more apposite and consequential ending. Nelson's reconstruction of a radically egalitarian current of republicanism inspired by classical example, from Machiavelli and More to Montesquieu and Rousseau, is compelling. But the climax of his narrative ought not to have been the American Revolution, with its faint echoes of the "Greek tradition," but rather the French. The epochal importance of what has been termed the "social republicanism" not just of the Jacobins, but of Babeuf as well, needs no demonstration – but nor does its debt to Montesquieu and Rousseau.[48]

The second feature of Rousseau's own republicanism was more original still – the "science of political right" set forth in on the *Social Contract*. Here we have been better served by recent scholarship, in which two books stand out in particular. Helena Rosenblatt's *Rousseau and Geneva* (1997) demonstrated in detail how much Rousseau's recourse to rights theory owed to a specifically Genevan intellectual inheritance, which constituted the "invisible thread" linking the Second Discourse to the *Social Contract*. Four years later, Jean Terrel's *Les théories du pacte social: Droit naturel, souveraineté et contrat de Bodin à Rousseau* provided us with the finest analysis we possess of the entire natural rights tradition, with Hobbes and Rousseau serving as its major figures. What may be added to these accounts is simply to stress the extraordinary originality of Rousseau's achievement in writing the *Social Contract* – bearing in mind that he regarded it as merely the "most considerable" surviving section of a far more ambitious but unfinished work. In his essay on *The Spirit of the Laws*, Louis Althusser famously suggested that Montesquieu's decisive innovation as a social thinker to have departed from the natural rights tradition, the dominant language of seventeenth- and eighteenth-century political ideology. It was precisely by setting aside the "abstraction and idealism" of the concepts of a "state of nature" and a "social contract" that Montesquieu was able to glimpse, from afar, the true "continent of history."[49] That judgment invites a certain nuance today. By the time of the publication of *The Spirit of the Laws*, the natural rights tradition might well have been regarded as residual rather than dominant. Its major figures – Grotius, Hobbes, Locke, Pufendorf – now belonged to a distant past, succeeded by

---

[48] For the concept of "social republicanism," see the recent collection of essays edited by S. Roza and P. Crétois, *Le républicanisme social: une exception française?* (Paris: Publications de la Sorbonne, 2014).

[49] See Althusser, *Montesquieu, Rousseau, Marx*, pp. 24–30, in particular.

a crowd of lesser commentators and popularizers, prominent among whom were Rousseau's compatriots Barbeyrac and Burlamaqui. David Hume's essay "Of the Original Contract" is there to show that Montesquieu was far from alone in expressing cutting-edge skepticism about the whole tradition. It is in this setting, in which natural rights theory might be thought to have become a closed inventory, that the profound originality of the *Social Contract* acquires its full relief. As Jean-Fabien Spitz has argued in his *La Liberté politique: essai de généalogie conceptuelle* – which can be added to the books by Rosenblatt and Terrel as the commanding works on the subject – Rousseau's unprecedented achievement was to grasp how to deploy the conceptual vocabulary of the natural rights tradition for what were plainly *republican* purposes, with the notion of the "general will" serving as the keystone of the synthesis.[50] In ideological context, the *Social Contract* is a classic example of how a certain kind of intellectual regression – returning to the apparently exhausted well of classical contract theory, that of Hobbes in particular – was the condition of possibility of an epochal leap forward. The passage from *Emile* suggests that Rousseau regarded his feat in establishing the "great and useless science of political right" as an exercise in futility. In fact, it was premonitory. Once the great cycle of "Atlantic" revolutions was underway – starting in his last years – hybrid combinations of rights-theories and republicanism rapidly became the common ideological coin of the age.

At all events, the passage from *Emile* brings us to a final set of issues having to do with the overall pattern of convergence and divergence between Montesquieu and his "critical disciple." The distinction Rousseau drew between "positive" and "political" right is central to the pattern. At first glance, the relation between the two, and thus between master and disciple, looks straightforward, suggesting a simple division of labor. If Montesquieu, alone among modern thinkers, was in a position to establish the science of "political right," it was surely owing to his command of "positive right," the particulars of which Rousseau largely accepted. Far from representing any kind of departure from *The Spirit of the Laws*, then, what the *Social Contract* offered was merely its complement or even completion. Yet that cannot be the whole story, for completion, in this instance, also clearly pointed to correction. For no sooner did Rousseau note Montesquieu's failure to move on from "positive" to "political" right, then he insisted on their interdependence, in

---

[50] J.-F. Spitz, *La liberté politique: Essai de généalogie conceptuelle* (Paris: Presses Universitaires de France, 1995).

a fashion that clearly involved criticism of Montesquieu: "Nevertheless, whoever wants to make healthy judgments about existing governments is obliged to unite the two. It is necessary to know what ought to be in order to judge soundly about what is."[51] What might Montesquieu have missed in his judgments about what is, by failing to have established what ought to be? Rousseau was of course in a better position than most to know that even if *The Spirit of the Laws* dispensed with any kind of contract theory, it nevertheless brimmed with normative judgments on political practices and institutions. It is perhaps Bernard Manin who has proposed the best formula for approaching this dimension of the text, in remarking that for Montesquieu, "reason shows that there is one political evil (despotism) but several political goods (moderate monarchy, republican govern-ment – especially of the commercial variety – and the English regime)."[52] However, if Montesquieu was a pluralist, in a way that no contract theorist could ever be, not a few commentators have detected clear rankings among his multiple political goods. For Strauss and his followers, England came out on top. But for an alternative viewpoint, which once commanded a widespread consensus among historians other-wise as different as Althusser and Robert Palmer, and which has returned in the work of Michael Sonenscher, Montesquieu's fundamental *parti pris* lay elsewhere. The ideological center of gravity of *The Spirit of Laws* was its portrait of "Gothic government" – the early modern estates-monarchies, whose origins could be traced to that "event which hap-pened once in the world and which will perhaps never happened again (the emergence of "feudal government"), and which reached their accom-plished form with the abolition of serfdom. Rousseau, in any case, would certainly have been familiar with the crucial passage that follows almost immediately after Montesquieu's analysis of the English constitution: "Here is the origin of Gothic government among us. It was at first a mixture of aristocracy and monarchy. Its drawback was that the com-mon people were slaves; it was a good government that had within itself the capacity to become better. Giving letters of emancipation became the custom, and soon the civil liberty of the people, the prerogatives of the nobility and of the clergy, and the power of the kings, were in such concert that there has never been, I believe, a government on earth as well

---

Rousseau, *Emile*, p. 458.
B. Manin, "Montesquieu," in *A Critical Dictionary of the French Revolution*, eds. F. Furet and M. Ozouf, trans. A. Goldhammer (Cambridge, MA: Harvard University Press, 1989), p. 730.

tempered as that of each part of Europe during the time that this government continued to exist."[53]

With this, we arrive at a fundamental point of divergence between master and disciple, which was doubtless crucial to the latter's recourse to contract theory. Rousseau obviously shared Montesquieu's condemnation of despotism and his admiration for the various forms of self-government that were its alternatives – the overlap in normative commitments that made their tag team contribution to modern republicanism possible. But they also clearly ranked forms of self-government differently. Paul Dubouchet's contrast between antithetical models, the "ancient or Roman" and the "modern or Germano-English," might exaggerate the distance between *The Spirit of the Laws* and the *Social Contract*. But it certainly captures something essential about the differences in their authors' normative horizons and historical ideals. When he wrote the *Persian Letters*, Montesquieu's political sentiments were radical enough: "Most European governments are monarchies; at least that is what they are called, for I do not know that there have ever been such things. At any rate, it would have been difficult for them to have existed for long in a pure form. Monarchy is a state of tension, which always degenerates into despotism or republicanism."[54] Over time, however, he moved in a steadily more conservative direction, first to his mid-career appreciation of the English constitution, before finally arriving at the historically grounded apology for "Gothic" monarchy that underpins *The Spirit of the Laws*. As for Rousseau, his adoption of an "ancient or Roman" – or "Greek," for Eric Nelson – model was the inaugural gesture of his intellectual career, and he never wavered from it, right through his last political writing, his reimaginings of the "actually existing" republics of Geneva, Corsica, and Poland. His one great innovation along the way was simply to furnish republicanism with something it had never possessed before: normative foundations borrowed from the rival political tradition of contract theory. In short order, this became the basic template for the revolutionary republicanisms of the succeeding epoch, though typically in forms more triumphant or agonistic than Rousseau's own version.

Yet if Rousseau parted company with Montesquieu at the juncture of "the science of political right," the conservative master and his radical disciple still had much in common. For Jean Erhard, the elective affinity

---

[53] Montesquieu, *The Spirit of the Laws*, p. 167.
[54] Montesquieu, *Persian Letters*, trans. C. J. Betts (Baltimore: Penguin Books, 1973), p. 187.

between the two owed much to social positions equally distant from the
emergent middle-class society of their time: "Before the civilization of
individual profit and material pleasures that was taking shape before their
eyes, the Baron de la Brède and the Citizen of Geneva had the same kinds
of reaction: the antipathy of the latter was seconded by the strong
reservations of the former." The aristocratic winegrower and the plebeian
music-copier led very different kinds of lives, of course. But they shared
a pre-modern sense of individual independence and self-sufficiency,
enjoying satisfactions left behind by their more "modern" contemporaries: "Both possessed enough in the way of inner resources not to expect
happiness to arrive from without. The 'secret joy' that Montesquieu felt
at sunrise every morning (*Pensées*, 213) is not inferior in quality to the joys
of the Solitary Walker."[55] The affinity between Montesquieu and
Rousseau was not just a matter of social position or eudaemonistic
temperament, however. It was also founded on a common conviction,
equally out of step with the intellectual milieu of that time, about the
centrality of *politics* in human affairs. We can be sure that Rousseau had
"the illustrious Montesquieu" in mind when he described his own
intellectual itinerary, toward the end of the *Confessions*: "Since then my
ideas had been greatly expanded through my historical study of morality.
I had seen that everything is rooted in politics, and that, whatever the
circumstances, a people will never be other than the nature of its government makes it. In other words, the great question, as to which is the best
possible form of government, seemed to me to come down in the end to
this one: what is the nature of the government most likely to produce the
most virtuous, the most enlightened, the wisest, and in short, taking this
word in its widest sense, the best people?"[56] The *Président* of the
Parlement of Bordeaux and the Citizen of Geneva answered that question
differently, but if their conceptions of the "best possible form of government" were not the same, neither were they completely antithetical. In
his essay on the "discrepancies" of the *Social Contract*, Louis Althusser
suggested that the limits of Rousseau's political thought were inscribed in
the contradiction between his prescription for a "flight backward in
economics" and a "flight forward in ideology." It might be argued that
Montesquieu reversed the formula, his sympathy for modern commerce
suggesting a "flight forward in economics," his endorsement of tri-

---

[55] J. Ehrard, "Le fils coupable," in *L'esprit des mots: Montesquieu en lui-même et parmi les siens* (Geneva:
Droz, 1998), p. 272.
[56] Rousseau, *Confessions*, trans. A. Scholar (Oxford: Oxford University Press, 2000), p. 395.

functional social hierarchy a "flight backward in ideology." The "dual revolution" of political upheaval and industrial transformation, already underway before Rousseau was in his grave, confounded the political hopes of both master and critical disciple, propelling the world forward, both economically *and* ideologically. What remains is the grandeur and provocation of *The Spirit of the Laws* and the *Social Contract*, the conjoined masterpieces of Enlightenment political thought, perpetual reminders that there was more than one kind of "liberty before liberalism."

Rousseau and Mendelssohn: "Enraptured Reason," Rousseau's Presence in Moses Mendelssohn's Thought

David Sorkin

The most famous example of Rousseau's impact on German thought, familiar to generations of undergraduates, is the amusing anecdote about Kant missing his afternoon walk, otherwise so punctual that his neighbors could set their clocks to it, because he was enthralled by his reading of *Émile*.[1] There is a developed scholarship on Rousseau's impact in eighteenth-century Germany with sustained attention to various themes as well as to a range of thinkers, from Wieland to Iselin, from Jacobi to Schlegel, from Lessing to Kant and Fichte. While Moses Mendelssohn (1729–86) invariably appears in the treatments of such individuals as Lessing and such topics as the theory of tragedy and the idea of "perfectibility," to the best of my knowledge there is no study devoted exclusively to Rousseau and Mendelssohn.[2] To be sure, there is a long list of articles devoted to Mendelssohn's relationship to other thinkers: Leibniz and Wolf, Locke and Hobbes, Spinoza and Maimonides. The lacuna with regard to Rousseau is remarkable, however, given Mendelssohn's importance for Rousseau's reception in Germany. Lessing was the first person in German-speaking Europe to review Rousseau's two discourses.[3] With Lessing's

---

I would like to thank my colleagues Helena Rosenblatt and Michah Gottlieb for their helpful comments and inspiring collegiality.

[1] E. Cassirer, *Rousseau, Kant and Goethe* (New York: Harper, 1963), p. 1.

[2] U. Kronauer, "Der kühner Weltweise: Lessing als Leser Rousseaus," in H. Jaumann (ed.), *Rousseau in Deutschland: Neue Beiträge zur Erforschung seiner Rezeption* (Berlin: Walter de Gruyter, 1995), pp. 23–45; F. Tubach, "Perfectibilité: der zweite Diskurs Rousseau und die deutsche Aufklärung," *Etudes Germaniques* 15 (1960): pp. 155–151; G. Hornig, "Perfektibilität: Eine Untersuchung zur Geschichte und Bedeutung dieses Begriffs in der deutschsprachigen Literatur," *Archiv für Begriffsgeschichte* 24 (1980) pp. 221–273 esp. pp. 225–230. The most sustained account in English is F. Beiser, *Diotima's Children: German Aesthetic Rationalism from Leibniz to Lessing* (Oxford: Oxford University Press, 2009), pp. 224–230.

[3] Lessing reviewed the first discourse in *Das Neueste aus dem Reich des Witzes* in April 1751; he reviewed the second discourse in the *Berlinischen Privilegirten Zeitung* on 10 July 1755. See H. Jaumann,

encouragement, Mendelssohn was the first to translate the *Second Discourse* (1756) which he published with an accompanying "open letter" to Lessing.[4] Mendelssohn also wrote one of the few detailed reviews of Rousseau's epistolary novel, *Julie or the New Héloise*. The lacuna is all the more remarkable given the recognition of Rousseau's importance for Mendelssohn. The first scholarly biographer of Mendelssohn (Kayserling, 1862) entitled a chapter "Rousseau."[5] A recent biographer, Dominique Bourel, asserted that in Rousseau Mendelssohn "found an interlocutor with whom he was in dialogue his entire life." What role did Rousseau play in Mendelssohn's intellectual career?[6]

Mendelssohn's publication of Rousseau's *Second Discourse* in German was in fact at the heart of his intellectual formation: he consistently engaged in translation as an act of intellectual mediation between diverse thinkers and disparate cultures that enabled him to constitute an independent intellectual position. Mendelssohn fashioned a truly cosmopolitan culture despite never traveling beyond the borders of the Holy Roman Empire. A native speaker of Yiddish, Mendelssohn claimed to think in, and translate his thoughts through, Hebrew.[7] He learned multiple languages with a minimum of assistance (German, French, English, Latin, and Greek) and polished his style, and developed the substance and presentation of his thinking, by rendering the prose of other writers into fluent, elegant German. He translated Shaftesbury from English, Plato from Greek, and the Pentateuch and Psalms from Hebrew. He translated

---

"Rousseau in Deutschland: Forschungsgeschichte und Perspectiven," in *Rousseau in Deutschland: Neue Beiträge zur Erforschung seiner Rezeption*, pp. 4–6. For Rousseau's "pervasive" impact on German writing about the relationship between the city and the provinces see M. Erlin, *Berlin's Forgotten Future: City, History and Enlightenment in Eighteenth-Century Germany* (Chapel Hill: University of North Carolina Press, 2004), esp. pp. 5–7; and C. Wiedemann "'Supplement seines Daseins'? Zu den kultur- und identitätsgeschichtlichen Voraussetzungen deutscher Schriftstellerreisen nach Rom-Paris-London seit Winckelmann," in idem. (ed.), *Rom-Paris-London: Erfahrung und Selbsterfahrung deutscher Schriftsteller und Künstler in den fremden Metropolen* (Stuttgart: Metzler, 1988), pp. 1–20.

[4] The playwright and poet Christian Felix Weisse (1726–1804) presented a copy of Mendelssohn's translation, as well as Mendelssohn's *Phädon*, to Rousseau in 1759 or 1760. Rousseau apparently responded that he wanted to read Mendelssohn's comments because they were written by a Jew. See J. Marks, "Rousseau's Use of the Jewish Example," *The Review of Politics* 72 (2010): p. 464; A. Altmann, *Moses Mendelssohn: A Biographical Study* (Tuscaloosa: University of Alabama Press, 1973), p. 148.

[5] Kayserling acknowledged Rousseau's lasting influence on Mendelssohn yet devoted half of the chapter to Mendelssohn's friendship with Lessing. See M. Kayserling, *Moses Mendelssohn: Sein Leben und seine Werke* (Leipzig, 1862), pp. 56–64, especially p. 60.

[6] D. Bourel, *La naissance du judaïsme moderne* (Paris: Gallimard, 2004), p. 113. Bourel convincingly demonstrates the extent to which French culture permeated eighteenth-century Berlin.

[7] *Gesammelte Schriften. Jubiläumsausgabe*. 27 vols. in 36 (Stuttgart: Frommann, 1972-) 3,2:89. Henceforth: JubA.

eighteenth-century German philosophical terms into Hebrew.[8] Indeed, the two books that crowned his dual reputation were in part translations. The *Phädon* (1767), the European-wide bestseller that won him the sobriquet the "Socrates of Berlin," was an enhanced reworking of Plato's dialogue on the immortality of the soul. The *magnum opus* that made him the preeminent figure of the Jewish Enlightenment or *Haskalah*, encapsulated in the phrase "from Moses unto Moses there was none like Moses," was *The Book of the Paths of Peace* (*Sefer Netivot ha-Shalom*; 1780–83; often referred to as the *Bi'ur* or "commentary"), his translation of the Pentateuch into High German (printed in Hebrew letters) accompanied by a general introduction and a verse-by-verse commentary in Hebrew. His translation of Rousseau, while it contributed to his growing reputation among German intellectuals, had an abiding impact: it resulted in a lifelong dialogue, at first manifest (1756–61), later latent.

At first glance there could not have been two men more radically different in character than Mendelssohn and Rousseau. Mendelssohn was the epitome, in the best sense, of the upright, disciplined and industrious aspiring bourgeois, a steadfast husband, a devoted father and a fiercely loyal friend. Mendelssohn was born poor, the son of a Torah scribe, suffered want in his adolescence after moving to Berlin in 1743 (he described counting off his meals for the week by making cuts in a loaf of bread), and slowly ascended the occupational and economic ladder. He was first a tutor to a wealthy family of silk manufacturers (Bernhard), then a bookkeeper for the firm, then a manager and finally, after the husband's death, a partner with the widow. Mendelssohn's courtship of his future wife Fromet was unusual for the time in that they had extended contact prior to the marriage. That contact was, however, a model of a chaste relationship informed by the best of the mid-century cult of sentimentality (which pervades their letters in Yiddish). Mendelssohn and Fromet had six children who lived to adulthood. He was a devoted father despite his crowded schedule. Mendelssohn was a fully observant Jew who punctiliously fulfilled the commandments and celebrated the holidays with his family. On many occasions he broke off writing a letter on Friday

---

[8] See, especially, *Biur Milot Ha-Higayon* (1760): Mendelssohn renewed the lexicon of philosophy in Hebrew by giving contemporary equivalents for Maimonides' Aristotelian terminology. For the Hebrew original see JubA 14. For a German translation of selections see JubA 2:197–230; for an English translation from the introduction see M. Gottlieb, *Moses Mendelssohn: Writings on Judaism, Christianity and the Bible* (Waltham: Brandeis University Press, 2011), pp. 233–240. For a brief account see D. Sorkin, *Moses Mendelssohn and the Religious Enlightenment* (Berkeley: University of California Press, 1996), pp. 18–22.

afternoon because of the approaching Sabbath. He initially undertook his translation of the Pentateuch for the education of his son. His daily schedule was a model of discipline and regularity: he rose early to read and write (his last book, *The Morning Hours*, reflects on and embodies that practice), then worked at the silk factory. He returned to his family and to an open house that was always filled with visitors and conversation. As a conversationalist Mendelssohn was famous for his humility, graciousness and dedication to avoiding conflict by discovering the root of a disagreement. To his mind many such disagreements resulted from the unintentional misunderstanding of terms. Mendelssohn was famous for his devotion to his friends, especially those of his early manhood, Lessing and Nicolai. Indeed, he spent the last years of his life defending Lessing's memory against the charge of Spinozism in the so-called "Pantheism debate." Mendelssohn would seem to have personified virtue in every aspect of his life. Indeed, Mendelssohn cast himself, in keeping with the way others viewed him, as "the virtuous Jew" who would endeavor to alter pernicious stereotypes not through polemics but by dint of his own exemplary behavior.[9]

In stark contrast was the tempestuous, petulant and wayward Rousseau who twice converted, participated in a *ménage à trois*, fathered numerous children out of wedlock whom he then consigned to the foundling home, and had violent conflicts with his erstwhile friends and supporters. Yet that same Rousseau could be said to have devoted all of his works to the issue of virtue. "His two great discourses indict the loss of virtue in the modern world; his political writings trace the contours of the virtuous state; his tract on education instructs how one individual might be raised to virtue; his novel describes virtue as 'sweetest sensuality'; and his autobiographical writings focus around the critical moment when he became 'drunk with virtue.'" And, of course, his "virtuous self" was later a "model for political discourse during the Revolution."[10]

Were these two figures perhaps connected by the fact that they were both "young men from the provinces" endowed with dissonant cultural capital? Rousseau was the Genevan rustic whose republican sentiments clashed with Louis XV's aristocratic Paris. Mendelssohn was the Dessau "yeshivah" student whose Judaism set him at odds with Frederick the Great's court and garrison boom town (not to mention that he suffered

---

[9] JubA 7:10. The book Mendelssohn had in mind was Iselin's *Philosophischen und Patriotischen Träume* (1755).

[10] C. Blum, *Rousseau and the Republic of Virtue: The Language of Politics in the French Revolution* (Ithaca: Cornell University Press, 1986), p. 13.

a precarious legal status in Berlin). Were Rousseau and Mendelssohn destined to be trenchant critics, however different, of society?

Rousseau's writings consistently fired Mendelssohn's moral imagination. Rousseau was not for Mendelssohn the "restorer of the rights of humanity" as he was for many German thinkers in the 1760s.[11] Mendelssohn admiringly labeled Rousseau's eloquence the "language of the heart [*Sprache des Hertzens*]" or "the language of enraptured reason [*die Sprache der begeisterten Vernunft*]" – which meant a rhetoric that had a direct impact, a captivating passion in discussing ideas and especially moral ideals that could affect actual behavior.[12] Mendelssohn valued and strove to create a philosophy not of cold abstractions, however cogent the logic, but one that could change minds and motivate actions by winning hearts. For that reason, he eschewed the encyclopedic or scholastic mathematical method of Wolff with its mania for definition. He also did not continue to write the kind of elegant treatise that won him first prize in the Berlin Academy of Sciences competition, *On Evidence in Metaphysical Philosophy* (1763). Instead, he opted for an exposition through essays or dialogues – the form he learned by translating Shaftesbury, Rousseau, and Plato – that emerged from the mouths of, and spoke directly to the hearts of, individuals. Nevertheless, Mendelssohn could not directly draw upon Rousseau's moral imagination. His philosophy, grounded in Leibniz and Wolff, empiricism and Judaism, diverged too much from Rousseau's, or at least the early Rousseau. Mendelssohn was a "guardian of the Enlightenment [*Aufklärung*]" and especially, in regard to Rousseau's *Second Discourse*, its tradition of "aesthetic rationalism" that turned on the role of the perception of beauty in the individual's perfection.[13] His embrace of the Enlightenment converged with, and promised to fulfill, his understanding of Judaism.[14] Before he could use Rousseau's views, he had to reshape them, or appropriate one side of a paradox or an ambiguous position, so that they supported his own philosophical optimism.[15] Such was the inception of Mendelssohn's enduring dialogue with Rousseau.

---

[11] Cassirer, *Rousseau, Kant and Goethe*, p. 13.

[12] "Sendschreiben," JubA 2:83; JubA 5,1:373. For Mendelssohn's emphasis on practical rather than abstract philosophy see D. Sorkin, *Moses Mendelssohn and the Religious Enlightenment*; M. Gottlieb, *Faith and Freedom: Moses Mendelssohn's Theological Political Thought* (New York: Oxford University Press, 2011); G. Freudenthal, *No Religion Without Idolatry: Mendelssohn's Jewish Enlightenment* (Notre Dame: University of Notre Dame Press, 2012).

[13] For the phrase see Altmann, *Moses Mendelssohn*, p. 638. For the tradition of aesthetic rationalism see Beiser, *Diotima's Children*.

[14] Gottlieb, *Faith and Freedom*, pp. 18–19.

[15] He similarly struggled with and attempted to purify some of Spinoza's ideas. In a large literature See Bourel, *Moses Mendelssohn*, pp. 98–109, 337–342, 391–450; A. Arkush, *Moses Mendelssohn and the*

Mendelssohn's "Open Letter to Lessing in Leipzig" and "Postscript" that accompanied his translation of the *Second Discourse* constituted a succinct confrontation with, and effort to recast, Rousseau's thinking. One recent commentator has called it, "one of the first and most subtle responses of the rationalist tradition [meaning rationalist aesthetics] to Rousseau's challenge."[16] Mendelssohn attempted to subvert Rousseau's radical dualism of the "state of nature" versus "society" by subsuming it to, or reconciling it with, his own emerging metaphysics that made sociability central to man's vocation, the striving for perfection. Rousseau should have employed his enviable eloquence "to defend a better topic," Mendelssohn asserted.[17] He assailed Rousseau's dualism by arguing that Rousseau's dedication to Geneva demonstrates a sociability at odds with his claims. If Rousseau could think of no place he would rather choose as a homeland than Geneva ("the fulfillment of all of his enthusiastic desires"), then he has demonstrated "an innate love for sociability": "he wishes to honor the laws and their virtuous administrators."[18]

Mendelssohn continued his analysis of the apparent tension between Rousseau's condemnation of society and his affirmation of sociability in his notion of pity. He asserted contrary to Rousseau that pity is "not a primordial urge" but is rather linked to sociability.

> Pity itself, this human feeling that Rousseau allows to the savage man, after he has robbed him of all other intellectual capacities, is not a primordial urge as he has deemed it. There is in us no explicit determination to feel displeasure at the weaknesses of other beings. No! Pity is based on love, love is based on the desire for harmony and order. Where we see perfection we wish it to grow.[19]

Mendelssohn reconceived Rousseau's understanding of pity to fit his own concept of sociability. By setting pity in relationship to "love" and "perfection" it became an intermediate "urge" linked to perfection. "Every need is

Enlightenment (Albany: State University of New York Press, 1994); Gottlieb, *Faith and Freedom*, pp. 9–12, 66–71; Freudenthal, *No Religion Without Idolatry*, pp. 40–45.

[16] Beiser, *Diotima's Children*, p. 225.

[17] "Sendschreiben," JubA 2:83. In an unpublished and undated essay (1757–60?), Mendelssohn asserted that Rousseau's method was faulty. Rousseau had gathered all the criticisms and accusations ever made against the "arts and sciences" and decided they were therefore corrupting. Mendelssohn asserted that Montesquieu would respond: one could do the same for "freedom" or "pity." See "Verwandschaft des Schönen und Guten," JubA 2: 181.

[18] "Sendschreiben," JubA 2:84–5.

[19] "Sendschreiben," JubA 2:86. Mendelssohn combined Leibniz's notions of order and perfection with Wolff's notions of pity and love. See Bourel, *Moses Mendelssohn*, p. 115.

an urge to perfection."[20] For Rousseau the urge for perfection was paradoxically both the "source of all miseries" (141) – it propelled man from the healthy state of nature to the corruption of society – and the source of improvement. For Mendelssohn, the urge for perfection was the root of sociability and the evidence of man's innate love of other men; it was the engine that drives each individual to fulfill his human vocation. Mendelssohn's "golden rule" or "categorical imperative" was: "Make your and your fellowman's internal and external condition, in due proportion, as perfect as you can."[21]

Mendelssohn tried to temper Rousseau's radical dualism by mediating between its terms: with the notion of perfection he introduced a natural development from the "state of nature" to "culture" or "civilization." That development represents neither decadence nor corruption; rather, "each development of our powers is the enlargement of our being."[22] Mendelssohn ascribed the urge for perfection to mankind at all stages: it is inherent whether in the state of nature or the most advanced culture. "But the law of nature requires us not only to be satisfied but primarily to make ourselves more perfect."[23] Indeed, he emphasized that Rousseau also acknowledged that man in the state of nature felt that urge to perfection.[24] Yet according to Mendelssohn, Rousseau mistakenly restricted that urge to physical capacities. "Rousseau inverts the character of human nature when he puts [physical needs] at the top, when he designates them as the sole obligation to which men are bound."[25] Rather, it is the soul's perfection that concerns Mendelssohn since it is "our true self" and only through it can we "raise all of our capacities to the fullest harmony."[26]

The quest for perfection rests on love: "True love considered to its total extent is the motivation, means and the end goal of all virtues." One of love's most important manifestations is friendship: "without [friendship] our soul cannot be improved." Mendelssohn attributed inordinate efficacy to friendship: "the omnipotent power of friendship . . . It [friendship] must accompany all of our duties; it must extend a hand to all of them; it must exalt them."[27]

---

[20] JubA 2:7.   [21] Abhandlung JubA 2:317. Cf. Orakel, JubA 6,1:20.
[22] "Sendschreiben," JubA 2:87. Tubach, "Perfectibilité: der zweite Diskurs Rousseau und die deutsche Aufklärung," pp. 146–148.
[23] "Sendschreiben," JubA 2:7.   [24] "Sendschreiben," JubA 2:88.
[25] "Sendschreiben," JubA 2:90, 97. For the same thought in Mendelssohn's notebook see JubA 2:8. "Haben die Bedürfnisse der Seele nicht eben so dringend seyn können als die Bedürfnisse des Körpers?"
[26] "Sendschreiben," JubA 2:89.
[27] "Sendschreiben," JubA 2:91. For the cult of friendship in the eighteenth century see Klaus Berghahn, "On Friendship: The Beginnings of a Christian-Jewish Dialogue in the 18th Century," in idem.

The crucial role of friendship exhibits perfection's absolute dependence upon sociability. Mendelssohn similarly praised friendship in his early Hebrew work, *Kohelet Musar* (1758?). There he defined love, following Wolff, as taking pleasure in another's increased perfection, for which Mendelssohn invoked the example of David and Jonathan's friendship in the Bible.[28] Mendelssohn would reiterate and reinforce this position in *Jerusalem* (1783), in which he argued that perfection requires benevolence – "perfection is inseparable from benevolence" – and benevolence in turn shapes society.[29]

Indeed, Mendelssohn argued that Rousseau committed a fundamental error in trying to abstract a conception of "man in nature" from the "savage condition," a matter of considerable importance to the natural law tradition that both he and Rousseau were adapting.[30] This is the equivalent, Mendelssohn averred, of a painter using the form of an infant as the model for the human body. Man's qualities cannot be inferred from mankind's infancy. Man should be studied in society, as he pursues his perfection. As a counterargument, Mendelssohn juxtaposed the degenerate to the savage: neither recognizes the soul's "merits," yet the former suppresses, while the latter simply lacks the ability to grasp, "the feeling of human value, of true morality and of the general love for order and perfection."[31] Mendelssohn discerns the "true middle" between the degenerate and the savage in the figure of Socrates. "He is a highly sensitive friend, a loving citizen and the most useful, instructive and charming companion in the world." Mendelssohn continues: "If sociability raised a Socrates, why should it be unable to bless us with more such divine examples."[32]

Mendelssohn asserted that Rousseau should have attacked the abuses and shortcomings of "sociability" rather than sociability itself.[33] Rather

---

(ed.), *The German-Jewish Dialogue Reconsidered: A Symposium in Honor of George L. Mosse* (New York: Peter Lang, 1996), pp. 5–24.

[28] KM4:109–112 p. 172 (Gilon's critical edition). For a similar view see Rhapsodie, JubA 1:406–407.

[29] *Jerusalem*, JubA 8:116 Cf., 110–111. Mendelssohn wrote in a letter of 1764 that his understanding of natural law and political theory was derived largely from Wolff. See JubA 12,1:44 (1 May 1764, to Abbt). For sociability in Wolff's theory see Bachmann, *Die naturrechtliche Staatslehre Christian Wolffs* (Berlin: Duncker und Humblot, 1977), pp. 86–89. For Mendelssohn's concept of benevolence see N. Rotenstreich, "On Mendelssohn's Political Philosophy," *Leo Baeck Institute Yearbook* 11 (1966), pp. 28–30; and M. Albrecht, "'Nunmehr sind Sie ein preussischer Untertan': Moses Mendelssohns Staatstheorie," in F. Rapp and H.-W. Schuett (eds.), *Philosophie und Wissenschaft in Preussen* (Berlin: Universitätsbibliothek, 1982), pp. 26–27.

[30] For Mendelssohn and Rousseau on natural law see Beiser, *Diotima's Children*, pp. 226–227.

[31] "Sendschreiben," JubA 2:94.

[32] "Sendschreiben," JubA 2:95. On this passage see M. Erlin, "Reluctant Modernism: Moses Mendelssohn's Philosophy of History," *Journal of the History of Ideas* 63:1 (2002): pp. 88–89.

[33] "Sendschreiben," (Nachschrift) JubA 2:104.

than criticizing all human societies he should have raised specific criticisms of certain kinds of governments (here Mendelssohn pointed to the example of another Swiss writer, Isaak Iselin (1728–82): ". . . the scandal of hypocrisy, deceit, flattery, oppression and other innumerable vices . . . that are associated with these forms of government. Thus all right-thinking minds would crown his statement with as much praise as his delivery."[34] For example, a lack of sociability causes wars: in fact, the more sociability, the more peace.[35] Similarly, language emerges from sociability: the ability to create associations between sounds and objects requires a "degree of attention that cannot be assumed of a savage man."[36]

Mendelssohn did not rest content with his vindication of sociability. He turned Rousseau's ideas into an argument for physico-theology and a Leibnizian-Wolffian theodicy. Rousseau's account of the savage man in the state of nature only attested to the stunning wisdom of God's creation: "God so wisely built the human body that, without the help of carping reason, it can arise, subsist and increase."[37] Rousseau eloquently defended man's exercise of freedom as his distinguishing characteristic; what about "the noblest gift of heaven," his reason, Mendelssohn inquired? In a passage built on wishful imputations ("perhaps"; *vielleicht*) Mendelssohn asserted: "He perhaps wanted only to vindicate wise providence that allowed savage man not to have capacities that would bring him no utility and perhaps even some harm." Or he tried to redirect Rousseau's universal animadversions to a particular audience: "He perhaps only wanted to chastise the pride of some this-worldly people who identify the entirety of moral being [*gesittete Wesen*], which men have worked on for centuries, with a few comforts, some coddling and a delicacy of behavior, and pass these off as the true advantages of humanity."[38] Moreover, freedom cannot exist without reason since it consists either in the "ability of a mind to act according to considered motives" or a condition of "no external coercion" that allows us "to satisfy our true needs in an innocent manner."[39] In short, for Mendelssohn freedom without reason had no value: "what a miserable gift is freedom without reason, without the inner certitude of the correctness of our actions."[40] Mendelssohn's validation of reason is crucial to his

---

[34] "Sendschreiben," JubA 2:93.   [35] "Sendschreiben," (Nachschrift) JubA 2:100–101.
[36] "Sendschreiben," (Nachschrift) JubA 2:106.   [37] "Sendschreiben," (Nachschrift) JubA 2:97.
[38] "Sendschreiben," (Nachschrift) JubA 2:98.   [39] "Sendschreiben," (Nachschrift) JubA 2:99–100.
[40] "Sendschreiben," (Nachschrift) JubA 2:100. In an unpublished and unfinished essay Mendelssohn had begun to explore the interactions of the various faculties e.g., reason, taste and common sense that created the relationship between the "beautiful and the good." See, "Verwandschaft des Schönen und Guten," JubA 2:181–185.

own theodicy: reason is God's gift that enables man to pursue his true vocation of perfection.

Mendelssohn has, as it were, made Rousseau's moral argument his own. He has assimilated Rousseau's denigration of society and sociability, however ambiguous or paradoxical, to his own understanding in which sociability is integral to man's pursuit of perfection and society itself is both positive and indispensable. At the same time, Mendelssohn was also aware, without formulating a full-blown theory, of the degree to which the pursuit of individual perfection was contingent upon the condition of society. In his postscript, Mendelssohn wrote:

> [A]ll of our effort to accustom a savage to our mode of life must be fruitless if we do not allow a series of fathers and children gradually to ascend the ladder which we have traversed in the course of many centuries. Does it follow from this that we have become worse? Or is it not rather a proof that our feeling has been ennobled and our being elevated a step?[41]

As we shall see below, in the 1780s Mendelssohn began to articulate, yet only partially formulated, a cyclical notion of the development of societies.[42] Mendelssohn did, however, circumvent Rousseau's contention that the negative aspects of society emerge in living through the opinions of others. Perhaps because of his commitment to sociability he did not engage that problematic. He similarly evaded Rousseau's contention that man's defining characteristic is freedom by arguing that freedom without reason is useless.[43]

Mendelssohn continued his recasting of Rousseau's thought in a tongue-in-cheek account that he published in a popular journal or "moral weekly" ("The Chamäleon," 1756), including a fictional letter about the reception of Rousseau's views in Switzerland – typical fare of a "moral weekly" – that was also, in part, an advertisement for his translation.[44] Mendelssohn parodied Rousseau's views in comically heightened formulations. As the subject of the first discourse: "[I]s it better to be a reasonable person or a fool?" in which Rousseau, "gave comfort to all fools by showing that people can do nothing more destructive than striving to be wise."[45] Or the *Second Discourse*: "would people have acted more in accordance with their nature if they had continued crawling around in the

---

[41] "Sendschreiben," (Nachschrift) JubA 2:103.
[42] For this issue see Erlin, "Reluctant Modernism: Moses Mendelssohn's Philosophy of History."
[43] Einleitung JubA 2:xxii–xxiii.
[44] "Betrachtung über die Ungleichheit und Geselligkeit der Menschen," JubA 2:137.
[45] "Betrachtung," JubA 2:134.

forest and remained equal to one another as one long-tailed monkey to another?"[46] "How happily, contentedly and peacefully do the apes, orangutans and pongos live!" He also made sure to articulate his own views about man's perfection being predicated upon sociability and the virtue of benevolence.

> One would have to be very unreasonable [. . .] to want to deny that there are also virtuous minds that have achieved perfection in society. Mere sentient animals have become thinking creatures, imitators of God and admirers of his magnificent works. Through society they have improved their reason and then used it for no other purpose than to recognize divine truths; and the power, which has come to them in part through possessions, serves them only to act benevolently towards others. The sublime feeling of their own worth; the internal conviction of their integrity; the love of fellowman; and the trust in an infinitely good creator; fill their souls with a divine reassurance that is so distant from the dull contentment of a savage man as is the felicity of an angel from the limited felicity of a person. All their needs are drives to felicity; and if they wish to achieve this adequately, then they must accept the inconveniences that are inseparable from societal life, which is the sole means to their felicity.[47]

In that same autumn and winter (August 1756 to March 1757) Rousseau's concern with "pity" played a central role in a correspondence on the nature of the theater that Mendelssohn conducted with his two close friends from Berlin, Gotthold Ephraim Lessing and the publisher Friedrich Nicolai. Here Mendelssohn and his friends assimilated Rousseau's penetrating idea to their own aesthetic and moral concerns while decisively contravening Rousseau's contention that the arts do not contribute to progress and moral perfection.[48]

Lessing wanted to reexamine Aristotle's conception of the nature of drama and especially tragedy. Echoing Rousseau he argued that "the compassionate man is the best man [*der mitleidigste Mensch ist der beste Mensch*] . . . Whoever makes us compassionate makes us better and more moral, and the tragedy that does the former also does the later, or it does the former in order to be able to do the later." He argued that it is in the nature of tragedy that it "should arouse passions," and that there is "no single passion that excites tragedy in the spectator as does pity." The other major emotions that spectators feel, such as fear (*Schrecken*) and admiration (*Bewunderung*), are but variations on pity. Fear is "the sudden surprise of pity"; admiration is "pity become dispensable." Thus "fear and

---

[46] "Betrachtung," JubA 2:136.   [47] "Betrachtung," JubA 2:139.
[48] Beiser, *Diotima's Children*, pp. 196, 224–230.

admiration are nothing but the first sprouts, the beginning and the end of pity." Thus for Lessing, "the tragedy must arouse as much pity as it possibly can," and the "best person [character in the play] must also be the most unfortunate," at least for the "duration of the play." And this contrasts sharply with the epic: "the admired hero is the theme of the epic, the pitiable [hero that of] the tragedy."[49]

Lessing additionally speculated about those qualities that arouse "admiration." He asserted that for a character to arouse pity he must have good qualities yet not heroic qualities: those are antithetical to pity. The character must feel his misfortune in order for the audience to feel it. Lessing emphasized the absolute superiority of pity to other emotions in tragedy. "Pity [...] improves directly. It improves without us having to contribute anything. It improves the man of reason as well as the simpleton."[50]

Finally, Lessing argued that "admiration" is the "resting place" of "pity." In a tragedy, the scenes that arouse pity must suffuse the play; there must be moments throughout in which "the perfections and misfortunes of his protagonist are shown in an arousing connection."[51] In the intervening moments, which he calls "empty scenes," the spectator can admire the protagonist and thereby have his sympathy renewed. "Tragedy should exercise pity in general rather than preparing us for pity in this or that circumstance."[52] Lessing criticized Aristotle's interpretation of the tragic flaw, understanding it as meaning that, "without the flaw that draws misfortune over him, his character and his misfortune would not constitute a whole."[53]

Mendelssohn at first offered an alternative to Lessing by emphasizing admiration's superiority to pity because it was more closely connected to perfection. Since admiration "modulates" pity, it can elevate it: "the sensuous sentiment of pity gives way to a higher sentiment, and its milder luster disappears when the glow of admiration permeates our mind."[54] Yet Mendelssohn also conceded that the Greek tragedians never put a morally admirable character on the stage. The ancient sculptors imbued their

[49] JubA 11:64–69 #33. Lessing acknowledges that such pity is also pleasurable: "a full half of pity . . . is pleasure."
[50] JubA 11:76–79. Lessing further distinguished three levels of pity. In the "emotional" we lack a clear idea of the character's perfections and misfortune. In the "tearful" we simultaneously learn of the character's strengths and disasters; "misfortune and merit are here of equal weight." In the anguished phase the scales tip to the side of genuine disaster. JubA 11:80–81 [29 November 1756].
[51] JubA 11:90 [18 December 1756].   [52] JubA 11:93 [18 December 1756].
[53] JubA 11:95 [18 December 1756].
[54] JubA 11:72 [23 November 1756]; Beiser, *Diotima's Children*, pp. 208–209.

passions with a "certain heroism."[55] Mendelssohn used Winkelmann's account of the Laocoon to elaborate his understanding of ancient sculpture: there "the painful sensation of pity is immediately overlain with a gloss of admiration and respect." The sculptor's version was preferable to Virgil's poetic account: "the more a mere pitiful feeling is set aside by a pity mixed with admiration and awe," the more powerful it is.[56] Mendelssohn echoed his argument in Rousseau's *Second Discourse* that freedom needed to function in combination with reason by emphasizing the importance of reason vis-à-vis "pity": "Pity can also lead us to bad habits when it is not ruled by reason."

Whatever Lessing and Mendelssohn's differences in the relationship between "pity" and "admiration," they were focused on the tragedy as an instrument of moral perfection. Not just aware of the aesthetic dimension, they were committed to understanding how the aesthetic can be made an efficacious means in the pursuit of moral ends understood as individual perfection. They transported Rousseau's emphasis on pity from the *Discourse on Inequality* directly into their own concerns while asserting the irrefragable contribution of a central art, tragedy, to moral perfection, that is, art was a form of education.[57]

Mendelssohn renewed his public encounter with Rousseau five years later when he wrote a review of the epistolary novel, *Julie or the New Héloïse* (1761). This may in fact have been one of only a handful of detailed critiques to appear in the German periodical press of the time.[58] Mendelssohn could hardly have been more critical of this widely admired bestseller.

> You know the avidity with which I am accustomed to take hold of a brief essay as soon as I see the name of the Genevan citizen glittering on its title-page. Would that Rousseau had written philosophical essays rather than a novel! You cannot believe the extent to which my anticipation has been disappointed. It cost me no little effort to read all six books of this novel with unbroken attention.[59]

---

[55] JubA ii:72–3 [23 November 1756].   [56] JubA ii:86 [December 1756].

[57] Beiser, *Diotima's Children*, pp. 216–217.

[58] D. Bourel, "Les Réserves de Mendelssohn: Rousseau, Voltaire et les Juif de Berlin," *Revue Internationale de Philosophie* 32 (1978): p. 314. Hamann wrote a counter-review in praise of the novel. See *Abaelardi Virbii Chimärische Einfälle über den zehnten Theil der Briefe die Neueste Literatur betreffend* (Königsberg, 1761). Mendelssohn wrote a brief reply, "Abälardus Virbius an den Verfasser der fünf Briefe die neue Heloise betreffend," JubA 5,1: 449–453. On this exchange see Beiser, *Diotima's Children*, pp. 233–235.

[59] "Briefe, die neueste Literatur betreffend," JubA 5,1:366 [4 June 1761].

Because of the novel's popularity, Mendelssohn at first mistrusted his own impressions. In the end, he found only the discourses truly outstanding. Rousseau, he thought, did not have the talents of a novelist (Mendelssohn compared him unfavorably with the English novelist Samuel Richardson).

> [H]is knowledge of the human heart is more speculative than pragmatic; the stories are uneven, now dragging, now in full gallop; he entirely lacks the talent to write dialogue, and his passions overshoot the reader's imagination. They are quickly in the clouds before the reader feels the slightest urge to ascend along with them.[60]

The Rousseau who writes brilliant essays is simply not suited to write novels.

> Mr. Rousseau, who writes so enchantingly beautifully when he speaks the language of enraptured reason, appears to speculate about the nature of passions but not to have felt them himself and therefore it is difficult for him to speak their genuine language.[61]

In fact, Mendelssohn judges Rousseau's "language of the passions [*Affektensprache*]" to be "abounding in metaphors, prolix and disorderly."[62] He found the novel lacking in structure and incident. Rousseau filled the gaps with "long moral sermons and amorous subtleties."[63] In sum, "I have already said it more than once, and will repeat it again, that the special subjects Mr. Rousseau treats in the novel are admirably presented. Only the novel, it seems to me, is unworthy and does not deserve the applause it has received."[64]

Despite these coruscating criticisms, Mendelssohn found his moral affinity to Rousseau in the main character. Mendelssohn judged the majority of Rousseau's characters to be neither convincing nor of "consequence." He did, however, single out Julie.[65] She is "the philosopher in this story": she "philosophizes incessantly" and does so "like a Rousseau, with the same fire and the same insight." As a character, she plays a "double role."

> At the outset she is a weak and even something of a seductive maiden and in the end becomes a woman who, as a model of virtue, exceeds those that have previously been devised. [. . .] She committed mistakes, for that very reason she is all the more perfect; she was less and becomes more than a virtuous lady; she becomes an angel.[66]

---

[60] "Briefe," JubA 5,1:367.   [61] "Briefe," JubA 5,1:373 [11 June 1761]
[62] "Briefe," JubA 5,1:381 [18 June 1761]   [63] "Briefe," JubA 5,1:370 [4 June 1761].
[64] "Briefe," JubA 5,1:379 [18 June 1761].   [65] "Briefe," JubA 5,1:373 [11 June 1761].
[66] "Briefe," JubA 5,1:373 [11 June 1761]. Mendelssohn recommended the novel to his wife-to-be, although he had not yet read the German translation that he sent. Fromet thought Julie's epistles the best in the novel; Mendelssohn of course agreed. See Altman, *Moses Mendelssohn*, p. 96.

Julie represents the very qualities that Mendelssohn had emphasized in his discussion of Rousseau's *Second Discourse*.

As far as I am able to ascertain, this was the last time that Mendelssohn addressed Rousseau's writings directly. It remains an open question why Mendelssohn neither reviewed nor even mentioned *Émile* and the *Social Contract*. It is difficult to believe that Mendelssohn did not read both of those inordinately influential books. Be that as it may, the manifest conversation ended, the latent one began. I will trace that conversation through three examples.

In 1769 Johann Caspar Lavater (1741–1801), a chiliastic Swiss pastor, later known as one of the founders of the pseudoscience of physiognomy, who was notorious for trying to convert celebrated figures, including Goethe, publicly challenged Mendelssohn's commitment to Judaism. In this confrontation with Lavater, Mendelssohn appears to have implicitly acted on, or indeed acted out, Rousseau's "Vicar of Savoyard" in *Émile* (1762). Lavater precipitately offered Mendelssohn a "golden bridge" to Christianity in the form of a dedication to a partial German translation of a French apology for Christianity (Charles Bonnet's *Palingenesie*). Lavater did so on the strength of conversations (1763–4) at Mendelssohn's home in which Mendelssohn expressed a "philosophical respect" for Jesus, as well as a wishful report that the "philosophical Jews" of Berlin were ripe for conversion.[67] Lavater invited Mendelssohn to repudiate Bonnet publicly or to "do what Socrates would have done, had he read this work and found it irrefutable," namely, convert.[68] Lavater's challenge to Mendelssohn was inordinately presumptuous in its public directness.

The Savoyard Vicar, after delivering his creed, suggested that Christians will never know what Jews actually think about Christianity until they have their own "free state, schools and universities" in which they can candidly discuss their views without the threat of censorship or punishment.[69] The Savoryard Vicar aptly articulated Mendelssohn's situation: Mendelssohn did not feel he could speak his mind freely about Christianity. He held a personal and non-transferable privilege of residence in Berlin (his exact status was that of an "*außerordentlicher Schutzjude*" or "unprivileged protected Jew" who was granted residence rights by virtue of practicing

---

[67] "Schreiben an den Herrn Diaconus Lavater zu Zürich," JubA 7:329.   [68] "Schreiben," JubA 7:3.
[69] *Émile*, Book IV. On this passage see Altmann, *Moses Mendelssohn*, p. 226. A reviewer at the time, Gottfried Less, a Professor in Göttingen, pointed to Rousseau's observation in the "Savoyard Vicar" that Jews were unable to speak the truth about Christianity. *Göttingsche Anzeigen* 1770 (January 11) no. 5 p. 44f. Quoted in Altmann, *Moses Mendelssohn*, pp. 238–239, 797 n. 21.

a useful profession).[70] He was acutely aware that the Prussian government could revoke his privilege at any moment, and that criticism of Christianity could in fact trigger such a revocation. He felt that Jews had to be grateful to those states that admitted them under "bearable conditions." To repay that debt by attacking the "religion of the majority" would be tantamount to an assault on "one's guardian at that point where the most virtuous men are the most sensitive," not to mention an attack on the state itself.[71] Mendelssohn felt compelled to have the Berlin Consistory review what he intended to publish to guarantee that he had neither insulted Christianity nor violated the terms of his privilege.[72]

Mendelssohn followed the example of the Savoyard Vicar, whether wittingly or unwittingly, by appealing to toleration. The Vicar had pointed out that two-thirds of mankind had no knowledge of Moses, Jesus or Muhammad; the virtuous of all faiths were capable of attaining salvation. Mendelssohn argued that philosophy could make no claim to absolute truth and therefore it was necessary to admit the legitimacy of other points of view: "[the philosopher] must never lose sight of the fact that this is only his conviction, and that other reasonable beings who begin from another point of departure, and follow a different guide, could reach entirely contradictory opinions."[73] Furthermore, while the philosopher should correct errors, he should desist from doing so if the apparently erroneous ideas did not subvert natural religion or natural law, were merely theoretical ("too far removed from practical life to be directly deleterious") or produced virtue.[74] This was Mendelssohn's politic way of indicating that he had criticisms of Christianity which he chose to withhold. Finally, Mendelssohn asserted that Judaism itself was a tolerant religion. It had no conversionary impulse and claimed no monopoly on salvation. The "righteous of the nations" would also gain eternal reward, and Mendelssohn pointed to the particular examples of Solon and Confucius.[75]

To be sure, there is no evidence that Mendelssohn read *Émile*, although given the book's enormous impact, and Mendelssohn's admiration for Rousseau's work, it is hard to imagine that he had not.[76] If Mendelssohn

---

[70] M. Breuer, "The Early Modern Period," in M. Meyer (ed.), *German-Jewish History in Modern Times*, 4 vols. (New York: Columbia University Press, 1996), I, pp. 148–149.

[71] "Schreiben," JubA 7:15.

[72] For the application to the Berlin Consistory see GS 1:20. Rawidowicz discussed it at JubA 7:xxiv.

[73] "Nacherinnerung," JubA 7:47.   [74] "Schreiben," JubA 7:13.

[75] Schreiben JubA 7:11; Gegenbetrachtungen JubA 7:95f.

[76] In the catalog of Mendelssohn's library compiled after his death the only book by Rousseau was a German translation of the Letter to D'Alembert. See *Verzeichniß der auserlesenen Büchersammlung des seeligen Herrn Moses Mendelssohn* (Berlin, 1786), p. 37. #331, *Rousseau patriotische Vorstellungen*

did in fact know the book and was emulating the Savoyard Vicar, then he once again drew upon Rousseau's moral imagination as the Vicar guided him past the shoals of theological polemic to the shore of toleration and a universally accessible salvation, which were foundational to morality.

The second example is drawn from part of his *magnum opus, The Book of the Paths of Peace.* In the conclusion to the translation and commentary on the book of Exodus (1781), Mendelssohn appended a long passage that addressed the related issues of sociability and luxury in which he seemed to continue his conversation with Rousseau on the *Discourse on Inequality.* Mendelssohn took up the theme of sociability in relationship to the Biblical children of Israel who had entered the desert and, living as a separate people under God's supervision, had begun to practice all of the arts required for society.

As we have already seen in his critique of the *Discourse on Inequality,* Mendelssohn posited, following Wolff, that mankind had an innate need for sociability. Without social relations individuals were unable to achieve their potential let alone their inherent possibility of perfection. Mendelssohn had given unequivocal expression to this view earlier in his commentary (Genesis 1:28). "Man is by nature social and will not achieve success without help from others of his kind; if he remains alone, his mental faculties and attributes will not pass from potentiality to actuality, and he will resemble the animals, and will perhaps not even achieve their merits."[77]

At the conclusion of Exodus he elaborated this issue. God understood that once the Israelites were gathered in their own land they would need to know all the skills and arts. Mendelssohn divided these into three. The "necessary" arts were those needed by individuals: food, clothing, and shelter. The "useful" arts were required both by individuals and by society: these included the building of roads and bridges, metalwork and tools, and everything associated with writing. The "ornamental" or "decorative" arts were those that bring "pleasure and delight," such as

---

gegen die Einführung einer Schaubühne in Genf (Zürich, 1761). Olga Litvak has recently asserted, though without any supporting evidence, that Mendelssohn "appropriated" Rousseau's distinction between ancient and modern law in *Jerusalem.* Thus, "Rousseau's evocation of the ancient 'language of signs' echoes in Mendelssohn's understanding of Jewish ritual as a 'living script' that engages the heart and the mind." She further asserts that "Mendelssohn's concept of the oral tradition likewise recapitulates Rousseau's notion of collective memory as an 'archive.'" See *Haskalah: The Romantic Movement in Judaism* (New Brunswick: Rutgers University Press, 2012), pp. 37–38.

[77] JubA 15, 2:26 (Genesis 2:18). Mendelssohn made a similar point in commenting on the book of Numbers (15:31). He argued that isolation is the greatest failure, connection to others the greatest success, for it alone enables us to enjoy the "spiritual pleasures." See JubA 18:130.

embroidery, painting, and goldwork. All of these arts contribute to the health of the nation so long as moderation prevails. Mendelssohn recognized the contingent nature of moderation: it depended upon each nation's size, resources, and relationship with its neighbors. Yet once the nation had mastered the "necessary" and "useful" arts a distinct danger arose of becoming unduly concerned with the "luxuries" of the third category.

Mendelssohn echoed Rousseau's famous denunciation of luxuries in his long note in the *Discourse on Inequality*. "Luxury is a remedy much worse than the evil it claims to cure; or rather, it is itself the worst of all evils in any State whatever, large or small, and in order to feed the crowds of lackeys and miserable people it has created, it crushes and ruins the farmer and the citizen . . . ."[78] For Rousseau luxury had only deleterious consequences for society. It neither brought wealth nor created employment; it impoverished the many and depopulated the state. Mendelssohn shared Rousseau's view of luxury as having the potential to unravel the very fabric of society. For Mendelssohn luxuries weaken the individual's body and create an undue desire for pleasure. The pernicious result of this process is a pervasive avarice that inflames relations. Luxuries promote "war among the inhabitants of the land itself"; luxuries not only disturb domestic tranquility and harmonious relations but can foment a civil war that has the potential to obliterate the social order.[79] In his essay, "What Is Enlightenment" (1784), Mendelssohn described this situation as a "misuse of culture [*Mißbrauch der Kultur*]."[80]

For Mendelssohn, the antidote to the omnipresent danger of luxuries was the offering of the "first fruits" that God commanded Israel. The fact that the Jews must dedicate to God the first fruits of all their arts which contribute to "the maintenance of state and society" means that they "will remember God in all their acts" and "will not pursue luxury and vanity." When Israel followed the commandments, it prospered: it was, for example, ordered to build the Temple. When it later failed to follow the law, then "the love of pleasure and glory grew among the king and the nation and overflowed into luxury, then what happened to them happened, as is well known from the books of our prophets." The commandments are Israel's special gift, its bulwark against the evils of luxury that can

---

[78] Cambridge edition, p. 201.   [79] JubA 16:406.
[80] JubA; English: "On the Question: What Is Enlightenment," in J. Schmidt (ed.), *What Is Enlightenment? Eighteenth-Century Answers and Twentieth-Century Questions* (Berkeley: University of California Press, 1996), p. 56.

potentially emerge from the society which is necessary to man's true vocation.

Mendelssohn interpreted the Bible and Jewish law in the light of Rousseau's critique of luxury. Just as Rousseau's depiction of "pity" in the savage man spoke to Mendelssohn and Lessing's concern with tragedy, here Rousseau's condemnation of luxury engaged Mendelssohn's understanding of society's inherent dangers.[81] It was, of course, Rousseau's moral condemnation that spoke to Mendelssohn. The eighteenth-century debate over luxuries was as much a discussion of morality as of political economy. Some thinkers endorsed luxuries for their salutary economic consequences: Hume, for example, thought they would help create a "middling rank" of men. Others endorsed luxury for their civilizing impact (*doux commerce*): Mandeville asserted that, "Luxury and Politeness ever grew up together."[82] Rousseau took the extreme negative position in direct opposition to *doux commerce*; it was this view that engaged Mendelssohn in his commentary.

The third example comes from Mendelssohn's famous work in German about church-state relations and Judaism, *Jerusalem, or on Religious Power and Judaism* (1783). Mendelssohn wrote this book in answer to a public challenge more serious than Lavater's. By the early 1780s, the late Enlightenment and enlightened absolutism in Central Europe had made the Jews' political status an issue of public debate and legislation. Christian Wilhelm Dohm in his *On the Civic Amelioration of the Jews* (1781) had advocated equal rights for the Jews. Joseph II's Edict of Toleration (1781) had begun to recognize Jews as potentially productive subjects and promoted their further integration into corporate society. Mendelssohn had requested Dohm to write his tract in response to the situation of the Jews in Alsace. He aimed to reinforce Dohm's tract by publishing a German translation of one of the pamphlets Menasseh ben Israel (1604–57) had written to gain Jews readmission to England in the 1650s. In his preface Mendelssohn advocated equality ("civic acceptance" *bürgerliche Aufnahme*) yet also took issue with Dohm's arguments that Jews should retain judicial autonomy in civil matters and that rabbis should continue to wield the power of excommunication. Mendelssohn insisted that Jews be

---

[81] JubA 16:407.

[82] H. Rosenblatt, *Rousseau and Geneva: From the* First Discourse *to the* Social Contract, *1749–1762* (Cambridge: Cambridge University Press, 1997), pp. 52–84; and idem., "Luxury," in A. Kors (ed.), *Encyclopedia of the Enlightenment,* 4 vols. (New York: Oxford University Press, 2003), II, pp. 440–445.

integrated into the state's legal mechanism and that the ban be abrogated since it was inimical to religion's very goals. That argument elicited a pamphlet that charged Mendelssohn with having repudiated Judaism itself: was not the rabbis' power of the ban fundamental to the maintenance of Jewish law?

In the course of his famous exposition of Judaism as a "divine legislation" (in contradistinction to a "revealed religion"), Mendelssohn addressed the issue of humankind's progress. He vehemently rejected Lessing's concept of the "education of the human race" in which mankind, as if it were a single entity, passed through the various stages of life, rising with each step to a more advanced condition. There was, Mendelssohn asserted, "no steady progress in [the human race's] development that brings it ever closer to perfection."[83] Mendelssohn suggested instead that progress is a matter of the individual rather than of the species:

> Individual man advances but mankind continually fluctuates within fixed limits, while maintaining, on the whole, about the same degree of morality in all periods – the same amount of religion and irreligion, of virtue and vice, of felicity and misery; the same result, if one compares like with like; of all these goods and evils as much as is required for the passage of the individual man in order that he might be educated here below, and approach as closely as possible the perfection which is apportioned to him and for which he is destined.[84]

Mendelssohn's dismissal of Lessing has always seemed to me curiously incomplete. The reason is that he omits to mention the other extreme. Mendelssohn characteristically chose the middle way. He identified the two poles and then found the balanced position that suited his moderate temperament and outlook. As we saw in his "Open Letter to Lessing," he presented Socrates as the "true middle" between the degenerate and the savage.[85] In one of his early works he charted the middle path between the Stoics and the Epicureans.[86] The polar opposite of Lessing' optimistic account of mankind's progressive education was of course Rousseau's pessimistic understanding of the development of

---

[83] *Jerusalem, oder über religiöse Macht und Judentum*, JubA 8:162–163; Arkush trs., 96.

[84] *Jerusalem*, JubA 8:163–164; Arkush trs., 97. On Lessing's and Mendelssohn's views of history see H. Liebeschütz, "Mendelssohn und Lessing in ihrer Stellung zur Geschichte," in S. Stein and R. Loewe (eds.), *Studies in Jewish Religious and Intellectual History* (University: University of Alabama Press, 1979), pp. 167–182.

[85] "Sendschreiben," JubA 2:95.

[86] *Rhadpsodie oder Zusätze zu den Briefen über die Empfindungen* (1761) JubA 1.

society in the *Discourse on Inequality* as inherently corrupting and retrograde.

In his critique of Rousseau Mendelssohn had recognized some collective progress: he wrote, for example, of the possibility of becoming a "moral being [*gesittete Wesen*], which men have worked on for centuries."[87] As cited earlier, Mendelssohn wrote in the Postscript,

> [O]ur entire effort to accustom a savage to our mode of life must be fruitless if we do not allow a series of fathers and children gradually to ascend the ladder which we have traversed in the course of many centuries. Does it follow from this that we have become worse? Or is it not rather a proof that our feeling has been ennobled and our being elevated a step?[88]

In the 1780s Mendelssohn articulated a stronger historical sense of the meandering path of progress within a particular society. In the second half of *Jerusalem*, for example, he argued that the proliferation of books and written culture had destroyed the sociability inherent in oral learning: there a student developed a true relationship with a teacher in which the teacher served as a model for emulation in every respect and thus a guide to human perfection. The predominance of the book subverted that complex intimate relationship: students just listened to a lecture that was intended to become yet another book. For Mendelssohn, the sociability of the teacher-student oral relationship was a prerequisite for man's attainment of perfection. In his essay "What Is Enlightenment," Mendelssohn pointed to the disjunction between the "destiny of man" and the "destiny of citizen" (again echoing Rousseau?) in which the individual's needs for the attainment of perfection comes into conflict with political conditions. Yet such historically conditioned progress was far from Lessing's view.

Rousseau was, then, the elided extreme that clarified Mendelssohn's own position. Mendelssohn was neither the globally optimistic advocate of sociability nor the globally pessimistic, let alone primitivist denigrator, of society. Mendelssohn was committed to sociability as the key to development and perfection yet he was also fully aware of the formidable obstacles. In the first part of *Jerusalem* he followed Wolff in arguing for benevolence (*Wohlwollen*) as the foundational characteristic of social relations and of human perfection, yet cautiously insisted that such development pertained only to the individual. In the second part of

---

[87] "Sendschreiben," (Nachschrift) JubA 2:98.   [88] "Sendschreiben," (Nachschrift) JubA 2:103.

Jerusalem he recognized the degree to which such sociability was impeded by the development of a book culture that undermined the relations between individuals. In response to Lessing's ideas, Mendelssohn returned to and reiterated his critique of Rousseau's *Second Discourse*: "If sociability raised a Socrates, why should it be unable to bless us with more such divine examples."[89]

Mendelsohn also rejected Lessing's phylogenetic appropriation of the ontogenic metaphor – mankind as the individual writ large – since it implied that man can discern a providential design for humankind. Such knowledge for Mendelssohn was, by definition, beyond mankind's ken; any claim to the contrary was preposterous hubris. In this instance, Rousseau and Lessing staked out the complementary extremes that enabled Mendelssohn to define a congenial middle way.

In conclusion, Rousseau's moral imagination had an abiding impact on Mendelssohn. The manifest impact was in the critique of the *Discourse on Inequality*, in which Mendelssohn assimilated Rousseau's moral force to his own understanding of sociability and perfectibility, while linking the emphasis on freedom to reason. In the correspondence on tragedy, Lessing and Mendelssohn used Rousseau's idea of "pity" from the *Discourse on Inequality* to reconceive the constellation of emotions required to make tragedy an effective instrument of moral perfection and a sterling example of the arts' direct contribution to moral perfection. Finally, Mendelssohn salvaged from *Julie or the New Héloise* the protagonist who embodied the drive to moral perfection and was "the philosopher" in the story. Rousseau's continuing if latent impact is discernible in the Lavater Affair, in which Mendelssohn seemed to emulate the "Savoyard Vicar"; in the conclusion to his commentary to the book of Exodus, in which he accepted Rousseau's condemnation of luxuries yet counterpoised the commandment of the offering of "first fruits"; and in his dissent from Lessing's *Education of Mankind* in *Jerusalem*, in which his choice of the middle way presumed Rousseau's extreme alternative to Lessing's extreme *Education of the*

---

[89] "Sendschreiben," JubA 2:95. This emphasis on oral instruction pervades Mendelssohn's introduction to his Bible translation, "Or la-Netiva." For an example see JubA 14:218.

"They did not pass on Holy Scripture to their children or pupils and leave them to read the written text alone . . . . Rather, they read Scripture in front of them and recited alongside them . . . and by these means they would transmit the accentuation of the Torah. They sweetened the appeal of its words for them until the words penetrated their hearts."

Human Race. As Dominique Bourel suggested, Rousseau was "an interlocutor with whom [Mendelssohn] was in dialogue his entire life." Yet after the initial five year encounter he was a silent interlocutor in an unspoken and heretofore largely unrecognized conversation.

CHAPTER 6

Rousseau and Smith: On Sympathy as a First Principle

Pierre Force

In the work of Adam Smith explicit references to Rousseau are few. The only extended treatment of Rousseau's views happened very early in Smith's career. In 1756 Smith published a critical review of the *Discourse on the Origin of Inequality*, just a few months after the publication of the book.[1] Smith scholars have generally seen the review as negative, but its ambiguous tone has allowed for diverging interpretations. I was one of the first commentators to argue, in a 1997 article[2] and in a 2003 book,[3] that Rousseau was an essential interlocutor for Smith and that the discussion of first principles in the *Theory of Moral Sentiments* and the *Wealth of Nations* appropriated key elements of Rousseau's philosophy (Keith Tribe's review described my analysis of the Rousseau-Smith connection as a "hitherto unwritten book").[4] I will structure this article as a critical discussion. I will summarize the claims I made at the time regarding how Smith's discussion of first principles was indebted to Rousseau. I will then summarize the objections made to these claims in reviews of my 2003 book, and will attempt to advance the discussion by responding to these objections. Finally, I will try to show how this debate about first principles was related to the story of the development of commerce as Smith told it in the *Wealth of Nations*.

Early Claims About the Rousseau-Smith Connection

Before I summarize the claims I made about the Rousseau-Smith connection in 1997 and 2003, I should indicate what the state of the question was

---

[1] *Letter to the Edinburgh Review*, in *Essays on Philosophical Subjects. The Glasgow Edition of the Works and Correspondence of Adam Smith* (Oxford: Oxford University Press, 1976–1983), III, pp. 242–256.
[2] P. Force, "Self-Love, Identification, and the Origin of Political Economy," *Yale French Studies* 92 (1997): pp. 46–64.
[3] P. Force, *Self-Interest before Adam Smith. A Genealogy of Economic Science* (Cambridge: Cambridge University Press, 2003), esp. chap. 1 and 4.
[4] K. Tribe, review of P. Force, *Self-Interest before Adam Smith, History of Economic Ideas* 12:3 (2004): pp. 123–125.

at the time. In the small number of studies that discussed the relationship between these two authors, Rousseau was almost always presented as a polemical target for Smith. According to E.J. Hundert, Smith's review of the *Second Discourse* was "an attack upon Rousseau."[5] To the extent that Rousseau had some importance for Smith, it was as someone whose theses should be refuted. E.J. Hundert argued that "for Smith, confronting Rousseau's picture of the development of civility and commerce as the last phase of a history of moral decline was the necessary preliminary to his qualified endorsement of competitive individualism in the *Theory of Moral Sentiments*."[6] Major Smith scholars such as A.L. Macfie and D.D. Raphael gave similar interpretations. According to A.L. Macfie, the *Letter to the Edinburgh Review* is a "statement of man's essentially social nature" in which Smith "criticizes Mandeville and Rousseau" for describing natural man as an unsociable being.[7] D.D. Raphael argued that in the passage in the *Theory of Moral Sentiments* about the invisible hand Smith "was implicitly contesting Rousseau's claim that the acquisition of property causes inequality."[8] Such conventional wisdom about the Rousseau-Smith connection was itself based on widely shared assumptions about each author. Rousseau was seen as the most eloquent critic of modern commercial society. Adam Smith was taken to be its most prominent advocate. It stood to reason that the latter had to be a critic of the former.

There were dissenting views, however. If we go as far back as Delatour's 1886 book on the life and works of Adam Smith, we'll see a more nuanced assessment of the relationship between these two authors.[9] Delatour noticed the ambiguity of Smith's review of the *Second Discourse* and took it to mean that Smith reserved judgment on Rousseau.[10] He also pointed out that that the critique of the division of labor one finds in the *Wealth of Nations* seemed to be borrowed from Rousseau: "In sum, it is civilization itself that the Scottish philosopher seems incidentally to put on trial, and in truth this reads not like a fragment of the *Wealth of Nations* but like a passage from Rousseau."[11] In the same interpretive vein R. Glenn Morrow noticed in the conclusion of his 1923 book that in ascribing the origin of government to the rise of private property Smith probably

[5] E. Hundert, *The Enlightenment's Fable: Bernard Mandeville and the Discovery of Society* (Cambridge: Cambridge University Press, 1994), p. 220.
[6] Hundert, *The Enlightenment's Fable*, p. 221.
[7] A. Macfie, *The Individual and Society. Papers on Adam Smith* (London: George Allen & Unwin, 1967), p. 44.
[8] D. Raphael, *Adam Smith* (Oxford: Oxford University Press, 1985), pp. 71–72.
[9] A. Delatour, *Adam Smith, sa vie, ses travaux, ses doctrines* (Paris: Guillaumin, 1886).
[10] Delatour, *Adam Smith*, pp. 84–85.   [11] Delatour, *Adam Smith*, p. 145.

followed Rousseau's *Second Discourse*.[12] In addition, "another point of agreement with Rousseau was his distrust of class interests in government, and his belief that the general welfare is best expressed by individuals, not by groups."[13] In 1938–39, Richard B. Sewall published a series of articles about the reception of the *Second Discourse* in England. According to Sewall, Adam Smith "was suspicious of Rousseau's sentimental picture of the state of nature, but there was much in the *Discourse* that he found to praise and even to make use of in future publications of his own."[14] Sewall added that the first paragraph of the *Theory of Moral Sentiments* was "little more than a restatement of Rousseau's conception of pity."[15] More generally, "when Smith summed up the essay as revealing 'only the true spirit of a republican carried a little too far,' he indicated a sympathy for Rousseau's political liberalism from which he never completely departed."[16] In the 1980s Michael Ignatieff and István Hont published several pieces, separately and together, which argued that Smith took Rousseau's positions seriously and shared many of his concerns about the rise of modern commercial society. According to Ignatieff, "Smith's [...] deep concern, for example, with the issue of standing armies, and his unconcealed preference for government by the independent landed class in preference to the ascendant commercial interests make it clear how deeply he shared Rousseau's anxieties, if not his solutions."[17] Ignatieff and Hont together claimed that "Rousseau is an important if unavowed interlocutor in the passages in the *Theory of Moral Sentiments* which Smith devoted to the pursuit of wealth in modern society."[18] Lastly, in his 1996 book on the history of British political economy, Donald Winch argued that "Smith's theory of sympathy, as expounded in the *Theory of Moral Sentiments*, is an augmented version of Rousseau's conception of *pitié*."[19]

---

[12] R. Morrow, *The Ethical and Economic Theories of Adam Smith: A Study in the Social Philosophy of the Eighteenth Century* (New York: Longmans, Green, and Co., 1923), p. 87.

[13] Ibid.

[14] R. Sewall, "Rousseau's Second Discourse in England from 1755 to 1762," *Philological Quarterly* 17:2 (1938): pp. 97–114, 98.

[15] Ibid.   [16] R. Sewall, "Rousseau's Second Discourse in England from 1755 to 1762," p. 99.

[17] M. Ignatieff, "Smith, Rousseau and the Republic of Needs," in T. Smout (ed.), *Scotland and Europe 1200–1850* (Edinburgh: John Donald, 1986), pp. 187–206, 197. Also see Ignatieff, *The Needs of Strangers* (London: Chatto & Windus, 1984), pp. 107–131.

[18] I. Hont and M. Ignatieff, "Needs and Justice in the *Wealth of Nations*," in I. Hont, *Jealousy of Trade: International Competition and the Nation-State in Historical Perspective* (Cambridge, MA: Harvard University Press, 2006), pp. 389–443, 400. Originally published in I. Hont and M. Ignatieff (eds.), *Wealth and Virtue: The Shaping of Political Economy in the Scottish Enlightenment* (Cambridge: Cambridge University Press, 1983), pp. 1–44.

[19] D. Winch, *Riches and Poverty. An Intellectual History of Political Economy in Britain* (Cambridge: Cambridge University Press, 1996), p. 72.

Winch qualified his claim by adding that, according to Rousseau, *pitié* diminished with civilization, while Smith saw civilized society as the vehicle for the perfection of sympathy.

Rousseau and Smith on First Principles

In my own work on the relationship between Smith and Rousseau, I focused on the discussion of first principles: the meaning of *amour-propre, amour de soi, pitié*, and *identification* in Rousseau, and how these concepts were appropriated by Smith in the *Theory of Moral Sentiments* and the *Wealth of Nations*. I made the following four claims:

1. **From the *Second Discourse* Smith borrowed the notion that *pity* cannot be derived from or explained by *self-interest* (based on a discussion of Mandeville).** The background of the discussion was the analysis of *amour-propre* by seventeenth-century French moralists such as La Rochefoucauld, who had claimed that pity was fundamentally a selfish feeling because it is our own misfortunes we feel in the suffering of other people. Mandeville was seen as the continuator and exponent of these theories that ascribed all human behavior to *amour-propre*. Yet as Rousseau, and Smith after him, showed, Mandeville acknowledged the existence of pity as a separate principle. The refutation of the "selfish hypothesis" came from inside the system of its most famous proponent.

2. **Smith appropriated Rousseau's concept of *identification* when he established *sympathy* as the cornerstone of his system in the *Theory of Moral Sentiments*.** In ancient and early modern accounts of sympathy, one "felt the pain" of others quite literally. Sympathy was described as a sort of emotional contagion that went from one body to another. Rousseau's innovation was to show that we experience pity by putting ourselves mentally in the position of the sufferer, a process he called identification. Smith appropriated this point and developed it as a paradox: through sympathy we do not have access to the feelings of others; we reconstruct these feelings through imagination in our own minds, based on our own feelings.

3. **Smith analyzed *vanity* (the engine of economic growth) as based on reason and reflection, like Rousseau's *amour-propre*.** For Rousseau, *amour-propre*, far from being a basic, instinctual impulse, was a product of reason and reflection (and as such a historically contingent development). This connection between *amour-propre* and

rational calculation was appropriated by Smith in both the *Theory of Moral Sentiments* and the *Wealth of Nations*. Smith insisted that in modern commercial society the acquisition of goods and luxuries was the most common way of securing the esteem and approbation of others.

4. **In the *Wealth of Nations*, Smith borrowed Rousseau's analysis of commerce as a form of persuasion, where self-interest was used as an argument, not as a first principle.** This last point was derived from the third one. The famous passage about the baker and the butcher in the *Wealth of Nations* is conventionally read as stressing the role of self-interest as an explanatory principle for economic behavior. Yet Smith's point, borrowed from Rousseau, was not that those who engage in commercial transactions are self-interested (this would be trivial or tautological). It was that commercial transactions are a form of persuasion where self-interest is used as an argument. Rousseau had shown that in modern commercial society, the only way of obtaining assistance from others was to appeal to their self-interest. Such appeal was therefore subject to debate and persuasion.

Summary of Objections

Before I take up the objections, I would like to quote Gilbert Faccarello's review,[20] which conflated these four points into two after stating that my study of the Rousseau-Smith connection "is certainly the book's strong point, its most novel and also most fascinating aspect."[21] According to Faccarello, the book established the following two main points:

1. The first move is to counter Mandeville's "doctrine of interest" by showing that human behavior is naturally founded upon other principles: Rousseau's *amour de soi, identification* or *pitié*, which correspond to self-love and sympathy in Smith (p. 43), all behaviors that cannot be "described as rational pursuit of self-interest"(p. 46).

2. But at the same time there is a recovery, though historicization, of the "selfish hypothesis": what we call the "rational pursuit of self-interest" certainly exists, but it is an "historically contingent phenomenon" (p. 247). The behavior described by Mandeville, far from being

---

[20] G. Faccarello, "A Tale of Two Traditions: Pierre Force's *Self-Interest before Adam Smith*," *European Journal of the History of Economic Thought* 12:4 (2005): 701–712.

[21] Faccarello, "A Tale of Two Traditions . . .," p. 704.

universal, is only "the description of human behavior in civilized society, a behavior that is in large part driven by the desire to obtain marks of esteem and approbation by others." (p. 44) At the conceptual level, this translates in Rousseau as the emergence of *amour-propre*: reason and reflection, allied to identification, engender it (p. 262) and the calculation of interest becomes a means to maximize our status in the eyes of other individuals. In Smith, this is translated by vanity – "a passion that does not originate in self-love [. . .] but rather in sympathy and the desire for sympathy" (p. 261) – which engenders the desire to ameliorate one's condition. *Amour-propre* and *vanity* are practically universal principles of conduct in commercial society: enjoyment is postponed so that the admiration and approbation of others might be obtained through accumulation.[22]

In the critical reaction to the book, the main contributions as Faccarello summarizes them have for the most part not been challenged. Most of the objections have been directed at the claims regarding sympathy and identification. Christopher Berry[23] criticizes my contention that Smith "bases sympathy on a psychological disposition that is very similar to what Rousseau calls identification."[24] Like me he quotes a passage from the *Second Discourse* where Rousseau speculates that identification with the sufferer must have been much greater in the savage man that it is in the civilized. He then brings up another, conflicting passage: "L'imagination qui fait tant de ravages parmi nous ne parle point à des cœurs sauvages" [*imagination, which causes so much damage among us, does not speak to savage hearts*].[25] Since identification requires imagination, and savage man had no imagination, savage man's pity cannot have been based on identification. Berry then brings a related objection, drawn from N.J.H. Dent's work on Rousseau, which he says points to a fundamental difference between Rousseau's pity and Smith's sympathy.[26] According to Rousseau, pity "moves us" and impels us to help the sufferer. However, there is no such impulse in Smith's sympathy, since we can sympathize even with the dead. Finally, as Berry points out, the development of civilization works in opposite ways for Smith and Rousseau regarding the efficacy of sympathy: "Whereas for Rousseau the development of 'civilization' is deleterious because it causes pity to be overlaid, for Smith civilization enhances the efficacy of sympathy because the interactions within a developed, complex

[22] Ibid.
[23] C. Berry, "Smith under Strain," *European Journal of Political Theory* 3 (2004): pp. 455–463.
[24] Berry, p. 455.   [25] Ibid.   [26] Berry, p. 456.

commercial society (an 'assembly of strangers'), more thoroughly abate 'the violence' of feelings than those that occur in face-to-face settings."[27]

Similarly, Jimena Hurtado points to major differences between Rousseau's pity and Smith's sympathy. She argues, based on Larrère's analysis,[28] that Smith's "system of sympathy allows the exclusion of the poor through their invisibility."[29] This stands in contrast to Rousseau's "system of pity, where the poor leads to the identification with the human condition shared in suffering."[30] Hurtado claims that for Rousseau "pity is the principle of moral, social, political and economic life." Sympathy, on the other hand, cannot be the foundation of social order because it generates a world of isolated individuals who hide behind false appearances.[31]

Gloria Vivenza's objections are in a similar vein.[32] According to her, I equate Mandeville's (and Rousseau's) "pity" with Smith's "sympathy."[33] Smith, however, "makes clear that to himself 'sympathy' is something more than pity."[34] Consequently, I have difficulty accounting for the "counterintuitive, straining or paradoxical [. . .] passages where Smith says that we sympathize more easily with the joy than with the sorrow of others."[35]

S.J. Pack's objections are of a different nature.[36] While the previous reviewers challenged the connections I establish between Rousseau's first principles and Smith's, Pack states: "Force's central point, that Smith was deeply influenced by Rousseau, and accepted many of Rousseau's criticisms of commercial society, is basically correct."[37] However, Pack claims priority for his own analyses, which he published in a 2000 article,[38] while my book appeared in 2003. On the priority claims, I confess that I was unaware of Pack's 2000 article when I published my 2003 book. However, my analysis of the Rousseau-Smith connection predates the 2003 book

[27] Ibid.
[28] C. Larrère, "Adam Smith et Jean-Jacques Rousseau: sympathie et pitié," *Kairos. Revue de Philosophie* 20 (2002): pp. 73–94.
[29] J. Hurtado, "Pity, Sympathy and Self-Interest: Review of Pierre Force's *Self-Interest before Adam Smith*," *European Journal of the History of Economic Thought* 12:4 (2005): pp. 713–721, 718.
[30] Ibid.   [31] Ibid.
[32] G. Vivenza, review of *Self-Interest before Adam Smith: A Genealogy of Economic Science*, EH.NET, September 2004: http://eh.net/book_reviews/self-interest-before-adam-smith-a-genealogy-of-economic-science/ (accessed September 16, 2014).
[33] Ibid.   [34] Ibid.   [35] Ibid.
[36] S. Pack, review of *Self-Interest before Adam Smith, Journal of the History of Economic Thought* 27:4 (2005): pp. 465–467.
[37] Ibid., p. 466.
[38] S. Pack, "The Rousseau-Smith Connection: Towards an Understanding of Professor West's 'Splenetic Smith,'" *History of Economic Ideas* 8:3 (2000): pp. 35–62.

since the main claims were stated in a 1997 *Yale French Studies* article. Essentially, S.J. Pack's response is that on the Rousseau-Smith connection my analysis is valid but he's the one who should get credit for these findings. As I will show later, my analysis is substantially different from Pack's. I will not discuss Schliesser's review here,[39] since I have already done it elsewhere,[40] and it does not mainly bear on the Rousseau-Smith connection (Schliesser, like Pack, seems to agree with me on the central importance of this connection).

Pity, Sympathy, and Identification

There is a good deal of convergence (Pack and Schliesser excepted) in the objections I have summarized above. The critics are on to something, but I'd like to show that the objections are based on a misunderstanding, which is itself the consequence of a major difficulty in Rousseau's thinking about pity and identification.

In his own analysis of the Rousseau-Smith connection, S.J. Pack states that "Smith's sympathy is fundamentally a generalization, a broadening of the idea of pity."[41] According to Berry, Hurtado, and Vivenza, my own analysis posits a similar equation between Rousseau's pity and Smith's sympathy. The point I made is a more complex one, however. It took two additional dimensions into account: first, the concept of identification, which is not synonymous for pity; second, Rousseau's stadial theory, in which pity works differently for primitive man, savage man, and civilized man.

As we have seen above, Berry points to a fundamental difference between Rousseau's pity and Smith's sympathy. For Rousseau, if I feel pity I feel compelled to help the one who suffers. There is no such impulse in Smith's sympathy. According to N.J.H. Dent, to whom Berry refers to support his point, the kind of identification that is at work in Rousseau's pity is far removed from "*projective* identification,"[42] i.e. what psychologists usually mean by identification today. As Dent puts it, "what 'identification' signifies is that just as when I feel a pain I am *immediately* and *directly* moved by distress to try to alleviate it, so in pity I am moved to try

---

[39] E. Schliesser, review of Pierre Force, *Self-Interest before Adam Smith*, *The Adam Smith Review* 3 (2007): pp. 203–211.

[40] P. Force, "Putting Categorizations in Context," *The Adam Smith Review* 3 (2007): pp. 211–214.

[41] S. Pack, "The Rousseau-Smith Connection . . .," p. 46.

[42] N. Dent, *Rousseau: An Introduction to his Psychological, Social and Political Theory* (Oxford: Blackwell, 1988), p. 130.

to alleviate the pain of another with that same immediacy and directness."[43] I am moved to respond to another person's hurts exactly as I am moved to respond to my own hurts. This stands in contrast to "sympathetic suffering,"[44] a process in which I trade places mentally with the other and experience the other's suffering thanks to the work of my imagination. What Dent calls "sympathetic suffering" is close to Smith's sympathy. In the *Theory of Moral Sentiments*, Smith insists that through sympathy I never have access to the feelings of the other. I reconstruct those feelings in my own mind based on my own feelings and my imagination. In that sense, Smith's sympathy is far removed from Rousseau's pity.

Rousseau's analysis of pity and identification is far more complex, however. Dent bases his analysis on two references to Rousseau. The first one is to *Emile*, where Rousseau describes pity as the first feeling that touches the human heart according to the order of nature:

> In fact how do we let ourselves be moved by pity if not by transporting ourselves outside of ourselves and identifying with the suffering animal by leaving, as it were, our own being to take on his being? We suffer only so much as we judge that it suffers. It is not in ourselves, it is in him that we suffer.[45]

The second one is the *Second Discourse*, where Rousseau had used similar language: "Commiseration will be all the more energetic as the observing animal identifies himself more intimately with the suffering animal."[46] For the purposes of our analysis, the main points of these two passages are the following: natural pity is based on identification; the stronger the identification, the stronger the pity; identification in this context means the ability to feel someone else's pain without mediation: we suffer not in ourselves but in the other. In that sense, pity is "prior to all reflection."[47]

However, another passage from the *Essay on the Origin of Languages* poses an exegetic difficulty. Pity alone cannot move us. It is effective only with the help of the imagination:

> Pity, although natural to the heart of man, would remain eternally inactive without the imagination that puts it into play. How do we let ourselves be moved by pity? By transporting ourselves outside of ourselves; by identifying ourselves with the suffering being.[48]

Similarly, in the passage from *Emile* that Dent quotes to support his analysis of pity as an unmediated feeling, Rousseau does mention the role

---

[43] Dent, *Rousseau*, p. 129.   [44] Dent, *Rousseau*, p. 130.   [45] *Emile*, CW XIII, p. 374.
[46] *Discourse on Inequality*, CW III, p. 37.   [47] Ibid.
[48] *Essay on the Origin of Languages*, CW VII, p. 306.

of imagination in triggering pity: "Thus no one becomes sensitive until his imagination is animated and begins to transport him out of himself."[49] This description of pity is much closer to Smith's description of sympathy: it is with the help of imagination that we identify with someone else's feelings. David Marshall has shown the central role that theatrical metaphors play in Smith's description of sympathy as well as in Rousseau's description of pity. As he puts it, "for Smith, sympathy depends upon a theatrical relation between a spectator and a spectacle."[50] Such a theatrical model is already present in the *Second Discourse*. In his analysis of pity in the state of nature, Rousseau states that pity will be stronger when the "observing animal" (*animal spectateur*) identifies more closely with the "suffering animal" (*animal souffrant*). What the English translation fails to convey properly is that the animal experiencing pity is a spectator and the suffering animal is a spectacle. The reference to theater is not coincidental. For Rousseau, the experience of theater is the best proof that the propensity to feel pity is an integral part of human nature:

> Such is the force of natural pity, which the most depraved morals still have difficulty destroying, since daily in our theaters one sees, moved and crying for the troubles of an unfortunate person, a man who, if he were in the Tyrant's place, would aggravate his enemy's torment even more.[51]

Rousseau may have misgivings about theater as a source of corruption but he argues that paradoxically the position of the spectator in the theater approximates the position of men vis-à-vis each other in the state of nature. Because the characters on stage are fictional no interests are at stake, thus the sight of suffering can trigger the full force of natural pity. On the contrary, in civilized society, calculations of self-interest stand in the way of our propensity to identify with others.

Marshall deals with the exegetical difficulty from a deconstructionist point of view. His comparative reading of Smith and Rousseau leads him to conclude that Rousseau's state of nature is "always already theatrical."[52] In his narrative of origins, Rousseau wants to posit pity as a pure, original, unmediated feeling, but the narrative of origins necessarily brings in language and concepts that are connected to civilization. In that sense, thanks to the theatrical metaphor, Smith's sympathy as a projective form of identification is already present in Rousseau's description of natural pity.

[49] *Emile*, 374.
[50] D. Marshall, *The Figure of Theater: Shaftesbury, Defoe, Adam Smith, and George Eliot* (New York: Columbia University Press, 1988), p. 190.
[51] *Discourse on the Origin of Inequality*, p. 36.   [52] Marshall, *The Figure of Theater*, p. 151.

Another way of dealing with the difficulty is Goldschmidt's analysis, which involves some measure of rational reconstruction of Rousseau but is very useful in clarifying the issues.[53] Goldschmidt makes distinctions based on Rousseau's stadial theory. He claims that the kind of pity that is prior to all reflection (simple pity) belongs to the primitive man. The pity that is based on identification (*pitié identifiante*, to use Goldschmidt's words) belongs to the savage man. There is a parallel evolution in the development of *amour-propre*. The rise in the ability to reflect marks the passage from primitive to savage man, and with it the transformation of love of oneself (*amour de soi*) into disinterested self-love (*amour-propre désintéressé* – Goldschmidt's expression again) i.e. a kind of self-love that only wants marks of esteem, and not the wealth that triggers esteem in civilized society. The third stage in the evolution is marked by the full development of human reason, which is itself closely tied to the ability to compute one's interest:

> Behold all our faculties developed, memory and imagination in play, amour-propre aroused, reason rendered active, and the mind having almost reached the limit of the perfection of which it is susceptible.[54]

The ability to make rational assessments of his interests has transformed man's self-love. It is no longer *désintéressé*. It has become *intéressé* ("aroused," as in the translation above, or more precisely "looking out for its interests"). In the third stage, the workings of pity and identification are also changed in fundamental ways. The "feeling that puts us in the position of him who suffers" is "obscure and lively in Savage man, developed but weak in Civilized man."[55] The capacity for identification evolves in two seemingly contradictory ways: from obscure to developed, and from strong to weak. Prior to the development of human reason, our ability to identify with the suffering of others always resulted in pity. When combined with reason and reflection, the capacity for identification is weaker, and therefore less likely to result in pity. For Rousseau, it is the philosopher, rational man par excellence, who says at the sight of the sufferer: "Perish if you will; I am safe."[56] Now, our capacity for identification is weaker because our reason tells us that it would be against our interests to help others, but at the same time it is more developed and more complete. With the development of reason, reflection, and imagination we

---

[53] V. Goldschmidt, *Anthropologie et politique. Les principes du système de Rousseau* (Paris: J.Vrin, 1974), pp. 337–341.
[54] *Discourse on Inequality*, CW III, p. 51.   [55] Ibid., p. 37.   [56] Ibid.

have a much greater ability to see things through the eyes of others, to trade places in fancy with them. This kind of reflective, projective identification is an essential component in the development of *amour-propre*, and it is very similar to what Smith calls sympathy.

Thus, Winch is right to notice that for Rousseau pity diminishes with civilization while for Smith sympathy is perfected by it. Berry, Hurtado, and Vivenza are right to state that there are major differences between Rousseau's pity and Smith's sympathy. However, in my 2003 book I did not attempt to equate Smith's sympathy with Rousseau's pity (differing on this key point from S.J. Pack). I showed that Smith's analysis of sympathy was borrowed from Rousseau's analysis of identification in civilized society.

Rousseau and Smith on the "Unnatural and Retrograde Order"

In order to see what was at stake in these discussions of first principles, I would like to show how the discussion of *amour-propre* and identification was related to the story of the development of commerce as Smith told it in the *Wealth of Nations*.

Adam Smith meant the *Wealth of Nations* to be an attack on the "mercantile system," which favored commerce at the expense of agriculture. This attack is carried out in Book IV of the volume. In the preceding book, Smith tells the prehistory of the mercantile system. He shows that commerce and cities were artificially developed by kings at the expense of agriculture. This was a historically contingent phenomenon that went against the natural course of things. Agriculture should have been developed first, commerce later.

For Smith, there are two classes of needs: natural and artificial. Agriculture addresses natural needs which should be satisfied first. Commerce addresses artificial needs whose satisfaction is secondary:

> As subsistence is, in the nature of things, prior to conveniency and luxury, so the industry which procures the former, must necessarily be prior to that which ministers to the latter. The cultivation and improvement of the country, therefore, which affords subsistence, must, necessarily, be prior to the increase of the town, which furnishes only the means of conveniency and luxury.[57]

Agriculture takes precedence over commerce as a matter of natural law. If one lets nature take its course, agriculture will develop before commerce,

---

[57] *Wealth of Nations*, in *The Glasgow Edition of the Works and Correspondence of Adam Smith* II, p. 377.

and commerce will develop only to the extent that it will help the development of agriculture:

> That order of things which necessity imposes in general, though not in every particular country, is, in every particular country, promoted by the natural inclinations of man. If human institutions had never thwarted those natural inclinations, the towns could no-where have increased beyond what the improvement and cultivation of the territory in which they were situated could support.[58]

This is not how things unfolded historically, however. The development of towns and commerce took precedence over the development of agriculture for an array of political and legal reasons. The main cause Smith gives is an alliance of convenience between kings and urban elites against the landed nobility:

> The burghers naturally hated and feared the lords. The king hated and feared them too; but though perhaps he might despise, he had no reason either to hate or fear the burghers. Mutual interest, therefore, disposed them to support the king, and the king to support them against the lords. They were the enemies of his enemies, and it was his interest to render them as secure and independent of those enemies as he could.[59]

The exact reasons given matter less than the broader point: the faster development of commerce and cities was the result of decisions made for reasons of convenience or ambition at particular points in time. These decisions were historically contingent but put together they fundamentally altered the "natural progress of opulence."[60] In the end, agriculture itself benefitted from the development of commerce, because the growing population of towns had to be fed, but the sequencing of events was such that the "natural order of things" was "entirely inverted."[61] The effect became the cause and the cause became the effect: "It is thus that through the greater part of Europe the commerce and manufactures of cities, instead of being the effect, have been the cause and occasion of the improvement and cultivation of the country."[62]

As István Hont has suggested, in telling this story of "unnatural and retrograde order"[63] Smith replicated a move made by Rousseau in the *Second Discourse*.[64] Hont pointed out that Rousseau did refer to the

---

[58] Ibid. [59] *Wealth of Nations, Works* II, p. 402. [60] *Wealth of Nations, Works* II, p. 376.
[61] *Wealth of Nations, Works* II, p. 380. [62] *Wealth of Nations, Works* II, p. 422.
[63] *Wealth of Nations, Works*, II, p. 380.
[64] I. Hont, *Politics in Commercial Society: Jean-Jacques Rousseau and Adam Smith* (Cambridge, MA: Harvard University Press, 2015).

four stages theory of human development, which was broadly used in the
eighteenth century and was understood to have been initially formulated
by Lucretius in his poem *On the Nature of Things*. The standard theory
posited four stages in the development of civilization: 1. Hunting/gather-
ing; 2. Pastoralism; 3. Agriculture; 4. Commerce.[65] Rousseau's move,
according to Hont, was to invert the order of stages 3 and 4. The standard
Lucretian story was that commerce arose as a consequence of the development of agriculture. Rousseau's intervention reversed the order of causes
and consequences-the development of agriculture was a consequence of the
development of commerce:

> The invention of the other arts was therefore necessary to force the human
> Race to apply itself to that of agriculture. As soon as some men needed to
> smelt and forge iron, other men were needed to feed them. The more the
> number of workers was multiplied, the fewer hands were engaged in
> furnishing the common subsistence, without there being fewer mouths to
> consume it; and since some needed foodstuffs in exchange for their iron, the
> others finally found the secret of using iron to multiply foodstuffs. From this
> arose husbandry and agriculture on the one hand, and on the other the art of
> working metals and multiplying their uses.[66]

According to Rousseau the development of agriculture was predicated on
the development of metal tools, and the development of metal tools was
itself predicated on the division of labor: those employed in metallurgy
could not cultivate the land themselves and had to buy food from farmers.
In that sense the development of commerce was a precondition of the
development of agriculture. There was never such a thing as subsistence
farming: the production of metal tools required the existence of a surplus in
food production that could be traded with artisans.

Smith made a very similar point in the *Wealth of Nations*. He argued that
farmers could not operate without a whole array of artisans who lived in
small towns and provided them with clothes and equipment:

> Without the assistance of some artificers, indeed, the cultivation of land
> cannot be carried on, but with great inconveniency and continual interrup-
> tion. Smiths, carpenters, wheel-wrights, and plough-wrights, masons, and
> bricklayers, tanners, shoemakers, and taylors, are people, whose service the
> farmer has frequent occasion for. Such artificers too stand, occasionally, in
> need of the assistance of one another; and as their residence is not, like that

[65] R. Meek, *Social Science and the Ignoble Savage* (Cambridge: Cambridge University Press, 1976),
pp. 5–36.
[66] *Discourse on Inequality*, CW III, p. 50.

of the farmer, necessarily tied down to a precise spot, they naturally settle in the neighbourhood of one another, and thus form a small town or village.[67]

In that sense the commerce between towns and country was not a recent development but rather a precondition of the development of agriculture itself, and the kings who favored towns at the expense of the countryside relied on a mechanism that was always already there.

As a deconstructionist would say, Rousseau, and Smith after him, reversed the hierarchy between origin and end. What was thought to be the end of the story was put at the beginning. Commerce was not a late development made possible by the growth of agriculture. It was precisely the development of commerce that made agriculture possible. In both Smith and Rousseau, we see the same dual move: on the one hand, the assertion of a natural norm, a natural course of things; on the other hand, the story of how this course was altered based on propensities in human nature that were there from the very beginning.

One sees a similar conceptual move here as in the story of pity and identification. Rousseau's state of nature, as Marhsall puts it, is "always already" theatrical. In that sense, the capacity for projective identification was there *in potentia* from the very beginning. In his description of pity in *Emile*, Rousseau says revealingly that pity is a *relative* feeling: "Thus is born pity, the first relative sentiment which touches the human heart according to the order of nature."[68] In another context he uses the exact same expression, *sentiment relatif*, to describe *amour-propre*:

> And that is how the love of self, which is a good and absolute feeling, becomes amour-propre, which is to say a relative feeling by which ones makes comparisons; the latter feeling demands preferences, whose enjoyment is purely negative, and it no longer seeks satisfaction in our own benefit but solely in the harm of others.[69]

We experience pity by comparing our position with that of others. The same operation of comparison is what makes *amour-propre* possible. In Rousseau, the story of agriculture and the story of *amour-propre* have a common root in the concept of *perfectibility*, "a faculty which, with the aid of circumstances, successively develops all the others, and resides among us as much in the species as in the individual."[70] Human nature is subject to change, and change is historically contingent; *amour-propre* a historically contingent phenomenon, like the development of cities and

---

[67] *Wealth of Nations*, III.i.   [68] *Emile*, p. 374.   [69] *Rousseau, Judge of Jean-Jacques*, CW I, p. 9.
[70] *Discourse on Inequality*, CW III, p. 26.

commerce. The discussion of first principles in the *Wealth of Nations* is not nearly as clear, but there are strong indications that Rousseau's story was a major implicit reference. At the beginning of Book 1, Smith poses the question of the origins of commerce and the division of labor. In response, he invokes "the propensity to truck, barter and exchange one thing for another."[71] Such propensity, however, is probably based on a more fundamental principle:

> Whether this propensity be one of those original principles in human nature, of which no further account can be given; or whether, as seems more probable, it be the necessary consequence of the faculties of reason and speech, it belongs not to our present subject to enquire.[72]

Smith declines to make a final call on the issue of first principles. This may be due in part to the fact the in the *Wealth of Nations* he proceeded analytically (starting with a problem and resolving it into simpler and simpler nations) while in the *Theory of Moral Sentiments* he proceeded *more geometrico* (starting with first principles). This may also be due to the fact that putting "the faculties of reason and speech" as a first principle was controversial. Smith's correspondence with Governor Pownall is revealing in that respect. In his September 25, 1776 letter to Smith, Pownall commented at length on the only passage in the *Wealth of Nations* where Smith brings up first principles. He agreed with Smith that the propensity to barter and trade could not be a first principle, but he felt that Smith's discussion was inconclusive: "I think you have stopped short in your analysis before you have arrived at the first natural cause and principle of the division of labor."[73] Pownall's own view was that the first principle of the division of labor was necessarily the same as the first principle of government. If one thought that the origin of government lied in the faculties of reason and speech, one had to believe that government was "an artificial succedaneum to an imagined theoretic state of nature."[74] In other words, invoking reason and speech as a first principle meant replicating the move Rousseau made in the *Second Discourse*: positing a conjectural state of nature and asserting that the division of labor and the invention of government were historically contingent developments that deviated from the natural course of things:

---

[71] *Wealth of Nations*, I.ii.1.   [72] *Wealth of Nations*, I.ii.2.
[73] Letter from G. Pownall to A. Smith in *Correspondence of Adam Smith, The Glasgow Edition of the Works and Correspondence of Adam Smith*, vol. 6, p. 338.
[74] Letter from Pownall to Smith, p. 339.

And as I think that great danger may arise [...] in deriving the source of community and government from passions and caprice, creating by will an artificial succedaneum to nature, I could not but in the same manner, *en passant*, make this cursory remark.[75]

Smith did not change the incriminated passage in response to Pownall's warning. What we can learn from the exchange is that for a perceptive early reader like Pownall, Rousseau's story about the development of civilization lurked in the background of Smith's account of the origins of commerce in the *Wealth of Nations*.

[75] Ibid.

CHAPTER 7

Rousseau and A.L. Thomas

Anthony La Vopa

On August 25, 1770 Antoine-Léonard Thomas delivered the first part of an address on "the character, the mores and the spirit [*l'esprit*] of women in different centuries" before a public audience at the *Académie française*. The entire address was published as an *Essai* in 1772 and as part of Thomas' *Essai sur les éloges* a year later.[1] An obscure figure now, Thomas was one of the most acclaimed authors of the French High Enlightenment, a "genius" in the new meanings the term acquired in the second half of the eighteenth century, and that marvel of a commercialized print culture, the "celebrity."[2] In the 1760s the Academy's patriotic eulogies of great men had become major events in the life of literary Paris and the overlapping circles of *le monde*, and Thomas was the acknowledged master of the genre. The Academy had awarded him no less than five prizes for eloquence from 1759 to 1765.[3]

The anti-*philosophe* party denounced the *Essay* as another coup by the "sect" of *philosophes*, paying tribute to certain salon women who had coddled them. Thomas seemed to be taking another step in the corruption of French society by the fashionable "philosophical spirit" of the *Encyclopédie*.[4] The reaction was not entirely paranoid; Thomas'

---

[1] *Essai sur les éloges, ou histoire de la littérature et de l'éloquence* (1773; repr. Paris, 1812). *Essai sur le caractère, les moeurs et l'esprit des femmes dans les différents siècles* (1772). I have used the edition of the latter text in E. Badinter (ed.), *Qu'est-ce une femme?* (Paris: P.O.L., 1989). All further references to this text are in parentheses in the text. My main source for biographical information is E. Micard, *Un écrivain académique au XVIIIe siècle, Antoine-Léonard Thomas (1732–1785)* (Paris: E. Champion, 1924). Its view of Thomas as a pre-Romantic is now dated, but it is soundly researched. It has been oddly ignored in most of the recent discussions of Thomas. Also useful is M. Henriet, *L'académicien Thomas (1732–1785) d'après des correspondances inédits* (Paris: H. Leclerc, 1918).
[2] D. McMahon, *Divine Fury: A History of Genius* (New York: Basic Books, 2013); A. Lilti, *Figures publiques: L'invention de la célébrité* (Paris: Fayard, 2014). On Thomas's extraordinary success as a eulogist see J.-C. Bonnet, *Naissance du Panthéon: Essai sur le culte des grands hommes* (Paris: Fayard, 1998), pp. 67–82.
[3] Bonnet, *Naissance du Panthéon*, p. 72.
[4] Ibid., p. 198 (quoting a critique of the Essay by Daillant de la Touche).

appointment to the Academy in 1767 *had* been a victory for the *philosophes* and their supporters. And yet the *philosophes* themselves – Denis Diderot, Melchior Grimm, Madame d'Épinay, and others – were even more dismissive of the *Essay*. In d'Épinay's words, it left the reader "not know[ing] what the author thinks, and whether his opinion on women is other than the received opinions." The modern reader is likely to agree; the essay abounds in puzzling compounds of discourses that would seem to resist mixing. D'Épinay flatly rejected Thomas' speculation, in places, that by nature women were intellectually as well as physically weaker than men. If she found Thomas' essay wrongheaded, Diderot found it anemic. He ridiculed the sexless erudition with which Thomas demonstrated, in other places in the text, that the character of women was determined by the educational and social institutions of their times.[5]

As maddeningly ambivalent as Thomas' essay was, its concluding critique of eighteenth-century society would seem to be emphatically Rousseauian. It reads as a summary statement of the moral critique that *mondanité* had engendered within itself, like an undertow, since the seventeenth century, and that had found its most powerful rhetorical expression in Rousseau's writings in the 1750s and early 1760s. In modern *politesse* Thomas saw sociability "pushed to excess" by rampant *amour-propre*. The art of pleasing (*complaisance*) in *politesse* thinly veiled "the fury of reputations," a ruthless competition for distinction. It was all a calculating game of false self-representations. The trick was to "conquer without having the air of combat." With the increased mixing of men and women "the two sexes denatured themselves." Women read to amuse and be amused, not to learn. Domestic life was no longer valued.

We are confronted with a dissidence. Thomas the academician can be fairly placed in the generation of "mandarins" who "grew fat," or at least well-nourished, in Voltaire's Enlightenment church in the closing decades of the old regime. They have been sharply distinguished from the much larger crowd of aspiring authors who came to Paris seeking fame and fortune and found themselves in a literary underground, scratching out livings as hired pens, using scabrous pamphlets and *libelles* to pour out a "gutter Rousseauism" that demonized the aristocracy of the court and *le monde* as parasitical and degenerate.[6] But if we take this dichotomy to refer to social psychology, and not just to social position, it does not do justice to

---

[5] Diderot, "Sur les femmes," in *Qu'est-ce qu'une femme?*, pp. 163–185; d'Épinay to Galiani (March 14, 1772), in ibid., pp. 189–194.

[6] R. Darnton, "The High Enlightenment and the Low-Life of Literature," in *The Literary Underground of the Old Regime* (Cambridge, MA: Harvard University Press, 1982), pp. 1–40.

the conflicted sense of self Thomas retained well after he achieved celebrity.[7] His psychological makeup is better understood by reference to d'Alembert's remarkable "Essay on the Society of Men of Letters and the Great," published in 1753. D'Alembert divided the "men of letters who court the great" into four "classes." His first class was "the slaves," who, unaware that they were slaves, were beyond rehabilitation. Second came the authors who might be called rationalizers, though d'Alembert did not use that term. They were "indignant" about the "disagreeable" role they had to play; but having "convinced themselves" that it was the only way to "fortune," they calculated the "*complaisances*" and "intrigues" (*bassesses*) required to purchase "the smallest service." Less numerous were the species of "amphibians," perpetually undecided. Having "formed in the morning the project of being free," they "return in the evening to being slaves." They were "at one and the same time bold and timid, noble and self-interested, seeming to "reject with one hand what they try to seize with the other." The last class was the worst: the authors who "*incensed* the great in public" and "tore them apart in private," and who "with their equals show off a philosophy that hardly costs them anything."[8]

Thomas obviously was not a hypocritical radical in d'Alembert's sense, but neither should he be placed among the hopeless sycophants. Even at the height of his career he was an undecided amphibian. "It is only too ordinary," he remarked in an address to the Academy in 1770, "that talents lack places."[9] The son of a modest commercial family in Clermont-Ferrand, the provincial capital of the Auvergne, he knew of the magnetic attraction of Paris for bright young men from the provinces; the hunger for fame; the craving for an intellectual "liberty" that life in a provincial town and a professional career would not provide; the danger of literary ambition ending in poverty and degradation. For young men with Thomas' ambitions, men who aspired to "celebrity" in Voltaire's church, the "party of humanity," a life in letters and a life in a profession – the law, let us say, or commerce – had nothing in common. To enter a profession was to be confined to a mere *état*, a conventional station that "suffocated" men of exceptional talent. Men of letters hovered above that world of narrowly focused labor.

---

[7] For a similar point on the world of the theater, see G. Brown, *A Field of Honor: Writers, Court Culture and Public Theater in French Literary Life from Racine to the Revolution* (New York: Columbia University Press, 2005).

[8] "Essai sur la société des gens de lettres et des grands sur la réputation, sur les mécènes, et sur les récompenses littéraires," in *Oeuvres complètes de d'Alembert*, vol. IV, Pt. 1 (Paris, 1822): pp. 355–356.

[9] "Discours pronouncé à la réception de l'Archevêque de Toulouse, Le 6 septembre 1770," in Thomas, *Oeuvres* IV, p. 224.

Among the authors who publicly expressed their contempt for the worldly man of letters was Thomas' protegé Jacques Delille, also a native of the Auvergne, who had been a younger member of the Thomas' literary circle in Paris in the late 1750s. He would follow Thomas into the Academy in 1769, with Voltaire's support, on the strength of his translation of Virgil's *Georgics*. In 1760, at age twenty-two, Delille submitted a poem titled "Epistle to the Utility of Retreat. For Men of Letters" for the Academy's prize competition. Thomas found it strong – so strong, in fact, that he feared it would eclipse his own entry.[10] Delille's poem was a slashing Rousseauian indictment of *mondanité* and its corrupting tyranny over men of letters. It begins with one friend asking another why he has made the error of retreating from "the ocean of the world." The rest of the poem is the solitary's uncompromising response. *Le monde* is "the imposture world," where the "vulgar" *bel esprit*, one of those "rampant parasites," "degrades his century by living to please it and devoting his pen to frivolity," and where art is perverted into performances in fakery. Transported to its "lazy circles," Malebranche or Pascal or Newton would yearn for the "the refuge (*l'asile*) where the soul lives and thinks." "Do you want to subject your manly character," he asks his friend, to "what is called the art of pleasing (*complaisance*)?" Only silence nourishes the profound sentiment of "manly eloquence." Only in retreat does the genius "dare elevate himself and listen to himself," because only there does his soul belong entirely to himself. In *le monde* women, "once content with being seduced, exercise their empire over talents," and "effeminate at once *les esprits* and *les moeurs*." Do not lower yourself before "the great," he tells his friend; such adulation "debases the soul and enervates genius." He himself will continue to embrace solitude and true friendship.[11]

A more scathing condemnation of *mondanité*, or a more radical denial of its claim to the unique honor displayed in its social aesthetic of play, would be hard to imagine. Though Delille's poem is arguably entirely derivative, its intense and rigid moralism may make it a singular moment in the process in which the social, cultural, and aesthetic values of mid-seventeenth-century France were being shaken. The once touted figure of the *bel esprit* has become the lazy parasite.[12] In *le monde* women "effeminate" men. The use of the verb (perhaps the first instance of it) underscores Delille's conviction that the demands of *complaisance* stifle genius by

---

[10] *Revue d'Histoire littéraire de la France*, 25 (1918), pp. 493, 498. Cited hereafter as RHL.
[11] J. Delille, *Oeuvres avec les notes de Parseval* (Paris, 1836), p. 850.
[12] E. Russo, *Styles of Enlightenment: Taste, Politics, and Authorship in Eighteenth-Century France* (Baltimore: Johns Hopkins University Press, 2007).

emasculating it. The only recourse was retreat to silent solitude and the mutual support of private friendship, which Delille separates from worldly sociability and the power it gives women. True friendship is not only private in practice; it is a deliberate mutual withdrawal into independence from polite sociability and its women-centered play of power.

Arguably Delille's poem was just a youthful gush of indignation; he went on to a comfortable academic career, cutting something of a gallant figure in *le monde*. More striking is that in 1772, at age forty, Thomas used his concluding critique of eighteenth-century society in the essay on women to issue a similar indictment, though with his own emphases. If Thomas' language was less inflammatory than Delille's, it was no less subversive of aristocratic cultural and social authority. As in Delille's poem, *complaisance* denatures men, which is to say that it effeminates them. Thomas' main difference with Delille was one of emphasis in judging the responsibility of women for this emasculation. Delille depicted the women of *le monde* as the power-hungry agents of corruption. To Thomas they were victims of the corruption they had done so much to create; they had deprived themselves of the natural joys of marital love and child-rearing. Echoing Rousseau directly, he lamented that only a few rare society women dared breast-feed their infants.

***

I want to come at Thomas' *Essay* through a friendship, a site in which Rousseau's *sensibilité* was absorbed selectively by the very world he despised, in the paradoxical, if not contradictory, phenomenon of Rousseauian *mondanité* or, perhaps better, worldliness with a Rousseauian shadow. In his concluding pages, Thomas paid tribute to the rare women of the century who combined a truly cultivated reason with a strong soul. It was common knowledge that his inspiration was Susanne Curchod Necker, the wife of the Genevan financier. She and Thomas had become close friends sometime in the mid-1760s, soon after she had started what would be the last great salon of the old regime, featuring, among others, Marmontel, Buffon, Diderot, Grimm, Morellet, d'Alembert, Raynard, and of course Thomas. Thomas and Necker made their sometimes daily private conversations a haven in which they reinforced each other's inner resistance to the *mondanité* they were both in fact practicing.

We know much more about Necker's conflicted interior life than we know about the much-published Thomas'. For reasons that are not clear, Jacques Necker, who had prevailed on his wife not to publish during her lifetime, published three volumes of "extracts" from her journals in 1798, four years after her death. The two volumes of *Nouveaux Mélanges* that appeared in 1801 brought the total number of pages to roughly 19,000.[13] As the full journals in the archive of the Necker chateau in Coppet, Switzerland, remain inaccessible to scholars, we are left wondering how representative the extracts are. Necker tells us in his introduction to the first volume that he had decided against organizing the extracts topically so as to avoid giving the false impression that his wife had aspired to be an author, when in fact her writings were intended to be "solitary." And yet many of the selected extracts contradict that claim. Thanks to Necker's editorial eclecticism, the extracts document, almost despite him, his wife's virtual authorship. Unfortunately, his apparently insouciant editing also makes the volumes a perilous source. The extracts are not dated; they were arranged with no thought to chronological order. They come at you like scraps of paper floating in the wind. In places it is hard to know whether Madame Necker was recording opinions and beliefs to which she was committed or simply bits of salon conversations she found noteworthy. Likewise, it is sometimes not clear where one entry ends and another begins. And so, I have approached the journal extracts as a wide but at times treacherous opening into the mind of a highly intelligent and well-read person, a woman who was, intellectually as well as socially, a central presence in one of the social spaces where *mondanité* and the world of letters met.[14]

***

Once Necker had made clear to Thomas that her marriage was sacrosanct, they conducted a kind of spiritual friendship, a union of souls. The spiritualized cult of male-female friendship had become commonplace in the culture of sensibility. It offered refuge from worldly imperatives in the performance of a rarified, febrile ideal of friendship between a man and a woman, an ideal in which, in principle, performance had no place. The rhetoric subsumed psychological particularity under an aspiration to

---

[13] *Mélanges extraits des manuscrits de Mme. Necker* (Paris, 1798), cited hereafter as M; *Nouveaux mélanges extraits des manuscrits de Mme. Necker* (Paris, 1801), cited hereafter as NM.

[14] Particularly insightful on Necker's syndrome of worldy ambition and alienation is C. Dubeau, "L'Epreuve du salon ou Le Monde comme performance dans les *Mélanges* et les *Nouveaux Mélanges* de Suzanne Necker," *Cahiers staëliens* 57 (2006): pp. 201–225. Dubeau gives this portrait a more psychological dimension in her *La lettre et la mère: Roman familial et écriture de la passion chez Suzanne Necker et Germaine de Staël* (Quebec: Presses De L'Université Laval, 2013). Recent portraits of Necker as a *salonnière* diverge markedly. See, e.g., D. Goodman, *The Republic of Letters: A Cultural History of the French Enlightenment* (Ithaca: Cornell University Press, 1994), pp. 79–82; B. Craveri, *The Age of Conversation*, trans. T. Waugh (New York: New York Review Books, 2005), pp. 367–371.

a kind of spiritual communion of sentiment. The "union" of "souls" had its
erotically suggestive base chords. In principle, though, union evoked the
purity of an incorporeal communion, free of the asymmetrical power and
the unequal dependence that both social rank and erotic desire intruded
into intimacy.

Necker regarded Thomas as one of the two true geniuses in her circle
(the other was Buffon), and he did not protest the label. They had nothing
new to say about genius; the concept had been in the air since the middle
decades of the century, and it was integral to the image of Rousseau among
his devotees. But this is a case, I think, in which the platitudinous is worth
close examination. As the friends shaped the concept, genius became
central to a cluster of ideas about selfhood, labor, authorship, and the
work of language in the formation of the *patrie* as a civic community.

For over a century the discourse of *honnêteté* had prescribed a relentlessly
performative culture, the practice of an exclusive social aesthetic of play,
particularly in the art of conversation. I want to stress that two of its elements
can fairly be called utopian. *Complaisance*, the art of always being *agréable*,
reigned in this imagined world. There would be complete harmony, no
appearance of open aggression or coercion. Polite conversation was idealized
as intersubjectivity without power. The second utopian element was distilled
in the term *aisance*, which evoked an apparent effortlessness that made
comportment and speech always seem natural, spontaneous, free. The
appearance of labor of any kind, including concentrated and sustained
intellectual labor, was taboo.[15] The virtuoso of this aesthetic was the *bel
esprit*, the man (or woman) of consummate wit and grace in conversation
and in *belles lettres*. The foil to him was the pedant, the laborious and
pugnacious academic, a boor and a bore, intent on impressing others with
his esoteric and tunnel-visioned academic expertise. Having been formed in
male ghettos of the *collèges* and the universities, the pedant was "intractable,
arrogant, uncivil, impolite, opinionated."[16] His voice grated; he interrupted
imperiously; he droned on. His combativeness betrayed the excessive
masculinity that conventional male education inculcated.

---

[15] A. J. La "Sexless Minds at Work and at Play: Poullain de la Barre and the Origins of Early Modern
Feminism," *Representations* 109 (2010): pp. 57–94.

[16] The quotation is from M. de Bellegarde, *Réflexions sur le ridicule* (Paris, 1696), p. 333, in Breiding,
Untersuchungen, p. 88. Important discussions of the meaning of the stereotype are N. Hepp, "La
belle et la bête, A.J. La Vopa, ou la femme et le pédant dans l'universe romanesque du XVIIe Siècle,"
Revue d'histoire littéraire de la France, 77:3/4 (1977): pp. 564–577; and F. Waquet, *Latin or the Empire
of the Sign*, trans. J. Howe (London: Verso, 2001), pp. 208–210.

Obviously the two friends did not emulate Rousseau's principled with-drawal from *le monde* to bucolic solitude. They were players in what Antoine Lilti has called the circulation of reputation or distinction. But even as they were ambitious to succeed in the game, they were resistant to it. In Necker's journals, and sometimes in Thomas' published writings, we hear the voice of the self-conscious outsider. Thomas would have remained a *collège* instructor, beneath public notice, if the Academy prizes had not catapulted him to fame. He was a reluctant and severe presence in *le monde*. His eloquence was underpinned by an erudition that opened him to the charge of pedantry. He could not avoid making the social rounds, but he did not master the art of conversation at polite gatherings. Necker noted in an incisive portrait of her friend in her journal that when he came back into society after a bout of work, he was "like an exile who returns to his country after a long absence and is frustrated by the fact that he recognizes no one; and so "he floats without ever being able to mix." It was not easy to maintain a friendship with a man "made more to die like Cato and Regulus than to live in the eighteenth century."[17]

But the friendship was maintained, and that was because the friends found in each other's company consolement for afflictions and a haven from the regimen of *mondanité* that seemed to aggravate, if not cause, them.[18] The journals give us a map of Madame Necker's psychic strains. She was the daughter of an enlightened Swiss minister who had taken great pains to educate her in ways that defied conventional strictures. If her salon would win her husband support in progressive circles, it would also prove her own ability to distinguish herself intellectually in *le monde*. She was vulner-able to ridicule as a provincial Swiss bourgeois, as a former governess, as a prudish Calvinist, and as *femme savante*. An unresolved tension runs through her journal entries. For all her devotion to her husband, she deflected his reproaches about her love of literature and philosophy. The journals include draft essays in several subjects, including philosophy and literary criticism. She wrote as if she would publish, even as she deferred to her husband's wish that she not publish.[19] And yet she also practiced another kind of secret labor – and was probably not the first *salonnière* to do

---

[17] M 3, 222, 226. See also Marmontel's portrait, quoted in Micard, *Un écrivain académique*, 33.

[18] The relationship between Necker's alienation from le monde and her physical and psychic sufferings is emphasized in S. Boon, *The Life of Madame Necker: Sin, Redemption, and the Parisian Salon* (London: Pickering & Chatto, 2011).

[19] D. Goodman, "Suzanne Necker's *Mélanges*: Gender, Writing, and Publicity," in E. Goldsmith and D. Goodman (eds.), *Going Public: Women and Publishing in Early Modern France* (Ithaca: Cornell University Press, 1995), pp. 210–223.

so. By reading extensively in the seventeenth-century literature of *honnêteté* she hoped to absorb the charm and the *aisance* – the "*je ne sais quoi*" – that a *salonnière* must exhibit. She crafted aperçus, hoping she would have occasion to offer them in her salon with apparent spontaneity, as flashes of insight. She labored in private to appear effortless in company, in a futile effort at methodical effortlessness.

It is tempting to dismiss the friends' Rousseauian rhetoric as Rousseau à la mode. We might, in fact, think of it as Rousseau for hypochondriacs. Thomas confided to his close friend Nicolas Barthe that he too experiences failures of manly self-disciple. What he called the excessive "movement" of sociability and ideas in *le monde* withered his inspiration, but his retreats to solitude, whether in Paris or in the Auvergne, often backfired, particularly when he had to struggle against the physical debility he described as a "weak chest." "I consume myself, I dessicate myself, I bore myself," he wrote on August 19, 1769; "my spirit languishes, my body is weak, and my soul, half the time, is devoured by melancholy."[20] "You have only one fault," Barthe concluded in his response, "that of not being at all happy."[21] In accounts of her state of health in letters to friends in Switzerland, Necker complained of what her husband called "painful nervous anxieties" and insomnia, as well as the usual fevers and tooth problems, and she sometimes felt herself to be close to death.[22] She described herself to Thomas as sometimes falling into "the abyss," a paralyzing state of indifference to everything. We have to suffice with saying that they both had psychosomatic bouts of depression, and that one of its manifestations, if not one of its causes, was an alienation from *mondanité* that was also a form of self-alienation, an inner aversion to their personas as social performers. In Rousseau's texts they found a voice for it.

***

In *Styles of Enlightenment* Elena Russo has shown how in the course of the eighteenth century, and particularly in its middle decades, the *bel esprit* came under attack as a superficial dazzler. Necker and Thomas shared this image; it was the counterpoint to their celebration of genius. Necker assured Thomas that his genius drew from his own "substance," in contrast to Fontenelle, one of those people who were "empty of any conscience, any center, any consistency in thought (*l'esprit*), because they have none in

---

[20] RHL 27 (1920), pp. 277–279, 600.   [21] RHL 27 (1920), p. 259.
[22] Boon, *Life of Madame Necker*, pp. 107–109.

character." Even as they disparaged figures like Fontenelle, the friends thought they were witnessing the corruption of the true *sensibilité* that Rousseau had done so much to articulate. Necker wrote to Thomas of a plague of "the affectation of sensibility." In their perception, *sensibilité* a la mode was being absorbed into – even coopted by – the worldly imperatives to perform, to impress others. They saw the eagerness to exhibit feeling as a new phase in the affectation of the natural and the spontaneous.

When Necker and Thomas assured each other of the "purity" of their friendship, they meant that they were bound by a conviction of unitary selfhood, a spiritual core that no social pressure could pull apart or dissolve. The conviction rested on two traditions of spirituality that we often see as divergent, one Calvinist and ultimately Augustinian, the other Stoic. The friendship, in fact, is a case study in how these traditions could enter dialogue and find common ground. Holding fast to her Calvinist spiritual heritage, Necker conceived God's presence in her in the form of an anterior sentiment of existence, mysterious but unshakeable. Thomas' Stoicism found its clearest expression in his eulogy of Marcus Aurelius, to whom he attributed an "enthusiasm of virtue." The labor of Stoic meditation had allowed Marcus "to assure [himself] of [himself]." His conviction of self-ownership was grounded in "a religious emotion," a belief in a God as "the universal mind," stampings its unity on all that exists, including the inner self.[23]

Perhaps the strongest bond in this friendship was a shared need for the meditative solitude of reading and writing. It was through this labor, grounded in the conviction of integral selfhood, that they achieved what Necker described as self-ownership. Necker's father had raised her in the enlightened Calvinism that had taken root in Geneva and several other Swiss cities in the early eighteenth century.[24] Recoiling against the psychological materialism of Diderot and others, she held fast to her Calvinist spiritual heritage by insisting on the immateriality and the immortality of the soul.[25] In several journal entries she tried to articulate how she experienced God's presence in her in the form of an anterior sentiment of existence, mysterious but unshakeable, an "unknown point."[26] On that intuition rested her conviction of the inner core that

---

[23] Micard, *Un écrivain académique*, 181.

[24] H. Rosenblatt, *Rousseau and Geneva from the* First Discourse *to the* Social Contract, *1749–1762* (Cambridge: Cambridge University Press, 1997), 10–17; J. Pocock, *Barbarism and Religion*, vol. I: The Enlightenments of Edward Gibbon, 1737–1764 (Cambridge: Cambridge University Press, 1999).

[25] M 3, pp. 110–114, NM 1, pp. 284–289.   [26] NM 1, pp. 363–370; NM 2, p. 3; M3, pp. 10–14.

she called the self, as opposed to the performative social being, the personality. Like Thomas, she too found meditative reflexivity imperative and thought of it as a kind of askesis, an inner struggle to achieve mastery of desires and impulses.[27] And yet, though she admired Malebranche, her faith had no place for Original Sin or sanctification through Grace. Now the inner struggle rested on the assumption that human beings were, by nature, capable of moral self-perfectibility, and that it was their duty to strive for it.

Thomas and Necker found their existential bedrock in the conviction of a transcendent self, anterior to any awareness of bodily existence, to any sense knowledge, and above all to a merely "external" existence, a false self existing only in the gaze of others. They reinforced each other's belief that, even as this self became particularized in social being, it remained unitary because of the indwelling presence of the Absolute in human interiority. Ultimately the sentiment of unitary selfhood was experienced in solitary self-examination. For Necker this self-awareness was solidified in a process of "self-ownership" through the solitary labor of reading and writing, which was itself a kind of meditation in which thoughts and sentiments found in print penetrated the self and became integral to it. With the use of *attention* in this sense of meditation, as opposed to the attention devoted to salon conversation, Necker was much closer in spirit to Malebranche. Such labor was the key to self-perfecting; it was a strenuous effort of acquisition, the kind of effort that had to be hidden in polite sociability.[28] It was in this sense that Necker called solitary reading "the secret of liberty." In the labor of selfhood, reading was not enough; only habitual writing confirmed that the sentiments one sought to express were not superficially derivative, but had become one's own. Truly "natural" self-expression lay not in the apparent ease of a social performance, but in the communication of something integral to the self labored on in solitude. The implication was that social knowledge – knowledge acquired in social interaction – deprives us of the self-distance needed to enter into our spiritual self, the unitary soul. Necker wanted to keep thought from being the mere stuff of performance, to make it instead a force that, rather than making an impression in the worldly sense, has a moral effect that ripples out beyond the arena of performance.

For geniuses like Thomas, the process ended in the manly eloquence that would move people to create a new civic community. Having undergone the arduous mental labor of acquisition, the genius could promote

---

[27] Micard, *Un écrivain académique*, p. 181.   [28] NM I, pp. 167–168, 179.

and perhaps even advance a great public end. His concentrated force could pull people into a *patrie* or a nation, a community united in civic action. Without such labor, thinking degenerated into the hyper-social performance of itself that the friends called mere *personalité*. The friends were reversing the order of priority between the spoken word and the written word in *mondanité*. The *bel esprit* wrote in symbiosis with a self-referential space of conversational sociability, never violating its parameters of the thinkable and the expressible. To Necker and Thomas such a man, for all his vaunted versatility, was fixed in his context, imprisoned within his performative role.[29] "The *homme d'esprit*," Necker observed, "always remains in his place [...] receiving his colors from all the objects that surround him, and rending them back to the [objects] in turn." "The man of genius always dashes forward, upward or in advance"; "and yet his ideas still precede him: one could say that he runs after them.[30] The great mind – the genius – broke out of social fixity. He could think outside society even as he remained in it. To speak to the "soul" and the "reason" of a public, Necker observed in another journal entry, one has to labor in retreat.[31] That summed up the paradoxical relationship between the solitary and the social, the private and the public, in the friends' ideal of the modern author. Solitude was the condition of the genius's societal mission. Only a work forged in solitary labor, withdrawn from social representations and unmediated by them, could galvanize a society into a civic community.

There was a political as well as a civic dimension to all this. Largely implicit, it became audible in the friends' fondness for the term "enthusiasm." Against the mere wit of the *bel esprit* they posed the eloquent enthusiasm of the genius. This was common practice. They were well aware that, in the tradition of religious and philosophical polemics, enthusiasm conjured the specter of uncontrollable social and political disorder, the preacher's emotion-laden abuse of figurative language to effect a contagion of collective frenzy, a mob running amok.[32] That Necker and Thomas nonetheless took up the new, positive usage of the term is a measure of their animus toward the self-referential trivialization of language in the conversational culture of *mondanité*. In the final chapter of his *Essay on Eulogies* Thomas did not hide his envy of the oratory of the ancient republics, where eloquence flourished under "liberty" and was indispensable to decision-making in the state. He reluctantly accepted

---

[29] M I, pp. 26–27, 370–371.   [30] NM 2, p. 31.   [31] NM I, pp. 69–70, 72.
[32] L. Klein and A. La Vopa (eds.), *Enthusiasm and Enlightenment in Europe, 1650–1850* (San Marino: Huntington Library, 1998).

the fact that in modern monarchies with the rule of law eloquence had to make do without either of these conditions. It could not be "political." Rather than communicating his natural impulsion of passion with a certain "abandon," the orator had to respect the constraints of politeness, the need to "please" and above all to not offend people of rank. And his oratory was in fact not really oratory. Rather than performing before a physically present assembly of "the People," he was limited to silent communication with isolated readers. All the more reason why his eloquence had to be driven by a unitary idea, developed in "profound meditation," and suffused with ardent and even "impetuous" sentiment. He advised aspiring authors to be as passionate as they could be within the limits of modern politeness: "Dare to mix a manly tone with songs of your century." He warned them above all against flattery, which had banished "truth" from the courts in every century"; and against "the softness [*mollesse*] of our mores," which banishes [truth] from our societies."[33] They were far from endorsing a radical repudiation of rationalism as such. They wanted eloquence to effect a contagion in the sense of moving the wills of listeners, or readers, immediately, like an electrical current, breaking through the distortions of socially generated opinion, but without collapsing individual wills into a collective hysteria. Necker called for a rhetoric of "grand intermediate ideas, uniting sensations and thoughts." The challenge was to put emotion-laden figurative language in the service of what she repeatedly called a "chain of ideas," a logic of argument which individual listeners were free to accept or reject. The eloquence of the genius – the eloquence Thomas already practiced – would be edifying, ennobling, inspiring, majestic, sublime, even commanding, but not manipulative or overpowering.

***

What role did Thomas' essay assign women in this regeneration of language and society? Here the text confronts us with a blatantly un-Rousseauian twist in a text so indebted to Rousseau. In his concluding paragraph, Thomas called for more women to publish their way of thinking. His ideal woman could do it all, engaging in solitary self-reflection and publishing her thoughts even as she retained all the social graces. This evocation had something of utopian fantasy, but it is also a point of entry for reconsidering Thomas' text as a whole. In his strides through the centuries, Thomas did not take Rousseau's meta-historical path from

---

[33] Thomas, *Essai sur les éloges*, p. 275.

the primal innocence of the species to its inexorable corruption. Reading the eulogies contextually, he made the Italian Renaissance the Golden Age, when women, within a still honorable culture of gallantry, had excelled in print as well as in conversation, in the study of language, in poetry, in philosophy, in law, and even in theology. The range of fields is striking. His grievance was with the French monarchy and its court. It was under Louis XIV, when the corrupt manners of the court shaped Parisian high society, that women had had to hide their learning for fear of being branded pedants. The extreme corruption of the Regency had drawn society women even more out of domestic life and into "the fury of appearing, the art of putting everything on the surface."

The prevailing view, which Madame Necker seems to have shared, was that no woman could do the intensely concentrated and grueling labor that genius required. But the labor of the genius was creativity on a grand scale, beyond most men as well as women. To Thomas and Necker intelligent and educated women were no less capable than their male peers of engaging in intellectual labor as a process of understanding and communicating, and of doing so as writers as well as readers. They had a legitimate place in the public discourse of civic life. This view ran against the grain of prevailing gender discourses and medical paradigms. By the early 1770s conceptions of sexual differences were positioned within at least two medical paradigms, both positing the natural physical and mental inferiority of women on materialist assumptions, but with different logics and implications. In the logic of mechanism, still quite common in medical thought, women differed from men in the degree of strength of the fibers through which forces – sensations, emotions, ideas – were transmitted. This view was being challenged by proponents of vitalist materialism, who had begun to argue that men and women had incommensurably different organic "organizations" or constitutions.[34] The physical and mental inferiority of women was not a matter of degree, but of kind. Sexuality was becoming the key to biological determinism in the strongest sense.

Necker was certainly familiar with the medical paradigms, and in her journals she sought ways to counter their implications. To be sure, the relevant entries are scattered and often contradict each other; Necker was often simply recording what she read and heard in conversations, thus

---

[34] A. Villa, *Enlightenment and Pathology: Sensibility in the Literature and Medicine of Eighteenth-Century France* (Baltimore: Johns Hopkins University Press, 1998); L. Daston, "The Naturalized Female Intellect," *Science in Context* 5 (1992): pp. 209–235.

offering a kind of potpourri of opinion on the much discussed question of female inequality.[35] She remained torn between her eagerness to fit the conventional mold of the *honnête femme* and her literary ambitions, which implied a quite different appraisal of female intellectual capacities. Refraining from publishing, she assured Thomas that she was quite content to share vicariously in his rise to immortality, as a lesser intellect; but that was because she knew herself to be one of the few who could understand his genius.[36] Her modesty in the face of genius had its note of envy. She yearned to connect with a public, as Thomas did. She approved of Buffon's dismissal of the common notion that "one must write as one speaks." For well-educated women, as for their male counterparts, conversation was "careless" (*négligé*), whereas writing was a difficult art requiring constant revisions.[37] In our long-term perspective, the implications, though left unstated, are of course huge. They cut the symbiosis between the *aisance* of conversation and style in the culture of *honnêteté*. In writing, educated women should not be free from labor; they should be free to labor, outside the constraints of effortlessness in polite conversation.

It is true, Necker noted in a brief entry, that women lack men's perseverance; but she adds that they can compensate with "habit." Persistent self-discipline, it would seem, could produce something of the same effect as sheer natural strength.[38] She faulted women in particular for publishing only to "shine," to exhibit their "personality" rather than to instruct others. But if properly educated in a wide range of fields, including history, ethics, and literature, women could order their thought into a "chain" of ideas; and in literary studies they could aim at "perfecting their style and acquiring eloquence, as much as that is possible."[39] As she used the terms here, style and eloquence meant a self-representation in writing and print that aimed at persuading others, not just at staging a pleasing performance. Several other entries elaborate Necker's critique of the *philosophes'* gender prejudice. What is called female "instinct" is in fact socially inculcated. If women dabble in everything and have no sustained focus, that is simply because they are trained from an early age only to please in the present moment.[40] The cultivation of their sensibility prevents them from having men's ability to "know how to live at a great distance from themselves."[41] If even celebrated women have been

---

[35] Cf. E. Harth, "The Salon Woman Goes Public . . . or Does She?" in E. Goldsmith and D. Goodman (eds.), *Going Public: Women and Publishing in Early Modern France* (Ithaca: Cornell University Press, 1995): pp. 192–193.
[36] M 3, p. 161.   [37] M 1, p. 248.   [38] M 3, pp. 30–32.   [39] M 3, pp. 30–32.   [40] NM 1, p. 79.
[41] NM 1, p. 81.

mediocre, that is because they have to had expended so much effort over-coming "obstacles." In a long entry she constructs a hypothetic plea for the "cause of women." The first part would show that "men cannot attribute the superiority of their talents to the difference in organs." The cause is "education." The second part would demonstrate that the objects of women's education "modify [their] esprit and their *penchans* without demanding any less intelligence and capacity." In the third part, she would cite "several treatises" that, if women are not as *susceptible* to application as great as men's, "they are more continually virtuous and more patient, a kind of constancy that is of considerable value in work (*travail*). "Perhaps," she speculates, "the force that supports sorrows is the same that gives genius."[42] She cannot deny the fact of men's greater physical strength, but she undercuts it by suggesting that intelligence is also a function of moral resources peculiar to women. Here her rejection of Diderot's materialism is critical. If the moral cannot be reduced to the material, then it is possible that the moral perseverance of women in the face of the suffering peculiar to their sex can contribute to intellectual strengths that are independent of their physical weakness. There may even be a sense in which they derive from that weakness; the sufferings attendant on weakness may generate a force that also empowers genius.

If Thomas wrote his *Essay* with medical theorists looking over one shoulder, he had Madame Necker looking over the other. In the *Essay's* concluding encomium to "the ideal woman," Thomas portrays a woman mastering all the "charms of society," its taste, grace, and wit (*esprit*) without falling into "false sensibility" or denying her need for repose in friendship, while cultivating philosophy and letters "for themselves" and not "for reputation." Such a woman would, at the risk of displeasing, sustain her esteem for virtue, her contempt for vice, and her sensibility for friendship in her home and outside it, and despite the desire (*envie*) of having an extended society, in the midst even of that society would have the courage to publish a way (*façon*) of thinking so extraordinary, and the greater courage of sustaining (*soutenir*) it (161).

Thomas pitted domesticity against the hyper-sociability of *le monde*; but he also imagined it offering educated women a kind of autonomy, devel-oped and protected in the solitude of the home, and allowing them, from that position, to question the "opinion" to which women were subjected. This was a call for a certain independence for women, a right to

---

[42] NM I, p. 76.

introversion over extroversion, to "being" within themselves, and not always to "pleasing," to "appearing" as required in the gaze of others.

To take Thomas' encomium seriously is not to deny that the more typical visions of a regenerated *patrie* had society women withdrawing from the stage lights into the privacy of domestic life. That was certainly Rousseau's view. In this friendship we see the worldly and the domestic, the public and the private, configuring in a different way. For women of the *haute bourgeoisie*, no less than for aristocratic women, the question was not whether women should be confined to the privacy of the domestic or given access to public occupations still reserved to men. The logic of gender and the logic of status fused to make remunerated work unthinkable. For them the issue of labor had a different valence. The question was whether well-educated women could be liberated, in the privacy of their homes, from the imperatives of a world that banned labor. For women, as for men, domesticity did not preclude authorship, it was the retreat – the space of solitude – that made serious authorship possible. This too was utopian. Thomas, one might say, used his Stoicism to square the circle, to reshape an emerging bourgeois ideal of domesticity. He floated the hope that women's domesticity, conceived as their habitual withdrawal from the performative imperatives of *aisance*, would become the site for their authorial labor.

If Rousseau read Thomas' essay, we can be fairly certain that he did not approve of it.

Rousseau and d'Holbach: The Revolutionary Implications of la philosophie anti-Thérésienne

Jonathan Israel

In the existing historiography of the Enlightenment the decidedly strained relationship between Rousseau and d'Holbach has mostly been treated as a relatively minor episode, an unfortunate quarrel, between two prominent Enlightenment figures with very different temperaments. Relations between these two who first met probably before 1750,[1] became tense just a few years later; from 1753, their feud intensifying and continuing down to their deaths and in a sense even after both men passed away. In his *Baron d'Holbach. A Study of Eighteenth-Century Radicalism in France* (New York, 1914), Max Peerson Cushing offers a distinctly anodyne summary of the seemingly not especially significant estrangement between the two thinkers:

> The account of their mutual misunderstandings contained in the *Confessions*, in a letter by Cérutti in the *Journal de Paris* Dec. 2, 1789, and in private letters of Holbach's to Hume, Garrick, and Wilkes, is a long and tiresome tale. The author of *Eclaircissements relatifs à la publication des Confessions de Rousseau* (Paris, 1789) blames the *club holbachique* for their treatment of Rousseau, but the fault seems to lie on both sides. According to Rousseau's account, Holbach sought his friendship and for a few years he was one of Holbach's society. But, after the success of the *Devin du Village* in 1753, the *holbachiens* turned against him out of jealousy of his genius as a composer. Visions of a dark plot against him rose before his fevered and sensitive imagination, and after 1756 he left the Society of the Encyclopedists, never to return. Holbach, on the other hand, while admitting rather questionable treatment of Rousseau, never speaks of any personal injury on his part, and bewails the fact that "l'homme le plus éloquent s'est rendu ainsi l'homme le plus anti-littéraire, et l'homme le plus sensible s'est rendu le plus anti-social." He did warn Hume against taking him to England, and in a letter to Wilkes predicted the quarrel that took place

---

[1] On this point, see T. L'Aminot, "D'Holbach et Rousseau ou la relation déplaisante," in *Corpus: Revue de philosophie* no. 22/23 (1993): pp. 117–128, here, p. 117.

shortly after. In writing to Garrick, he says some hard but true things about Rousseau, who on his part never really defamed Holbach but depicted him as the virtuous atheist under the guise of Wolmar in the *Nouvelle Heloïse*. Their personal incompatibility is best explained on the grounds of the radical differences in their temperaments and types of mind and by the fact that Rousseau was too sensitive to get on with anybody for any great length of time.[2]

My object in what follows is to present a somewhat different picture of the clash between Rousseau and d'Holbach placing it, and especially the several conflicting interpretations of its meaning dating from the years 1789–94, in the context of the war of Enlightenment ideologies within the French Revolution. As I and others have frequently stressed, the "society" that made up the *philosophes* increasingly polarized in the 1770s and 1780s, following publication in 1770 of d'Holbach's *Système de la nature*, the most forthright statement of materialism, philosophic monism and atheism of the Enlightenment, and the *Histoire Philosophique des Deux Indes* (1770), published under the name of "Raynal" but actually composed in large part by others including an increasingly radicalized Diderot. The latter was the most widely published affirmation that the peoples of the world lived in misery under systems of oppression and exploitation jointly wrought by kings, aristocrats and priests. As they polarized, one side pressed for rejection of the deistic compromise of separating God from man and the material world in favor of a monistic view of man as "a being purely physical," as d'Holbach thought, and for outright rejection of belief in God, the other for Voltaire's deistic compromise and sanctioning the work of divine providence – and hence the existing social order.[3]

Rousseau, however, found himself very much at odds with both sides, accepting the "deistic compromise" with regard to nature but not with respect to society which he too thought predominantly lived "in chains." This gave the late Enlightenment something of the character of a triangular fight between "moderates," "radicals" and Rousseau.[4] This triangular philosophical format was then paralleled in important and interesting ways by the ideological clashes within the French Revolution. The Rousseau-d'Holbach quarrel arguably developed into a far from

[2] M. Cushing, "Baron d'Holbach: A Study of Eighteenth Century Radicalism in France" (PhD Dissertation: Columbia University, 1914), pp. 16–17; L'Aminot, "D'Holbach et Rousseau," p. 120.

[3] G. Garrard, *Rousseau's Counter-Enlightenment: A Republican Critique of the Philosophes* (Albany: State University of New York Press, 2003), p. 26; J. Israel, *Democratic Enlightenment: Philosophy, Revolution and human Rights 1750–1790* (Oxford: Oxford University Press, 2011), pp. 648–683.

[4] Garrard, *Rousseau's Counter-Enlightenment*, p. 27; Israel, *Democratic Enlightenment*, pp. 633–647, 813–814.

insignificant strand of the three-cornered conflict between the principal ideological tendencies within the Revolution rivaling each other for control of France and of the international revolutionary movement.

The French Revolution is best understood, I have argued, as a struggle between three warring, incompatible and fundamentally different ideological streams. In one corner stood a liberal constitutional monarchism aiming at a restricted suffrage and aligned with Montesquieu, the "British model" and mixed government which can fairly be said to be the heir of the "moderate Enlightenment." From 1788 until the rising of 10 August 1792, and the overthrow of the French monarchy, the "moderate" Revolution's chief rival was the democratic republicanism of the Brissotins and some Dantonists – figures such as Condorcet, Cérutti, Carra, Lanthenas, Pétion, Gorsas, Robert, and Desmoulins, as well as Tom Paine who, during 1792, operated in Paris as an ally of Brissot and Condorcet. Theirs was the far more sweepingly reformist ideology of the "Radical Enlightenment." During the early part of the Revolution, the great strength of this democratic republican tendency culminating in the world's first modern democratic constitution (February 1793) – and chief weakness of the "moderates" – was these republicans' powerful hegemony over the pro-Revolution press.

By 1792, however, both the "moderates" and the radicals found themselves literally locked in a life and death struggle with a third powerful tendency entirely distinct from both – the authoritarian populism of Marat and Robespierre, a form of Counter-Enlightenment which dominated the Jacobin Club completely from August 1792 onwards and aimed at crushing all dissent. Violently intolerant and dictatorial, in its stress on uniformity, eliminating dissent and the primacy of "the ordinary," this third Revolution was proto-Fascistic. What in June 1793 became the group dictatorship of the Montagne, its leadership presided over by Robespierre, shut down the Brissotin as well as the liberal monarchist press, outlawed Condorcet (July 1793), imprisoned Paine, and generally imposed the dogma of the overriding legitimacy of "the ordinary," the backbone of the ideology of the Terror.[5]

During the French Revolution, many voices, including that of Mirabeau, claimed that Rousseau's writings played a crucial role in the "regeneration" of 1789,[6] and agreed with the revolutionary writer Louis

---

[5] J. Israel, *Revolutionary Ideas: An Intellectual History of the French Revolution from the Rights of Man to Robespierre* (Princeton: Princeton University Press, 2014), pp. 695–708.

[6] E. Lemay, "La Part d'*Émile* dans la « régéneration » de 1789," in R. Thiery (ed.), *Rousseau, l'Émile et la Révolution* (Paris: Universitas, 1992), pp. 375–383.

Sebastien Mercier (1740–1814), in his *De Jean-Jacques Rousseau considéré comme l'un des premiers auteurs de la Révolution*, published in June 1791, that no other philosopher had as profound an impact on the Revolution as a whole. Although not all scholars agree that Rousseau's influence on the Revolution was fundamental, I and others have argued, like Mercier, that Rousseau always and everywhere loomed large as a cultural force within the Revolution, in my view doing so from the outset figuring to some extent and at some level, in all three ideologies.[7] But if we pay close attention to "structures of ideas" rather than names we soon realize each of the three competing ideologies used Rousseau, or rather different parts of his political thought, in sharply divergent ways. The third of the Revolution's competing tendencies promoted Rousseau much more vigorously than the others, creating a veritable cult, lionizing Rousseau but also in some respects simplifying and debasing his thought while continually stressing his hostility to the *philosophes*, and doing so with a passion diverging markedly from the guarded and qualified admiration for and use of Rousseau characteristic of such figures as Mirabeau, Sieyes, Cérutti, Brissot, and Desmoulins.

Condorcet, for his part, was distinctly unimpressed with both Rousseau and his writings. He very rarely mentions him and when he does allude to him it is invariably with unconcealed sarcasm.[8] On the other hand, Rousseau was decisive in the intellectual formation of Brissot and Desmoulins. The young Brissot's temperament was such that he was powerfully attracted to Rousseau's refusal to adjust to the etiquette and demands of elite culture. Brissot's exceptional sympathy for the persecuted and the underdog, continually evinced in his writings of the 1780s, was largely inspired by Rousseau – especially at first.[9] Yet to insist on his being essentially and above all a Rousseauist and on his calling Rousseau "Jean-Jacques" (when everyone did so, friend and foe), is to miss the point.[10] If Brissot's concern with penal reform owes something to Rousseau it owes more to Beccaria; if his view of nature was partly inspired by Rousseau it stood closer, as has been acknowledged, to the conception of natural forces

---

[7] J. Swenson, *On Jean-Jacques Rousseau Considered as One of the First Authors of the Revolution* (Stanford: Stanford University Press, 2000), p. 172; see also Israel *Revolutionary Ideas*, pp. 20–22.

[8] R. Trousson, *Jean-Jacques Rousseau* (Paris: Tallandier, 2003), p. 737; see also *Correspondance inédite de Condorcet et Mme Suard, M. Suard, et Garat (1771–1791)*, ed. E. Badinter (Paris: Fayard, 1988), pp. 210–211, 226.

[9] L. Loft, *Passion, Politics and* Philosophie: *Rediscovering J.P. Brissot* (Westport: Greenwood Press, 2002), pp. 55–67.

[10] See L. Hunt's remarks about Brissot, in "Louis XVI wasn't killed by Ideas. This is what happens when you ignore the role of Politics in Intellectual History," *New Republic*, 27 June 2014.

expounded in the work of atheist materialists like La Mettrie and d'Holbach;[11] if Brissot's advocacy of universal human rights owes something to Rousseau it owes more to Raynal, Diderot, and d'Holbach, especially with respect to his idea that slaves, serfs, savages and others degraded and dehumanized by oppression or living in the "natural state" must be rescued and elevated through education, the civilizing process, and revolutionary action.[12]

No-one could have guessed from the thoroughly uncontroversial *nécrologie* d'Holbach's close confidant, Jacques André Naigeon (1738–1810), published nineteen days after his death in the *Journal de Paris* for 9 February 1789, that d'Holbach's political and social as well as religious thought was politically, as well as religiously, highly controversial and subversive. Nor would they guess that his thought already infused the democratic republicanism of some revolutionary leaders such as, most obviously, Carra,[13] and that, especially behind the scenes, d'Holbach would posthumously play a role in the revolutionary conflict of ideologies. D'Holbach, Naigeon reminded readers, had furnished numerous "excellent articles" on politics as well as natural history and philosophy for the *Encyclopédie* and was esteemed by "all the savants of Europe," but communicated nothing new to the reader.[14]

Very different was the piece appearing in the same journal, on 2 December 1789, in which the ex-Jesuit revolutionary pamphleteer, republican ideologue and reformer, Joseph-Antoine Cérutti (1738–92), set out to rescue a worthy figure – an "homme estimable" (d'Holbach), unjustifiably attacked by a "celebrated man" (Rousseau). If many authors dismissed the *Système de la nature* (1770) as an "abominable work,"[15] Rousseau not only abhorred d'Holbach's philosophy, contended Cérutti, but positively vilified d'Holbach himself in a cruel, even outrageous fashion. It was Diderot who had originally brought the two into regular contact and tried to mend fences when the quarrel first commenced. Cérutti recalled meeting d'Holbach at the bath resort of Contrexéville in the Vosges, before he died, and hearing the latter's frank account of the feud. It was their "philosophie anti-thérésienne," d'Holbach assured

---

[11] Loft, *Passion, Politics and* Philosophie, pp. 30, 33, 60–62, 90.
[12] Loft, *Passion, Politics and* Philosophie, p. 203.
[13] Israel, *Revolutionary Ideas*, pp. 110, 112, 117, 142, 150, 167–168.
[14] J. Naigeon, "Lettres sur la mort de M. le baron d'Holbach," *Journal de Paris* 40 (9 February 1789): pp. 176–177; see also P. Naville, *Paul Thiry d'Holbach et la philosophie scientifique au XVIIIe siècle* (Paris: Gallimard, 1943), pp. 128, 452–455.
[15] M. Curran, *Atheism, Religion and Enlightenment in pre-Revolutionary Europe* (Woodbridge: Boydell Press, 2012), p. 139.

Cérutti, the disgust Diderot, d'Holbach, and their German colleague, Grimm, conceived for Rousseau's relationship with his companion, Thérèse Levasseur (1721–1801), and attempts to break up what to their minds was an thoroughly unsuitable union, that chiefly caused Rousseau's estrangement and subsequent animosity.

Thérèse, as has been noted, they regarded "as stupid and narrow."[16] A servant and washer-girl working in the Hotel Saint-Quentin close to the Luxembourg palace, Rousseau first met her around 1745 and was greatly attracted by what he construed as her modesty, timidity, and need for protection from others. In the early stages of their relationship, Rousseau often told others his relationship with her was merely one of convenience, referring to her as the "supplement I needed."[17] He did not so much love or adore as felt attached to her, relying on her sturdy practicality to enable him to preoccupy himself entirely with himself, his writings and thoughts without getting entangled in either daily life or in "dissipation." Although not always loyal to her, and she not to him, their relationship and his close dependence on her as his cook, minder, and nurse whom, before their marriage, he tended to call "tante" [aunt] in company, remained solid for the rest of their lives. "I lived with my Thérèse," he writes in the *Confessions*, "as with the finest genius in the universe."[18] They had five children together, the first late in 1746 or early 1747, all of whom he abandoned much to the detriment of his later reputation, doing so, he himself later claimed without any scruples on his part, but with the "greatest difficulty in the world in getting her to accept this means of preserving her honor."[19]

Thérèse's arithmetic was dreadful; and although rudimentarily literate, she never learned to tell the time by the clock, correctly "count change," or remember the months of the calendar, and her spelling was bizarrely phonetic. "At first," reports Rousseau, in his *Confessions*, "I wanted to form her mind. I wasted my effort. Her mind is what nature has made it: cultivation and effort do not take hold there. I do not blush at all to admit that she has never known how to read very well, although she writes passably."[20] Later, during the time she and Rousseau spent in England, she further gained the reputation, according to Hume, of being vulgar, quarrelsome, and a compulsive talebearer.[21] While Rousseau's relationship

---

[16] L. Damrosch, *Jean-Jacques Rousseau* (Boston: Houghton Mifflin, 2005), p. 188.
[17] L. Müller, "Marie-Therèse Lavasseur," in R. Trousson and F. Eigeldinger (eds.) *Dictionnaire de Jean-Jacques Rousseau* (Paris: H. Champion, 2006), pp. 539–544.
[18] J.-J. Rousseau, *The Confessions*, CW V, p. 279.
[19] Quoted in Damrosch, *Jean-Jacques Rousseau*, p. 191.   [20] *Confessions*, CW V, pp. 278–279.
[21] Damrosch, *Jean-Jacques Rousseau*, p. 429.

with Thérèse started considerably before he joined the d'Holbachian circle toward the end of the 1740s, his ties to her indubitably aggravated his, from 1753, increasingly quarrelsome relations with d'Holbach. "The more we tried to lead him back to his former principles and his former friends," complained d'Holbach to Cérutti, the "more he abandoned both the one and the other." Their final break d'Holbach recounted in a manner placing Rousseau in a decidedly unfavorable light. "The most eloquent of men," d'Holbach later concluded, became "the most anti-intellectual, the touchiest of men became the most anti-social." The satisfaction Cérutti professed to feel in setting the record straight was tempered by a lively sense of ideological "danger." While he too admired Rousseau – like d'Holbach, he added – zealous Rousseau enthusiasts will perhaps find it something "bad that I dare to challenge their enthusiasm and even my own."[22]

A particular kind of *intolérance* characterized the fervor of Rousseau admirers for their hero and when it came to publicly criticizing Rousseau, "opinions fanatiques" created a situation which made Cérutti feel as if he was "setting foot on a savage island." But he also felt he had to risk possibly "being devoured by cannibals" since there was a friend needing to be rescued from "fanatical hands," a cherished reputation to "defend from their insults." Cérutti pronounces it a "horrible thing" that anyone, even a démi-god like Rousseau, should when dying immolate on his literary tomb all the friends he had possessed in life, compelling their plaintive ghosts to follow after his, plunged in opprobrium for the rest of posterity. One sees what Cérutti meant: in his *Confessions*, Rousseau claims d'Holbach arranged various petty "conspiracies" against him while admitting that "Diderot and d'Holbach were not, at least I cannot believe it, people to scheme very black plots, the one was not wicked enough to do it the other not skillful enough: but by this very fact the party [i.e. the d'Holbach conspiracy against Rousseau] was bound together better";[23] Rousseau was delighted by the success of his *Lettre à d'Alembert* (1758) which "taught the public to distrust the insinuations of the Holbachic coterie."[24] Due to such passages, d'Holbach, noted Cérutti, considered Rousseau's *Confessions* a compendium of "fury and infamy."[25] Some readers did react angrily to Cérutti' intervention, claiming his "unjustified" account reflected discredit not on Rousseau but solely on d'Holbach and Diderot.[26]

[22] J. Cérutti, *supplément* to *Journal de Paris* 336 (2 Dec. 1789) pp. 1567–1568.
[23] *Confessions*, CW V, p. 412.   [24] *Confessions*, CW V, p. 420.
[25] J. Cérutti, *supplément* to *Journal de Paris* 336 (2 Dec. 1789), p. 1568.
[26] See I. de Charrière (Belle van Zuylen), "Eclaircissements relatifs à la publications des *Confessions* de Rousseau," in De Charrière, *Oeuvres complètes* (Amsterdam: van Oorschot, 1979–1984), X, pp. 193–194.

If Rousseau's central but complex role in the ideological battles of the Revolution is hard to dispute, and often invoked, that of d'Holbach is scarcely known at all. Indeed, at the start of the Revolution, d'Holbach had not yet fully emerged from the general obscurity in which he had lived, researched, and (anonymously) published his writings. In notes on d'Holbach published in the journal *Correspondance littéraire, philosophique et critique* in March 1789, the editor, the Zurich *érudit* resident in Paris, Jakob Heinrich Meister (1744–1826), recalled having known d'Holbach personally during the last years of his life, confirming he was indeed the author of the *Système de la nature* (1770) which had created such a massive stir nineteen years before. But he also stressed something still more noteworthy: d'Holbach was the author too of the subsequent books, the *Système sociale* (1773) and *La Morale universelle* (1776). Even if the latter had caused far less controversy at the time of their original publication than the *Système*, they better demonstrated, he explained, the essentially political and social reforming goals of d'Holbach's endeavors. It was to be via education and by "good laws" (*de bonnes lois*), by being rescued from men's profound ignorance, that humanity could and would secure a better future and "all the well-being of which our nature is capable."[27]

Hence it definitely deserves emphasis not just that the political writings of d'Holbach were important to the likes of Condorcet, Carra, Brissot, Naigeon, and Volney but that where the late 1770s and 1780s had undoubtedly witnessed a marked receding of the torrent of d'Holbach editions sweeping France and all Europe from the end of the 1760s (down to the mid-1770s), the revolutionary years witnessed a noticeable resurgence of interest in his books. Figure 8.1 shows the number of editions of key d'Holbach subversive works for each of the six quinquennia between 1770 and 1800 partially reflects this revival of interest, though what was chiefly significant here was the increasing attention being paid to d'Holbach's pleas for political and social reform.

Historians have rarely taken note of the relevance of d'Holbach's central political message to the Revolution. Mark Curran in his otherwise excellent book on d'Holbach and the reception of the latter's publications, on this point gives what I believe is a misleading impression, implying d'Holbach's writings had very little impact.[28] In 1790, Condorcet took a dramatically different view in his analysis of *La Politique naturelle* (1773)

---

[27] J. Vercruysse, *Bibliographie descriptive des écrits du Baron d'Holbach* (Paris: Minard, 1971), p. 16; Meister's text reproduced in Naville, *Paul Thiry d'Holbach* p. 458.
[28] Curran, *Atheism, Religion and Enlightenment*, pp. 71–72, 109.

	1770–74	1775–79	1780–84	1785–89	1790–94	1795–99	1800–04
10							
9							
8	<						
7							
6	–						
5			.				
4	+	<					
3	*	= –			= – <	* –	
2				<		= +	<
1	*	<		+		<	
0		+	= + *	= * –	+ *		= + –

– *Système de la nature* (1770); < *Le Bon Sens* (1772); * *La Politique naturelle* (1773)
+ *Système sociale* (1773); = *La Morale universelle* (1776)
See Jeroom Vercruysse, *Bibliographie descriptive des écrits du Baron d'Holbach* (Paris, 1971) see unpaginated lists for 1770–1804

Figure 8.1 D'Holbach editions per quinquennium (1769–1800)
(*Système de la nature, Politique naturelle, Système sociale, Le Bon Sens, Essai sur les préjugés*)

in the *Bibliothèque de l'Homme Public* where, as Vercruysse affirms, he regretted not being free to reveal the author's name.[29] There, Condorcet pronounces *La Politique naturelle* an outstanding work and among "those which we believe did most to prepare minds for the Revolution which has regenerated France."[30] Politics until recently had been an entirely obscure and problematic science, a "chaos impénétrable" dominated by the "imaginary interests of princes" and the "metaphysical ideas of theology." "Ignorance and lies," concludes Condorcet, echoing d'Holbach in true Radical Enlightenment style, are the "true sources of the ills by which we see human societies afflicted."[31]

The *Politique naturelle* (1773) like his other major work published that year, the *Système social* (1773) does indeed expound an essentially republican political stance, d'Holbach's argument that "the rights" of peoples and individuals are universal: all laws not democratic in the sense

---

[29] "Condorcet s'excusa de ne pouvoir nommer l'auteur," see Vercruysse, *Bibliographie descriptive*, section 1773, p. A2; Naville, *Paul Thiry d'Holbach*, p. 129.

[30] [Condorcet] in *Bibliothèque de l'Homme public; ou Analyse raisonnée des principaux ouvrages françois et étrangers sur la politique en général, la législation* [. . .] *et surtout le droit naturel et public* (Paris, 1790), VI, pp. 62–226, here p. 129.

[31] [Condorcet], *Bibliothèque de l'Homme public*, VI, p. 69.

of serving the "common benefit," the interest of society as a whole, are "disavowed by reason." Hence, upholding the people's "rights" essentially means ensuring governments do not prey on the majority, or serve minority interests, but are actively and continually obliged by the people (the true sovereign), preferably through representative institutions, to promote the interest of society as a whole, that is *l'Utilité générale, la volonté publique* or the general will, "general utility" being defined as the worldly interest of the greatest number which d'Holbach pronounces the only just and rational basis of the law.[32] The "rights" of peoples hence operate in close conjunction with equality, the interest of the majority, and blocking the selfish initiatives of kings, aristocrats, lawyers, and clergy. Above all, d'Holbach's universal "rights" promote to the maximum the freedom the individual enjoys in the state of nature insofar as the "common good" or *volonté générale* permit these to carry over into society. The distinctly anti-Hobbesian idea that most individual and group free-doms and autonomy are, or should be, carried over directly from the state of nature is a key radical doctrine common to Diderot, d'Holbach, Raynal, Helvétius, Condorcet, and Volney and in a different, more particularist, less universalist way also Rousseau.[33] It is an idea Diderot and Rousseau derived either indirectly or (more probably) directly from Spinoza – Riley most unfortunately missed this – and which constitutes the chief difference between Hobbesian and Spinozist political theory.[34]

All laws not operating in the interest of the greatest number are, for these political thinkers, unreasonable and cannot embody, be based on, or protect any "rights." They are the products of tyranny and violence and must always be rejected and opposed by society. Force may legitimately be used to secure "rights" but only when these genuinely conform to equity and justice, a rule applying to peoples no less than individuals. Since men are always entitled to enjoy the "rights of nature" on the basis of reciprocity and justice, the "rights" of peoples and individuals are "eternal and

---

[32] P. d'Holbach, *La Politique naturelle, ou Discours sur les vrais principes du gouvernement* ("Londres" [Amsterdam], 1773), pp. 26–29, 44, 47; one of the few recent works to note the significance of d'Holbach's non-Rousseauist conception of *volonté générale* is Swenson, *On Jean-Jacques Rousseau*, pp. 162, 164–165.

[33] On the differences between Rousseau's "general will" and that of d'Holbach and Diderot, see, Israel, *Democratic Enlightenment*, pp. 636–640, 813, 865, 948.

[34] See M. Villaverde, "Rousseau, lecteur de Spinoza," *Studies on Voltaire and the Eighteenth Century* 369 (1999), pp. 107–139; M. Villaverde, "Spinoza, Rousseau: dos concepciones de democracia," *Revista de estudios políticos* 116 (2002): pp. 85–106; D. Williams, "Spinoza and the general Will," *The Journal of Politics* 72 (2010), pp. 341–356; Israel, *Democratic Enlightenment*, pp. 100–108, and esp. pp. 637–647.

inalienable." Societies can adopt laws that vary; but insofar as laws are worthy of respect, and can be expected to be durable and to contribute to the "happiness" of society, all laws without any exception, held d'Holbach, must conform to the principle of equity which never varies.[35] "Let us conclude," d'Holbach summed up, in 1773, that there "cannot be any legitimate rights except those which are founded on nature, justice, utility, and the true interest of society."[36] While he did include "property" among the most important "rights," unfortunately for mankind "princes, aristocrats and the rich seem only to be occupied with finding ways to appropriate the fruits of labor of others," thus infringing their "rights." The privileged classes, all too often "useless and harmful" members of society, usurp whether by acquiescence or force the advantages which nature or industry made the property of their fellow citizens: they abolish their liberty, violate their persons, and appropriate their possessions. They claim the incontestable "right" to be unjust, oppression that is unchallenged wherever it "continues for a long time, and ignorance, prejudice, feebleness, and inertia have prevented their subjects resisting or complaining." In short, "the happiness of society is the goal of all government," and d'Holbach's *volonté générale* is the general push in society toward securing them.[37]

Universal "Rights" within this conceptual framework are also a measure by which to evaluate and criticize governments and by which any reader, through the journals, newspapers and debates, can involve himself in international politics; "rights" understood thus provide, d'Holbach repeatedly stresses, a regulatory tool for imposing an invariable moral order on relations between nations and peoples and making judgments about rulers, laws and constitutions. Here, in 1773, we find clearly stated that revolutionary new conception of "human rights" eternal and inalienable underpinning the principles infusing Jefferson's concept of universal natural rights in the American *Declaration* of 1776, and the slightly earlier and epoch-making Virginia *Declaration of Rights* of June 1776 composed by George Mason, as well as the 1789 French Declaration and Paine's later text, *Rights of Man* (1791).

This whole topic – the difference between radical and Rousseauist "general will" and "rights" – is relevant to the American as well as the French Revolution because, as has recently been demonstrated, the "architecture of ideas" buttressing "universal basic rights" appeared in

---

[35] D'Holbach, *La Politique naturelle*, pp. 34–35.   [36] D'Holbach, *La Politique naturelle*, pp. 36–37.
[37] D'Holbach, *La Politique naturelle*, p. 48.

the English language, in the 1770s, only suddenly and abruptly. Contrary to what scholars once assumed, the American revolutionary usage in 1776 owed practically nothing to Locke and other pre-1770 British writings and usages. Neither did it stem from social practice and reading novels, or any gradual "invention" of universal human rights through some long-term cultural shift toward greater empathy for the other.[38] On the other hand, neither did it derive from Rousseau. Though thoroughly steeped in Enlightenment literature from his youth onwards, neither Locke nor Rousseau, we should note, were particularly significant in either Jefferson's development or his mature thought.[39] Some rights could be derived from Rousseau's thought and he undoubtedly had some impact on the human rights debate in France during summer of 1789.[40] But in general Rousseau's conception of "general will" proved more useful for overriding than protecting individual rights.

From the very outset, both thinkers employing the term "general will" in different articles of the fifth volume of the *Encyclopédie* (1755), Diderot and Rousseau each imparted to the term *volonté général* a distinctive but substantially different twist.[41] The essential difference is that Diderot's, d'Holbach's, and Condorcet's "general will" refers to the sum of all individuals' drives for happiness and well-being understood as something universal providing a universal code of morality for the whole of humanity,[42] whereas Rousseau's refers to the individual's oneness with and absorption into the collectivity of a particular people so that it is less tied to individual well-being and more tied to citizenship and belonging to a particular society. Rousseau's conception of "general will" was also more likely to vary from one people to another, was more particularist and less universal, and apt to clash with Diderot's and d'Holbach's (and Jefferson's)

---

[38] For L. Hunt's thesis being "wide of the mark," see P. De Bolla, *The Architecture of Concepts: The Historical Formation of Human Rights* (New York: Fordham University Press, 2013), p. 48.

[39] A. Jayne, *Jefferson's Declaration of Independence: Origins, Philosophy and Theology* (Lexington: University Press of Kentucky, 1998), pp. 2–6, 244; M. Valsania, *The Limits of Optimism: Thomas Jefferson's Dualistic Enlightenment* (Charlottesville: University of Virginia Press, 2011), pp. 28–29.

[40] J. Cohen, *Rousseau: A Free Community of Equals* (Oxford: Oxford University Press, 2010), pp. 146–148; B. Gagnebin, "L'Influence de Rousseau sur la *Déclaration des droits de l'Homme et du citoyen*," in S. Harvey et al. (eds.), *Reappraisals of Rousseau: Studies in Honour of R. A. Leigh* (Manchester: Manchester University Press, 1980), pp. 75–89.

[41] P. Riley, *The General Will before Rousseau: The Transformation of the Divine into the Civic* (Princeton: Princeton University Press, 1986), p. 203; R. Wokler, *The Social Thought of J.J. Rousseau* (New York: Garland, 1987), pp. 57–64; M. Hulliung, *The Autocritique of Enlightenment: Rousseau and the Philosophes* (Cambridge, MA: Harvard University Press, 1994), p. 27.

[42] Riley is good on explaining the difference between Diderot's and Rousseau's general will but strangely make no mention of d'Holbach, Condorcet, or Volney in this connection, see Riley, *The General Will*, pp. 203–206.

universalist conception. Diderot's and his followers' "general will" also stood in an emphatically different relationship to philosophical reason from Rousseau's particularist "general will." D'Holbach consistently opted for Diderot's, not Rousseau's conception.[43] According to d'Holbach, the citizen only obeys the general will, the law, the *volonté publique*, the sovereign authority, "because he hopes these will guide him more surely to a durable happiness than his own particular desires and fantasies which very often draw him away from [that happiness]"; individual self-interest lies at the heart of radical "general will."[44]

The unceasing posthumous philosophical battle between Rousseau and d'Holbach was fought out as a mostly behind-the-scenes clash of symbols and reputations. This posthumous philosophical battle indeed proceeded always quietly, only hinted at in the articles of Cérutti and Condorcet, and those of Ginguiné and Naigeon published later, avoiding noisy, confrontational, public form. This lack of explicit discussion of the clash between two different conceptions of "general will" and "rights" in the dramatic revolutionary context might seem puzzling but appears less so when we consider the general unawareness in the France of 1789–94 of who d'Holbach was and his significance, and the immense cultural clout of the Rousseau cult, the overwhelming sense of allegiance among the pro-revolutionary public to Rousseau which Cérutti nervously emphasized. Early in the Revolution an official canon of major *philosophes* who had prepared the Revolution was widely propagated in society through the system of revolutionary fêtes and celebrations held in every town and place of any importance and this became a powerful cultural force in itself. The Idéologue medical theorist and writer, Jean-Georges Cabanis (1757–1808) was responsible for one such event, as town administrator, at Auteil, on 5 August 1792, to mark the anniversary of the abolition of feudal dues and obligations in August 1789. Busts of the *philosophes* were ceremonially carried into the town hall as part of the public ritual – Rousseau in first place, Voltaire as "enemy of privilege," Franklin as a titan of science, philosophy and American liberty and, finally, Mirabeau.[45]

Diderot, d'Holbach, and Helvétius were decidedly not part of this public revolutionary ritual and canon. Condorcet who mentions Rousseau as little as possible (in fact practically never) in his political writings presumably proceeded thus because Rousseau's stature in both

---

[43] Israel, *Democratic Enlightenment*, pp. 624, 636–640, 644, 809, 811, 815–816.
[44] D'Holbach, *Politique Naturelle*, p. 52.
[45] M. Staum, *Cabanis: Enlightenment and Medical Philosophy in the French Revolution* (Princeton: Princeton University Press, 1980), pp. 126–127.

public rituals and in literary and café culture, as well as among his Brissotin allies, was such – while the earlier efforts of Diderot and d'Holbach to counteract it had had so little success – that any such open confrontation was apt to be counter-productive and unnecessarily divisive among those supporting popular sovereignty, general will, republicanism and democracy. An open clash among the adherents of popular sovereignty could only have benefited the moderates seeking to repel democracy and the populists more and more driving the Rousseau cult.

By July 1791, Mirabeau and Voltaire had been magnificently pantheonized, but Rousseau considered by most people, then as now, the Revolution's chief inspirer, had not. How could Rousseau be omitted or fail to be presented as one of the leading revolutionary *philosophique* triumvirate? The artist Baudon, then preparing elaborate portrait engravings of all three founding titans – Mirabeau, Voltaire, and Rousseau – expected these preeminent figures to grace buildings and offices throughout the eighty-three departments of France.[46] However, during the early Revolution circumstances ensured that Rousseau could not to the same extent as Mirabeau or Voltaire be useful as a political rallying device and unifier of the revolutionary center and Left. During the months of the Feuillant ascendancy following Louis XVI's flight to Varennes, in June 1791, and the National Assembly's efforts to check the rise of republicanism and consolidate the constitutional monarchist Revolution, Rousseau looked to the then dominant moderates more threatening and divisive than a useful tool.[47]

During 1791, the Revolution was presided over by an anti-republican and increasingly aggressive *modérantisme* presided over by Barnave, Bailly, and the De Lameths to which they managed to recruit Lafayette and which now launched an all-out intellectual campaign to promote Montesquieu, moderate Enlightenment, and admiration for the British constitution based on mixed monarchy (which both Rousseau and d'Holbach despised). These "moderate" revolutionary leaders were supported by everyone seeking to prevent democracy and ensure a limited suffrage and were helped by the antipathy widespread among lawyers, the commercially-minded and much of the public generally to *la philosophie moderne*. Republicanism was impracticable the National Assembly and public were assured, a turbulent sea continually agitated by storms, easy prey to

---

[46] *Archives Parlementaires*, Series 1 (1787–94) (ed.) M.J. Mavidal et al., 102 vols. (Paris, 1879–2005), XXIX, p. 736–737. Hereafter AP.
[47] [Ginguené], *Petition to Assemblée nationale*, 27 Aug. 1791, p. 2, in AP XXIX (27 Aug, 1791), p. 736–737; P.-L. Ginguené, *Lettres sur les* Confessions *de J.J.Rousseau* (Paris, 1791), pp. 63–65.

conquest by an aspiring Sulla, Cromwell, or some other great scoundrel. With such rhetoric, Barnave swayed most of the then still predominantly "moderate" Jacobin Club, reported Carra in his paper, and "all the ignorant and unaware."[48] Barnave and his allies, Alexandre and Charles de Lameth, incorporated Rousseau into their moderate-conservative stance to a limited extent where useful to them. But this consisted mainly of highlighting his doctrine that the republican form is unsuited to large states like France, a Rousseauist proposition that republicans, of course, vigorously denied.[49]

By July 1791, Mirabeau and Voltaire had received major public honors, magnificent ceremonies of interment in the Panthéon, while Rousseau still had not. This blatant discrepancy seemed outrageous, astounding, and insufferable to the innumerable Rousseau enthusiasts. In protest, an impressive deputation of writers, artists, and others on 27 August 1791 submitted a formal petition to the National Assembly bearing no less than 311 signatures, including those of Mercier, Chamfort, Clavière, Lanthenas, Roland, Gorsas, Duroveray, Perlet, and Fanny Beauharnais, eloquently demanding Rousseau's *panthéonisation*.[50] If Voltaire had deservedly been installed for crushing fanaticism "under the feet of philosophy" helping clear the way for the Revolution, how could the Revolution fail to discharge its debt to Rousseau, according to this petition "the first founder of the French constitution"? Despite defending Calas and "all the oppressed," Voltaire hardly compared with Jean-Jacques as a "foe of oppression." Many elements of the 1791 liberal monarchist Constitution, and especially the principle of equality, alleged the petitioners, stemmed from Rousseau's ideas. First to establish "equality of rights among men" and "sovereignty of the people," the very "idées-mères" from which the Revolution arose, Rousseau had accomplished all this "under the eyes of despotism itself."

This August 1791 petition was composed by Chamfort's friend, the Breton reformer Pierre Louis Ginguené (1748–1816), an ardent admirer of Rousseau and future member of the Convention's Committee of Public Instruction. Some of Rousseau's doctrines did not conform to the National Assembly's principles and the new (constitutional monarchist) constitution, conceded Ginguené, referring in particular to his claiming the "general will" cannot be represented in a representative assembly, an

[48] J.-L. Carra, *Annales patriotiques et littéraires de la France* DCXLV (9 July 1791), p. 1655.
[49] Carra, *Annales patriotiques* DCXLIII (7 July 1791), pp. 1648, 1651; Lemny, *Jean-Louis Carra (1742–1793): parcours d'un révolutionniare* (Paris: Harmattan, 2000), p. 208.
[50] [Ginguené], *Petition to Assemblée nationale*, p. 5; Trousson, *Jean-Jacques Rousseau*, p. 753.

important divide not only between Rousseau and republican theorists like Paine and Condorcet, as has been pointed out, but also between Rousseau and d'Holbach, a prominent early advocate of "representation" stripped of privilege.[51] However, Ginguené did not cite the full list of inconvenient features of Rousseau's thought that Mercier had set out in his book on Rousseau published a few weeks before. In particular, Ginguené does not mention Mercier's point about Rousseau's citizenship-orientated doctrine of "general will" being unsuited,[52] in fact in some ways a barrier to, the doctrine of the universal rights of mankind so fundamental to the Revolution. Rousseau was chiefly useful to the National Assembly's currently dominant ideology of constitutional monarchism, Ginguené acknowledged, agreeing here with the Brothers de Lameth, through his insistence that republican forms are appropriate only for small states and inappropriate for France.[53]

As far as the general public was concerned no one else deserved to be recognized as the Revolution's spiritual author to the same degree as Rousseau. Besides Rousseau's *panthéonisation*, Ginguené's petition demanded implementation of a December 1790 decree authorizing a public statue of Rousseau for central Paris honoring the *Contrat social's* and *Émile's* author under the rubric "La nation française libre, à J.J.Rousseau," and implementation also of the article of the same decree assigning an annual state pension of 1,200 livres to Rousseau's widow, Thérèse Levasseur.[54] In Paris and throughout France generally there was doubtless considerable support for these proposals.

Nevertheless, Ginguené's petition stood little chance of succeeding then or in the near future. *Panthéonization*, besides violating Rousseau's last testament, answered Charles de Lameth, would infringe on the property rights of the landowner, on whose land he was presently entombed, and who had sheltered him in his last days. Rousseau had stipulated in his last

---

[51] N. Urbinati, *Representative Democracy: Principles and Genealogy* (Chicago: University of Chicago Press, 2006), p. 168; on d'Holbach and representative government, see Israel, *Democratic Enlightenment*, pp. 813–817.

[52] L. Mercier, *De J.J.Rousseau considéré comme l'un des premiers auteurs de la Révolution* (Paris, 1791), II, pp. 32–34; Israel, *Democratic Enlightenment*, p. 644. Olivier-Henri Bonnerot regrettably fails to provide anything like the full list of what Mercier considered the inconvenient aspects of Rousseau's thought from a French revolutionary perspective, see O.-H. Bonnerot, "Louis-Sebastien Mercier: lecteur et éditeur de Jean-Jacques Rousseau," in Thiery (ed.), *Rousseau, l'Émile et la Révolution*, pp. 415–423, here pp. 421–422.

[53] AP XXIX, p. 756; Swenson, *On Jean-Jacques Rousseau*, p. 10.

[54] AP XXIX, pp. 755–756; A. Jourdan, "Le Culte de Rousseau sous la Révolution: la statue et la panthéonisation du Citoyen de Genève," in T. L'Aminot (ed.), *Politique et révolution chez Jean-Jacques Rousseau* (Oxford: Voltaire Foundation, 1994), pp. 62–63.

testament that he should not be buried in the city he loathed (Paris), preferring rural solitude. His present resting place, near Montmorency, accorded with his wishes. On these grounds, prompted by the De Lameths, the National Assembly deferred any final decision.[55] The *Panthéonization* of Rousseau was again petitioned for, on 4 September, and again deferred.[56] The Feuillants, much preferring Montesquieu, were simply unwilling to concede the same level of honors to Rousseau as had been bestowed upon Mirabeau and Voltaire, and still less publicly portray him as the chief inspiration of their Revolution.

Barnave and the Lameths opposed promoting Rousseau's reputation and image to the level most revolutionaries urged. But there was a further barrier: the chief difficulty, admitted Ginguené in his petition, was that opinion concerning the real character of Rousseau's thought remained seriously split not just in the National Assembly but among opinion leaders more generally. Experts on the Revolution's essential principles and *habitués* of philosophical debate in the Paris cafés were seriously divided over Diderot's claim that he had supplied the original inspiration for Rousseau's early major work, the *Discourse on Inequality*: had Diderot lied or told the truth? Were the *philosophes* right to claim Rousseau, over whom so many enthused, was an "homme à paradoxes" whose moral thought is really just a ridiculous bundle of contradictions?[57] There was no denying the revolutionaries' great debt to Diderot and the *Encyclopédie*. Yet, having closely studied the quarrel between Rousseau and the *philosophes*, and reread all Voltaire's works, Ginguené was convinced responsibility for this unhappy and ruinous rift lay mainly with the *philosophes* – and especially d'Holbach.[58]

This was indeed the moment, Ginguené's remarks confirm, in which d'Holbach for the first time emerged as a controversial and concrete personality in his own right in the public consciousness and an active force in intellectual debate. Cérutti, Condorcet, Volney, Naigeon, and others were all now promoting his reputation. Diderot and Voltaire had unjustly persecuted the man of "virtue"; but it was especially the "good and honest M. d'Holbach, eulogized in December 1789 by Cérutti in the *Journal de Paris*, "a figure who was now becoming influential," Ginguené acknowledged, in the minds of many revolutionary leaders, who had wronged him. Like Cérutti, Condorcet, and Volney, Ginguené had known d'Holbach and his "intimate circle" personally. He agreed with

---

[55] AP XXIX, pp. 760–761.   [56] AP XXIX, p. 191.   [57] Ginguené, *Lettres* pp. 30, 53.
[58] Ginguené, *Lettres*, pp. 80–82.

"everything Cérutti and d'Holbach's other friends affirmed honorable to his memory." Yet d'Holbach showed a penchant for "banter, a tendency to jeer" that was decidedly reprehensible and the battle between Rousseau and the *coterie d'Holbachique*, as Cérutti's eulogy itself concedes, had produced much personal rancor.[59] Other evidence confirms that after the final rupture, in 1757, and during Rousseau's quarrel with Hume, d'Holbach had indeed condemned Rousseau's ideas in a harsher more implacable manner, as well as frequently referred to Rousseau personally in a more insulting fashion, than Diderot or virtually anyone else even though Rousseau himself more keenly resented the role of Grimm in orchestrating the "coterie d'Holbachique" against him more than that of d'Holbach himself.[60] Years after their rupture, d'Holbach still continued to harp on Rousseau's relationship with his companion, Thérèse Levasseur, and an exemplar of the latter's supposedly abysmal moral standards, Rousseau having treated her in a degrading fashion as well as abandoned their children and, in 1766, allegedly allowed her abandoned mother to die penniless of hunger.[61]

The quarrel, though, as reported by Ginguené and perpetuated during the Revolution, was far from just a matter of personal rancor. Rather, it focused on the status of "the ordinary" in morality, education, and ultimately politics. Rousseau's "war" on the *philosophes* was retaliation, as d'Holbach's conversations with Cérutti at the Contrexéville baths confirmed, for d'Holbach's and his friends' scorning his humble and worthy companion, Thérèse, retaliation against their "philosophie anti-Thérèsienne."[62] It was especially their "aristocratic disdain" for the ordinary, held Ginguiné, that rendered the *philosophes* inferior to Rousseau as a revolutionary icon. Had not the Citizen of Geneva taught men to penetrate behind the mask of false social convention, and understand man as he truly is, fostering contempt for vain titles and illusions of grandeur, fomenting that preference for simple tastes, natural sentiment, virtue, and liberty that permeated all his publications and that had enthused the public and inspired the Revolution?[63]

The status of "the ordinary" remained fiercely controversial subsequently and indeed defined in a most remarkable way the lines of the conflict between the democratic republicans, or Brissotins and the Montagne during

---

[59] Ginguené, *Lettres* pp. 87–88, 131–135; L'Aminot, "D'Holbach et Rousseau," p. 121.
[60] Naville, *Paul Thiry d'Holbach*, pp. 78, 82–83; L'Aminot, "D'Holbach et Rousseau," pp. 21, 124–125, 127.
[61] L'Aminot, "D'Holbach et Rousseau," pp. 122, 124.   [62] Ginguené, *Lettres*, p. 132.
[63] [Ginguené], *Petition to Assemblée nationale*, pp. 3–4 in AP XXIX, p. 756.

1792 and 1793, indeed throughout the course of the Terror. Only in late July 1792, did Robespierre begin moving tentatively toward republicanism. But he did so incessantly complaining that his democratic republican adversaries were seducing the common people with superfluous talk of "republicanism," and of his being maligned by the pro-Revolution democratic press. For him, the main issue was that "sovereignty of the people" was being falsely and hypocritically proclaimed by the Assembly and the Brissotin press, not being promoted and emphasized as he urged.[64] In his speeches, Robespierre continually expounded the cosmic dualism infusing all his attitudes – stressing the purity, disinterestedness, generosity, and "moderation" of ordinary folk and their being abused by those insidiously seeking to raise themselves above them. The latter, in his Manichaean worldview, included the "writers" and intellectuals he accused of scheming to betray the ordinary and innocent, these men too being "aristocrats." The "people alone is good and just, and magnanimous," went Robespierre's interminable refrain, corruption and tyranny being the exclusive attributes of those who disdain "the ordinary."[65]

The pivotal point of dispute involving Rousseau and Rousseau's writings during the ideological battles of the Revolution from 1792 was thus the status of "the ordinary." If Cérutti, Brissot, Condorcet, and Volney aligned with the *philosophes*, Robespierre stood with the common people, with "des hommes simples et purs."[66] Plainly, Marat's, Hébert's, and Robespierre's anti-intellectualism and emphatic populism were closely linked. *Philosophes*, according to Robespierre, were the people's enemies. How vastly preferable was the common artisan with robust understanding of the *Rights of Man* to *philosophes*. There was an urgent need to purge all doctrines as well as persons detrimental to the quick, sure instinct of the ordinary person. Admittedly, the *philosophes* had been republicans long before himself and others – Robespierre did not move tentatively toward republicanism until July 1792 – and were predominantly republicans before the Revolution, in 1788 he correctly reminded his audience during one of his major speeches. This was the case with Condorcet, Brissot, Mirabeau, and other radical *philosophes*. But afterwards they had "stupidly defended" the royal cause [resisting execution of Louis without an *appel au public*], in 1793.[67]

---

[64] Robespierre, *Le Défenseur* II (July 1792), p. 538.
[65] R. Scurr, *Fatal Purity: Robespierre and the French Revolution* (London: Vintage, 2006), pp. 182, 184; P. McPhee, *Robespierre: A Revolutionary Life* (New Haven: Yale University Press, 2012), pp. 91, 123.
[66] Robespierre, *Le Défenseur*, I, p. 45, and IV, pp. 174–177.
[67] Israel, *Revolutionary Ideas*, pp. 561–569.

What was the correct meaning, the real character and nature of the "general will"? Could representative democracy express the general will, and how far should Rousseau's educational principles should be embraced? The quarrel between d'Holbach and Rousseau played a behind-the-scenes but subtly pervasive part in all of these political-intellectual controversies as it did also in another conspicuous area of intellectual and ideological disagreement – international dissemination of the democratic Revolution and call for black emancipation around the Caribbean colonies. In general, the anticolonial fervor of the *Histoire philosophique des Deux Indes* was reflected much more in the ideology and actions of Condorcet and the Brissotins than in the fiercely opposing ideologies of either the Feuillants or the Montagne. When Raynal personally was publicly discredited in May–June 1791 for declaring against the principles of equality and democracy,[68] the previously glowing revolutionary reputation of the *Histoire philosophique* itself was salvaged by pointing out that Raynal was not its real author: that indispensable text had been composed by a whole group, it was revealed to the public, led by Diderot in which d'Holbach supposedly participated but Rousseau did not. In the attacks on Raynal by Cloots in the *Chronique de Paris* and others, it was repeatedly stated that d'Holbach was among the authors of the *Histoire Philosophique*, though no one ever seems to have identified any particular passages that issued from his pen. According to Cloots, no admirer of Rousseau, everything in the *Histoire philosophique* was really the work of Diderot, d'Holbach, Naigeon, and Pechméja.[69] The anonymous *T.G. Raynal démasqué, ou Lettres sur la vie et les ouvrages de cet écrivain* (1791), states that it was not Raynal who composed the *Histoire* but Diderot, Deleyre, Pechméja, Guibert, Kniphausen, d'Holbach, and Diderot's classicist assistant, La Grange, the translator of Lucretius.[70]

At bottom the post-1792 posthumous contest between Rousseau and d'Holbach was a fight between two fundamentally incompatible conceptions of equality. D'Holbach's three major political books lent themselves to a conception of rights and equality that strengthened the individual's freedom and status; Rousseau's thought lent itself more to the mobilization of the collectivity to render the revolutionary state more efficient as an equalizing force. Admittedly, not all opponents of the Montagne were as aware of this crucial rift as Department Du Nord deputy François Poultier

---

[68] Israel, *Revolutionary Ideas*, pp. 157–159.   [69] Vercruysse, *Bibliogrphie descriptive*, pp. 36–37.
[70] *T.G. Raynal démasqué, ou Lettres sur la vie et les ouvrages de cet écrivain* (Paris, 1791), p. 6; see also Israel, *Democratic Enlightenment*, p. 936; Israel, *Revolutionary Ideas*, pp. 158–159.

Delmotte (1753–1826), or Jean Debry (1760–1844), another fierce antago-
nist of Robespierre's views both before and after the Montagnard coup of
2 June 1793, who defined *volonté générale* as participation of all in the *force
publique* understood as a system of rights allowing the majority no right to
mistreat, impoverish or intimidate minorities.[71]

Poultier Delmotte wanted it expressly affirmed in the Brissotins' pend-
ing democratic republican Constitution that the "allegedly general will
voted by the majority cannot bind the minority when it evidently violates
the *Rights of Man*. The minority always remains free to remind the majority
who is the true sovereign – *la raison universelle* [universal reason], the
sovereign that dictated those rights."[72] "In the cases of Diderot and
Holbach," Mark Hulliung – one of the very few writers on Rousseau
who has rightly stressed the strong republican tendency in d'Holbach's
political writings[73] – has observed, "it is remarkable to see how little
volition enters into their constantly used expression, the 'general will.'"
While I agree with Hulliung that "one cannot imagine a view more distant
from Diderot's and Holbach's than Rousseau's," I do not altogether agree
with his conclusion that "for Diderot and d'Holbach, the general will is
already there, given by nature; for Rousseau it must be constructed with
painstaking effort and at a high human cost, within the walls of
a republic."[74] For while it is true, in a certain sense that d'Holbach's
"general will," like Diderot's, is already there in the laws of nature,
awareness of it and the need for its primacy when organizing laws and
institutions ensues only when prejudice, superstition and ignorance are
overcome and (radical) Enlightenment widely propagated. According to
Condorcet, Poultier Delmotte, and the Montagne's democratic republican
opponents, the majority's will itself can involve unjustly subjecting the
weakest to the strongest and hence become a gateway to a new tyranny.
Volonté générale untreated, taken in its *Rousseauiste* sense, facilitates
subjection to tyranny and oppression, blighting everyone's rights. "Let us
assert, then, that reason is the only veritable sovereign among men; and
that to reason alone belongs the right to make laws. Laws not dictated by
reason are never obligatory, even when sanctioned by the majority."[75] Here
was the true language of d'Holbach as well as of the late Diderot,
and Radical Enlightenment more generally, a language more and more
opposite to the Montagne's ideology.

---

[71] AP LXVII, p. 289.   [72] Poultier Delmotte in AP LXVII, p. 383.
[73] Hulliung, *Autocritique*, pp. 5–6, 139–143, 204.   [74] Hulliung, *Autocritique*, pp. 171–172.
[75] Poultier Delmotte in AP LXVII, p. 382.

The idea that republican reeducation of society must overcome ignorance, prejudice, and superstition, and hence that all praise of the natural state, *l'état sauvage*, is misplaced and harmful, an idea powerfully expounded in all d'Holbach's late works, operated contrary to Rousseau's moral and educational theories. The doctrine of d'Holbach's was also inherently revolutionary. Plying "un politique aveugle" controlled by vested interests, the "two classes of civil and sacred tyrants" (i.e. kings and priests) working against the interests of society as a whole, do not willingly permit men to become enlightened either about their own rights and interests or the true ends of the social body that it continually subverts.[76] Various key educational reformers during the Revolution, and not least François Xavier Lanthenas (1754–99), among the most active ideologues of anti-*esclavagisme*, education reform and press freedom in the *Cercle social* and reforming circles around Brissot and Roland during the early Revolution, and later Volney, were keen to use the principles set out in *La Politique naturelle* and the *Système social* to forge a new public civic consciousness in revolutionary France by means of public primary education.[77]

D'Holbach is indeed at his most hostile to Rousseau when discussing educational matters. In d'Holbach's eyes Rousseau's "paradoxes" about science, learning, and reading derived from love of contrariness, or madness and were such as to destroy virtue itself through their wrong-headedness. To denounce and seek to discredit learning and the sciences is to ensure men have no means to form sound judgments and distinguish what enhances our existence from what harms and curtails it.[78] The "natural man" invoked by the "eloquent sophist" would be a contemptibly ignorant creature lacking the means to safe-guard his own well-being. Where Rousseau believed ancient Sparta and Rome were especially well-equipped to uphold the *volonté générale*, his frequent eulogies of the pristine "virtue," austerity, and prowess of the ancient Spartans and Romans struck d'Holbach as unedifying and absurd, the ancient Romans in his opinion being aggressive and intolerably oppressive toward all their neighbors, anything but a model for modern citizens to emulate.[79]

---

[76] D'Holbach, *Politique naturelle*, pp. 119–121; Israel, *Democratic Enlightenment*, p. 612.

[77] Israel, *Revolutionary Ideas*, p. 132.

[78] P. d'Holbach, *La Morale universelle, ou Les Devoirs de l'homme fondés sur sa nature*, 3 vols. (Amsterdam, 1776), II, pp. 204–205.

[79] P. d'Holbach, *Le Bon-Sens du curé J. Meslier suivi de son Testament* ("Londres" [Amsterdam], 1772), pp. 177–178.

At the heart of Robespierre's ideology was a populist anti-intellectualism that plainly owed much to Rousseau's concept of virtue, the ordinary, and to the educational philosophy Rousseau expounds in *Émile* with its bias against reading and learning from books and toward manual skills and moral formation. Rousseau's strictures on education in *Émile* were reflected in most remarkable fashion in the ideological clashes over education during the Revolution. Against Condorcet's stress on education being about learning how to form judgments and prove assertions, about learning history, geography, science, and civics, and having primary and secondary education supervised by *philosophes*, a concept that later materialized in the shape of the Institut de France, Robespierre, Marat, and their allies sought to eliminate the academies of science, suppress intellectual elitism and lessen the stress on academic study in primary and secondary education, emphasizing rather moral formation, gymnastics, and rural simplicity.[80]

This drama reflected a good deal in the original antagonism between the sublime "Jean-Jacques" praised to the skies by Robespierre at every turn and Rousseau's foes, the *philosophes* – whose heirs Robespierre identified with those he regarded as his own principal political enemies, Brissot and Condorcet.[81] If Robespierre too, after becoming virtual head of the Montagnard group dictatorship from June 1793, proved distinctly reluctant to install Rousseau's remains in the Panthéon, this was because, to him, it was an edifice mired with the remains of Mirabeau and Voltaire, a monument "debased," though his rather similar reluctance to see Marat interred in the Panthéon probably owed as much to jealousy of the latter's reputation as to principle. In any case, associating and mixing Rousseau with *philosophes* struck him as sacrilege – "quel décadence de l'esprit public!"[82]

Rousseau's ideas and the cult promoting his fame were central to Robespierre's and Saint-Just's ideology. This is illustrated by speech after speech in which they invoked Rousseau and also by Robespierre's actions. Only one thinker (Rousseau), he insisted, in his great speech of 7 May 1794 (18 Floréal) to the Convention in which he reviewed the whole course of the Revolution and set out the theology of his cult of the Supreme Being, showed true grandeur prior to the Revolution and true purity of doctrine, that is presented "virtue" and the Divinity as drawn from nature – expressly

---

[80] On the two conflicting educational ideologies in 1793–4, see Israel, *Revolutionary Ideas*, pp. 374–395.
[81] Robespierre, *Le Défenseur*, IV, pp. 184–186; McPhee, *Robespierre*, pp. 107–108.
[82] Robespierre, *Le Défenseur*, IV, p. 186; Scurr, *Fatal Purity*, pp. 248–249.

in opposition to *la philosophie*. On 5 December 1792, at the Jacobins, Robespierre vehemently denounced the deceased *philosophe*, Mirabeau, the hero of the early Revolution, inciting those present to pull down and smash Mirabeau's bust together with that of Helvétius, busts hitherto presiding over the Jacobin Club's meetings. Helvétius Robespierre declared a *philosophe* whose presence should not be tolerated in their debating hall, since he was a complete unbeliever in religion and foe of Jean-Jacques. Both busts were pulled down and trampled to dust under foot.[83] This was the signal for Jacobin clubs across France to topple Mirabeau and "philosophy," and intensify the offensive against Brissotin intellectualism. Busts of Mirabeau and Helvétius were torn down in the "clubs populaires" of Dijon, Langres, Châtillon-en-Seine, and many other places. Mirabeau "is not a great man any more" sneered the Abbé's Feller's journal, "what true *philosophe* would not make salutary reflections on the meandering course of fleeting reputations to which certain madmen sacrifice honor, virtue and religion!"[84]

In Robespierre's eyes, humanity's true teacher, Rousseau, assailed tyranny in every way, spoke of the Divinity with enthusiasm, and defended immortality of the soul and reward and punishment in the hereafter. Rousseau's "invincible" contempt for the "sophistes intrigants" usurping the name of *philosophes* provoked the lasting hatred of his rivals (Diderot, d'Holbach, and Helvétius). Had Rousseau witnessed this Revolution of which he was the chief precursor, his generous soul would ecstatically embrace the cause of justice and equality. By contrast, what had Rousseau's *philosophique* adversaries contributed to the Revolution? They fought the Revolution from the moment they feared it would raise up the common people. Some questioned republican principles, prostituting themselves to the political factions, especially the Orléanist clique; others withdrew into cowardly neutrality (Raynal, Naigeon). Overall, the intellectual elite "dishonored themselves in the Revolution" and left the "reason of the people" to carry the burden to the eternal disgrace of the *philosophique* sect. These rascals should blush with shame, the achievements of the Revolution being accomplished without and in spite of them by ordinary folk. Good sense, without education or intrigue, brought France to perfection, arousing their disdain and revealing their nullity.[85]

---

[83] Scurr, *Fatal Purity*, p. 218; M. Culoma, *La Religion civile de Rousseau à Robespierre* (Paris: Harmattan, 2010), p. 191.

[84] [Feller], *Journal historique* (Maastricht, 15 January 1793), p. 148.

[85] Robespierre, *Discours*, pp. 31–32; T. Crow, *Emulation: David, Drouais, and Girodet in the Art of Revolutionary France* (New Haven: Yale University Press, 2006), pp. 175–176, 178.

For the Montagne, Rousseau towered above every other thinker who had contributed to preparing and shaping the Revolution and in no respect more than their cult of "the ordinary." On 14 April 1794, the Convention summoned Thérèse Lavasseur and paid homage to her in full session prior to voting unanimously, once again, for a report from the Comité d'Instruction on the question of the transfer of Rousseau's ashes from Ermenonville to the Panthéon.[86] This was nine days after the guillotining of Danton and Desmoulins with their leading associates and just three weeks after the guillotining of Hébert and his chief adherents. Very likely, there is some connection between this fresh publicity exercise to promote Rousseau's status and the ending of the de-Christianization campaign along with Robespierre's effort to promote deism and the cult of the Supreme Being. But for whatever reason, perhaps because Robespierre was still very much in two minds about the whole concept of the Panthéon, no report materialized as yet and no action was taken with respect to panthéonizing either Rousseau or Marat prior to Thermidor.

The situation changed in this as in so many other respects following Robespierre's downfall. The Thermidorians needed to boost their revolutionary legitimacy and in early September 1794 the mechanism for Rousseau's panthéonization was re-activated. On 9 September, it was decided to raise Thérèse's pension by another 300 livres.[87] When finally Joseph Lakanal did produce the *Comité*'s report recommending panthéonization, it was agreed to proceed and prepare a major public fête and ceremony to take place on 20 Vendémiaire (11 October 1794), three weeks after Marat's entombment. At this point there was some question in the Convention whether the Republic had yet done enough for Thérèse who was venerated not just as the great Rousseau's widow but as in some sense the guardian of his manuscripts and literary legacy, the living symbol of his thought. She was honored yet again, appearing before the assembly on 26 September to present the manuscript of Rousseau's *Confessions* to the Convention.[88] Ginguené was sent by the Convention to Ermenonville to supervise the exhumation. Finally, on 11 October, the transfer of Rousseau's remains to the Panthéon was finally effected amid public eulogies and hymns celebrating humanity's foremost prophet of "equality."

[86] Trousson, *Jean-Jacques Rousseau*, p. 754.
[87] Müller, "Marie-Therèse Lavasseur," p. 542; Israel, *Revolutionary Ideas*, pp. 597–598.
[88] Trousson, *Jean-Jacques Rousseau*, p. 755; R. Wokler, *Rousseau, the Age of Enlightenment and Their Legacies* (Princeton: Princeton University Press, 2012), p. 136.

Although there are several important points, notably the importance of d'Holbach's "republicanism" and theory of "general will" where I decidedly agree with Mark Hulliung – against the mainstream of Enlightenment historiography which has tended to overlook these features – I do not subscribe to his innovative and important yet, I believe mistaken, conclusion that the "closer the *philosophes* moved to the ground long held by Rousseau, the more sharply drawn were the lines of battle, the less feasible was a reconciliation; the more public and celebrated was their conflict."[89] For, on the contrary, as Hulliung himself concedes in the case of the "general will," in reality the core political concepts of republicanism, general will and "rights" only drove Rousseau and d'Holbach (together with Diderot) apart. Rousseau's essential ideas, undeniably fundamental for Robespierre and the Montagne though they were, were really quite alien to the democratic republicanism based on Radical Enlightenment notions of reason, universalism, and the *Rights of Man*, infusing the democratic republican Revolution' of 1789–93, the *Declaration of the Rights of Man*, and the world's first democratic constitution.

If this is accepted, it means that there is a pressing need to re-evaluate the collective role of Diderot, d'Holbach, Helvétius, and Raynal in the Revolution and analyze their fundamental contribution more fully than has been done in the past. Within this context the particular role of d'Holbach seems likely to emerge as appreciably more important than has been supposed.

[89] Hulliung, *Autocritique*, p. III.

CHAPTER 9

Rousseau and Diderot

Joanna Stalnaker

Jean-Jacques Rousseau and Denis Diderot were born within one year of each other, in 1712 and 1713 respectively, and died within six years of each other, in 1778 and 1784. They became close friends in their thirties shortly after Rousseau arrived in Paris. During the early years of fusion and heady philosophical exchange, they collaborated on the *Encyclopedia*, planned a literary journal in imitation of Joseph Addison's *Spectator* to be called *Le Persifleur*, and debated how Rousseau should respond to the Académie de Dijon's question about the moral effect of the arts and sciences. But by the end of their lives, they had been separated by a bitter quarrel, equal parts personal and philosophical, and had exchanged mutual attacks in their published and unpublished writings.[1] Diderot was foremost among the "modern philosophers" Rousseau excoriated in his late autobiographical writings – the materialists he accused of co-opting the name of nature for their own purposes and reducing man to a mere machine. For Diderot, Rousseau was a brilliant sophist, an orator duped by his own eloquence, not a philosopher who could be counted on in the quest for truth.[2]

Recent scholarship has magnified the divide between Diderot's radical materialism and Rousseau's sentimental philosophy of man. Jonathan Israel's interpretation of the Enlightenment starkly opposes radical materialists such as Diderot to figures from the moderate and counter-Enlightenment, who unlike the radicals sought to reconcile philosophical

---

[1] The classic discussion of the quarrel is J. Fabre, "Frères ennemis: Diderot et Jean-Jacques," *Diderot Studies* 3 (1961): pp. 155–213. More recent discussions include Y. Citton, "Retour sur la misérable querelle Rousseau-Diderot: Position, conséquence, spectacle et sphère publique," *Recherches sur Diderot et sur l'Encyclopédie* 36 (2004): http://rde.revues.org/index282.html; E. Gatefin, *Diderot, Sénèque et Jean-Jacques: Un dialogue à trois voix* (Amsterdam: Rodopi, 2007); and E. Russo, "Slander and Glory in the Republic of Letters: Diderot and Seneca Confront Rousseau," *Republics of Letters: A Journal for the Study of Knowledge, Politics, and the Arts* 1:1 (2009): http://rofl.stanford.edu/node/40.

[2] D. Diderot, *Réfutation d'Helvétius, Oeuvres complètes*, eds. H. Dieckmann et al. (Paris: Hermann, 1975-), vol. XXIV, p. 546. Subsequent references to this work will be made parenthetically in the main text.

ideas with existing social structures or to resist the advance of philosophy altogether. Although Rousseau has proved difficult to classify as a radical, moderate, or counter-Enlightenment figure, Israel points to his religious beliefs, his defense of patriarchy, and his sentimentalism as signs of his fundamental divergence from the radical camp.[3] He has even argued that the split between Diderot and Rousseau paved the way for the violent ideological struggle that set the French Revolution on its course to Terror, between those who believed that philosophy should be democracy's ultimate guide and those who favored "uneducated man's unspoiled nature."[4] But I will argue here that at the end of their lives, Rousseau and Diderot converged around a shared philosophical concern, and that this convergence is ultimately more important for understanding their late philosophy than the opposition between radical materialism and senti-mental individualism. At stake for both of them in their late works was the question of how we can gain knowledge of man, and more specifically whether our knowledge of man should come from within or outside the self. These questions went to the heart of the Enlightenment definition of the *philosophe*, according to which "the source of our knowledge is entirely outside of ourselves."[5] Diderot remained a steadfast materialist until his death, and his last project was an encyclopedic survey of the physiological sciences of his time. But he was nonetheless deeply dissatisfied with the account of man he found in the works of his fellow materialists. In his *Réfutation d'Helvétius*, written between 1773 and 1776–77, Diderot aligned himself with Rousseau in refuting Claude-Adrien Helvétius' philosophy of man. As Jean Fabre argued in a classic article published in 1961, Diderot's late work can only be understood "by a perpetual reference, manifest or secret, to that of Rousseau."[6] But according to Fabre, this late dialogue was anything but mutual, for during the same period "Diderot had ceased to exist for Jean-Jacques."[7] I will suggest, on the contrary, that Rousseau's last work, *Reveries of the Solitary Walker*, written between 1776 and his death in

---

[3] In the second volume of his four-volume series on the Enlightenment and the French Revolution, *Enlightenment Contested*, Israel distinguishes between an early, radical Rousseau and a later, counter-Enlightenment Rousseau. In his third volume, *Democratic Enlightenment*, he characterizes Rousseau as a contradictory mixture of radical, moderate, and counter-Enlightenment tendencies. See *Enlightenment Contested: Philosophy, Modernity, and the Emancipation of Man 1670–1752* (Oxford: Oxford University Press, 2006), p. 11; and *Democratic Enlightenment: Philosophy, Revolution, and Human Rights 1750–1790* (Oxford: Oxford University Press, 2011), p. 21.

[4] Israel, *Democratic Enlightenment*, p. 109.

[5] C. du Marsais, *Le Philosophe*, University of Chicago: ARTFL Encyclopédie Project, Winter 2008 ed., gen. ed. R. Morrissey, http://encyclopedie.uchicago.edu/, pp. 177–178.

[6] J. Fabre, "Frères ennemis," p. 203.   [7] Ibid., p. 189.

1778, testifies to a shift in his philosophical thought that brought him back into dialogue with Diderot at the end of his life, despite his sense of isolation and his claim to write for himself alone. Rousseau was no materialist, but he developed in his last work a local, embodied understanding of the self, abandoning his previous attempts to ground universal definitions of man in his personal sentiments. For all their differences, Rousseau and Diderot both came to believe at the end of their lives that the philosophy of their day, including their own, had failed to account adequately for man, and they sought in their late works to address that problem, each in his own way.

***

The issue that would preoccupy Rousseau and Diderot at the end of their lives was already in germ in the definition of the *philosophe*, put forth by César Chéneaux Du Marsais in his 1743 work *Le Philosophe*, and later reformulated in the *Encyclopedia*. After observing that true *philosophes* were "convinced that the source of our knowledge is entirely outside of ourselves," Du Marsais took up the question of what a *philosophe* could know about himself:

> The *philosophe* applies himself to gaining knowledge of the universe and himself; but since the eye cannot see itself, the *philosophe* knows that he cannot know himself perfectly, because he cannot receive external impressions from within himself, and we know nothing if not from such impressions. This thought is in no way distressing to him because he takes himself as he is, and not as it seems to the imagination that he could be.[8]

This passage suggests that the *philosophe* will have difficulty following in the Delphic tradition of self-knowledge evoked in the opening pages of Rousseau's *Discourse on Inequality*. Introspection appears futile since the *philosophe* "cannot receive external impressions from within himself." Given his adherence to sense-based knowledge, he must content himself with an imperfect and partial knowledge of the self. Rousseau may well have had Du Marsais' definition in mind when he opened his *Discourse on Inequality* by skewering his contemporaries for their impoverished knowledge of man. It is significant that Rousseau drew on the authority of the naturalist Georges Louis Leclerc de Buffon to make his point. In keeping with the precepts of *Le Philosophe*, Buffon was an empiricist whose multivolume *Histoire naturelle* focused largely on the world outside the self, from the earth, to quadrupeds, to birds, to minerals. But in his *Histoire naturelle*

---

[8] Du Marsais, *Le Philosophe*, ARTFL, pp. 177–178.

de l'homme, he nonetheless insisted that we must cultivate a *sens intérieur*, or inner sense, to gain knowledge of man. It was this passage that Rousseau quoted in a key footnote appended to the opening sentence of the *Discourse on Inequality*:

> Whatever interest we have in knowing ourselves, I do not know if we do not know better everything that is not ourselves. Granted by Nature with organs destined solely to our survival, we use them only to receive foreign impressions, we seek only to scatter ourselves on the outside, and to exist outside ourselves; too busy multiplying the functions of our senses and increasing the external expanse of our being, rarely do we make use of that inner sense that reduces us to our true dimensions, and that separates from us everything that is not a part of us.[9]

In the passage quoted by Rousseau, Buffon rejected the central precept of *Le Philosophe*, asserting that our knowledge does not come solely from outside the self, and emphasizing the importance of introspection in the knowledge of man. He even implied that engaging in encyclopedic projects like his own threatened man's capacity to perceive the limits of the self and its place in nature – as if the quest for empirical knowledge would necessarily distract the *philosophe* from the more crucial task of looking within. Over the course of his career, Rousseau would build upon this insight, developing a philosophy of man that was grounded less in the anthropological footnotes of the *Discourse on Inequality* than in his inner sense and exploration of himself. He would pursue his inquiry into man's original nature through his depiction of the state of nature – which he acknowledged was quite possibly fictional – and through the autobiographical works that occupied him until his death. What he only acknowledged late in his life, however, was that these two facets of his investigation into man were inextricable from one another.

The deep connections between Rousseau's philosophy of man and his autobiographical works have long been overshadowed, due to our tendency to divide his corpus along various dichotomies: the Enlightenment Rousseau versus the pre-Romantic Rousseau, the philosopher Rousseau versus the writer Rousseau, the communitarian Rousseau versus the individualist Rousseau. This oversight has been exacerbated by the long-standing neglect of the second work in Rousseau's autobiographical triptych, *Rousseau juge de Jean-Jacques* or the *Dialogues*, which he wrote during a period of acute mental anguish between 1772 and 1776. It was in this work of self-justification that Rousseau spelled out the underlying

---

[9] J.-J. Rousseau, *Discours sur l'origine de l'inégalité*, PL III, pp. 195–196.

connections between his vision of natural man and his autobiographical project. In the third dialogue, the Frenchman, who is initially suspicious of Jean-Jacques but ends up defending him after reading his works, offers a succinct account of the vilified author's philosophical system. In doing so, he explains that Jean-Jacques must be a good man, because he took the idyllic vision of nature portrayed in the *Discourse on Inequality* from his own heart: "Where could the painter and apologist of nature, today so disfigured and so slandered, have taken his model, if not from his own heart? He described it as he felt himself to be."[10] The implication is that the *Discourse on Inequality* is not merely conjectural history, but finds an empirical basis in the operations of the inner sense identified by Buffon as essential to self-knowledge. The Frenchman goes on to explain that if Jean-Jacques was able to uncover man's original nature as no other philosopher could do, it was because of his solitary life and habit of introspection: "A retiring and solitary life, a strong taste for reverie and contemplation, the habit of withdrawing into the self and seeking there in the calm of passions those first traits that have disappeared for the multitude, only these things could make him find them again. In a word, it was necessary that a man paint himself to show us primitive man in this way, and if the Author hadn't been just as singular as his books, he never would have written them."[11] Through this third-person account of his philosophical system, Rousseau made it clear that he perceived no split between his philosophical investigation into the state of nature in the *Discourse on Inequality* and his literary exploration of the self in his autobiographical works. In order to pursue the study of man he had first called for in the *Discourse on Inequality*, he had to begin by rejecting the notion that all knowledge comes from outside the self. Only by relying on his inner sense and engaging in introspection could he uncover the original nature of man. Only by engaging in the literary tradition of self-portraiture could he communicate his inner perception of natural man to other men. His philosophical system – based on the principle of man's natural goodness – was thus inseparable from his autobiographical project.[12]

By his own account, Rousseau's philosophical system first came to him as an illumination on his way to visit Diderot at the Vincennes prison in 1749. Both he and Diderot later recounted the exchange they had during that visit. Although their accounts differ in important respects, both agreed

---

[10] Rousseau, *Rousseau juge de Jean Jaques: Dialogues*, PL I, p. 936.   [11] Ibid.
[12] On the natural goodness of man as the central tenet of Rousseau's philosophical system, see A. Melzer, *The Natural Goodness of Man: On the System of Rousseau's Thought* (Chicago: University of Chicago Press, 1990).

that the discussion turned on how Rousseau should respond to the Académie de Dijon's question about the moral effect of the arts and sciences.[13] Diderot later gave Rousseau feedback on an early version of the *Discourse on the Sciences and Arts* and helped him to get it published. In other words, he played a key role in the earliest elaboration of Rousseau's philosophy of man. But by the time Rousseau turned to autobiography, deciding in 1764 to write his *Confessions*, the two men had broken all ties and would have no further contact for the rest of their lives. Not only did Diderot play no role in the elaboration of Rousseau's *Confessions*, he went so far as to vow that his eyes "would never be sullied by the reading of his piece of writing."[14] This did not prevent him from attacking the *Confessions* and its author in his last published work, the *Essai sur les règnes de Claude et de Néron*, the initial version of which appeared shortly after Rousseau's death. Diderot's harsh assessment of the *Confessions* makes it clear that he did not see Rousseau's autobiographical project as part of a broader philosophical inquiry into the nature of man. Rather, he saw it as a grotesque and unethical magnification of the self at the expense of others: "It must be acknowledged that it is crazy, that it is atrocious to sacrifice, in dying, one's friends, one's enemies to provide a procession for one's shade; to sacrifice gratitude, discretion, loyalty, decency, domestic tranquility to the arrogant mania of having oneself talked about in the future; in a word, to want to drag one's entire century into one's tomb, to magnify one's dust."[15] This attack reflected Diderot's fear that in addition to revealing Rousseau's darkest secrets, the *Confessions* would reveal the secrets of his former friends, including Diderot himself. But it also had a curiously Rousseauian ring to it: in effect, Diderot accused his former friend of succumbing to the very *amour propre* Rousseau had assailed as an effect of social corruption in the *Discourse on Inequality*. As Diderot saw it, Rousseau engaged in self-portraiture not to gain a broader knowledge of man, but merely to magnify his already inflated self-image.

Nonetheless, Diderot agreed with his former friend that there was something seriously lacking in his fellow materialists' account of man. According to Fabre, it was during the 1770s, when he was able to devote himself fully to his own philosophical projects after the completion of the *Encyclopedia*, that Diderot began to develop his own philosophy of man

---

[13] It is striking that both Diderot and Rousseau referred to this incident much later in their lives, Rousseau in the *Confessions* and Diderot in the *Réfutation d'Helvétius*. See Rousseau, *Confessions*, in PL I, pp. 350–352; and Diderot, *Réfutation*, pp. 497–498.

[14] Diderot, *Essai sur les règnes de Claude et de Néron*, in *Oeuvres complètes* XXV, p. 120.

[15] Diderot, *Essai*, p. 121.

and, in doing so, returned to Rousseau.[16] In his *Réfutation d'Helvétius*, Diderot reaffirmed his materialist beliefs and accused Rousseau of sophistry. But he nonetheless aligned himself with Rousseau in refuting what he saw as Helvétius' reductive and overly superficial view of man. Diderot expressed two main objections to Helvétius' philosophy of man: first, that he failed to acknowledge the specificity of man with respect to other species, and second that he failed to acknowledge the specificity of each individual with respect to other men. The latter objection brought Diderot into dialogue with one of the driving questions of Rousseau's autobiographical corpus: what role does self-knowledge play in our attempts to gain a broader knowledge of man? In the *Confessions*, Rousseau asserted his fundamental unlikeness from other men, but he also offered his work as a "first article of comparison for the study of man, which is certainly yet to have begun."[17] Whereas Helvétius, in Diderot's reading, naively offered his own self-portrait as a portrait of man, Rousseau posed the intractable question of how an idiosyncratic self-portrait could contribute to a general philosophy of man.

According to Fabre, Diderot was bitterly disappointed by Helvétius' posthumously published *De l'homme* because he felt that "no man worthy of that name could recognize his humanity in it."[18] In his effort to pinpoint the deficiencies of the work, Diderot aligned himself with Rousseau. The commentary in question specifically concerns the sixth book of *De l'homme*, in which Helvétius offers a materialist explanation of man's propensity to compare ideas:

> Here is a conclusion that is quite far-fetched. It is more suited to animals in general than to man. To move abruptly from physical sensitivity – that is to say the fact that I am not a plant, a stone, a metal – to the love of happiness, from the love of happiness to self-interest, from self-interest to attention, from attention to the comparison of ideas. I cannot put up with such generalities. I am a man, and I need causes that are proper to man. The author adds that in going back up two steps, or in going down two steps further, he moved from physical sensitivity to organization, from organization to existence, and that he said, I exist, I exist in this form, I feel, I judge, I want to be happy, because I sense; it is in my interest to compare my ideas, because I want to be happy. What utility will I draw from this string of consequences that are equally suited to the dog, the weasel, the oyster, the dromedary. If Jean-Jacques denies this syllogism, he is wrong. If he finds it frivolous, he could well be right. (p. 523)

---

[16] Fabre, "Frères ennemis," pp. 203, 213.   [17] Rousseau, *Confessions*, p. 3.

[18] Fabre, "Frères ennemis," p. 204.

The conclusion to this passage underscores the uneasiness of Diderot's philosophical position. On the one hand, he wanted to defend Helvétius' materialist logic in the hopes of building a philosophy of man on its basis. On the other hand, he was dissatisfied with the conclusions Helvétius drew on the basis of that logic. He thus attempted to take something from each writer, favoring the principles of Helvétius and the conclusions of Rousseau: "The big difference between you and Rousseau is that the principles of Rousseau are false and his conclusions true; whereas your principles are true and your conclusions false" (p. 546). It seems that for Diderot to develop a satisfying philosophy of man, some sort of synthesis between Helvétius and Rousseau was needed.[19]

Yet the challenge of achieving such a synthesis is indicated by Diderot's exclamation of humanity – "I am a man, and I need causes proper to man." This suggests that it was Diderot's own experience of being a man that allowed him to perceive the shortcomings of Helvétius' philosophy. Why then did Helvétius not see them himself? Was he like Buffon's distracted empiricist, too caught up in observing the outside world to look within? Or did he believe with Du Marsais that the *philosophe*'s self-knowledge must be limited to what he could glean from external sense impressions? In either case, the picture of Helvétius that emerges from Diderot's reading of *De l'homme* is of a man curiously lacking in self-knowledge and even interiority. In fact, Diderot's reading of Helvétius is not so far from Rousseau's damning portrait of the materialists in the *Reveries*, when he describes himself as inhabiting a world populated by machine-like beings whose inner life is either inaccessible to him or simply nonexistent:

> When, after having searched in vain for a man for ten years, I finally had to extinguish my lantern and cry out to myself, there are no more. Then I started to see myself alone on the earth and I understood that my contemporaries were nothing in relation to me but mechanical beings who acted only by impulse and whose actions I could calculate only by the laws of movement. Whatever intentions, whatever passions I could have supposed in their souls, these never would have explained their conduct toward me in a manner that I could understand. It is thus that their inner dispositions ceased to be anything to me. I no longer saw anything in them but masses transformed in various ways, lacking any morality in relation to me.[20]

---

[19] Fabre, "Frères ennemis," p. 206.
[20] Rousseau, *Rêveries du promeneur solitaire*, PL I, p. 1078. Subsequent references to this work will be made parenthetically in the main text.

Rousseau's ironic depiction of the materialists is best understood in light of Du Marsais' precept that the *philosophe* cannot gain knowledge of his inner self because all knowledge must come from external sense impressions. After years of following Diogenes' search for a man, Rousseau has finally given up his quest. If he is alone in the *Reveries*, it is because he has finally come to view his fellow men as *Le Philosophe* requires them to view themselves: solely on the basis of external impressions. He no longer seeks to draw any analogy between his inner self and those of other men. And this in turn makes it impossible for him to develop a general philosophy of man on the basis of his introspective inquiry, as he had long sought to do.

Diderot, as we have seen, rejected Rousseau's autobiographical project as a monstrous act of self-aggrandizement. But self-portraiture was in fact central to the *Réfutation d'Helvétius*, both as an object of criticism and as a personal practice. On the one hand, Diderot's most damning criticism of Helvétius was that he failed to realize that *De l'homme* was actually a self-portrait masquerading as a portrait of man. If Helvétius claimed that the quest for sensual pleasure was one of man's primary motives, it was simply because his "ribbon" – the thing he desired most of all – was women: "The ribbon, the ribbon; I want the ribbon. Here is the story of nineteen out of twenty men; and, thinking you were writing the story of the human race, you have only written your own; and because women were your ribbon, you supposed that they were the ribbon of everyone else" (p. 535). The problem, as Diderot saw it, was not so much that Helvétius had written a self-portrait. It was that he had overlooked the philosophical question underpinning Rousseau's entire autobiographical project: what implications did one man's self-portrait have for our understanding of human nature in general? But on the other hand, in highlighting the shortcomings of Helvétius' portrait of man, Diderot did not hesitate to draw on personal anecdotes and experiences. On the question of genius, for example, he set Helvétius' lack of genius in opposition to his own occasional forays into the land of genius:

> If we were not to mince words, the system of Helvetius is that of a man of great intelligence who demonstrates with each sentence that the tyrannical impulsion of genius is unknown to him and who speaks of it like a blind person of colors. Perhaps I am myself in the same situation. There will nonetheless be this difference between us, that everything he does is due to meditation and hard work. [...] He guesses many things about the land he speaks of, but I who have walked through it, I see that he never set foot there. (pp. 583–584)

This passage is especially revealing not just for what it says about Diderot's judgment of Helvétius, but for what it says about his self-perception as a *philosophe* and writer. As Roland Desné has observed, Diderot frequently engaged in self-portraiture in the *Réfutation*.[21] At another especially self-reflective moment, he offered his rueful reflections on the role that chance and necessity played in shaping his career as a writer:

> Chance and even more than that the necessities of life dispose of us according to their fancy; who knows it better than me. It is the reason that for about thirty years in a row, contrary to my preference, I did the *Encyclopedia* and I did only two plays. It is the reason that talents are displaced and that the professions are filled with unhappy men and mediocre subjects, and that he who would have been a great artist is nothing but a poor *sorboniste* or a dull jurisconsult. And here is the true story of life, and not all these sophistical suppositions where I notice a lot of wisdom, without any truth; charming details, and absurd conclusions: and always the portrait of the author offered as the portrait of man. (pp. 540–541)

In response to Helvétius' optimistic claim that education is all that is required to attain genius, Diderot offered his own personal experience as proof that the most fertile minds could be distracted from their vocation by the material circumstances of life. Crucially, this meant that one should not judge men's capacity for genius solely on the basis of the works they produced. The genius of some men would forever remain enclosed within their inner selves: "How many men have died, and how many other will die without having shown what they were. I would readily compare them to superb paintings hidden in a dark gallery, where the sun will never enter, and where they are destined to perish without having been seen or admired" (p. 499). If Diderot found Helvétius' account of man so unsatisfying, it was both because it was too particular in its account of human motives – in the end, it was simply a self-portrait of the author – and because it was too general in its disregard for the individual circumstances of each man's life. What was missing from Helvétius' philosophy, in Diderot's view, was any serious consideration of how one man's interiority could be linked to the broader nature of man – in other words, precisely the question Rousseau raised in his autobiographical works.

---

[21] In his introduction to the *Réfutation*, Desné characterizes the autobiographical dimension of the work as follows: "En réponse à Helvétius qui recourt à l'abstraction d'‘un homme communément bien organisé' et qui considère le comportement humain d'un point de vue global, Diderot, plus attentif à la diversité concrète des individus, peut opposer aux ‘généralités' de *L'Homme* sa propre singularité. De là, de nombreuses références à sa propre expérience qui sont autant de notations ou de souvenirs autobiographiques." See Diderot, *Réfutation*, p. 437.

In the eighth promenade, Rousseau characterized the machine-like men surrounding him as lacking not just interiority, but also any sense of the moral significance of human life. Here too, we find a surprising convergence between Diderot and Rousseau in their late years. Although Diderot's commitment to materialism was unwavering in the last decades of his life, he did share Rousseau's preoccupation with the potentially immoral, or amoral, implications of materialist philosophy. In one especially evocative passage, Diderot accused the materialist Helvétius of reducing all human motivations to the desire to ejaculate in the morning and to defecate in the evening:

> I beg the reader's forgiveness; I am going to say something filthy, something dirty, of the worst tone, in very bad taste, words from the market; but more decisive than a thousand arguments. Well, Mr. Helvetius, all the projects of a great king, all the efforts of a great minister or of a great magistrate, all the meditations of a politician, of a man of genius, are thus to be reduced to ejaculating a good shot in the morning and making a stool in the evening. And you call that moralizing and knowing man. (p. 529)

The problem with Helvétius' philosophy was not just that it was frivolous, when compared to that of Rousseau, or that it offered a self-portrait in place of a portrait of man. The problem, above all, was that it stripped human life of all moral significance. In the end, Helvétius was not so different from Rameau's cynical nephew, who found no greater meaning or end in human life than the production of shit: "The important point is to go easily, freely, copiously, every evening to the toilet; *o stercus pretiosum!* here is the grand result of life in all stations."[22] Taken together, the *Réfutation d'Helvétius* and *Rameau's Nephew* make it clear that Diderot had serious doubts about the potentially cynical moral percussions of materialist philosophy.[23] At the end of his life, he longed to reconcile Helvétius and Rousseau, to develop a philosophy of man that acknowledged man's material nature, while also doing justice to his rich inner life and his sense of moral purpose.

***

It was precisely this kind of synthesis between man's material, corporeal nature on the one hand and the moral significance of his life on the other that Rousseau sought for the first time to achieve in his *Reveries of the*

---

[22] Diderot, *Le Neveu de Rameau, Oeuvres complètes* XII, p. 96.
[23] For a perceptive reading of *Le Neveu de Rameau* along these lines, see L. Shea, *The Cynic Enlightenment: Diogenes in the Salon* (Baltimore: Johns Hopkins University Press, 2009).

Solitary Walker. Rousseau wrote this work in the last two years of his life and claimed to write it for himself alone with no concern for whether it would reach posterity. The work was nonetheless published posthumously in 1782, just two years before Diderot's death and the same year the expanded version of the *Essai sur les règnes de Claude et de Néron* was published. We have no reason to think Diderot ever laid eyes on it, but it is tempting to imagine what he would have thought if he had. In this "appendice de [s]es *Confessions*," Rousseau pursued the autobiographical project Diderot attacked with such vehemence in his *Essai sur les règnes de Claude et de Néron* (p. 1000). But he did so in a way that marked a turning point in his philosophy of man, one that in my view brought him closer to Diderot's materialist account of man than he had ever been before. Just as Diderot turned to Rousseau in his effort to refute Helvétius' materialist philosophy of man, Rousseau turned to Diderot in developing a more local, materially grounded understanding of the self. For the first time, in the *Reveries*, he gave up his longstanding attempt to found a philosophical system on the basis of introspection and self-depiction. Instead, he initiated an empirical inquiry into the self, one that was grounded in the physical experiences of the body. At the same time, he introduced a new way of understanding the moral purpose of human life, one based not in essentialist claims to natural goodness, but in the modest efforts of a solitary man attending to the operations of his body and soul and working toward their improvement on a day-to-day basis. In this way, Rousseau answered Diderot's call for an ethics that acknowledged man's material nature without reducing his rich inner life to purely physical motives in the manner of Helvétius.

To understand Rousseau's project in the *Reveries* one must first consider the meaning of his claim to solitude. On one level, this claim was the logical conclusion to his failed quest for a sympathetic reader, as recounted in the postface to the *Dialogues*. Having been frustrated in his repeated attempts to find a reader who could explain the plot against him and acknowledge his essential goodness, Rousseau resolved at the end of the postface to accept his fate at the hands of his enemies and give up any attempt to salvage his reputation. He signaled the logical connection between his last two works with the word "donc" in the opening sentence of the *Reveries*: "So here I am alone on the earth [*Me voici donc seul sur la terre*], no longer having any brother, kin, friend, society but myself. The most sociable and the most loving of humans has been proscribed from humanity by a unanimous accord" (p. 995). Rousseau's solitude was that of the monster, the social pariah who has been proscribed from humanity by other men. But on another level, his solitude signaled his renunciation of the entire philosophical system he had worked so hard to build. This system, as the Frenchman explained it in the *Dialogues*, was based on an analogy between the (possibly fictional) state of nature as depicted in the *Discourse on Inequality*, and the natural goodness of Rousseau's heart as illustrated in his *Confessions*. The pathos of the *Dialogues* lies just in Rousseau's anguished attempts to prove his innocence in the face of an all-encompassing plot against him, but in his desperate efforts to prove that his own natural goodness had broader implications for human nature in general.

In the *Reveries*, in contrast, Rousseau explicitly rejected the possibility of building a philosophical system on the basis of his introspective inquiry:

> I will perform on myself in a certain sense the operations that physicists perform on air to know its daily state. I will apply the barometer to my soul, and these operations if well conducted and long repeated will be able to provide me with results just as certain as theirs. But I do not extend my endeavor that far. I will content myself with keeping the register of the operations without seeking to reduce them to a system. (p. 1001)

Although the *Reveries* is peppered with ironic references to the scientific spirit of Rousseau's time, we should nonetheless take his claim to engage in an empirical study of his soul seriously. With this claim, he once again rejected Du Marsais' view that the *philosophe* could not gain knowledge of the self through empirical means. But he also pointed to an important shift in his philosophy of man, by underlining the limits of his introspective inquiry. Whereas he had presented his *Confessions* as a "first article of comparison for the study of men, which is certainly yet to have begun," he initiated in the *Reveries* a study of the self in isolation from other men: "I would have loved men in spite of themselves. It was only in ceasing to be men that they could evade my affection. So here they are foreign, unknown, nothing for me after all because they wanted it so. But me, detached from them and from everything, what am I myself? Here is what remains to me to find out (p. 995). In other words, the inquiry Rousseau pursued in the *Reveries* was no longer an inquiry into man, but simply, and more modestly, an inquiry into the self.

The *Reveries* also marked a shift in Rousseau's philosophy of man in its emphasis on the physical presence and materiality of his body. It is significant that the title of the work as a whole refers to *rêveries* whereas the title of each chapter refers to *promenades*, thereby establishing a connection between the operations of Rousseau's soul and the movements of his body. As an old man whose sole remaining task is to learn how to die, Rousseau frequently evokes the departure of his soul from his body and his hope for its continued existence after death. In the first promenade, he characterizes his body as a mere obstacle from which he hopes he will soon be freed: "My body is no longer for me but a burden, an obstacle, and I extricate myself in advance from it as much as I can" (p. 1000). But this view of the body is belied by Rousseau's increasing insistence, as he progresses from walk to walk, and from chapter to chapter, on the constraints his declining body impose on his soul. Already in the second promenade, he suggests that his physical decline is such that it threatens his capacity to engage in reveries. His physical decline may even make it impossible for him to pursue the project he has just outlined in the first promenade:

> I soon sensed that I had put off executing this project for too long. My imagination, already less lively, no longer inflames itself as in the past in the contemplation of the object that animates it, I am less intoxicated by the frenzy of reverie; there is more reminiscence than creation in what it produces now, a tepid languor enervates all my faculties, the life spirit is extinguished in me in stages; my soul no longer projects itself except with difficulty outside its lapsed envelope, and without hope for the state to which I aspire because I feel I have a right to it, I would no longer exist except through memories. (p. 1002)

Reverie is an operation, a movement of the soul that Rousseau wishes to describe. But this movement depends upon the physical movements and sensations of the body, and as he approaches death, he finds himself not gradually freed from the body, as he had hoped, but increasingly trapped within it. Although the passage concludes by evoking the afterlife Rousseau longs for, the negative formulation – "sans l'espérance de l'état auquel j'aspire" – conveys instead a lack of hope. This impression is exacerbated by the following promenade, in which Rousseau describes the genesis of the religious beliefs recorded in his "Profession of Faith of a Savoyard Vicar," the famous chapter from *Émile* that led to the work being banned. In describing his efforts to refute materialist philosophy earlier in his life, Rousseau makes it clear that he fixed his religious beliefs not by resolving all of the doubts provoked by his discussions with the materialists, but by determining what doctrine he needed in order regain his peace of mind. It is striking that Rousseau refers in this chapter to his religious doctrine as a system, just two chapters after rejecting any effort to build a system on the basis of his self-exploration:

> No, vain arguments will never destroy the affinity that I perceive between my immortal nature and the constitution of this world and the physical order that I see reigning in it. I find there in the corresponding moral order and of which the system is the result of my inquiry the support I need to put up with the miseries of my life. In any other system I would live without resources and I would die without hope. I would be the unhappiest of creatures. Let us then stick with the only one that suffices to make me happy in spite of fortune and men. (p. 1019)

The religious system Rousseau developed in writing *Émile*, just like his philosophical system, was based on an analogy between his own nature and the moral and physical order surrounding him. Yet it is precisely this kind of systematic "reduction" on the basis of an analogy between inner self and outer world that Rousseau rejects in the *Reveries*.

The evocation of Rousseau's body becomes especially pronounced in the eighth promenade. Not coincidentally, this is the moment in the genesis of the *Reveries* when Rousseau's rapidly declining health interrupted his writing and threatened to bring his project to a close. This interruption even affected the form in which the work has come down to us, since Rousseau copied the first seven promenades neatly into a notebook, whereas he left the last three in draft form. In the eighth promenade, Rousseau's body – from which he has recently suffered – appears both as an empty shell and as an unbearably heavy collection of organs that drags down his soul and prevents its escape from the material world:

> Reduced to myself alone, I nourish myself it is true with my own substance but it does not use itself up and I suffice to myself even though I ruminate as it were on empty, even though my dried-up imagination and my extinguished ideas no longer provide any nourishment to my heart. My offended soul, obstructed by my organs sags down from day to day and under the weight of these heavy masses no longer has the vigor to throw itself as in the past outside of its old envelope. (p. 1075)

The metaphor of the body as an envelope, which appears here for the second time after being introduced in the second promenade, suggests that the true self lies in the text of a letter that can only be read after tearing the envelope apart and discarding it. But the physical evocation of the body as a collection of organs or heavy masses gives more weight to the envelope than to the letter it contains. This idea is significant for the work as a whole since Rousseau professed a lack of concern for the actual text of the *Reveries* and its posthumous survival:

Whether one spies on what I am doing, worries about these pages, takes possession of them, suppresses them, falsifies them, all of that is equal to me from now on. I neither hide them nor show them. If they are taken away from me during my lifetime, it will not take away from me the pleasure of having written them, nor the memory of their contents, nor the solitary meditations of which they are the fruit and of which the source can only be extinguished with my soul. (p. 1001)

Rousseau suggests here that the meaning of the *Reveries* lies not in the pages themselves, but in the transient, embodied experiences integral to their composition: the pleasure he took in writing them, the memories of their contents, and the solitary meditations that produced them. All these things are preserved within Rousseau's physical self and will die with it.

Yet we can also see in the *Reveries* Rousseau's effort to create a form of writing that reproduces the transience of his bodily experience. The chapters are walks – temporary movements of the body through space – and reveries – a state of the body and soul that appears to lie outside of time but is fleeting at best. At the same time, Rousseau compares the *Reveries* to the herbarium in which he preserves the fragile plant specimens he has collected during those walks:

I will never again see these beautiful landscapes, these forests, these lakes, these groves, these boulders, these mountains of which the aspect has always touched my heart: but now that I can no longer roam these happy lands I can simply open my herbarium and it soon transports me there. The plant fragments that I picked there suffice to remind me of this entire magnificent spectacle. This herbarium is for me a journal of botanical expeditions that allows me to begin them anew with a new charm and produces the effect of an optical device that would paint them once again to my eyes. (p. 1073)

As a collection of plant fragments, the herbarium preserves the physical traces of Rousseau's botanizing, an activity that depends upon the actions of his body: his stooping back leaning over to observe the tiny flowers, and his fingers reaching out to pick them. To read the work as an herbarium is to read it as a record of the experiences of a body that is no longer present. Unlike Rousseau, we cannot use the work as an optical device to reproduce the full experience of walking through nature. Instead, we must accept a form of writing that merely preserves the dead fragments of that experience without allowing us to access it.

***

Diderot's last work, unfinished at his death, was an encyclopedic survey of the physiological sciences of his time, the *Éléments de physiologie*. This work

was a consummate expression of Diderot's materialism, offering a philosophy of man that was grounded in the physiological operations of the
body. But it also contained the richest evocation we have of Diderot's inner
life: of the workings of his brain, of his perceptions of nature and art, and of
his inner experience of memory and the imagination.[24] In some ways, the
Éléments de physiologie is utterly unlike the *Reveries of the Solitary Walker*: it
engages so deeply in dialogue with the writings of Diderot's contemporaries that its status as an original work has been questioned, whereas the
Reveries has been seen as Rousseau's literary masterpiece in large part
because it bears so little resemblance to any work before or since.
The ambitions of the *Éléments de physiologie* are so vast that it has been
called Diderot's "second encyclopedia," whereas the *Reveries* seeks no
readership and aspires, in its form, to the humility and fragility of a mere
herbarium.[25] But in other ways, these works capture the late philosophical
convergence between Diderot and Rousseau that I have argued for in this
essay. Both works give greater place to the physical presence of the author's
body than any of their previous works. Both depict a rich inner life that is
inextricable from the physical movements of the body. And both capture
the fragility of that inner life – and of that body – through a fragmentary
form of writing that belies the overarching system of Rousseau's earlier
thought and the encyclopedic ambitions of Diderot's career. These works
remain as the fragile, fragmentary external traces of an inner life of which
we can only catch partial glimpses, the last, tenuous connection Rousseau
and Diderot sought to establish between themselves and the selves of
other men.

---

[24] For an analysis of the *Éléments* that interprets the form of the work as a means of representing the
inner workings of Diderot's brain, see my "Diderot's Brain," in A. Conway and M.H. McMurran
(eds.), *Philosophical Turns: Eighteenth-Century Literature, Thought, and Aesthetics* (forthcoming).
[25] K. Ballstadt, *Diderot: Natural Philosopher* (Oxford: Voltaire Foundation, 2008), p. 209.

CHAPTER 10

Rousseau and Kant: Rousseau's Kantian Legacy

Susan Shell and Richard Velkley

A Rare Thought and a Hidden Law

Perhaps no one read Rousseau with more admiration and instruction than Immanuel Kant. Even so, he expressed reservations, at least in a provisional way. In a fragment from the 1760s,[1] Kant writes:

> The first impression that an understanding reader, who does not read only out of vanity or in order to pass the time, acquires from the writings of Mr. J. J. Rousseau is that he has encountered an uncommon acuity of mind, a noble impetus of genius and a sensitive soul in such a high degree as has perhaps never before been possessed by a writer of any age or people. The impression that follows next is bewilderment at strange and absurd opinions [*seltsame und wiedersinnische Meinungen*] which oppose what is generally held so much that one could easily form the suspicion that, by means of his extraordinary talents, the author only wanted to prove the magical power of eloquence and play the eccentric [*den Sonderling machen wollen*] who stands out among all rivals in wit because of a disarming novelty. The third thought, to which one comes only with difficulty because it happens only rarely

The fragment breaks off, causing one to wonder how the third thought would restore Rousseau to positive estimation, as no doubt it would, given that it would speak of a rare experience that comes only after a difficult and sustained engagement with the author. One suspects it is a level of philosophic insight that is achieved rarely, and if this is so, one wonders if that level is reached in spite of the absurd novelties of Rousseau's writing,

---

[1] *Bemerkungen zu den 'Beobachtungen über das Gefühl des Schönen und Erhabenen,'* Kants gesammelte Schriften (Berlin: G. Reimer, 1902-), XX, pp. 43–44. Parenthetical references in the text, unless otherwise noted, are to the volume and pages of this edition. See the English translation of the *Bemerkungen* in P. Frierson and P. Guyer (eds.), *Observations of the Feeling of the Beautiful and Sublime and Other Writings* (Cambridge: Cambridge University Press, 2011). M. Rischmüller's definitive scholarly edition of the *Bemerkungen* (Hamburg: F. Meiner Verlag, 1991) should also be consulted.

or rather because of them and through them. The latter more befits the triadic dialectic that Kant's fragment suggests is inherent in reading this author. For Kant does not say "The first impression I acquired" then "The impression I had next" and "The third thought, to which I came . . ." but speaks impersonally of an order of insights that the writings compel "one," an understanding reader, to pass through. But what is the "rare" thought which arrives with such difficulty?

That Kant underwent a philosophic rebirth at about age forty in 1764–65 is widely recognized, and it is generally admitted that Kant's intense reading of Rousseau at this time played an important role in this revolution. It is also known that Kant's contemporary conversations with his student Johann Herder, another enthusiastic reader of Rousseau, were a factor in Kant's attention to Rousseau's works. The *Observations on the Feeling of the Beautiful and Sublime*, published in 1764, already reveals some significant engagement with Rousseau's thought, but the marginal notes Kant made in his copy of the *Observations* known as *Remarks in the 'Observations'* (1764–65) offer clear signs of a deeper investigation of Rousseauian themes and questions, turning above all on the problematic status of nature and reason. It is as if Kant had been set on a certain path by the Swiss thinker and in pressing forward on it had found himself in a tangled thicket of questions. In order to proceed Kant had to reconsider Rousseau's first principles and arguments, which up to this point he had imperfectly mastered. The outcome is Kant's breakthrough in the *Remarks* in understanding the human essence in ideal and rationally legislated terms, a breakthrough ushering him into new territory which in the end is in many ways distant from Rousseau's thought. Kant's declaration of a Rousseau-inspired change of orientation is the best-known passage of the *Remarks*: "I am by inclination a seeker of truth . . . there was a time when I thought that this alone could constitute the honor of mankind, and I despised the rabble. Rousseau set me right [*hat mich zurecht gebracht*]. This blind prejudice vanishes; I learn to respect humans, and I should consider myself far more useless than the common laborer if I did not believe that this consideration could give worth to all others, to establish the rights of man" (20: 44).

Although the *Observations* marks a highpoint in Kant's interest in British common sense philosophers, it is a particularly revealing document on Kant's emerging views on morals and aesthetics and the influence of Rousseau upon them. Like Addison's *Spectator* (which is in many ways its model), *Observations* addresses itself to a general (and largely feminine) audience, and takes up subjects that reappear in Kant's successive treatments of anthropology through the rest of his career. These topics include both the rudiments of what he will later treat under the rubric of empirical psychology, and subjects ranging from basic categories that will inform his later aesthetics to issues of gender, religion, and race. *Observations* can plausibly be read as an experiment along the provisionally "Rousseauist" lines that in Kant's words seeks what "lies in" (rather than what "accords with") nature. As such *Observations* provides clues both to what Kant found unsatisfying in Rousseau on a first and second reading, and to the "rare" thought that Kant claimed to uncover on further reflection. In *Observations* Kant seems still to believe – naively, in retrospect – that nature is directly accessible through observation of the varieties of human taste.

That Kant claims in *Observations* to speak "more as an observer than a philosopher" (2: 207) already places him in an ambiguous position *vis à vis* his earlier claims (in the *Universal Natural History*) as to the supreme value of speculative science. On the one hand, the essay's expressed goals are largely practical and civic: to improve aesthetic taste and help cultivate morality (or a "feeling for the beauty and the dignity of human nature" [2: 217]) in the society around him. He does not address an elite group of actual and potential "scientists," but the general literate public, male and female (or every potential "young world citizen" [2: 256]). At the same time, in treating "finer feeling" and its peculiarly "universal" pleasures, Kant specifically abstracts from the "even finer feeling" that he reserves to the few capable of genuine scientific inquiry [2: 208]. Removing himself from his earlier position without necessarily wholly abandoning it, Kant stands somewhere between his encomium to the poet-scientist, in the *Universal Natural History* (1755), and his decisive elevation, in the *Remarks*, of practical over theoretical ends. In short, *Observations* appears to mark the transition from Kant's earliest opinion of Rousseau, based on a first (and second) reading to the final, more stable and considered view elaborated in the *Remarks*.

The text that has come to be known as the *Remarks* consists of hand-written notes inserted into Kant's own copy of his *Observations*. *Remarks* has a freshness and immediacy that will surprise most readers who are mainly familiar with his later published writings. It addresses topics as diverse as ethics (including an early formulation of the categorical imperative), the moral basis of religion, the relation of the sexes, republicanism, and the negative role of metaphysics (or what he calls "the limits of reason"). It sets out a remarkably coherent philosophic position in its own right while also anticipating many key elements of his later critical philosophy. Why Kant chose to write such extensive and substantive notes into his own copy of the *Observations* is a matter of some speculation. Kant's handwritten comments do not obviously form a continuous argument; they are rich in allusion, sometimes fragmentary, and often elusive as to tone and meaning. One does not always know in whose voice Kant is speaking or on which sources he draws. The notes do not seem to have been made with revision of the *Observations* directly in mind. Few of the notes bear directly on contiguous passages in the printed text. Indeed, the *Observations* were subsequently reprinted several times in Kant's own lifetime essentially unchanged. What cannot be doubted is the deeply searching character of these notes, which sketch out or otherwise anticipate essential elements of Kant's mature theoretical and practical philosophy.

In one of his more famous statements on Rousseau in the *Remarks*, Kant compares Rousseau to "Newton who saw for the very first time order and regularity combined with great simplicity" in the celestial bodies, whereas Rousseau "discovered for the first time, beneath the manifold forms adopted by the human being, the deeply hidden nature of the same and the hidden law according to which providence is justified by his observations" (20: 58–59). What Kant calls the hidden human nature and the hidden law is an insight concerning the source of the greatest evils befalling the human, namely, that these evils are not due to the unchangeable natural order, but to the faulty development of the human powers, for which, in the end, human reason alone is responsible. Human evil is self-inflicted and as such is corrigible. According to Kant, Rousseau discovers a "law," hitherto hidden, of the proper development of reason, according to which the human individual by means of a focus on self-imposed rational order overcomes the alienating power of desires and inclinations that enslave the individual to what is not its true self. Out of this thought Kant eventually develops his account of the moral law and the will's autonomous determination under its guidance. Kant claims that by exposing this principle of human dignity, Rousseau reveals what alone gives philosophy its true worth: to establish the rights of humanity.

Further light is shed on this line of thought by Kant's *Announcement* of lectures for the winter of 1765–66, wherein Hutcheson, Shaftesbury, and Hume are mentioned as guides in ethics and Rousseau is absent by name. Yet the *Announcement* contains a remark that shows that Rousseau is on Kant's mind. Kant says that his method in the study of man [*Mensch*] will distinguish between "the mutable form" shaped by contingencies, which has nearly always been misunderstood by philosophers, and "the unchanging nature of man and his distinctive position within the creation." Kant

adds "my purpose will be to establish which perfection is appropriate to
him in the state of *primitive* innocence and which perfection is appropriate
to him in the state of *wise* innocence." Kant concludes that this "method of
moral investigation is one of the most beautiful discoveries of our time and
was [. . .] wholly unknown to the ancients" (2: 311). This passage points to
Kant's taking his central bearings from Rousseau's "state of nature" understood in a peculiar sense. The state of nature for Kant (following Rousseau)
is not, principally a historical condition, though it may also be this, but
a hypothetical construction, resting on certain grounding insights or
assumptions as to the goodness of nature and the freedom of man.
It means any condition in which free yet mortal, and hence dependent
beings (like us) can coexist harmoniously. On the basis of this construction, which bears certain affinities with Newton's methodological presup-
position of a frictionless universe, the "deeply hidden law" is disclosed as a
"return" to the ideal of this unchanging nature of man (and hence a
condition of "wise innocence"). The state of nature as a condition of
freedom, Kant also says, functions as an "Archimedean point" from
which to "move the emotions" of men.

Rousseau as Critic of the Age and Reformer

The meaning of the rare thought and the hidden law cannot be adequately
addressed without first having a good grasp of Rousseau's philosophical
intentions and arguments. A brief sketch with Kant's reception in view
must be offered here. Kant's debt to Rousseau is usually thought to focus
on the formulation of the *volonté générale* in the *Social Contract* as
a principal source of Kant's idea of autonomy as self-legislation under
the imperative of practical reason. But this narrow focus misses the crucial
dimension of Kant's encounter with questions about nature, reason,
desire, freedom, and history, as Rousseau develops them in the *Social
Contract*, the two *Discourses*, *Julie*, and *Emile*. In this area of questions
Kant finds in Rousseau a formidable challenger of modern conceptions of
progress and Enlightenment, and thus of the dominant modern accounts
of the relations between the rational and scientific improvement of the
species on the one hand, and moral perfection and happiness on the other.
In this regard, one must recall that Rousseau's thought brings to a logical,
or at least radicalizing conclusion the arguments of early modern philosophy about natural rights as grounded in an original presocial condition, the
beginnings of society in contract, and the non-teleological science of
human nature conducted in the style of Hobbes, Locke, and

Montesquieu. Rousseau goes further than his predecessors with his claim that the movement from the presocial to the social entails more fundamental changes in the structure of human thought and desire. That is, he argues that taking wholly seriously the idea of a presocial condition requires the assumption that the original human lacks any actualized rational powers, and hence has neither articulate speech nor social and moral sentiments and passions. Yet this proto-human possesses incipient self-awareness in the form of the "sentiment of existence," and in "perfectibility" it has the latent capacity for the acquisition of rational powers of judgment, comparison, future-oriented calculation, and speech. Rousseau also mentions "the property of being a free agent" as a distinguishing feature of the human and asserts "it is mainly in the consciousness of this freedom that the spirituality of his soul manifests itself." But after referring to "difficulties surrounding all these questions" he adduces perfectibility as a specific human property "about which there can be no argument." Kant in the *Remarks* seems to have fewer hesitations about the reality of free agency, although his distinction between metaphysical and moral senses of freedom probably reflects Rousseau's thought. We shall see, furthermore, that perfectibility plays a major role in the *Remarks* in what Kant calls "freedom."

The core "paradox" of Rousseau's thought centers on his effort to employ his radicalized version of the state of nature as a means to move beyond the utilitarian spirit of modern philosophy which grounds social life in self-interest. On a novel basis, Rousseau seeks to restore certain elements of classical political and philosophical virtue. A key to this project is the indeterminacy of human perfectibility, which for the most part is the source of human inequality, corruption, and misery, since the indeterminate enlargement of thought (the invention of ideas) entails the expansion of desire beyond our limited powers of satisfaction. On this basis, Rousseau argues that the Enlightenment's expectation of universal well-being arising from unlimited progress in the arts and sciences (or "luxury") is a deluded vision, since such progress involves increasing enslavement to artificial desires and passions. Liberation from primary material wants does not entail psychological and moral freedom. On the other hand, Rousseau proposes that the malleability of the human as a thinking and desiring being contains the foundation for the self-correction of its disorders, insofar as it allows one to assume that human nature can be refashioned according to the artifices of legislators and educators. These pedagogic artifices are the foundation of virtue. They employ models of human perfection that dictate the best means of bringing human desire into accord with human power. In devising the model of the socially formed human who retains original naturalness (or freedom from opinion), Rousseau makes use of insights that are available only to a thinker in a highly civilized and corrupted order, as it offers the vantage point for observing the psychological phenomena of self-enslavement, above all entrapment in the snares of *amour-propre*. At the same time, Rousseau expresses doubts about the general efficacy of such reforms and is less hopeful than many of his followers about the improvement of civilization through philosophically inspired legislation.

Reason's Self-Correction and Freedom

Kant's more hopeful account of human prospects starts from Rousseau's critique of modern accounts of reason, nature, and society. It is seldom noticed that Rousseau's historical conception of human powers is central to this appropriation. Rousseau's radical questioning of whether reason has a natural end and destination beyond the original condition of simplicity, and whether inclination and passion can give salutary ends to reason in an instrumental role, points Kant toward the reflection that reason needs to give itself ends and to regulate itself apart from natural desire. Certainly, Rousseau does not propose a "pure" or "noumenal" account of reason as lawgiver, capable of determining itself without regard for inclination, in the mode of the mature Kant. Accordingly, he does not argue for the superiority of moral willing over the pleasures of solitary reflection or happiness based on contemplation, which he acknowledges to be unavailable to most human beings. At the time of the *Remarks* Kant is himself not ready to take the leap into the pure morality of unconditioned imperatives, although the first steps on the path to that terminus appear at this time. But if Rousseau offers no theory of pure or noumenal willing, what does he adduce that is so provocative for Kant?

In the first place, Rousseau makes Kant aware of an unprecedented crisis in the intellectual and moral life of modern Europe. This is central to Rousseau's historical account of the human, which does not see this crisis as due to historically necessary processes, but rather as a consequence of the malleable and expansive human faculties that develop without plan, partly in response to circumstances and partly spontaneously. As a result, human life is burdened by luxury, vanity, and factitious desires. The *Remarks* makes many references to the crisis as one in which the natural human good is effaced, while at the same time the crisis offers an unprecedented opportunity to place human affairs on a new foundation. Thus Kant writes of the "hard to apply principle" that something "does not lie or does lie in nature," which Rousseau follows because "human reason has taken on such wasted form that the natural foundations have become doubtful and unrecognizable" (20: 47.13–48.7). Similarly, Kant observes that "in the social condition so many unnatural desires come forward, and thereby the provocation to virtue and the sciences arises." This contrasts with the natural condition in which virtue and science are unnecessary (20: 11.9–13). "Virtue becomes ever more necessary and also impossible in our present regime" (20: 98.9–10). And further: "When man strives against the niche [*Zuschnitt*] of the order which nature assigned to him, so will he disturb the beautiful order of nature and spread corruption to himself and others . . . he has stepped outside the circle of humanity and become nothing, creating a void that spreads its corruption to the adjacent parts" (20: 41.21–30). Such striving is a general feature of modern society. Rousseau's educational efforts try to address the problem of the loss of simplicity and freedom that progress entails and to "restore the flower of society" (20: 175.5–12) or in other terms to educate a free human being (20: 167.3–4). The historical account thus places human freedom at the center of human misery and well-being, since both the growth of unnecessary desires and the attainment of virtue rest on the power of the human to give itself ends other than immediately given natural ones. Thus Kant writes of "freedom, in the genuine sense (moral and not metaphysical) is the highest principle of all virtue and also of all happiness." And he meditates: "Everything goes past in flux; the changing tastes, the diverse forms of humanity make the whole play of things uncertain and deceptive. Where can I find the firm point of nature that man cannot overthrow and that can offer him the markers on the shore that will sustain him?" He raises a related question, echoing the Cartesian search for the Archimedean point, and then answers it: "The question is whether I shall find the fulcrum point outside this world, in order to set the affects in motion, I answer: I find it in the state of nature, that is, of freedom" (20: 31.10–12, 20: 46.11–15, 20: 56.3–5).

Kant's account of the human, as historically malleable yet finding a firm principle in freedom, is directly linked to the conception of the moral order as an "ideal" that is the free projection of human reason. Kant writes that the beast is below the nature of man and the luxurious life transgresses the limits of nature, but also the morally constructed human (*der moralisch gekunstelte*) goes beyond nature (20: 60.1–3). Human rationality by an inherent tendency departs from the natural, and the dangerous longings that result can be corrected only by an opposing principle, also grounded in reason and lying beyond nature. In this self-correction of reason moral education makes use of a negative rule or idea, rather than a teleological notion of perfection, one of moving out of the condition of luxury and back to the natural. But as Kant notes, "if one assesses the happiness of the primitive man it is not in order to return to the forests but it is in order to see what one has lost and at the same time gained" through the progress of the faculties (20: 31.13–24). Rousseau's counsel that original acquisition of the troublesome passions must be avoided as much as possible through sound educational procedure, and that the educator's task is not to overcome presupposed passions, is endorsed by Kant (20: 17.27–30; 20: 39.11–16) although he admits having doubts about the practicality of the radical project of *Emile*, Rousseau's treatise on education. Kant writes that the first impression given by Rousseau's writings is of "an uncommon acuity of mind, a noble flight of genius and a sensitive soul on such a high level as perhaps has never" been found in an author of any age. But the impression that follows is "alienation over strange and nonsensical opinions" (20: 43.13–22). Kant in particular wishes that Rousseau would show how Emile's education can be made practical for instruction in the schools (20: 29.4–16). In sum the educational ideal that moves Kant is Rousseau's goal of preventing the acquisition of what is unnatural and to allow only original simplicity to flourish. "Virtue consists not in overpowering acquired inclinations in particular cases but in learning to dispense with such inclinations and seeking to be free of them" (20: 77.24–78.3). The idea of natural simplicity or of the state of nature, used rationally as corrective to social corruption, or better, as preventive rule for education, is not a return to the primitive but rather the "wise innocence" of which Kant writes in the *Announcement* (20: 77.13–19; also 20: 77.6–12 on Socrates, and 20: 30.16–19). Kant clearly is moved by Rousseau's central project of *constructing* naturalness on the social-rational level, where naturalness means an accord of human ends or desires with human powers. And he grasps that this project is different from two other possible projects, each of which has often been understood as Rousseau's true project: the *return* to original simplicity (self-unity) and the *expression* of a presumed naturalness ("sentiment") available to humans in the present era.

Although Kant criticizes Rousseau's program as too radical to be practical, all the same he finds it to rest on an insight of first importance: that an unchangeable natural order is not the source of the greatest human evils, for these are due rather to the faulty development of human powers for which human reason alone is responsible in the end. Human evil is self-inflicted (20: 45.6–8, 20: 68.17–22). Reason's self-inflicted disorder has overwhelmed the good immediate natural inclinations and feelings, and thus these cannot be the ground for moral judgment and virtue, as Kant was still assuming in 1762 before the *Remarks*. The force of the immediate natural inclinations does not extend beyond a condition of freedom and equality, which condition is no longer available. Rousseau seeks the reconstruction of original nature but he recognized that it could not be attained by an appeal to feeling or passion alone. But in the realm of construction Kant already sees a difference between his approach and Rousseau's. Kant describes Rousseau's procedure as "synthetic" insofar as Rousseau tries to bring the natural condition as an external standard into relation with the corrupted human condition. "Rousseau. Proceeds synthetically and begins with the natural man and I proceed analytically and begin with the morally formed [*gesitteten*]" (20: 14.5–6). Kant's analytic procedure assumes that consciousness of freedom and of the will's power to be virtuous is currently available to humans and contains the standard, even for corrupted beings, of the rectification of rationally inflicted evils. In his view, human beings do not have to be constructed from the ground up by an all-seeing tutor, as in *Emile*, since human reason inherently possesses an idea of dignity grounded in self-rule – an immediate sense of justice – adherence to which leads to the search for freedom from acquired inclinations and as well as for recognition of one's power of self-rule by other humans (20: 88.3–12). The individual has an immediate awareness of the injustice of servitude, whether that be servitude to luxurious wants (internal "injustices" of reason) or to the tyrannical passions of others (arising only in beings with reason) who desire to appropriate the individual's power of will (20: 65.21–67.4). Servitude to another will contradicts the uniquely human sense, inherent in the consciousness of existing, that the thinking subject (or "I") possesses a will as the ground of a completeness of being lacking in other animals (20: 93.14–25).

Rousseau's educational plan calls for the creation of an individual whose self-sufficiency is grounded in an active principle built upon the "preventive" habits assuring indifference to opinion. Pride in benevolent activity sustains the moral life as keeping a precarious distance from the ordinary motives of human praise and blame. Rousseau writes of a morality of generalized pity, extended to the whole of mankind, in which acts of beneficence give rise to "inner enjoyment."[2] This phase of Emile's moral education is the non-philosophic version of moral freedom, "obedience to the law one has prescribed to oneself," which famously the *Social Contract* calls the highest form of freedom (above natural and civil), although its

---

[2] Rousseau, *Emile*, PL IV, pp. 547–548, 520.

nature is not elaborated there. Kant comes forward with a related proposal in the sense of an active self as the true source of moral feeling (20: 145.6–8). This is an early suggestion of "moral feeling" as a non-empirical feeling. Activity of the self offers a basis for a universally effective morality not provided by sympathy, for "sympathy is an instinct that is effective only on rare and very important occasions" (20: 145.14–15). At the same time freedom as supplying a universal principle (20: 145.21–23) also grounds a state of perfection independent of empirical satisfactions, "the greatest inner perfection arising from the subordination of all our powers and receptivities under a free will" (20: 145.16–18). As Paul Guyer has noted, Kant adumbrates in the *Remarks* a conception of human freedom or spontaneity as an absolute ground of worth directly allied to the basis of morality in reason's legislating for itself a non-contradictory rule.[3] Most of the elements of Kant's mature account of autonomy are thus present, but their internal connections are only suggested at this time.

Rousseau, Kant, and the Relation Between the Sexes

Rousseau's treatment of the relation of the sexes was a primary driver in Kant's turn, in the early 1760's, from a "speculative" to a "moral" understanding of the "intelligible world" and accompanying reevaluation of the "end" of human reason, as documented in the famous confessional note in his *Remarks* (20: 44–45). If Rousseau is now the "Newton" of the "moral world" (20: 58–59), it is no small part because the drive to unity (abetted by the force of sexual desire) and that toward independence (abetted by that of the natural desire for freedom) mirrors the relation between Newtonian attraction and repulsion:

> The drive of honor is grounded on the drive for equality and the drive for unity. Two powers that move the animal world, as it were. The instinct for unity is either unity in judgments and thoughts or also in inclinations. The former brings about logical perfection, the latter moral one.
>
> The only naturally necessary good of a human being in relation to the will of others is equality (freedom) and, with respect to the whole, unity. Analogy: repulsion, through which the body fills its own space just as everyone [fills] his own. Attraction, through which all parts combine into one [. . ..] The natural instincts of active benevolence towards others consist

---

[3] P. Guyer, "Freedom as the Foundation of Morality: Kant's Early Efforts," in *Kant's 'Observations' and 'Remarks': A Critical Guide*, eds. S. Shell and R. Velkley (Cambridge: Cambridge University Press, 2012), pp. 77–98.

in love toward the [other] sex and towards children. That toward other human beings merely concerns equality and unity. (20: 165–166)

Love of women, aided by her "refusal," and related propensity to appear better than she is, is here the stepping stone to morality proper. A clue to the transformative insight prompted by Kant's reading of Rousseau lies in the following passage, from Book Five of *Emile*, which lays out, through the "history" of Emile and Sophie's courtship, a template, as it were, for the various "cosmopolitan histories" Kant would sketch in the coming decades.

> If I enter here into the perhaps too naïve and too simple history of their innocent love, people will regard these details as a frivolous game, but they will be wrong. They do not sufficiently consider the influence which a man's first liaison with a woman ought to have on the course of both their lives [. . . .] We are given treatises on education consisting of [. . .] bloated verbiage about the chimerical duties of children, but we are not told a word about the most important and most difficult part of the whole of education – the crisis that serves as a passage from childhood to man's estate. If I have been able to make these essays useful in some respect, it is especially by having expanded at great length on this essential part, omitted by all others [. . .]. If I have said what must be done, I have said what I ought to have said. It makes very little difference to me if I have written a romance. A fair romance it is indeed, the romance of human nature. If it is to be found only in this writing is this my fault? This ought to be the history of my species.[4]

Rousseau's ideal history, rewritten as a romance, is usefully compared with the dystopian analysis presented in the *Second Discourse*, which describes both the "golden age" at which man should have remained, and the fatal steps that brought about our downfall.[5] In each of these pivotal moments – both the fragile point of equilibrium between human freedom and equality, on the one hand, and the full development of all our faculties, including both reason and *amour-propre* – and the blind progression toward mutual enslavement that subsequently followed – are deeply marked by the relations between the sexes. In the former case, an incipient condition of sexual rivalry makes possible the emergence of "the sweetest sentiments known to man" – namely filial and romantic love – without yet compromising men's (though not women's) economic independence. Still self-reliant with regard to what they need, men can enjoy the ideal pleasures associated with self-display without relinquishing their natural freedom. In the latter case, human progression toward ever greater mutual

---

[4] PL IV, pp. 777–778.   [5] PL III, pp. 168–169.

enslavement is mediated and abetted by the coquetry of women, who manipulate the free-floating reason and imagination of men in ways that are increasingly destructive to both. The "romance of Emile and Sophie" that ought, as Rousseau puts it, be the history of our species, is presented as the remedy, at least in principle, offering an example for how, through the proper intellectual and moral education of both sexes, the full development of human faculties might be achieved without sacrificing human freedom.

Whether or not Rousseau ever seriously intended his "romance" to serve as a practical guide in other than isolated and sporadic ways, Kant seems to have taken it to heart as a model for general reform, lamenting, in the *Remarks*, that Rousseau had not shown how from *Emile* there might spring forth schools (20: 29).

Kant's hopes for, and consequent reliance on, the reeducation of men and women as key to the moral transformation of the species and related fulfillment of our cosmopolitan destiny reached its apogee in the decade following his early reading of Rousseau (or from the mid-1760's to the mid-1770's) – a period coinciding both with his absorption with the subject of "anthropology" and increasing frustration in his attempts to bring his long promised "critique of reason" to completion (the *Critique of Pure Reason* was published in 1781).

The *Friedländer* Lectures on Anthropology (1776), for example, present a proper understanding of feminine perfection (along Rousseauist lines) as key to the project of a philosophically chastened "idealism" capable of overcoming the gap between man's "animal" and "rational" perfection, a gap that lies at the source (as Rousseau showed) of the main ills of civilization. Kant's three examples of idealism gone awry – misology, misanthropy, and misogyny – share both a common root, and a common cure:

> Misology is a property of reflective [*nachdenkender*] people, who undertake investigations into their future vocation [*Bestimmung*] and chief ends, investigations that culminate in this, that the human being has insight into his ignorance [*Unwißenheit*]. Now if reason cannot do enough with regard to knowledge [*Wissen*], if it cannot satisfy one in this ... so that the human being cannot look toward the goal and end of all things [*das Ziel und Ende aller Dinge nicht absieht*],[6] the human being betakes himself to simple-mindedness and renounces reason entirely, in the same way that someone becomes a misanthrope through the feeling of virtue – not because he hates human beings, but because he doesn't find them as he wishes them to be

---

[6] Cf. Kant's later essay entitled *The End of All Things* (1794) (8: 325–340).

[. . ..] Accordingly] one does not become a misologist out of hatred of reason; indeed one esteems it, but because it gives poor service. One who has become accustomed to using reason [*die Vernunft zubrauchen*], one who has a propensity [*Hang*] thereto, [. . ..] thinks for the entire rest of his life [. . ..] Misogyny, or hatred of women, occurs in the same way. It also arises from an ill humor [*Laune*], not because one despises them, but because one does not find in them what one believes, thus from an entirely too great a demand for their perfections. (25.1: 553)

Following Rousseau, Kant argues that female nature can only be fully observed under conditions of refinement, in which certain dispositions of her nature compensating for her weakness have been able to develop (25.1: 700). Among these is a natural artfulness in ruling men without (external) compulsion.

The greatest union of society and the most perfect state of society must happen without compulsion. This, however, only occurs through inclination, and hence through women [. . ..] True, by means of compulsion the civil order produces a civil society, yet a perfect inner unity should be established, and to this inner union, which happens without constraint, woman contributes everything [*trägt das Frauenzimmer alles bei*]. (25.1: 701)

In the perfected domestic union at which "nature aims," the woman dominates [*herren*] through inclination, while the man rules [*regieren*] through understanding, the one according to mood [*Laune*], the other in accordance with law [*Gesetz*] (25.1: 717–18).[7] Without such moving forces of "action and reaction," human beings would "fuse together" into "lifeless" inactivity and quiet (25.1: 719). That women are not capable of "principles," but aim only to maintain the household, is thus no matter for reproach (25.1: 720). And it may help counter a certain rule-bound "pedantry," in matters of domestic economy, to which men especially are susceptible (25.1: 469, 338, 635).

In short, according to the schema set out in the Friedländer Lectures, natural misanthropy, misogyny, and misology (the three perversions of "reflection" that Kant had earlier specifically compared) are to be resolved by related pedagogical means, making possible a "world history" or "history of the human race" that gives reason's demand to know "the end of things" an at least pragmatic sort of satisfaction.

In the event, Kant's confidence in the sufficiency of pragmatic anthropology to determine the limits of human nature proved short-lived.

---

[7] For Rousseau by way of contrast, wives are the "ministers," husbands the "monarchs" (cf., for example, *Emile*, PL IV, p. 766).

The 1777–78 Pillau Lectures on Anthropology now describe the very "concept of human nature" as a "problem" with "many difficulties" (25.2: 839). Nature and freedom now stand in opposition without apparent means of reconciliation (25.2: 733). And history no longer culminates in a potential "paradise on earth," but remains open-ended, with a new emphasis on the role of invention and discovery (almost entirely eclipsing the relation of the sexes, his discussion of which is now perfunctory), from agriculture and writing to Rousseau's "essay on inequality."

Despite its increasing distance from the center of his philosophic thought, the relation between the sexes viewed through the prism of Rousseau never ceased to play a crucial role in Kant's understanding of civil and moral education. In the *Conjectural Beginning of Human History* (1786), he calls woman's sexual refusal "the first artifice" that leads "from merely sensed stimulus over to ideal ones," and hence to that "propriety" which serves as "the foundation" of "true sociability":

> *Refusal* was the first artifice for leading from the merely sensed stimulus to ideal ones, from merely animal desire gradually over to love, and with the latter from the feeling of the merely agreeable over to the taste for beauty, in the beginning only in human beings but then, however, also in nature. Moreover, *propriety* [*Sittsamkeit*], an inclination by good conduct [*guten Anstand*] to influence others to respect for us (through the concealment of that which could incite low esteem), as the genuine foundation of all true sociability, gave the first hint toward the formation of the human being as a moral [*sittlichen*] creature. (8: 113)[8]

Feminine refusal is, to be sure, only the second of four "steps" in the development of reason, one that is followed by both "expectation of the future," and man's self-comprehension as the true "end of nature." Still, it remains "epoch-making," insofar as it gives an "entirely new direction" to "the way of thinking," and is as such "more important," as Kant here insists, than all the "extensions of culture that follow from it" (8: 113).

One is here reminded of Rousseau's "golden age," which had likewise linked feminine "refusal" with the appearance of the "sweetest sentiments known to man," namely, "conjugal and paternal love," followed by "ideas of merit and beauty" along with "sentiments of preference" and a related competition and rivalry – i.e., what Kant will later call man's "social sociability."[9]

---

[8] Translated by A. Wood, in Kant, *Anthropology, History, and Education*, ed. Günter Zöller (Cambridge: Cambridge University Press, 2007), pp. 166–167. Cf. *Remarks* (20: 184).

[9] Rousseau, *Discourse on Inequality*, PL III, pp. 168–169; cf. Kant, *Idea for a Universal History from a Cosmopolitan Intention* (8: 20).

And the theme continues into Kant's late *Anthropology* (1798), in which women's weakness, both physical and moral, is balanced by a natural "artfulness" that "imperceptibly fetter[s]" men's desire, and thus "prepar-[es] for" its transcendence:

> Since nature . . . wanted to instill the finer feelings that belong to culture – namely those of sociability and propriety – it made this sex man's rule through her modesty and eloquence [. . . .] It made her clever while still young in claiming gentle and courteous treatment by the male, so that he would find himself imperceptibly fettered by a child through his own magnanimity, and led by her if not to morality itself, to that which is its cloak, moral decency [*gesitteten Anstande*], which is the preparation for morality and its recommendation. (7: 306)

The great "problem" of educating the human race so as to achieve its destiny of cultivating, civilizing, and moralizing itself is determined, in the first instance, by the gap between men's natural and civil maturity. According to the stages of his natural development, "at least by his fifteenth year," he "is *driven* by the *sexual instinct*, and he is also *capable* of procreating and preserving his kind." According to the stages of his civil development, he can "hardly venture upon" doing so "before his twentieth year": he must "learn a trade" before he can set up a household, and "in the more refined classes" may pass his twenty-fifth year before "mature for his vocation," with "vices" filling up the interval "of a forced and unnatural abstinence" (7: 325).

To be sure, this gap, and related violence that human culture does to nature (7: 326), is only one of three problems – along with violence through civilization and through pseudo-moralization – that must be solved if man is to achieve the destiny for which his higher nature suits him (7: 327–328). Still, it is enough to suggest an ongoing fascination on Kant's part with the problem that surrounds the relation of the sexes, one reflected in his late description of the fact of sexual difference as a "chasm" [*Abgrund*] of thought that human reason cannot fully fathom.[10]

The Problem of Science and Reason's Limits

The thoughts of the 1760s inspired by Rousseau are of the greatest importance not only for his moral philosophy but for Kant's entire critical approach to reason. Rousseau is decisive for the first germs of Kant's critical idea of reason as a self-correcting power in all its uses. Rousseau's insight into reason's subversion of natural freedom and equality applies in Kant's

---

[10] Letter to F. Schiller, March 30, 1795 (12: 10–11).

judgment to the theoretical use of reason in philosophy and the sciences. Once again, the problem is reason's tendency to awaken strivings that exceed human powers of satisfaction, thus undermining contentment with concerns more fitting to human limitations, and provoking the undue estimation of intellectual attainments that causes invidious comparisons (20: 37.5–10). Motivated often by vanity, science deviates from sound inquiries into empty speculations. All the same, reason can proceed in a self-corrective way here as well (20: 39.20–27, 20: 78.4–6). The sciences should be guided by a "method of doubt" that defends the sound understanding (20: 175.13) by exposing speculative excesses and drawing reason's interests toward moral simplicity and essential human ends. It should abjure complex argumentative supports for moral principles, thereby establishing harmony between theoretical science and common moral reason (20: 6.6–11). "One must teach the young to hold in honor the common understanding on both moral and logical grounds" (20: 44.6–7). This gives rise to the project of developing a new critical science of reason as the highest science or first philosophy. "One could say that metaphysics is a science of the limits of human reason" (20: 181.1–2). Kant's project relates, in his view, to the Socratic understanding of philosophy as calling for "dispensing" with unnecessary inquiries, which is the theoretical counterpart to Rousseau's demand that society reject the pursuit of luxury and return to the self-sufficiency of the natural state. Socrates "needs little because he can dispense with much" (20: 77.6–12). This gives rise to Kant's distinction between primitive and wise innocence. "Simplicity is either ignorant or it is rational and wise" (20: 180.6–7). In the *Remarks* one finds an early adumbration of the two central goals of the criticism of reason: to establish the limits of reason in speculative-metaphysical inquiry and to support thereby the conceptions of human dignity and the virtuous life inherent in the sound common understanding. It also points to the common methodological basis of these undertakings: to see problems of human life as rooted in reason's authorship of disorder or what Kant later calls "dialectic," and to propose that reason can restore order through self-corrective legislation. Science is, like war, slavery and religion a consequence of "deterioration" of the human away from its true vocation (20: 78.4–6). But science can also be used for the "preventing of the evil it has instituted" (20: 39.20–27).

One could call this a methodological principle of rational autonomy, in that it gives reason sole responsibility for its condition, and not a transcendent divine or natural principle. The nature that is to be respected and fulfilled is the nature of reason itself. The nature of reason, thus understood, is Rousseau's discovery of the true essence of the human and thereby of the "hidden law" that "justifies Providence": reason's free capacity for self-alienation and self-rectification. This capacity as found in all humans, the common laborer as well as the philosopher, is what gives worth to all reflections. To clarify its nature and defend it against distorting accounts of reason is the true task of philosophy. By undertaking that defense philosophy is not only concerned with promoting a universal benefit but also engaged with securing its own possibility.

Now to summarize the picture of the problems of reason and nature as they emerge from the *Remarks*. As the human develops its rational capacities in the arts and sciences it moves further away from original simplicity, and becomes burdened by the many ills of civilization. Yet all these ills are self-inflicted, which indicates that reason should be able to correct what it has instituted. Human reason discloses a historical character with disastrous consequences, insofar as man can step outside the circle of humanity and become like nothing, being lower than any animal if he does not make fitting use of his reason. Yet this same freedom from natural determination means that reason has a self-rectifying power. This freedom shines forth as a ground for reverence, since the subordination of all inclinations and talents to the free will brings the human into harmony with itself and nature; this is a simplicity that has the advantage of being wise and not merely innocent. This rational power for self-imposed order is an object of greater respect than mere acquisition of knowledge. To defend this power is what gives worth to all inquiry, and thus philosophy should take up a Socratic critique of knowledge that does not promote the true end of man. Philosophy has been able to discover its proper vocation only through the historical experience of deterioration and disorder, of the unprecedented dangers of the modern regime. This is the hidden law of historical development, that man discovers his essence through extreme alienation. The genuine science of reason rests on this historical insight: "If there is indeed a science that man needs, it is one that teaches him to fulfill properly his appointed place in creation and to learn what he must do to be a human being" (20: 45.17–20). As Kant also writes, "the whole aim of science" is to contribute "to making the human more intelligent and also more content in the world appropriate to human nature" (20: 7.8–11). But grasping this aim presupposes the experience of abandoning that world. Such reflections have been characterized by scholars as belonging only to the sphere of moral anthropology, but this is an error, for it is clear that they relate directly to the fundamental motives for a critical approach to reason wherein reason discovers or, as

Kant later will say, legislates its limits in the speculative realm for practical ends. Indeed, the object of critical philosophy is to secure the possibility of the self-legislative power of reason which cannot be grounded in either speculative knowledge of things in themselves or in empirical psychology. The correction of the errors of philosophy requires the full exposure of these errors; Kant later calls that exposure the dialectic of pure reason. But such arguments and their role in the critical defense of reason would take Kant over a decade to articulate.

CHAPTER 11

Rousseau and Wollstonecraft: Solitary Walkers

Barbara Taylor

The mythic Rousseau that accrued to the living Rousseau from the mid-1750s was above all a *solitaire*. As Rousseau's celebrity – and notoriety – increased, he sought refuge in a series of mostly rural retreats; by his death he had become Europe's star recluse. Often he was fleeing persecutors, real or imagined, but a lifelong passion for aloneness was the main driver. As he wrote to his friend Malesherbes in 1762,

> I was born with a natural love for solitude which has done nothing but increase in proportion as I have gotten to know men better. I find my advantage better with the chimerical beings that I assemble around me than with the ones I see in the world . . . .[1]

By modern standards, this famed solitariness was far from solitary. In whatever haven Rousseau found himself – country houses large and small, foreign boltholes – he was accompanied by others; sometimes he was so surrounded by people that he hid to avoid them. And – like most male solitaries – even at his most reclusive Rousseau was serviced by a woman, in his case the long-suffering Thérèse Levasseur who was a constant presence in his life from 1745 until his death thirty-three years later. Thérèse, Rousseau said of his lower-class mistress, was his "supplement," his adjunct with whom he shared "a single soul."[2] He could not bear to be without her, and although he regularly described dependence on others as a form of enslavement,[3] he also acknowledged the impossibility of a completely solitary existence: "absolute solitude is a state that is sad and contrary to nature." "[W]hat sentient being can live forever [. . .] without attachments? That is not a man; that is a beast or a god."[4]

---

[1] J.-J. Rousseau, *Four Letters to M, the Président de Malesherbes Containing the True Picture of My Character*, 4 January 1762, CW V, p. 572.
[2] L. Damrosch, *Jean-Jacques Rousseau: Restless Genius* (New York: Houghton Mifflin, 2005), pp. 88, 460.
[3] See for example, Rousseau, *Emile or On Education*, trans. A. Bloom (London: Penguin, 1991), p. 85.
[4] Rousseau, *Judge of Jean-Jacques: Dialogues* (1782), CW I, p. 118; Rousseau, *Emile and Sophie; Or, The Solitaries* (1782), CW XIII, p. 686.

Nevertheless, Rousseau's self-image as a loner ("a hermit," "a bear") was very powerful, and in his final decades he became a veritable apostle of solitude, limning its joys to all who would listen. Solitary walking was his particular delight. "Never did I think so much, exist so vividly, and experience so much, never have I been so much myself – if I may use that expression – as in the journeys I have taken alone and on foot."[5] Botanising during these lone walks made them even more pleasurable. It was "in this way," he wrote in *Reveries of a Solitary Walker*, "that I learnt that the source of true happiness is within us, and that it is not in the power of men to make anyone truly miserable who is determined to be happy."[6]

This happy state was much more than mere aloneness.[7] Solitude for Rousseau was an achieved condition, a distinctive mode of being facilitated by physical solitude but not dependent on it. It had many registers, from the blissful daydreaming of his months on Isle Saint-Pierre, as recalled in the *Reveries* ("where time is nothing [...] where the present runs on indefinitely [...] with no feeling of deprivation or enjoyment, pleasure or pain, desire or fear than the simple feeling of existence, a feeling that fills our soul entirely"),[8] to the simple joys of woodland strolls and reading while eating alone ("as if my book were dining with me"),[9] through to the sterner pleasures of moral introspection ("conversing with my soul") which, echoing Montaigne, Rousseau depicted as an act of the moral will, a deliberate stilling of the "din of the world" until the "voice of the soul" could be heard.[10] "The solitude in question," Rousseau instructed his one-time *inamorata*, Sophie d'Houdetot in 1758, "is less to have your door closed and to stay in your apartment than take your soul out of the throng [...] and [...] close it against the alien passions that assail it at every moment." The virtuous life, which is also the happy life, is founded in solitude:

> The conscience is fearful and timid, it seeks solitude, the world and noise scare it [...] it flees or keeps quiet before them, their noisy voices stifle its voice and prevent it from making itself heard [... until] it finally gives up,

---

[5] Rousseau, *The Confessions*, trans. J. Cohen (London: Penguin, 1973), p. 157.
[6] Rousseau, *Reveries of a Solitary Walker*, trans. P. France (London: Penguin, 1979), p. 36.
[7] Rousseau's solitude is explored in scores of books and articles. For this chapter I have made particular use of the following: J. Starobinski, *Transparency and Obstruction* (Chicago: University of Chicago Press, 1988); M. Berman, *The Politics of Authenticity: Radical Individualism and the Emergence of Modern Society* (New York: Atheneum, 1970); J. Seigel, *The Idea of the Self* (Cambridge: Cambridge University Press, 2005), pp. 210–247; T. Todorov, *Imperfect Garden: the Legacy of Humanism* (Princeton: Princeton University Press, 2002).
[8] Rousseau, *Reveries*, p. 88.   [9] Rousseau, *Confessions*, p. 255.
[10] Rousseau, *Reveries*, p. 32; Rousseau, *Moral Letters*, CW XII, p. 199.

no longer speaks to us [. . .] Commune with yourself, seek out solitude, there to begin is the whole secret.[11]

Coming from a man whose writings on women have made him a *bête noir* of feminists, this counsel is striking. It stands in stark contrast to Rousseau's notoriously belittling account of the female character as set out in *Emile* and elsewhere. But contradictions of this sort never worried Rousseau ("I prefer to be a paradoxical man than a prejudiced one").[12] Nor did they much trouble his most famous feminist critic, Mary Wollstonecraft. "I love his [Rousseau's] paradoxes," Wollstonecraft wrote in 1787, and one of the more paradoxical aspects of Rousseau was his appeal to a woman whose sexual equalitarianism was fashioned in direct opposition to him.[13] But then Wollstonecraft too was a person of contradictions: a solitary who yearned for loving companionship, a radical whose philosophy centred on the "social affections" but who found everyday sociability demanding and irritating. A female Rousseau? The label would surely have raised a Wollstonecraftian eyebrow, but she probably would not have spurned it.

***

Rousseau's career as a solitary began in the spring of 1756 when he withdrew from Paris into the Hermitage, a cottage on Mme d'Epinay's estate at Montmorency. The move delighted him: "I began to live only on April 9, 1756."[14] Others were less pleased. Two years earlier Rousseau's prelapsarian account of the solitary life of primitive man (in *Discourse on the Origins of Inequality)* had attracted fierce criticism, not least from Voltaire. Now his apparent determination to live out this "savage" existence in the forests of Montmorency was greeted with accusations of egoism and solipsism. All the "literary people," he later recalled, "shouted [. . .] that a man by himself is useless to everyone and has not fulfilled his duties in society."[15] His fellow *Encyclopedistes* were especially hostile, with Grimm, Mme D'Epinay's lover, warning her that residing in the Hermitage was likely to drive Rousseau mad ("He is a poor devil who torments himself, and does not dare to confess the true subject of all his sufferings, which is his cursed head and his pride; he raises up imaginary matters, so as to have the pleasure of complaining of the whole human race").[16] Diderot mocked him for

---

[11] Rousseau, *Moral Letters*, pp. 198–199.   [12] Rousseau, *Emile*, p. 93.

[13] M. Wollstonecraft to E. Wollstonecraft, 24 March 1787, *Collected Letters of Mary Wollstonecraft*, ed. R. Wardle (Ithaca: Cornell University Press, 1979), p. 145.

[14] Rousseau, *Letters to Malesherbes*, 26 January 1762, CW V, p. 577.

[15] Rousseau, *Letters to Malesherbes*, 28 January 1762, CW V, p. 580.

[16] Quoted in W. Noyes, "The Insanity of Jean-Jacques Rousseau," *The American Journal of Psychology* 3:3 (1890): p. 414.

retreating into "brute stupidity under a bearskin mantle."[17] Not content
with this jibe, Diderot followed it up by sending Rousseau a copy of his
new play, *The Natural Son*, containing the line "Only the wicked man lives
alone." Assuming this was a reference to him – which it probably was –
Rousseau shot back a reproach which elicited an apology from Diderot for
derogating his friend's lifestyle. But "[a]ll the same," Diderot couldn't
resist adding, "a hermit is a strange sort of citizen."[18]

The criticisms were echoed across the Channel, with Edmund Burke
condemning Rousseau's "unsociable fierceness" while the *Critical Review*
cast him as a modern Diogenes, "a recluse of the gloomy, misanthropic
type."[19] Similar charges had been levelled at solitaries from antiquity
onward, but the rise of Enlightenment had sharpened the censure. Man,
the *philosophes* insisted, was a naturally social animal; solitaries were
misanthropes, monsters, madmen.[20] Yet in an age of high sentiment
Rousseau's preference for solitude also elicited applause, as a token of his
"exquisite sensibility" and "Roman simplicity," his Cato-like hatred of
luxury and artifice. Visiting Rousseau in his "romantick retirement" at
Moitiers in 1764, James Boswell came away singing his praises and raging
against the corruptions of society.[21] "He is a musical instrument above the
concert pitch," another English fan eulogised shortly before Rousseau's
death, "and therefore too elevated for the present state of society."[22]

A few commentators, including David Hume, were shrewder in their
perceptions. In 1766, Rousseau took up residence for a time in an isolated
house in Staffordshire. "He will be unhappy in that situation, as he has
indeed been always in all situations," Hume predicted. "[H]is sensibility
rises to a pitch beyond what I have seen any example of: but it still gives
him a more acute feeling of pain than of pleasure. He is like a man . . .
stripped not only of his clothes, but of his skin."[23] Hume spoke from
experience: he and Rousseau had been close friends until Rousseau decided
that Hume was plotting against him. The paranoia was not new –
Rousseau had manifested it since boyhood – but by the 1760s it had

[17] L. Shea, *The Cynic Enlightenment: Diogenes in the Salon* (Baltimore: Johns Hopkins University Press, 2010), p. 101.
[18] P. Furbank, *Diderot: A Critical Biography* (London: Minerva, 1993), p. 151.
[19] E. Duffy, *Rousseau in England: The Context for Shelley's Critique of the Enlightenment* (Berkeley: University of California Press, 1979), p. 11.
[20] R. Sayre, *Solitude in Society: A Sociological Study of French Literature* (Cambridge, MA: Harvard University Press, 1978), pp. 49–50.
[21] R.A. Leigh, "Boswell and Rousseau," *The Modern Language Review* 47:3 (1952): pp. 290–318.
[22] P. France, "Introduction," Rousseau, *Rêveries*, p. 9.
[23] E. Mossner, *The Life of David Hume* (Oxford: Oxford University Press, 1980) p. 523.

become acute. And it bred loneliness: how could Jean-Jacques ever know, truly know, what was going on in other people's minds when they thought about him? That he could never know frightened and enraged him, and he filled the gap between himself and others with imputed feelings and motives to which he then reacted violently.[24] The anxiety showed itself at its starkest in his misogyny, but it pervaded all his relationships to a greater or lesser extent, driving him into the narcissistic cocoon so wonderfully evoked in the *Reveries*.

> Always too strongly affected by what I see or hear, and particularly by signs of pleasure or suffering, affection or dislike, I let myself be swayed by these outward impressions and can only avoid them by running away. A sign, a gesture or a glance from a stranger is enough to disturb my pleasure or ease my suffering. It is only when I am alone that I am my own master, at all other times I am the plaything of all who surround me.[25]

This phobic dread was lost on most of Rousseau's critics and admirers. But Hume detected it – and so too did Mary Wollstonecraft who, reviewing *The Confessions* in 1790 for Joseph Johnson's *Analytical Review*, described Rousseau's solitariness as arising from "the excess of his affection for his fellow-creatures," combined with his "extreme timidity":

> The bustle of society will ever harass a man accustomed to think or profoundly feel the vices and follies of mankind – such a man lives in a continual warfare, and the grand passions, which in solitude would carry him out of himself, only serve to torment him by having the contrary effect. Contending with the world [... Rousseau] was not more than that timid man, rather bashful than modest, who dared not present himself, nor speak, whom a sportive word disconcerted, and the glance of a woman made blush, but in solitude he became himself again.[26]

The classic feminine descriptors – affectionate, timid, bashful, blushing – came straight from *The Confessions*, where Rousseau at one point described himself as a man of "effeminate" character.[27] Wollstonecraft disliked stereotypical femininity in either sex; nonetheless, Rousseau's susceptibilities

---

[24] "The first, the greatest, the strongest, the most inextinguishable of all my needs was entirely one of the heart. It was the need for intimate companionship, for a companionship as intimate as possible [...] This singular need was such that the most intimate physical union could not fulfil it; only two souls in the same body would have sufficed. Failing that, I always felt a void" (Rousseau, *Confessions*, p. 386).

[25] Rousseau, *Reveries*, p. 148.

[26] Wollstonecraft, "*Seconde Partie des Confessions de J. J. Rousseau,*" *Analytical Review*, in *The Works of Mary Wollstonecraft* (London: Pickering, 1989), VII, p. 232.

[27] Rousseau, *Confessions*, p. 23.

clearly touched her. It was "impossible to read" his *Confessions*, she wrote, "without loving the man despite the weaknesses of character that he himself depicts, which never appear to have arisen from depravity of heart."[28]

Wollstonecraft's attitude to Rousseau is usually described as militantly adversarial, and certainly her treatment of him in the *Rights of Woman* is very quarrelsome. But a closer look at her *corpus* leaves a very different impression. And even in the *Rights of Woman*, where she rakes him with critical fire, her tone is much more that of an infuriated acolyte than an intellectual enemy. As discipleships go, this was an exceptionally ambivalent one, but that Wollstonecraft *was* a disciple of Rousseau, right from the start, is indisputable.[29] "I am now reading Rousseau's Emile," she wrote excitedly to her sister Everina from Ireland in 1787: "He chuses [sic] a *common* capacity to educate – and gives as a reason, that a genius will educate itself."[30] Six months later, she announced the completion of *Mary: a Fiction* (1788), "a tale, to illustrate an opinion of mine, that a genius will educate itself."[31] It was "Rousseau's opinion respecting men" which she "extend[ed] to women," she wrote in *The Rights of Woman*, in the midst of the argument with him that occupies so much of the text.[32] "I have always been half in love with him," she confided in 1794.[33]

But if one half of Wollstonecraft loved Rousseau, the other half clearly identified with him. "He rambles into that *chimerical* world in which I have too often wandered – and draws the usual conclusion that all is vanity and vexation of spirit," she told her sister Everina. "He was a strange inconsistent unhappy clever creature – yet he possessed an uncommon portion of sensibility and penetration" – a condition with which Wollstonecraft was all too familiar.[34] Reading Rousseau's personal writings, she immediately recognised a fellow "Solitary Walker," as she described herself in a letter to William Godwin; another of those restive spirits who "lost in a pleasing enthusiasm . . . live in the scenes they represent; and do not measure their steps in a beaten track."[35] Like her hero, polite society made her nervous

---

[28] Wollstonecraft, "Letters on the Confessions of J J Rousseau. By M Guigne," *Analytical Review*, in *Works* VII, p. 409.

[29] This summary account of Wollstonecraft's attitude to Rousseau derives from my *Mary Wollstonecraft and the Feminist Imagination* (Cambridge: Cambridge University Press, 2003), pp. 72–74.

[30] Wollstonecraft to E. Wollstonecraft, 24 March 1787, *Collected Letters*, p. 145.

[31] Wollstonecraft to Rev. H. Gabell, 13 September 1787, *Collected Letters*, p. 162.

[32] Wollstonecraft, *A Vindication of the Rights of Woman*, *Works* V, p. 90.

[33] Wollstonecraft to G. Imlay, 22 September 1794, *Collected Letters*, p. 263.

[34] Wollstonecraft to E. Wollstonecraft, 24 March 1787, *Collected Letters*, p 145.

[35] The "Solitary Walker" reference appeared in a letter to Godwin (7 August 1796) where, following a sudden loss of confidence in Godwin's feelings for her, Wollstonecraft told him she would once

and tetchy. "I commune with my own spirit," she wrote to Everina in 1787 from the Irish Kingsborough estate, where she was labouring away miserably as a governess, "and these reveries do not tend to fit me for enjoying the *common* pleasures of this world."[36]

Uncommon women, like maverick *philosophes*, needed open space in which to stretch their wings. There was of course a problem here. Rousseauite woman, as prescribed in Book Five of *Emile*, was emphatically not a solitaire. Common pleasures and well-beaten tracks were her destiny. Solitary reveries were a masculine prerogative. Women, Rousseau explained in *Emile*, are entirely social animals; deprived of worldly distractions, they succumb to "the vapours": "a horrible illness which sometimes deprives them of their reason and finally their lives."[37] Women's feelings are too cold, their imaginations too weak, for the "sublime transports" of a solitary existence. Women should lead a reclusive, domestic life – unlike most of his enlightened contemporaries, Rousseau was a great fan of the classical sequestration of women – but for men's sake, not for themselves. "To please men, to be useful to them [. . .] to make their lives agreeable and sweet – these are the duties of women at all times."[38]

Wollstonecraft's extended rejoinder to this, in *A Vindication of the Rights of Woman*, was the most influential of the period. But her career too became an implicit rebuttal, as she displayed to the world a woman of "peculiar character" determined to live life on her own terms. "I long for a little peace and *independence!*" she wrote to her employer and patron Joseph Johnson in 1787 as she searched for a suitable London home.[39] She had just launched herself on her writing career and was resolved on living alone. "I have determined [. . .] *never* to have my Sisters live with me," she wrote to a friend, "my solitary manner of living would not suit them, nor *could* I pursue my studies if forced to conform."[40] Nearly a decade and many turbulent experiences later, her attitude remained the same. "I am not fatigued with solitude," she wrote to Godwin in 1797 from the separate home she maintained during their relationship. "I wish you, from my soul, to be riveted in my heart; but I do not desire to have you always at my elbow."[41]

---

again become a "Solitary Walker" (*Collected Letters*, p. 337); Wollstonecraft, *Mary: A Fiction*, *Works* I, p. 5.

[36] Wollstonecraft to E. Wollstonecraft, 24 March 1787, *Collected Letters*, p. 144.
[37] Rousseau, *Emile*, p. 350.   [38] Ibid., p. 365.
[39] Wollstonecraft to J. Johnson, 13 September 1787, *Collected Letters*, p. 159.
[40] Wollstonecraft to G. Blood, 16 May 1788, *Collected Letters*, p. 175.
[41] Wollstonecraft to W. Godwin, 6 June 1797, *Collected Letters*, p. 396.

The "generality" of women, Wollstonecraft wrote in the *Rights of Woman*, "fly" from solitude as from a "fearful void." Trained to submission, leached of inner resources, most women find aloneness intolerable.[42] Against this she set her own self-image as a solitary walker, not just metaphorically but literally: nearly all her self-portrayals show her rambling alone, from the eponymous heroine of the semi-autobiographical *Mary: A Fiction* (1788) who enjoys solo walks along "gloomy" mountain paths, pausing along the way to read poetry in a hidden mountain cavern (which she dubs the "Temple of Solitude"), through to the final work published in her lifetime, "On Poetry" (1797), where she depicts herself walking outdoors on an early morning while the rest of the world sleeps: "pacing over the printless grass" watching the sun rise "in solitary majesty, whilst my eyes alone hailed its beautifying beams."[43] Letters to friends and family described returning from such walks with muddied skirts and high spirits. This was dodgy behaviour: when Jane Austen's feisty heroine Elizabeth Bennett did it two decades later, in *Pride and Prejudice*, the reaction was sharp. "[A]lone, quite alone!" the genteel Miss Bingley exclaims as the bedraggled Elizabeth arrives from walking across the fields to Netherfield Park. "It seems to me to show an abominable sort of conceited independence."[44]

"Conceited independence" was the improper face of female solitude. By and large, eighteenth-century women sought to avoid this. Throughout western history, women with a preference for solitude had been regarded with suspicion. "When a woman thinks alone," it was said by witch-obsessed priests in the fifteenth century, "she thinks evil"; and while the censure had lost most of its psychotic edge by Wollstonecraft's day, weaker versions of it persisted.[45] The solitary woman – unobserved, unregulated – was a deviant figure. Single women and widows might endure aloneness, but to choose it was the prerogative only of female religious recluses, who in Enlightenment France were the butt of much salacious satire, and in post-Reformation England were virtually a defunct species. Protestant Englishwomen who continued to yearn for religious seclusion were suspected of papist tendencies, or accused of low-church "enthusiasm." Retiring to one's closet periodically for reflection and prayer was praiseworthy, but to shun society for solitary worship was reprehensible. "T'is

---

[42] Wollstonecraft, *A Vindication of the Rights of Woman*, Works V, pp. 242, 190.
[43] Wollstonecraft, *On Poetry, Works* VII, p. 7.
[44] J. Austen, *Pride and Prejudice, The Complete Novels* (London: Penguin, 2006), p. 229.
[45] *The Malleus Maleficarum of Heinrich Kramer and James Springer* (1486), quoted in P. Koch, *Solitude: A Philosophical Encounter* (Chicago: Open Court, 1994), p. 252.

a sin against Nature for women to be Incloystred, Retired or restrained," the solitude-loving Margaret Cavendish had a male character exclaim in a 1662 play, "[T]hose women which restrain themselves from the company and use of men, are damned."[46] Light learning and a measure of piety were meritorious in a woman, but a life of lone thought or spirituality ran contrary to the female character and violated women's social obligations. "We [women] must have company," a woman wrote to *The Spectator* in 1711:

> We are made for the Cements of Society, and came into the World to create Relations among Mankind; and Solitude is an unnatural Being to us.[47]

The attitude survived throughout the century, with even well-known literary women expressing such views.[48] But – as with Rousseau and his critics, of which more below – the meaning of these sentiments needs some unpicking.

"Solitude" was many things in the eighteenth century: country retirement, religious devotion, scholarship, leisure, introspection, daydreaming, a melancholy disposition. Only rarely did it mean total aloneness ("absolute solitude," as this was denominated). "Retirement poetry," a popular neoclassical genre, eulogised a quiet rural life surrounded by books, family, a few close friends. Secluded in some rustic retreat "far from the clamorous world" (that is, in a comfortable country house with plenty of servants), the happy recluse would commune with Nature, share intimacies, sink into a pleasurable melancholy.[49] Both men and women published many such poems, celebrating the delights of leisure and companionship in tranquil rural settings.[50] The solitariness they evoked was, for the most part, richly sociable, albeit with moments of isolation and lone introspection ("inward retirement") which increased as the century progressed, and writers of both sexes became imbued with sensibility: that "tender and delicate disposition

---

[46] B. Hill, "A Refuge from Men: The Idea of a Protestant Nunnery," *Past and Present* 117 (1987): p. 128.

[47] *The Spectator* 158, 31 August 1711.

[48] The most eminent of these women were the "Bluestockings" who enjoyed spells of country retirement during the off-season but were adamant that such solitariness should not become habitual. "The love of retirement seems to grow upon you," Catherine Talbot wrote to her fellow "Blue," the Epictetus translator Elizabeth Carter. "But it ought not. The use of retirement is to fit us for moving more reasonably, more beneficially in the world" (Talbot to Carter, 13 November 1752, quoted in S. Bending, *Green Retreats: Women, Gardens and Eighteenth-Century Culture* [Cambridge: Cambridge University Press, 2013], p. 82).

[49] P. Spacks, *Privacy: Concealing the Eighteenth-Century Self* (Chicago: University of Chicago Press, 2003), pp. 197–199; Bending, *Green Retreats*, pp. 1–172.

[50] P. Backscheider, *Eighteenth-Century Women Poets and Their Poetry* (Baltimore: Johns Hopkins University Press, 2005), pp. 233–267.

of the soul which renders it easy to be moved and touched," and which by the final decades of the eighteenth century – thanks in no small part to Rousseau – had become a hallmark of the modern personality.[51]

Sensibility was a baggy cultural invention, a medley of enlightened moral science, aesthetic and medical theory, literary fashion. At its core were the traditional Christian virtues of compassion and neighbourly love naturalised into "social instincts" or "moral sentiments": deep, involuntary responses to the suffering of others. "How selfish soever man be supposed," Adam Smith's *Theory of Moral Sentiments* famously opens,

> there are evidently some principles in his nature, which interest him in the fortunes of others, and render their happiness necessary to him, though he derives nothing from him except the pleasure of seeing it. Of this kind is [. . .] is the emotion we feel for the misery of others, when we either see it, or are made to conceive it in a very lively manner.[52]

The operative faculty here was the imagination. "By the imagination we place ourselves in [the other person's] situation," Adam Smith wrote. "[W]e enter as it were into his body, and become in some measure the same person with him"; or as Rousseau put it in *Emile*: "It is not inside ourselves; it is in him [our fellow creature] that we suffer. Thus, no one becomes sensitive until his imagination is animated and begins to transport him out of himself."[53] Long regarded as a lower-order mental function – a mere conduit between sensations and mind (or, in minds where it had become detached from sensory reality, dangerously delusory) – now this sympathetic imagination was celebrated as a primary agent of social cohesion, transforming spontaneous responses into emotional links in the "great chain of society."[54]

In an age of accelerating commercial individualism, affective solidarity of this order was at a premium.[55] If, as some Enlightenment moralists warned, modern man was becoming an isolate (a "detached and a solitary being," Adam Ferguson described him, "in competition with his fellow-creatures [. . .] for the sake of the profits they bring") then the highly

---

[51] J. Brewer, "Sentiment and Sensibility," in J. Chandler (ed.), *The Cambridge History of English Romantic Literature* (Cambridge: Cambridge University Press, 2009), p. 25.

[52] A. Smith, *The Theory of Moral Sentiments* (1759; Cambridge: Cambridge University Press, 2002), p. 11.

[53] Smith, *Moral Sentiments*, p. 12; Rousseau, *Emile*, p. 223.

[54] E. Burke, *A Philosophical Enquiry into the Origins of Our Ideas of the Sublime and Beautiful* (1759), p. 57.

[55] J. Mullan, *Sentiment and Sociability: The Language of Feeling in the Eighteenth Century* (Oxford: Oxford University Press, 1988), p. 4 and *passim*.

sociable version of human selfhood promulgated by Smith, Rousseau *et al.* offered a powerful counter to such atomism.[56] Solitariness in this sociable self could only ever appear as lack or loss. Yet the individual susceptibilities on which this self drew for its other-directed responses were ineluctably subjective: a private realm of emotions, desires, imaginings whose tendency, especially in people of acute sensibility like Rousseau and Wollstonecraft, was to draw individuals away from the crude and bruising insensitivities of "the world"; to turn them, in John Mullan's apt formulation, into "solitary epicure[s] of sentiment."[57] The result was a tension between sociality and solitariness that was felt throughout the eighteenth century, long before "Romanticism" arrived on the scene to claim the lone self as its representative figure. Solitariness became the apotheosis of sensibility, simultaneously glamorised as a mark of "exquisite refinement" while signalling sensibility's pathological downside, its fostering of morbid self-concern and an egoistical distaste for the "endearments of life."[58]

By the second half of the century this solipsistic element in sensibility was overshadowing its social virtues. Popular overuse of the concept, especially in its more hyperbolic tearstained versions, sent it into a decline which by Wollstonecraft's day had become so precipitous that it was difficult to find a literary figure of either sex promoting sensibility. Even writers, like herself, who continued to write in the sentimental mode made great play of repudiating sensibility's "excesses." These excesses – hyper-emotionalism; self-absorption; moral complacency; erotic fantasy; a wide range of psychosomatic ailments including hysteria, hypochondria, and melancholia – were not wholly new; related evils had long been associated with solitude. But now these evils took on heightened significance as men and women imbued with sociable values grappled with the nature and limits of the feeling self. Ciceronian strictures against solitude were dusted off and pushed back into circulation, alongside cautionary tales about sentimental recluses succumbing to gross eccentricity or melancholy, and thus becoming "lost to themselves and society."[59] Even writers like Henry Mackenzie, author of the most popular sentimental novel of the century, inveighed against "that sickly sort of refinement" which favoured "imaginary blessings and enjoyments" over the

[56] A. Ferguson, *An Essay on the History of Civil Society* (1767), I:iii, p. 28.
[57] Mullan, *Sentiment*, p. 17.   [58] Bending, *Green Retreats*, p. 50.
[59] See for example the story of Mr Umphraville in *The Mirror* (1779–1780); also S. Johnson, *The History of Rasselas: Prince of Abissinia* (1759) and the many examples listed in R. Havens, "Solitude and the Neoclassicists," *English Literary History* 21:4 (1954): pp. 251–273.

real-life pleasures of social intercourse.[60] The criticisms were fiercest when directed at women, or rather at Woman, that construct of eighteenth-century gender ideology whose relatively weak intellect, strong passions and "over-active" imagination were seen to predispose her to sentimental excess. Far from the large-souled, outward-reaching Man of Feeling conjured by sensibility theorists, the classic Woman of Feeling was either a self-abnegating saint (Richardson's Clarissa provided the template) or a sentimental solipsist: narrow and maudlin in her affections, morally indifferent, given over to "romantick whimsies."[61] Misogynist caricatures of such women proliferated. But men whose intense sensibilities induced them to shun social intercourse came in for some harsh censure as well:

> The most vicious of men is he who isolates himself the most, who most concentrates his heart in himself; the best is he who shares with affections equally with his kind.[62]

The dictum is Rousseau's, from his *Letter to D'Alembert on the Theatre* (1758). Whatever Rousseau the man felt about solitude, in the intellectual tug-of-war between solitude and sociality Rousseau the philosopher came down firmly on the side of social being.[63] His private inclinations were to be no example to others. As his letters to Sophie Houdetot show, Rousseau could be as inconsistent in this as he was in so many things. But his pronouncements against solitude were of a piece with the Augustinian exhibition of his vices in *The Confessions*, the *Dialogues* and elsewhere. The exculpatory tone of *The Confessions* has persuaded many scholars that for Rousseau "*tout comprendre, c'est tout pardonner.*" But the person from whom Rousseau most needed forgiveness was Jean-Jacques himself, in the echo chamber of his psyche, and this he could never bestow. Vehement self-vindications were repeatedly hollowed out by guilt. His self-portrayals as a solitaire were typical. "Detached from the whole world, what am I?" he

---

[60] H. Mackenzie, *The Lounger* 20, 18 June 1785.

[61] The literature on women and sensibility is large; for a good summary discussion of the issues see J. Todd, *The Sign of Angelica: Women, Writing and Fiction, 1660–1800* (London: Virago Press, 1989), Part 2.

[62] Rousseau, *Letter to D'Alembert on the Theatre* (1758), in *Politics and the Arts*, trans. A. Bloom (Ithaca: Cornell University Press, 1991), p. 117.

[63] The solitary/citizen opposition has been the focus of much Rousseau scholarship, although to my knowledge no previous study has explored the relationship between this division and Rousseau's views on women. For an interesting recent discussion of the solitary/citizen binary see J. Neidleman, "Rousseau and the Desire for Communion," *Eighteenth-Century Studies* 47:1 (2013): pp. 53–67.

asked at the beginning of his *Reveries of a Solitary Walker*, and the answer he gave there and elsewhere was an individual of supreme sincerity and moral sensitivity, but also one too lazy, too unobliging, too sensual (too "savage" we might say, in Rousseau's use of the word) for civilised company.[64] Rousseau was a compulsive masturbator, regularly dreaming up women "celestial in their virtue and in their beauty," and then enjoying their company "in my own fashion," sometimes to the point of exhaustion. Readers of *The Confessions* were treated to an unbuttoned account of the orgy of sexual fantasies which, he claimed, inspired the writing of *La Nouvelle Héloïse*.[65] And even when – in the long tradition of Christian solitaries – the lone Rousseau felt himself in the presence of God, his descriptions of this "delirious" sensation (a "stupefying ecstasy ... which sometimes made me cry out in the agitation of my raptures, 'Oh great being! Oh great being'") were heavily charged with erotic emotion.[66] Small wonder that he regarded his solitariness as a forbidden pleasure, permissible only to Jean-Jacques because of his suffering at the hands of his enemies:

> It would not be desirable in our present state of affairs that the avid desire for these sweet ecstasies should give people a distaste for the active life that their constantly recurring needs impose upon them. But an unfortunate man who has been excluded from human society ... may be allowed to seek in this state a compensation for human joys.[67]

Above all, however, it was Rousseau's "indomitable spirit of freedom" which made him a true solitary. "I have never really been fitted for civil society, where everything is discomfort, obligation and duty," he wrote shortly before his death. "My independent nature has always made me incapable of enduring the constraints that are necessary for anyone who wants to live among men."[68] When the Jacobins came to venerate Rousseau they made this primal passion for liberty into a cardinal political virtue. But Rousseau himself would have had none of this. Free-spirited individuals – mavericks, nonconformists, solitaries – are the enemies of a well-ordered polity. The argument runs throughout his corpus, but its most psychologically developed treatment comes in *Emile*, as Rousseau wrestles with the relationship between self and society, solitude and sociality, and – not incidentally – men and women, and comes to some famously contentious conclusions.

---

[64] Rousseau, *Reveries*, p. 27; Rousseau, *Letters to Malesherbes*, CW V, pp. 572–583.
[65] Rousseau, *Confessions*, pp. 398–401.   [66] Rousseau, *Letters to Malesherbes*, CW V, p. 579.
[67] Starobinski, *Transparency*, p. 264.   [68] Damrosch, *Rousseau*, p. 41.

Emile is a work which tries – and fails – to reconcile the private self with the public good. At its heart is the opposition, first laid out in the *Second Discourse*, between "natural man," a "Savage [who] lives within himself," and "civil man" who is "always outside himself, is capable of living only in the opinion of others" and thus "derives the sentiment of his own existence solely from their [other people's] judgment."[69] Emile's education is intended to safeguard his natural autonomy while turning him into a model of civil manhood. The goal is impossible. To be a good citizen Emile must become what Rousseau most feared for himself: a person whose selfhood is defined wholly by his relations with others.

> Natural man is entirely for himself. He is numerical unity, the absolute whole which is relative only to itself or its kind. Civil man is only a fractional unity dependent on the denominator; his value is determined by his relation to the whole, which is the social body. Good social institutions are those that best know how to denature man, to take his absolute existence from him in order to give him a relative one, and transport the I into a common unity, with the result that each individual believes himself no longer one [...] and no longer feels except within the whole. A citizen of Rome was neither Caius or Lucius; he was a Roman.[70]

At the centre of this "denaturing" process is the suppression of the imagination. "All of Emile's early rearing," Alan Bloom has noted, "is an elaborate attempt to avoid the emergence of the imagination [...] the faculty that turns man's intellectual progress into the source of his misery."[71] As in all children, Emile's imagination remains dormant during his pre-adolescent years. Its awakening, at puberty, is accompanied by a host of dangers which "reading, solitude, [and] idleness" will all encourage. To prevent this, Emile's Mentor sets up a programme of study and physical activities aimed at inhibiting Emile's imagination by distracting him from solitary pursuits. "I would rather see him [Emile] in the midst of the worst society of Paris than alone in his room [...] given over to all the restlessness of his age. No matter what one does, the most dangerous of all enemies that can attack a young man [...] is himself."[72] The immediate risk is masturbation – that "dangerous supplement" – against which the Mentor insists on twenty-four hour surveillance of his pupil.[73] But the larger hazard is a world of social refuseniks who, seeking "to preserve the primacy of the sentiments of nature" in the civil order, end up as "double men," that is

---

[69] Rousseau, *Discourse on Inequality*, G1, p. 187.   [70] Rousseau, *Emile*, p. 40.
[71] A. Bloom, "Introduction," *Emile*, p. 7.   [72] Rousseau, *Emile*, p. 333.   [73] Ibid., p. 333–334.

miserable individuals like Rousseau himself who, "[s]wept along in contrary routes by nature and by men [. . .] end [our lives] without having been able to put ourselves in harmony with ourselves and without having been good either for ourselves or for others."[74]

How is Emile to be saved from this unhappy fate? "Emile is not a savage to be relegated to the desert. He is a savage made to inhabit cities."[75] Such an urban savage is truly a chimera; nonetheless, in pursuit of this vision the Mentor imposes on Emile an education which oscillates between a fierce repression of self masquerading as moral discipline, and a robust anti-authoritarianism. The boy is given *Robinson Crusoe* as an object lesson in self-dependence, while his Mentor covertly dictates his every thought and action.[76] Even in solitude there can be no privacy for Emile, whose mind and heart have been surreptitiously colonised.

But when it comes to Emile's future wife, Sophie, open repression is the watchword. Sophie, as portrayed in Book Five of *Emile*, is a paragon of Rousseauite femininity: sweet, shy, sexy: "made to please and to be sub-jugated." No pretence of self-rule for her. "Girls," Rousseau dictates, "must be enslaved to the most continual and most severe of constraints – that of the proprieties [. . . T]each them above all to conquer themselves."[77] Thus enslaved, Sophie becomes, as all wives must, her husband's lesser complement, a "fractional" creature; "a fanciful kind of half being," as Wollstonecraft characterises her. "She ought," Wollstonecraft says of Sophie, in her excoriating attack on *Emile* in the *Rights of Woman*,

> to sacrifice every other consideration to render herself agreeable to him [Emile]: and let this brutal desire of self-preservation be the grand spring of all her actions [. . .] to fit which her character should be stretched or contracted.[78]

To Wollstonecraft, Sophie is female oppression personified, in which guise she acted as a lightning rod for feminist opinion for half a century. But viewed within the wider frame of Rousseau's civic philosophy, we see that Sophie is in fact much more than this: she is the denatured citizen *par excellence*. Once "stretched or contracted" into Woman, Sophie becomes the ideal Rousseauite subject, the wholly acculturated individual who – like the good citizen of any well-ordered republic – "when he is alone, he is nothing."[79] Never let children "play by themselves," Rousseau counsels,

---

[74] Ibid., p. 41.   [75] Ibid., p. 205.   [76] Ibid., p. 185.   [77] Ibid., p. 369.
[78] Wollstonecraft, *Rights of Woman, Works* V, p. 148.
[79] Rousseau, "Considerations on the Government of Poland," G2, p. 189.

"but all together and in public, so that there is always a common goal to which all aspire."[80]

Woman is what civil man must become: a being estranged from his inner world, without the capacity or inclination for solitary fantasy. Or so it would seem. In fact in the heroine of *La Nouvelle Héloïse*, Julie D'Etange, Rousseau created one of the great solitaries of western fiction, a woman whose "passions" are all "born in solitude" and whose romantic dreams of her tutor-lover St. Preux provided thousands of European women with a model for solitary reverie.[81] And even Sophie, for all her prescribed docility, has her moment, as about halfway through Book Five of *Emile* an alter-Sophie suddenly appears who, abandoning domestic duties, hides herself in her room to dream and cry. What has happened? Sophie has fallen in love with Telemachus, son of Odysseus and eponymous hero of Fénelon's didactic novel on which *Emile* is based. Like so many romantic solitaries, Sophie has been overcome by love for a fictive object, one whose image is "imprinted on her soul." "Why," she demands, "cannot this someone exist, since I exist – I who feel within myself a heart so similar to his?" The result is near-disaster – enraged parents, a persecuted Sophie heading for the grave – until Rousseau directly intervenes in the story to whip the rebel back into line, depriving her of her "lively imagination," and replacing her copy of Fénelon with the *Spectator*. "I wanted to depict an ordinary woman, and by dint of elevating her soul I have disturbed her reason."[82]

Retrieved from her solitary dreams, Sophie is then whisked into marriage to Emile – and all seems well, until in a startling sequel to *Emile* (*Emile and Sophie; or The Solitaries*) she is corrupted by urban life and commits adultery. The couple separate and Emile is left heartsick and lonely. Eventually he ends up on a desert island, from where he writes to his erstwhile Mentor: "oh my master! My heart has been torn apart by all its attachments, it no longer holds anything."[83]

> What a void is made in us, how much does one lose of one's existence when one has depended on so many things and one must no longer depend on anything but oneself – or what is worse, on what makes us ceaselessly feel our detachment from the rest. I had to seek whether I was still that man who knows how to fill his place in his species when no individual takes an interest in it any longer.[84]

---

[80] Ibid., p. 191.   [81] Rousseau, *Julie or the New Eloise*, CW VI, p. 86.
[82] Rousseau, *Emile*, pp. 403–405.   [83] Rousseau, *Emile and Sophie*, CW XIII, p. 685.
[84] Ibid., p. 705.

The "void" in Emile is the loneliness of a man who has lost not only his life-partner but also his species-being. Emile is a second Crusoe stranded on his desert island, and his solitariness is not just wretched but inhuman. "It is man's weakness which makes him sociable," Rousseau writes,

> it is our common miseries which turn our hearts to humanity; we would owe humanity nothing if we were not men. Every attachment is a sign of insufficiency. If each of us had no need of others, he would hardly think of uniting himself with them. Thus from our very infirmity is born our frail happiness. A truly happy being is a solitary being. God alone enjoys an absolute happiness. But who among us has the idea of it? If some imperfect being could suffice unto himself, what would he enjoy according to us? He would be alone; he would be miserable. I do not conceive how someone who needs nothing can love anything. I do not conceive how someone who loves nothing can be happy.[85]

Rousseau knew this kind of lonely misery all too well. Again and again he expressed his yearning for love, and his terror of it. "I dread intimacy," he told a friend late in life. "I have closed my heart – but I have a leaden one."[86] "I carry a source of unhappiness in myself whose origin I don't know how to untangle," he wrote in his twenties, and all his attempts to alleviate this unhappiness – through friendship, sexual affairs, philosophy, solitary fantasy – ultimately failed him.[87] Dreaming alone in natural land-scapes would cheer him for a time, but even then "the nothingness of my chimeras sometimes suddenly c[o]me to sadden it [. . .] I found an inexplicable void in myself that nothing could fill."[88]

Perhaps if he were a woman . . .? Men of high sensibility were frequently accused of womanliness, of "effeminacy" and "foppery."[89] A worry no doubt for some; but for others – an opportunity? Rousseau always felt himself to be at least "half a woman," as he joked to a female friend when he started to wear his famous robes. "I thought as a man, I wrote as a man, and they disapproved; I'm going to turn myself into a woman."[90] But what sort of woman? A Sophie d'Houdetot perhaps, with her dashing male riding gear and "romantic air"?[91] Or better still a Julie, with her "heart [that] takes orders only from itself"?[92]

[85] Rousseau, *Emile*, p. 221.   [86] Damrosch, *Rousseau*, p. 470.   [87] Ibid., p. 234.
[88] Rousseau, *Letters to Malesherbes*, CW V, p. 579.
[89] G. Haggerty, *Men in Love: Masculinity and Sexuality in the Eighteenth Century* (New York: Columbia University Press, 1999), p. 96; P. Carter, *Men and the Emergence of Polite Society: Britain, 1660–1800* (London: Longman, 2001), pp. 101, 132.
[90] Damrosch, *Rousseau*, p. 372; J. Schwartz, *The Sexual Politics of Jean-Jacques Rousseau* (Chicago: University of Chicago Press, 1984), pp. 107–108.
[91] Damrosch, *Rousseau*, p. 267.   [92] Rousseau, *Julie*, p. 173.

Certainly not a Mary Wollstonecraft who, like Rousseau, loved freedom and solitude and longed to be "independent in every sense of the word" but, like Rousseau also, was haunted by feelings of loss and loneliness. All her life Wollstonecraft sought to reconcile her passionate desire for a self-governed existence with a "heart feelingly alive to all the affections of my nature."[93] For most of her life she could not achieve this, in part because – like Rousseau again – she found intimacy acutely difficult, but also because her feeling heart was female, which pitched her straight into the cultural anxieties surrounding lone womanhood.

If, as we saw earlier, the solitary woman was a suspect figure in Wollstonecraft's day, then this was even more so when aloneness was twinned with extreme sensibility. Passionate feelings in women (even religious or beneficent feelings) had always been perceived as having a strong sexual element: an equation eagerly exploited by commercial novelists who, by the late eighteenth century, had flooded the literary marketplace with sentimental heroines sighing and swooning their way through heart-palpating romances. The prurience of many of these "French" novels (many *were* French imports but even those that weren't often had the tag) led to an outpouring of public anxiety about the corruption of women readers, especially when reading alone.[94] Moralists inveighed against the "diseased books" favoured by women which "pollute the heart in the recesses of the closet [. . .] and teach all the malignity of vice in solitude."[95] Pornographic prints depicted women masturbating while reading in the privacy of their bedrooms.[96] Never before had the perils of female solitude seemed so great, or been so widely trumpeted.

For a woman who cherished aloneness, this equation between solitude, sensibility, and sexual pleasure posed a major dilemma. Wollstonecraft's novels show this very clearly. The fictional Mary of her first novel is a girl of "exquisite" sensibility who, as we saw earlier, loves solitary walks and reading poetry in isolated country spots. Deeply pious and intensely – indeed morbidly – benevolent, Mary spends most of her waking hours in lone spiritual reflection or in caring for others.[97] Thus far, so conventional.

---

[93] Wollstonecraft to G. Imlay, 6 September 1795, *Collected Letters*, p. 311.

[94] R. Porter, *Enlightenment: Britain and the Creation of the Modern World* (London: Penguin, 2000), pp. 286–287; J. Pearson, *Women's Reading in Britain, 1750–1835: A Dangerous Recreation* (Cambridge: Cambridge University Press, 1999).

[95] Porter, *Enlightenment*, p. 287.

[96] In 1772 the *Critical Review* described romantic novels as "companions of [women's] pillows" (T. Laqueur, *Solitary Sex: A Cultural History of Masturbation* [New York: Zone Books, 2003], p. 321).

[97] Wollstonecraft, *Mary: A Fiction, Works* I, pp. 11–17.

Yet this fictive Mary also demonstrates the feminist potentials of sensibility. Created while Wollstonecraft was reading *Emile*, she is many respects an anti-Sophie: a woman whose tender sensibilities are partnered by a "sublime imagination," a stringent moral code and "thinking powers [...] not subjugated to opinion."[98] Mary, in the language of the *Rights of Woman*, is a "human creature" first, and only secondarily a woman; she lacks a "sexual character," by which Wollstonecraft means the degraded femininity of a Sophie.[99] But she also lacks sexual passion: for much of the novel her "ardent affections" are directed at God. When they finally turn earthward, they fix on a sickly philosopher who soon dies, leaving Mary to expire in a spirit of pious resignation.[100]

Mary, Wollstonecraft wants her readers to understand, is a woman in whom strong sensibility is wedded to unassailable virtue, hence the chaste sublimity of her solitary ruminations. This is in sharp contrast to the "diseased sensibility" of her neglectful mother, whose hours of solitude are spent reading "those most delightful substitutes for bodily dissipation [...] sentimental novels."[101] A lady of fashion who cares nothing for her daughter, this woman embodies corrupt sensibility, her "false sentiments" and "voluptuous reveries" evoked by Wollstonecraft with a sneer of priggish disdain. Four years later the *Rights of Woman* picked up the theme, attacking novels that induce "a romantic twist of the mind" in their female readers, including Rousseau's *La Nouvelle Héloïse* which by the 1790s had acquired an awesome reputation for provoking its female readers into "sighs and torments" of an onanistic variety, or even inducing them to succumb to seduction.[102] The censorious note is unremitting, as the *Rights of Woman* flays the "depravity of the appetite which brings the sexes together" and the women who allow sensual appetite to get the better of them.[103] The woman of feeling must fix her heart on God, Wollstonecraft warns, lest she is "surprised by her sensibility into folly – into vice; and the dreadful reckoning falls heavily on her own weak head."[104]

This fierce hostility to the erotic did not last very long. Wollstonecraft was a virgin when she wrote *Mary* and the *Rights of Woman*. By the time she died, only five years after publishing the *Rights of Woman*, she had had at least two passionate sexual affairs, one of which had nearly killed her.

---

[98] Ibid., p. 5.   [99] Wollstonecraft, *Rights of Woman, Works* V, pp. 74, 88.
[100] Wollstonecraft, *Mary: A Fiction, Works* I, pp. 27–73.   [101] Ibid., I, p. 8.
[102] Wollstonecraft, *Rights of Woman, Works* V, p. 255; Laqueur, *Solitary Sex*, p. 323.
[103] Wollstonecraft, *Rights of Woman, Works*, V, p. 116.   [104] Ibid., p. 195.

Love had battered at her solitude, as it did at Rousseau's, leaving her bruised in ways that her fellow Solitary Walker had known all too well, but also changed in ways that only a woman could experience and express.

***

In June 1795 Wollstonecraft travelled to Scandinavia to sort out some business matters for her lover, Gilbert Imlay. She set out accompanied by her one-year-old daughter Fanny and her maid Marguerite, but as she moved northward these were left behind to be gathered up on the return journey. It was a wretched period in Wollstonecraft's life. Imlay, who prior to Fanny's birth had been a devoted paramour, had been involved with other women since. She clung to him desperately, as if life itself were at stake – as it had been two months earlier when, wild with misery, she had attempted suicide. Now, journeying through strange lands with neither lover nor child, she was wracked by the grief of abandonment. Yet, as always, the literary professional was on the *qui vive*, alert to possibilities. Shortly after returning to London Wollstonecraft brought out a volume of letters addressed to an errant lover, but in fact written for publication and never sent to Imlay. *Letters Written During a Short Residence in Sweden* was one of her best-received works, a favourite especially with the young Coleridge and Southey who enjoyed her self-portrayal as a melancholy solitaire, a companionless voyager in a loveless world.[105] The image of a lone woman of feeling ("fraught with imagination and sensibility," as Godwin later described her), shorn of all domestic ties, was touching but also pleasurably outré, a startling contrast to the stock sentimental heroines of the day.[106]

Relocated to the "half-savage" lands of Europe's northern fringe, Wollstonecraft meditated on her aloneness in new ways. She was lovesick, yet also deeply interested in her peculiar situation, and her prose reflects this, offering vivid, unsentimental evocations of her inner states, a repertoire of intense – and divided – reactions to her solitude. The miseries of a forsaken heart are set against the exaltations of a mind freed from constraint. "Here I am writing quite alone," she reports from Portor in Norway, after

[105] Wollstonecraft, *Letters Written During a Short Residence in Sweden, Norway and Denmark, Works* VI. For the young poets' reception of the book, and general Romantic enthusiasm for it, see Richard Holmes, "Introduction," in Mary Wollstonecraft and William Godwin (eds.), *A Short Residence in Sweden and Memoirs of the Author of a 'Vindication of the Rights of Woman'* (Harmondsworth: Penguin, 1987), pp. 36–42.
[106] Godwin, *Memoirs*, p. 249.

a hair-raising sea journey, "something more than gay, for which I want a name."[107] Yet returning to her lodgings in Tonsberg, she quails at entering the room, "without lighting-up pleasure in any eye – I dread the solitariness ... and wish for night to close my eyes on a world where I am destined to wander alone."[108]

As well as the letters which make up the *Short Residence*, Wollstonecraft also wrote privately to Imlay during her Scandinavian journey. These letters record her desperate struggles to survive the relationship. "Adieu! adieu! My friend," she wrote to him as the ship set sail from Hull, "your friendship is very cold [...] I may perhaps be, some time or other, independent in every sense of the word [...] I will break or bend this weak heart."[109] The trip itself, with its inevitable partings, became a replay of old losses and a rehearsal for the final solitude of death. "Black melancholy hovers around my footsteps," she wrote, as one lonely sight after another – an aged pine wood, a mountain waterfall, a deserted palace – filled her with thoughts of mortality, "the only thing of which I ever felt a dread."[110] Fear and misery stalked her. "Why am I forced to struggle thus?" she screamed to Imlay in letters written for his eye only, "I have never suffered in my life so much [...] from despair."[111]

Yet as the journey proceeded solitude showed her another face. Striding along mountain paths, rowing across fjords, writing alone in foreign rooms away from the world's "gaudy bustle," she felt herself expanding into the space around her, and gloried in the sensation. "I am more alive than you have seen me for a long, long time," she wrote to Imlay after a day spent scrambling over rocky hillsides.[112] Thrilling to the dramatic countryside, she flexed her imaginative muscles, producing a series of vivid landscape sketches that delighted her readers, especially the young romantics of her circle. "How often do my feelings produce ideas that remind me of the origin of many poetical fictions," she wrote exaltingly after a wonderful walk through a Norwegian pine forest.[113] The sense of renewal drew her thoughts gratefully upward to God and inward, as "turn[ing] over in this

---

[107] Wollstonecraft, *Short Residence, Works* VI, p. 293. The account of Wollstonecraft's Scandinavian journey that follows is derived from my "Separations of Soul: Solitude, Biography, History," *American Historical Review* 114:3 (2009): pp. 640–651.
[108] Ibid., p. 298.   [109] Wollstonecraft to G. Imlay, 21 June 1795, *Collected Letters*, p. 299.
[110] Wollstonecraft, *Short Residence, Works* VI, pp. 303, 281.
[111] Wollstonecraft to G. Imlay, 17 June 1795, *Collected Letters*, pp. 296–297.
[112] Wollstonecraft to G. Imlay, 4 July 1795, *Collected Letters*, p. 303.
[113] Wollstonecraft, *Short Residence, Works* VI, p. 286.

solitude a new page in the history of my own heart," she read what she found on it.[114] The introspection triggered a fierce inner conflict, as she struggled to imagine a life apart from Imlay. She had become his creature – the object once of his love and desire, now his resentment and pity – and repudiated this: "I am not, I will not be, merely an object of compassion – a clog to teize you," "I am content to be wretched, but I will not be contemptible."[115] The Imlay who obsessed her, she began to suspect, was a fiction born of need and solitude, and she fought to free herself from the "delusion." But she was haunted, possessed, and could not let go. "I cannot tear my affections from you though every remembrance stings me to the soul."[116] Being in the company of others intensified the sense of dependence. "I cannot live without a passion – and I feel the want of it more in society, than in solitude."[117] As the journey neared its end the conflict became unbearable. "I am unable to tear up by the roots [...] an affection which has been the torment of my life," she wrote to Imlay from Dover, "but life will have an end!"[118] Even God seemed to have abandoned her, as she returned to emotional disaster. Back in London she found Imlay living with a new mistress and attempted suicide for the second time, this time nearly succeeding. "I seem to have no home," she had written to Imlay from Norway, "now" she wrote in her suicide note, "I go to find comfort."[119]

Solitude is border country, the zone where self and other negotiate for possession of what Wollstonecraft would have called her soul. Early on in her Scandinavian journey, reflecting on her love for her child – that other continuous presence in her mind – Wollstonecraft brooded on the "imperious sympathies" that bound to her life.

> I have considered myself as a particle broken off from the grand mass of mankind [...] alone, till some involuntary sympathetic emotion, like the attraction of adhesion, made me feel that I was still part of a mighty whole, from which I could not sever myself [... even] by snapping the thread of existence.[120]

The lone "I" adheres to others in an involuntary relation that is sometimes replenishing, sometimes depleting, always risky. For Rousseau, the risks proved

[114] Ibid., p. 289.
[115] Wollstonecraft to G. Imlay, 26 August, 27 September 1795, *Collected Letters*, pp. 310, 313.
[116] Wollstonecraft to G. Imlay, 4 July 1795, *Collected Letters*, p. 303.
[117] Wollstonecraft to G. Imlay, 5 August 1795, *Collected Letters*, p. 308.
[118] Wollstonecraft to G. Imlay, 4 October 1795, *Collected Letters*, p. 316.
[119] Wollstonecraft to G. Imlay, 10 October 1795, *Collected Letters*, p. 317.
[120] Wollstonecraft, *Short Residence, Works* VI, pp. 248–249.

too great and he hid from them. Wollstonecraft too was almost scuppered, but she survived to forge a happy – sadly short-lived – relationship with Godwin. But the love of solitude never left her, and she continued to think about its meanings for women. She also never stopped thinking about Rousseau, and two years after her affair with Imlay ended she began writing a novel that brought together these preoccupations for the final time. *The Wrongs of Woman, or Maria* (1798) was incomplete at Wollstonecraft's death and published posthumously by Godwin, to a torrent of outraged criticism.

Like *Mary: A Fiction, The Wrongs of Woman* depicts a woman of sensibility fallen foul of cruel circumstances.[121] The novel is set in a lunatic asylum where Maria, an heiress, has been confined by her wicked husband. Alone in her cell, she finds refuge in Rousseau: a male prisoner, learning of her presence, has a warder take her his copy of *La Nouvelle Hèloïse*. Reading it, she promptly falls in love with St. Preux and invests her fellow prisoner with the tutor's attributes; they become lovers. "We see what we wish, and make a world of our own," Wollstonecraft tells her readers warningly, before unfolding a tale of disillusionment and betrayal (the prisoner-lover is an Imlay clone).[122] Solitude plus Rousseau has made Maria dangerously romantic, but also defiant. Her adultery discovered, she is hauled up with her lover before a judge. But Maria is uncowed, and in court she defends a woman's right to love whom she chooses.

> To this person [...] I voluntarily gave myself [...] I wish my country to approve of my conduct; but if laws exist, made by the strong to oppress the weak, I appeal to my own sense of justice.[123]

Like Sophie with her Telemachus, Maria is a fabulist, a concocter of amorous fictions for whom solitude spells misery, but also peril, excitement, opportunity. However, unlike Sophie, Maria has no Rousseau to rob her of her aloneness. Her adventurous solitude belongs to her, is inherent to her humanity, which – in an age that increasingly valued docile, socialised Sophies over wayward visionaries of either sex – represented no small triumph for the female spirit. Responding to a male friend who on reading a draft version of the *Wrongs of Woman* told Wollstonecraft that he found Maria's marital situation insufficiently "important," Wollstonecraft retorted that "[f]or my part I cannot imagine any situation more distressing than for a woman of sensibility with an improving mind" to be "bound" to

---

[121] Wollstonecraft, *The Wrongs of Woman, or Maria, Works* I, pp. 79–184.
[122] Ibid., pp. 95–96, 104–106, 173. [123] Ibid., p. 180.

"such a husband as I have sketched." Better to be a sexual outlaw, a social outcast, a Solitary Walker, than a woman subject to "matrimonial despotism." A life apart could be hard, sometimes very lonely; but for a freedom-loving woman, like a maverick *philosophe*, in this hard world it was often the only life worth living.

CHAPTER 12

Rousseau and Madame de Staël:
A Surprising Dialogue

Aurelian Craiutu

L'on se sent entraîné par lui comme par un ami, un séducteur, un maître.
~ Madame de Staël

Although Madame de Staël's youthful admiration for Rousseau, as expressed in her *Lettres sur les écrits et le caractère de J. J. Rousseau* (1788), has been noted and studied, especially by feminists and comparative literature scholars, relatively little scholarly attention has been devoted to exploring how her *political* thought articulated in her later writings – *Réflexions sur la paix intérieure* (1795), *Des circonstances actuelles qui peuvent terminer la Révolution et des principes qui doivent fonder la république en France* (1798), and *Considérations sur les principaux événements de la Révolution française* (1818) – relates to Rousseau's political and philosophical ideas. This is all the more surprising since Rousseau's politics of authenticity and his theory of the general will exercised a powerful influence on many postrevolutionary writers in France and were, along with Montesquieu, unavoidable reference points in public and parliamentary debates during the first years of the Revolution. In this chapter, I examine the extent to which Rousseau's political ideas, as mediated by the experience of the French Revolution, inspired and provoked Jacques Necker's daughter to articulate her own republican and liberal doctrine. Under the influence of her father's ideas, and through conversations and engagement with the ideas of other members of the famous Coppet group, including Benjamin Constant and Sismonde de Sismondi, Madame de Staël developed an original political agenda that made her one of Napoleon's staunchest enemies and inspired an entire generation of political thinkers who came of age during the Bourbon Restoration.

If Necker[1] was undoubtedly the most important source of inspiration for his daughter throughout her entire life, Rousseau came in second place,

---

[1] On Necker's political (economic and religious) thought, see H. Grange, *Les idées de Necker* (Paris: Klinksieck, 1974). I have analyzed Necker's political moderation in Chapter 4 of my book, *A Virtue*

ahead of Montesquieu. That Madame de Staël was deeply influenced by
the author of *Émile* should not come as a surprise after all. For one thing,
Rousseau had been a favorite subject of conversation in her mother's
Parisian salon in which she made, so to speak, her first sentimental
education. Rousseau's restlessness, his radical individualistic leanings,
and romantic longings resonated with the restiveness of his younger
admirer. In 1796 she wrote an entire volume about the importance of
passions, *De l'influence des passions sur le bonheur des individus et des
nations*, that was, in some respects, a Rousseauian book (unfortunately,
the political part was never completed). On several occasions, Madame
de Staël acknowledged Rousseau's irresistible spell and his powerful
literary influence and referred to him (in the first volume of *De la
littérature*) as the most eloquent among all French writers. Rousseau's
intense quest for authenticity and autonomy exercised a powerful mys-
tique over his younger admirer who admitted that, if Rousseau had not
discovered anything new, he had certainly set on fire everything he
touched.[2] She often considered him as a model and indispensable partner
of dialogue in her own project of self-examination, self-revelation, and
self-knowledge carried out with the same dramatic brilliance.

What should strike us, however, is how much their political projects
differed in several important respects, in spite of the sentimental and
literary affinities between them. The last book written by Necker's daughter turned out to be unlike anything Rousseau ever wrote and stood for.
It offered a strong endorsement of the English constitutional monarchy,
that is, the very system which had been flatly rejected by Rousseau in *Du
contrat social* because of its allegedly illusory freedom and factitious stability. It is the transition from the lyrical praise of Rousseau in *Lettres sur
Rousseau* to the moving eulogy of England in Part VI of *Considérations* that
I shall analyze here. If Madame de Staël's political allegiances evolved over
time, back and forth between constitutional monarchy and republicanism,
I believe that in all of these changes her reflections retained a remarkable
thematic and conceptual unity and coherence, built around the concept of

for Courageous Minds: Moderation in French Political Thought, 1748–1830 (Princeton: Princeton
University Press, 2012), pp. 113–157.
[2] See S. Génand, "'Une lecture qui nous interesse comme un événement de notre vie': Rousseau et la
refléxion biographique chez Germaine de Staël," in F. Lotterie and G. Poisson (eds.), *Jean-Jacques
Rousseau devant Coppet* (Geneva: Slatkine, 2012), pp. 35–53. On Rousseau and Madame de Staël, also
see L. Marso, *(Un)Manly Citizens: Jean-Jacques Rousseau's and Germaine de Staël's Subversive Women*
(Baltimore: Johns Hopkins University Press, 2001).

political moderation, the red thread that can be found in all of her political writings.[3]

Lettres sur Rousseau

In her first book written in 1788, which revealed her talent as a writer and consisted of six letters (chapters), a young and enthusiastic Anne Louise Germaine Necker, who had just tied the knot of her first (unhappy) marriage to the much older Swedish Baron Staël von Holstein, linked her literary destiny to that of Rousseau, whose writings she compared to a magic personal mirror. *Lettres sur Rousseau* are an intense personal text that displays the profound sentimental affinities between the two authors. Not only did the young Germaine confess her fascination with Rousseau, but she went a step forward in claiming that all pure souls devoted to liberty and justice must recognize Rousseau as their friend, in spite of his complex personality, not devoid of some flaws (among them, Madame de Staël half-heartedly acknowledged Rousseau's pride and vanity). She considered Rousseau, after her beloved father, an inspiration for an entire generation and referred to him as Necker's "*ange tutélaire.*"[4]

The irony of associating the extremely rich banker and Prime Minister of Louis XVI with his fellow Genevan citizen who had been a staunch critic of monarchy should not go unnoticed.[5] Yet, it was not so much Rousseau's political ideas that came to the fore in this early writing of Madame de Staël as his complex and contradictory character. To be sure, Rousseau's political writings are discussed in the fourth letter (and a brief reference to the second *Discourse* as a "great effort of genius" can be found in the first chapter),[6] but the analysis is quite short and does not go into much detail. Still, a few details are worth pointing out. Comparing Rousseau with Montesquieu, Madame de Staël argued that the latter is "more useful to already formed societies"[7] while the former can be a source of inspiration for those that are being formed for the first time. Rousseau was presented as a friend of a true form of liberty that does not artificially separate people, but can bring them closer together. After highlighting the importance of

---

[3] On Madame de Staël's political moderation, see Craiutu, *A Virtue for Courageous Minds*, pp. 158–197.

[4] G. de Staël, *Lettres sur les écrits et le caractère de J. J. Rousseau* in *Œuvres Complètes de Madame la Baronne de Staël publiées par son fils* (Paris: Treuttel and Würtz, 1821), I, p. 16.

[5] She goes as far as to claim that had he been alive, Rousseau would have loved and approved of Necker's ideas as much as she did. This is an implausible claim, to put it mildly.

[6] Ibid., p. 2.   [7] Ibid., p. 16.

the social contract which provides the "foundations of all legitimate power,"[8] Madame de Staël somewhat timidly suggested that Rousseau, who admired direct democracy and famously rejected political representation in *Du contrat social*, might have misunderstood the nature of the English government. A brief (and surprisingly positive) reference to Rousseau's method also appeared in this fourth letter. Madame de Staël compared him to a geometer who seeks to be as rigorous as possible and applies calculus to political matters. Oddly, she seemed to endorse this approach, without asking herself whether or not it might be in tension with Rousseau's (and her own) powerful imagination and sensibility.

Not surprisingly, the last – and arguably the most interesting – of the six letters comprising this short book was entitled "Sur le caractère de Rousseau"[9] and was devoted to Rousseau's *Confessions* (observations about Rousseau's character can be found, however, throughout the entire text). Madame de Staël described Rousseau as a friend made to live in nature and seclusion rather than in society and she praised the astonishing variety of Rousseau's sentiments, his restless soul and powerful imagination, nourished by his equally profound eloquence, sincerity, and enthusiasm. There are certain truths, she wrote, "*vérités de sentiment*"[10], whom only a profound soul can feel and grasp. Rousseau's blessing was to have been born with exactly such a penetrating soul that could see directly into the heart of reality where the gaze of his fellow citizens could hardly reach. Among all the people in the world, she argued (in the third letter), Rousseau was the one least likely to take and write about things lightly and he systematically applied this attitude to all the subjects he examined, including religion. Far from being an atheist, as some accused him, Rousseau was, in her opinion, a believer *sui generis*.[11] Madame de Staël also resonated with Rousseau's "somber melancholy,"[12] so evident in his literary and autobiographical writings, which echoed her own restless disposition, prone to anxiety, depression, and despair and fearful of solitude (they both seem to have had difficulty in sustaining long-term intimate relationships).

---

[8] Ibid., p. 15.
[9] The previous five ones touched upon Rousseau's style in his first writings on inequality and arts and sciences, on Héloïse and Émile. Rousseau's passion for music and botany is the subject of the fifth letter.
[10] Ibid., p. 16.
[11] "Rousseau croyait à l'éxistence de Dieu, par son esprit et par son cœur" (ibid., p. 14).
[12] Ibid., p. 23.

In her view, the author of *Émile* managed, better than anyone else, to combine intellectual depth, literary eloquence, warmth, excess, and moderation (!) in his writings and own life. Toward the end of the book, she waxed lyrically – "*Renais, donc, o, Rousseau! renais donc de ta cendre !*"[13] – encouraging her readers to be gentle toward her controversial idol who had been a constant defender of the weak and unfortunate ones and a passionate lover of virtue. Rousseau, Madame de Staël claimed, "was a man who had to be left alone thinking without asking anything more from him; he had to be guided as a child and listened to as an oracle!"[14]

If many of his contemporaries hailed her call and drew (or thought they were drawing) inspiration from Rousseau's ideas, when time came to build a new and legitimate form of government on the ruins of the absolute monarchy, their efforts had unintended consequences and, in some cases, even perverse outcomes. The famous *Declaration of the Rights of Man and of the Citizen* signed on August 1789 contained several Rousseauian ideas and borrowed a few concepts that bore striking resemblance to those of the *Social Contract*. Yet, the "oracle" Rousseau could do little to ensure the successful application of his theories or to make sure that those who were invoking his name were true to his real intentions. Under the undeniable influence of his ideas, a political culture of generality developed that allowed the Jacobins to make and justify their problematic distinction between revolutionary and constitutional government.

All this became obvious in the intense debates in the Constituent Assembly (and beyond) during the summer and fall of 1789 on the rights of man, representation (mandates), bicameralism, veto power, and balance of powers. In these debates, the name of Rousseau was invoked by supporters and critics alike, but in the end, his ideas were misinterpreted and distorted to the point that Rousseau himself might not have agreed with those who, consciously or unconsciously, borrowed his language of virtues and duties and invoked his theory of liberty and general will while pursuing their own dreams of power. While it is virtually impossible to clearly specify the extent to which the Terror of 1793–94 was the work of circumstances, social structure, and/or ideology, it is beyond doubt that, in the short-run, Rousseau's reputation suffered after 9 Thermidor.

[13] Ibid., p. 17.   [14] Ibid., p. 19.

Réflexions sur la paix intérieure and Des circonstances actuelles

For all of his sincere enthusiasm for liberty, Rousseau seemed an unlikely source of inspiration for those who sought to contribute to the debate on "ending" the French Revolution after the fall of Robespierre. A "liberalism of fear" grounded in a system of checks of balances *sui generis* eventually became the order of the day, replacing the romantic republicanism of Rousseauian extraction. Consequently, during the Directory liberal-minded thinkers such as Madame de Staël and Constant felt compelled to take (some) distance from Rousseau's ideas. To be sure, in Madame de Staël's two most important political writings from this period, *Réflexions sur la paix intérieure* (1795)[15] and *Des circonstances actuelles* (1797–98), the admiration for Rousseau the political writer seems to have faded away, but the image of Rousseau remained, as it were, behind the curtain. If enthusiasm is allowed in "sentiments and personal life," she now believed, it had no place whatsoever in "practical projects."[16] Although she now unambiguously placed Necker above Rousseau and distanced herself from her initial enthusiasm for the latter, Madame de Staël continued her dialogue with her egregious predecessor, sometimes without even quoting him.

In many ways, *Réflexions sur la paix intérieure* and *Des circonstances actuelles* were highly political writings in which Madame de Staël addressed the enemies and friends of the new republic and openly declared her allegiance to the new republican government. "I sincerely wish the establishment of the French Republic upon the sacred bases of justice and humanity," she confessed. "I desire it because it has been made clear to me that, under the current circumstances, only the republican government can give France peace and liberty."[17] There were several reasons that might have convinced her, a previous defender of constitutional monarchy (also

---

[15] The *Réflexions sur la paix intérieure* were printed but never distributed, mostly out of prudential considerations suggested by her close friend, François de Pange. The reference work on this period of her life remains B. Munteano, *Les idées politiques de Madame de Staël et la Constitution de l'an III* (Paris: Les Belles Lettres, 1931).

[16] G. de Staël, *Des circonstances actuelles qui peuvent terminer la Révolution et des principes qui doivent fonder la république en France*, ed. L. Omacini (Geneva: Slatkine, 1979), p. 328. A recent updated and enlarged version was published in G. de Staël, *Œuvres Complètes, Série III: Œuvres historiques, Tome I, Des circonstances actuelles et autres essais politiques sous la Révolution*, ed. L. Omacini (Paris: Honoré Champion, 2009). For a review of this volume, see A. Craiutu, "Flirting with Republicanism: Madame de Staël's Writings from the 1790s," *History of European Ideas* 36:3 (2010): 343–346.

[17] Quoted in G. Gwynne, *Madame de Staël et la Révolution française* (Paris: A.G. Nizet, 1969), p. 29. The irony is that the new republican regime viewed Madame de Staël with skepticism and monitored her movements. In October 1795, she was ordered her to leave France and was placed under constant surveillance across the border.

supported by her beloved father), that the republic was the best form of government for France under the Directory. One such reason, if not the most important one, was the fact that the republic was already a *fait accompli* and the republican government seemed the best available protection against instability and anarchy (Necker, however, thought otherwise). A sincere belief on her part in the theoretical superiority of republicanism should not be excluded either, but it is likely that her allegiance to republicanism, without being entirely opportunistic, combined both prudential and principled considerations. It was also, at times, a bit excessive, as her father believed.

One thing is clear though. If republicanism had been the doctrine advocated by Rousseau, the conservative form of republicanism endorsed by Madame de Staël's in her writings during the Directory had, at least on surface, remarkably little in common with his ideas. It may not be an accident that Rousseau's name did not appear in her *Réflexions sur la paix intérieure*, an ambitious short but dense text in which she called upon all the friends of liberty to rally around the new French republic. Madame de Staël's main preoccupation in 1795 was to help France build a new center based on the principles of constitutionalism and political moderation. While she embraced the ideal of a liberty above or beyond all parties and referred to the "sacred love of freedom [. . .] which electrifies all souls,"[18] her words carried surprisingly few or no Rousseauian connotations whatsoever. The liberty she referred to in *Réflexions sur la paix intérieure* and, later, in *Des circonstances actuelles* was to be provided by representative government, that is, the very form of government that Rousseau thought incompatible with liberty.

Moreover, she came to believe that the fledgling French Republic needed a vital political center in order to survive the ever more menacing attacks of its opponents, left and right. She took to task radical republicans for having been immoderate in their attachment to democratic principles and took the legitimists for living only in the past and being unwilling to open their eyes and try to understand the present. In order to exorcise the specter of anarchy, she insisted, France needed political moderation and the rule of law, and the principles of representative government were the only effective remedies through which the wounds of the past could properly heal. That meant, among other things, divided sovereignty, a proper balance of powers in the state, and the participation of the people through their elected representatives in the exercise of the legislative power.

---

[18] Staël, *Œuvres Complètes*, I, p. 46.

Her text advocated three other principles which, not surprisingly, had also been endorsed by Necker: bicameralism, a strong and independent executive, and respect for private property. Needless to say, Rousseau would have rejected all these solutions and one might surmise that he would have dismissed Madame de Staël's call to moderation as a form of complacency or, worse, a pernicious combination of blindness and opportunism.

She renewed her appeal to moderation located in a hypothetical *juste milieu* between extremes in *Des circonstances actuelles qui peuvent terminer la Révolution et des principes qui doivent fonder la république en France* written in 1798. The long title of this important manuscript (which has not appeared in print in its integral form until 1979) reveals the ambitious scope and the difficult nature of her task. A political manifesto and treatise at once, written after the fateful events of 18 Fructidor (which she initially supported before coming to regret her imprudent position), *Des circonstances actuelles* was described by some commentators as "one of the most representative texts of republican constitutionalism"[19] ever written, and a true "discourse of method of the new republicanism."[20] It was to be her most complex writing and it requires (at least) two levels of interpretation. On the one hand, it can be interpreted as a circumstantial work that sought to offer a reasonable policy of cohabitation and reconciliation. Madame de Staël continued to believe the republic could be saved only if all of the *honnêtes hommes* rallied to support the new republican institutions and principles. On the other hand, the book rests upon a sophisticated theoretical foundation that marked a notable departure from her previous admiration for Rousseau.

Madame de Staël's manuscript, drafted at a point in time when her salon at Coppet began rising in prominence, was the outcome of an intense dialogue with Benjamin Constant and Sismonde de Sismondi. Already active in 1798, the Coppet group witnessed its golden age from 1804, when Necker died, to 1810, when Staël's *De l'Allemagne* was published in London. The group also included other prominent figures such as Mathieu de Montmorency to Sismonde de Sismondi, Friedrich Tieck, and Charles-Victor de Bonstteten.[21] Their political writings, in spite of

---

[19] M. Barberis, "Constant, Madame de Staël et la constitution républicaine: un essai d'interprétation," in F. Tilkin (ed.), *Le groupe de Coppet et le monde moderne: conceptions-images-débats* (Geneva: Droz, 1998), p. 193.

[20] G. Gengembre and J. Goldzink, "Une femme révolutionnée: le Thermidor de Mme de Staël," *Annales Benjamin Constant*, 8–9 (Lausanne & Paris: Institut Benjamin Constant & Jean Touzot, 1988), p. 275. Also see R. Mortier, "Comment terminer la Révolution et fonder la République," *Annales Benjamin Constant*, 8–9, pp. 293–307.

their differences, reveal many important similarities and point to a common discourse which made the Coppet circle (located in today's Switzerland), in the words of Lucien Jaume, "*le creuset de l'esprit libéral*"[22] in France. They all shared a strong commitment to liberty and moderation and were highly cosmopolitan in their intellectual proclivities and tastes.

When Madame de Staël sat down to write *Des circonstances actuelles* in 1798, she reflected on much the same topics as her friend Constant would do in *Fragments d'un ouvrage abandonné sur la possibilité d'une constitution républicaine dans un grand pays* which he began around the same time and completed in 1802 or so.[23] In his own book, which also remained unpublished during his life, Constant examined the possibility of creating a republic in a large modern state. Recent scholarship has demonstrated that the two thinkers commented on each other's drafts, and borrowed freely from each other's ideas to the point that it virtually impossible in some places to distinguish their voices clearly.[24] Equally worth noting is the fact that at about the same time, Sismondi was writing his own *Recherches sur les constitutions des peuples libres*. Started in 1797, this important (and still little-known) book manuscript was completed four years later but was never published either (Constant and Sismondi would meet in 1801).[25] There was a clear affinity between the three books by Madame de Staël, Sismondi, and Constant and any reader of them can easily discover that their authors had a surprisingly similar attitude – respectful but critical –

[21] I have commented on the political moderation of the Coppet group in A. Craiutu, "Moderation and the Group of Coppet" in K. Szmurlo (ed.), *Germaine de Staël's Politics of Mediation: Challenges to History and Culture* (Oxford: Voltaire Foundation, 2011), pp. 109–124. The place of Madame de Staël in the context of modern French thought is analyzed in L. Jaume, *L'Individu effacé ou le paradoxe du libéralisme français* (Paris: Fayard, 1997), pp. 25–62.

[22] See L. Jaume (ed.), *Coppet, creuset de l'esprit liberal: les idées politiques et constitutionnelles du group de Madame de Staël* (Marseille & Paris: Presses Universitaires d'Aix-Marseille & Economica, 2000).

[23] Constant's *Fragments d'un ouvrage abandonné sur la possibilité d'une constitution républicaine dans un grand pays* was published posthumously in 1991 under the editorship of Henri Grange at Aubier. A critical edition of the text has recently been published in Constant, *Œuvres Complètes, vol. IV. Discours au Tribunat. De la possibilité d'une constitution républicaine dans un grand pays (1799–1803)*, eds. M. Sánchez-Mejía and K. Kloocke (Tübingen: Niemeyer Verlag, 2005), pp. 355–761.

[24] On this issue, see E. Paulet-Grandguillot, *Libéralisme et démocratie. De Sismondi à Constant, à partir du Contrat social (1801–1806)* (Geneva: Slatkine, 2010).

[25] Sismondi's *Recherches sur les constitutions des peuples libres* were edited and published by Marco Minerbi at Droz (Geneva) in 1965. The published text represents, however, only the last batch of the entire manuscript which consists of three other parts. The second part was published in R. di Reda (ed.), *Libertà e scienza del governo in Sismondi, vol. II: Essais sur les constitutions des peuples libres* (Rome: Jouvence, 1988). For a detailed analysis of this important yet neglected text, see Paulet-Grandguillot, *Libéralisme et démocratie*. For a review of the latter, see A. Craiutu, "A Tale of Two Moderates," *History of European Ideas*, 39: 1 (2013): 141–150.

toward Rousseau. They did not consider him *"un adversaire à combattre"*[26] and never joined the ranks of his detractors, so numerous in France and abroad. Instead, they felt compelled to seriously engage with Rousseau's ideas, in a direct or oblique manner, while seeking to correct his alleged errors and amend his theories.

To be sure, almost everything in *Des circonstances actuelles*, from Madame de Staël's defense of *la liberté des modernes* to her embrace of constitutionalism, represented the opposite of what Rousseau advocated in his three *Discourses* and the *Social Contract*. Her previous idol would have been disappointed by her cavalier dismissal of direct democracy and her endorsement of representative government grounded in respect for individual rights and security of property.[27] Democracy, he would have answered, should not be equated with mobocracy and the corrupted form of popular sovereignty that had been used to legitimize the Jacobin dictatorship. He would have disagreed even more, perhaps, with Madame de Staël's final stated goal, the creation of a genuine aristocracy of talent capable of correcting the shortcomings of extreme equality. Such a system would have placed power in the hands of a small number of citizens rather than the majority, corrupting the general will. It would have made little difference, Rousseau might have said, if this elite were comprised of "the most enlightened, most virtuous, and most courageous,"[28] for it would be the opposite of direct democracy and as such, it would be illegitimate.

Most likely, the greatest point of contention between the two would have been Madame de Staël's conception of liberty and the claim that legislators must give priority to the protection of individual independence against collective power. In *Des circonstances actuelles*, her allegiance to political liberty was obviously informed by the experience of the Revolution and the Terror, and the need to cure the country of its previous revolutionary fervor. "Ignorant people want to be free," she once wrote, "but only the enlightened minds know how one can be free."[29] Liberty, she suggested again in 1798, requires a difficult and

[26] Paulet-Grandguillot, *Libéralisme et démocratie*, p. 49.
[27] I note in passing that it is (and was) possible to choose representative government over direct (pure) democracy and also give, in a Rousseauian vein, an almost unlimited power to the people's representatives. Such a hybrid position was, in fact, espoused by Sieyès, an unconventional disciple and critic of Rousseau.
[28] Staël, *Des circonstances actuelles*, p. 188. Also: "C'est par l'élection libre et sagement combinée que vous consacrerez l'inégalité naturelle, seule remède aux suites funestes de l'inégalité factice" (ibid., p. 40).
[29] Staël, *Œuvres Complètes*, I, p. 46.

arduous apprenticeship and a distinctive set of mores. In making this claim, she might have borrowed a trope from Rousseau, but the gist of her argument took her in the opposite direction. She parted company with Rousseau when claiming that the love of liberty needs to be combined with respect for the liberty of the moderns, a concept dismissed and derided by her predecessor.

While Rousseau, who was a modern mind with an ancient soul, unambiguously preferred the liberty of the virtuous ancients to the superficial and illusory freedom enjoyed by his contemporaries (preoccupied only by material gain), Madame de Staël held a different view. She believed that the main role of laws in modern society is to protect private property and the private sphere from any form of illegitimate interference. "The liberty of present times," she wrote, "consists of everything that guarantees the independence of citizens against the power of government."[30] This includes the protection of private property which, unlike Rousseau who regarded it as the main source of a lack of freedom in modern society, she considered to be "the origin, the basis and the link of the social pact."[31] She preferred modern society, in which citizens are allowed to freely pursue their private interests, to ancient republics which asked their citizens to sacrifice their individual interests for the sake of the common good. Such a strong demand, Madame de Staël argued, can hardly be made in the more diverse modern society in which it is no longer possible to identify a "common good" which all citizens should virtuously follow. In France of today, she wrote in 1798, one becomes attached to the cause of the republic and comes to love it only when one feels one's life and property duly protected by it. The only liberty suitable to modern mores, she concluded, is that which protects the private individual sphere against any form of undue social and political interference.

This modern form of liberty, Madame de Staël insisted, further departing from Rousseau, could be achieved only through a complex institutional architecture at the heart of which lies a system of checks and balances that distribute and limit sovereignty and power. Rejecting Rousseau's understanding of sovereignty articulated in the first four chapters of Book II of *Du contrat social*, Madame de Staël opposed his doctrine of the indivisibility, infallibility, and inalienability of the general will. Much like Sismondi, she believed that Rousseau's theory was marred by important

---

[30] Staël, *Des circonstances actuelles*, p. 111.   [31] Ibid., p. 47.

contradictions. It was difficult to argue simultaneously for the total alienation of individual rights and deny at the same time that the general will can
ever be represented. It was impossible to maintain that people may be
forced to be free and affirm at the same time that the social contract offers
the most effective protection of individual liberty as absence of
domination.

Madame de Staël must have been particularly concerned about
Rousseau's monist theory of sovereignty which claimed that "limited
sovereignty" was a contradiction in terms. Rousseau had famously asserted
that the will of the people could only be represented by a single and simple
organ (the legislative body) and he regarded plurality of interests as
a synonym for disunion and factionalism, preferring instead social homogeneity and unanimity. Such an illiberal perspective was alien to Madame
de Staël's outlook which followed in her father's footsteps. "The sovereignty in a free country, in a wisely organized political society," Necker
had argued in *Réflexions philosophiques sur l'égalité*, published as an appen-
dix to *De la Révolution française* (1796), can never exist in a simple manner,
and a mere majority may never serve as a title and justification for the
unlimited exercise of sovereignty. In other words, both Necker and his
daughter believed that, in order for sovereignty to be limited, it may never
be simple.

Des circonstances actuelles spelled out the implications of such a liberal
view even if the notion of mixed government did not loom large in this text
(as it did in Sismondi's work, for example). Madame de Staël sought to
demonstrate the possibility and the legitimacy of a representative government that expresses the national will and protects the pluralism of interests
and groups that comprise the nation. This view was pregnant with several
important implications. One of them had to do with representation,
a topic on which Madame de Staël and Rousseau's ideas clashed.
Representation looms large in her book manuscript and it is obvious that
she considered it a pillar of modern liberty. The nation, she argued (relying
again on one of his father's main ideas rather than on Rousseau), cannot be
free as long as absolute power is allowed to exist unchallenged in society, be
that the power of a monarch, a group, or the representatives of the nation.
The nation is truly free only when two important conditions are met: (1) its
representatives give voice to the interests of the people and earn their trust;
and (2) they have their hands tied by a constitution. On this view, political
liberty emerges not simply as the outcome of the implementation of the
sovereignty of the nation, but as the result of an equilibrium or balance of
powers. Such a complex institutional arrangement gives individuals

effective means of resisting the encroachment of their rights and puts effective limits on any sovereign power.

The other important implication concerns pluralism and intermediary bodies, two related issues toward which Rousseau had a dismissive attitude in most of his political writings. Like Sismondi and Constant, Madame de Staël questioned Rousseau's alleged identity between the general interest of the people and the myriad of individual interests that people follow. Legislators in modern society, she argued, must allow all the groups that comprise a nation to share in its sovereignty in order to prevent any entity from dominating over others. As a result, she shifted the emphasis from the Rousseauian claim that all citizens must equally participate in politics to the need for securing a balanced and orderly participation of all groups in the collective exercise of sovereignty. On this view, the legitimacy of intermediary bodies can no longer be questioned, nor can Rousseau's distrust of them be justified. No intermediary bodies, no liberty, she concluded. Montesquieu would have been very happy to see his insight vindicated decades after his death!

Considérations

If Rousseau remained an important interlocutor for Madame de Staël in *Des circonstances actuelles*, albeit in an oblique way, he almost entirely disappeared from sight in her last, unfinished, and posthumously published book on the French revolution, entitled *Considérations sur les principaux évènements de la Révolution française* (1818). There are only three minor references to Rousseau in this big book, and one of them is a claim attributed to Napoleon who allegedly described Rousseau as the cause of the French Revolution. *Considérations* were in many ways a strange book and a highly polemical one. "Fundamentally a composite,"[32] it was part memoir, part reflections on lived events, yet like all of her previous writings, Madame de Staël's reflections on the causes and events of the Revolution, too, bore the mark of her sparkling personality and profound wit. She wanted to vindicate the wisdom of her father and one of the main goals of the book was precisely to demonstrate the reasonableness of Necker's ideas. Some accused her of writing a hagiography and they had their own reasons to think so. Others

---

[32] M. Gauchet, "Staël," in *A Critical Dictionary of the French Revolution*, eds. F. Furet and M. Ozouf (Cambridge, MA: Harvard University Press, 1989), p. 1009.

took her to task for offering a selective and subjective reading of the past. In 1798, she had maintained that in France, liberty was ancient and despotism modern, and now she set out to justify that claim in further detail.[33] On the eve of the Revolution, she notes (in a tone that reminds one of Rousseau), France was a country where no fixed political principles existed. "France," Madame de Staël wrote, "has been governed by custom, often by caprice, and never by law. [. . .] The course of circumstances alone was decisive of what everyone called his right."[34] Rousseau could have agreed with this and would have probably endorsed her claim that in the Old Regime France, classes were separated from each other and absorbed in the pursuit of power under the domineering effect of vanity and arrogance.

Nonetheless, Rousseau would have strongly disagreed with the conclusions in Part VI of the book in which Madame de Staël went beyond her main stated goal – to offer a more or less comprehensive view of the principal events of the French Revolution – and championed a vigorous liberal agenda grounded in the principles of constitutionalism and representative government. The latter had previously loomed large in *Des circonstances actuelles*, but now it was explicitly linked to the concept of constitutional monarchy. The book ends with a long and moving eulogy of England presented as a political model for France. In these pages, Madame de Staël's tone was nothing but neutral and she was far from being an impartial observer of the English scene. Her approach was normative rather than descriptive and she called upon the French, only a few years after the crushing defeat at Waterloo, to imitate the political institutions of England in order to overcome their legacy of despotism, absolute power, and centralization. Madame de Staël also had great things to say about England's "mixture of chivalrous spirit with an enthusiasm for liberty"[35] and she praised the English aristocrats for identifying themselves with the nation at large and for having avoided becoming a privileged caste, detached from the management of local affairs, as it happened in France. The economic prosperity of English she attributed it to the rule of law, their morality, and religion which serve as pillars of their civil and political freedoms, along with publicity and

---

[33] Staël, *Des circonstances actuelles*, p. 273.
[34] G. de Staël, *Considerations on the Principal Events of the French Revolution*, ed. A. Craiutu (Indianapolis: Liberty Fund, 2008), p. 143. For an overview of Madame de Staël's political thought, see Gauchet, "Staël" and my own introduction ("A Thinker for Our Times: Madame de Staël, Her Life and Works") to *Considerations*, pp. vii–xxiv.
[35] Staël, *Considerations*, p. 243.

freedom of the press. In England, she noted with approval, the government, benefiting from the existence of a genuine balance of powers between Crown and Parliament, "never interferes in what can be equally well done by individuals: respect for personal liberty extends to the exercise of the faculties of every man."[36]

It should be obvious by now that the political vision undergirding the last part (VI) of *Considérations* was in many ways the opposite of Rousseau's political ideas. He would have been utterly disappointed by Madame de Staël's warm praise of the very country that he disliked so much. And he would have certainly been taken aback by Madame de Staël's shift of allegiance from republicanism to the constitutional monarchy *a l'anglaise* (under Louis XVIII). Such a change, he might have thought, amounted to nothing else than treason or opportunism. But would he have been right to think so? My hunch is no.

The Enigma Called Rousseau

"If she knew how to govern herself, she would have ruled over the entire world,"[37] Benjamin Constant once said about his brilliant friend and former lover. The same applied to Madame de Staël's first idol, Rousseau, the author who charmed her in her youth and continued to exercise a spell on her ever after. That she was far from being alone in sharing this fascination for Rousseau should be evident by now; everyone interested in individual autonomy, equality, liberty, and justice had to come to terms, in one way or another, with Rousseau's ideas.[38] His imprint, Constant wrote referring to the author of *Émile*, was evident on everything he addressed. Because nothing seemed to him to be in the right place in modern society, he sought to change everything.[39] But, if Rousseau the perceptive critic was a true genius endowed with a "prodigious force" that allowed him to unmask and condemn the prejudices of entire centuries, he was a poor architect when it came to building the institutional framework of free government.[40]

---

[36] Ibid., pp. 208–209.

[37] Constant as quoted on the back cover of G. de Diesbach, *Madame de Staël* (Paris: Perrin, 1983).

[38] The classical book on this topic remains J. Roussel, *Jean-Jacques Rousseau en France après la Révolution, 1795–1830* (Paris: Armand Colin, 1972).

[39] Constant wrote: "Il a tout ébranlé, non qu'il voûlut, comme on l'a dit, tout détruire, mais parce que rien ne lui semblait à sa place. Il a, dans sa force prodigieuse, arraché de leurs fondements antiques les colonnes sur lesquelles réposait, tant bien que mal, l'éxistence humaine." The quote is taken from Constant's *De la religion*, vol. I, as quoted in K. Kloocke, "Le sentiment religieux chez Rousseau et Constant" in Lottérie and Poisson (eds.), *Jean-Jacques Rousseau devant Coppet*, p. 107.

Madame de Staël eventually came to accept this sad truth, in spite of her admiration for Rousseau the writer. She also slowly realized that, unlike Rousseau, she could be (more or less) happily at home in the dynamic and cosmopolitan world that was emerging from the ruins of the Old Regime. For unlike her former idol, she came to believe that one can become free and live authentically even in the context of modern bourgeois society; in other words, one can prudently deal with the tensions between the self and the world without losing one's self, even if such antinomies may never be fully solved.[41] In the end, the political moderation Madame de Staël inherited from her father and which was, as mentioned before, the red thread in all of her writings, triumphed over the youthful and romantic impulses inspired by her beloved Rousseau.

There was one other important paradox in Rousseau's case. For all of his unambiguous commitment to liberty and individual autonomy, some of his concepts and ideas such as the general will or the Legislator were used to legitimate grave political errors and they furnished the most terrible auxiliary to all forms of despotism. This was unfortunate because, even many of those who invoked Rousseau during the initial period of the revolution and the Terror, drew on other sources as well to justify their political agendas. Yet, as François Furet once put it, "if Rousseau's political program was not present in the revolution, his spirit certainly was . . . Jean-Jacques Rousseau may not have left the revolutionaries any political formulas, but his writings remain indispensable to the interpretation of their experience."[42] Rousseau's indictment of factions, for example, can account for the subsequent French distrust of intermediary bodies and associations as well as political parties. It would be hard to deny that this skepticism was, in part, a direct legacy of Rousseau's theory of indivisible sovereignty and the general will which Madame de Staël, Constant, and Sismondi rejected. Not surprisingly, all these prominent members of the Coppet group were political moderates.

A little over three hundred years after his birth, one thing is clear. A great part of modern French political thought has developed and remained in his shadow rather than Montesquieu's. In spite of their impracticality,

[40] Again Constant: "Architecte aveugle, il n'a pu, de ces matériaux épars, construire un nouvel édifice. Il n'est résulté de ses efforts que des déstructions, de ces déstructions qu'un chaos où il a laissé sa puissante empreinte" (Ibid.).

[41] On Rousseau's quest for authenticity, its implications, and contemporary relevance, see M. Berman, *The Politics of Authenticity: Radical Individualism and the Emergence of Modern Society*, second edition (London: Verso, 2009).

[42] F. Furet, "Rousseau and the French Revolution," in C. Orwin and N. Tarcov (eds.), *The Legacy of Rousseau* (Chicago: University of Chicago Press, 1997), p. 178.

Rousseau's political ideas continue to fascinate and provoke us (much like Madame de Staël herself) while his legacy remains a highly contested one. As her admirer once so well put it, *"l'on se sent entraîné par lui comme par un ami, un séducteur, un maître."*[43] As such, much like Machiavelli, Rousseau is likely to remain an open-ended question which will probably never be fully settled or closed.

---

[43] Madame de Staël quoted in Roussel, *Jean-Jacques Rousseau en France après la Révolution*, p. 315.

CHAPTER 13

Rousseau and Proudhon: Human Nature, Property, and the Social Contract

K. Steven Vincent

Jean-Jacques Rousseau was a central reference for intellectuals of the early nineteenth century, and this was as true for socialists and self-proclaimed anarchists as others. Some were attracted to his rehabilitation of sentiment; others to his critique of the "arts and sciences"; others to his vision of asocial "natural man"; others to his views of education; others to his proto-socialist critiques of property and inequity; others to his appeal to the unity of the "general will"; others, finally, to his views of the "social contract."

Pierre-Joseph Proudhon (1809–1865), like his contemporaries, frequently referred to Rousseau in his notebook and published writings. Extracts from Jean-Jacques's works are present in Proudhon's first notebooks dating from the late-1820s, and he returned frequently to renew his acquaintance with his *oeuvre*.[1] He undertook a detailed analysis of the *Social Contract* in April 1839;[2] studied Rousseau's *Emile* in August 1839; analyzed the *Discourse on the Origins of Inequality* in January 1840; commented on Rousseau's "Letter to d'Alembert on the Theater" in January 1840; and, he carefully studied Rousseau's writings again in 1842. There are around two hundred direct references to Rousseau in Proudhon's published writings, and many more in his correspondence.

Proudhon's assessment of Rousseau was mixed. He enthusiastically recommended Rousseau's style,[3] and he at times identified with what he imagined was the intellectual isolation that Rousseau experienced.[4]

---

[1] See P. Haubtmann, *Pierre-Joseph Proudhon: sa vie et sa pensée (1809–1849)* (Paris: Beauchesne, 1982), pp. 72 n74, 175, and especially 250–251.

[2] In early 1839, Proudhon wrote: "I have begun reading the Social Contract," noting that he was impressed with its "powerful, vigorous, and energetic" style. (Bibliothèque National, Manuscrits français. MS 18256, f. 93; cited by D. Kelley and B. Smith, "Introduction," Pierre-Joseph Proudhon, *What Is Property?* [Cambridge: Cambridge University Press, 1994], p. xvii.)

[3] About Rousseau and Diderot, Proudhon wrote the following in December 1840: "avec quelle supériorité ils ont sustenu leurs thèses." Cahier V, p. 48 [cited by Haubtmann, p. 270].

[4] On 2 July 1840, worrying about the reaction to his first memoire on property, Proudhon wrote to his friend Ackermann: "Depuis le jour où J.-J. Rousseau écrivit la profession de foi du Vicaire Savoyard,

Proudhon also warmly embraced some elements of Rousseau's thought: his theory of education; his insistence that woman adopt a passive socio-political role; his analysis of property, which Proudhon judged to have opened an important debate. He could celebrate Rousseau as "the apostle of liberty and equality."[5] But, he was critical of other dimensions of Rousseau's thought. He judged the *Discourse on Inequality* as filled with "thoroughly mediocre argumentation."[6] After reading Rousseau's attack of d'Alembert, he wrote that Rousseau was "an eloquent *amplifier*, a subtle dialectician, but deprived of method, of depth, in a word of philosophy."[7] More substantively, Proudhon disagreed with Rousseau's view of human nature, as discussed below. He also lamented that Rousseau's critique of property did not go far enough. But most troubling, in Proudhon's estimation, was Rousseau's analysis of sociopolitical organization. Rousseau's views of the general will and the social contract, Proudhon argued, were deeply flawed and gave theoretical support to dangerous conceptions of society.

Human Nature

Proudhon did not have an overly optimistic view of human nature, and was critical of those writers, including Rousseau, who began with the assumption of human innocence. Rousseau, of course, famously claimed that there were two "sentiments prior to reason" – self-respect (*amour de soi-même*) and pity (*pitié*) – that, when uncorrupted, would support humanity and virtue. Rousseau referred to pity as the sentiment that "inspires in us a natural repugnance at seeing any other sensible being, and particularly any of our own species, perish or suffer."[8] When combined with self-respect, it would naturally lead to what was best in human relationships. Unfortunately, according to Rousseau, these natural senti-ments were corrupted by historical developments, as humanity had passed from the savage natural state, through the primitive social stage, and on to

---

aucun homme peut-être n'a eu une conscience plus forte de la vérité de ses écrits: aucun n'a été livré à une tristesse plus profonde que la mienne." [*Correspondance de P.-J. Proudhon*, ed. J.-A. Langlois (Paris: Lacroix, 1875), I, p. 221.]

[5] P.-J. Proudhon, *Deuxième mémoire sur la propriété* [1841], ed. M. Augé-Laribé (Paris: Rivière, 1938), p. 99.

[6] Studying the *Discourse on Inequality*, Proudhon wrote: "Le style est d'un rhéteur [. . .] Il y a du talent, de l'énergie, du paradoxe, des choses très profondes: mais l'auteur est tout à fait en dehors de la vérité." Cited by Haubtmann, p. 250.

[7] Cahier II, pp. 51–52; cited by Haubtmann, p. 250.

[8] J.-J. Rousseau, *Discours sur l'inégalité*, PL III, pp. 125–126.

the civilized societies in which Europeans found themselves living in the
late eighteenth century. He was particularly critical of modern civiliza-
tions, of the unfortunate effects of the "arts and sciences," of salons, and
more generally of the overrefined affectations of luxurious urban living.
These later influences and contexts encouraged inauthentic interactions,
defined as *amour propre*, and prevented individuals from honestly speaking
their minds and enjoying "transparent" relations.[9] Modern society, in
short, crippled natural sentiments and created unwholesome dependences
among individuals. Rousseau believed, as explored in more detail below,
that one of the primary functions of a properly constructed political
association was to eliminate such personal dependencies.

Proudhon also wrote positively of pity, describing it as "a sort of
magnetism awakened in us by the contemplation of a being similar to
ourselves."[10] But he did not believe that it naturally led to virtuous social
action, even when combined with self-respect. Such a sentimental calculus,
he reasoned, failed to take into account the deeply flawed elements of
human nature. "The cause of evil," he wrote in 1846, "must be traced [. . .]
to a primitive perversion, to a sort of congenital malice in the will of
man."[11] Like Rousseau, he believed that society often fostered passions that
encouraged selfish and morally suspect actions. But he strongly disagreed
with the claim that society was the *sole* cause of all that was perverse in
human action and all that was wicked in the world. "The organic contradictions of society," he wrote, "cannot cover the responsibility of man."[12]

> Does it require an effort of genius to see that [. . .] the pretended perversion
> of society is nothing but the perversion of man, and that the opposition of
> principles and interests is only an external accident, so to speak, which
> brings into relief [. . .] both the blackness of our egoism and the rare virtues
> with which our race is honored?[13]

Without the inherent egoism of man's nature, society would not have
evolved to the pitiable state in which it found itself.

> Man, I say faithless to the law of charity, has, of himself and without any
> necessity, made the contradictions of society so many instruments of harm;

---

[9] The classic account of this is J. Starobinski, *J.-J. Rousseau, la transparence et l'obstacle, suivi de sept
essais sur Rousseau* (Paris: Gallimard, 1948). See also, R. Grimsley, *The Philosophy of Rousseau*
(Oxford: Oxford University Press, 1973).

[10] P.-J. Proudhon, *Qu'est-ce que la propriété?* [1840] ed. M. Augé-Laribé (Paris: Rivière, 1926), p. 303.

[11] P.-J. Proudhon, *Système des contradictions économiques ou philosophie de la misère* [1846], ed. R. Picard
(Paris: Rivière, 1923), I, p. 349.

[12] Ibid., p. 359.   [13] Ibid., p. 365.

through his egoism civilization has become a war of surprises and ambushes; he lies, he steals, he murders, when not compelled to do so, without provocation, without excuse. In short, he does evil with all the characteristics of a nature deliberately maleficent, and all the more wicked because, when he so wishes, he also knows how to do good gratuitously and is capable of self-sacrifice.[14]

Proudhon's conviction of the inherent evil of human nature had a number of implications. He viewed the dogma of the Fall, of original sin, as historically false but philosophically true, because it accurately captured the evil inclinations of mankind. "The Fall," he wrote, "is the spontaneous confession in a symbolic phrase of this fact as astonishing as it is indestructible, the culpability, the inclination to evil, of our race."[15]

The depravity of humans was also, according to Proudhon, not simply a stage in humanity's evolution, a stage that at some future time could be transcended. It was a constituent element of humanity's makeup. He attacked those who argued to the contrary.

> Certainly we should be very near an understanding if, instead of considering the dissidence and harmony of the human faculties as two distinct periods, clean-cut and consecutive in history, you would consent to view them as I do simply as the two faces of our nature, ever adverse, ever in course of reconciliation, but never entirely reconciled.[16]

The inherent inclinations of humans toward selfish and evil acts did not lead Proudhon to suggest that there was no possibility of improvement. Human depravity did not excuse evil, nor did it make it necessary. Rather, its presence should call forth our most vigorous efforts. In *Système des contradictions économiques* (1846), he put it in these terms: "Man is by nature a sinner – that is, not essentially *ill-doing* [*malfaisant*], but rather *ill-made* [*malfait*] – and it is his destiny perpetually to recreate his ideal in himself."[17] What he obviously meant by this statement was that philosophers were correct to view humans as inherently prone to sin and as not naturally inclined to virtuous action: they were, in a word, "ill-made." Nonetheless, humans did not need to be perpetual sinners, because they had the capacity to overcome these inherent inclinations; that is, they were not necessarily "ill-doing."

What was it in the nature of man that caused ill-made humanity to be ill-doing? What caused flawed humans to act so poorly? It was, according to Proudhon, a combination of inherent passions and the failure of

---

[14] Ibid., p. 354. [15] Ibid., p. 368. [16] Ibid., p. 368. [17] Ibid., p. 372.

256 K. STEVEN VINCENT

intelligence and will. What could promote improvement and encourage humanity to act morally? It was the triumph over negative passions of intelligence and will. This was not that different from Rousseau's view. Humanity, both believed, had the requisite mental and emotional qualities for the growth of order and progress, though both could express pessimism concerning the current state of society and its members. Proudhon believed that moral action leading to improvement would not be the result of standards imposed on the individual from the outside, but rather from nurturing the elements of his own nature in accordance with the principles that his reason recognized as conforming to justice. Rousseau's thoughts about the moral development of the individual took a similar form. Morality, for Rousseau, was rooted in sensibility, in the "sentiments prior to reason" that were the primordial impulses of humans. These did not exist in isolation, however, but needed to develop in accordance with the order and progress of our sentiments and our knowledge. Proudhon's view was much the same. Moral actions required the careful cultivation of positive sentiments and the application of reason and will.

Proudhon termed the resulting recognition of correct action "immanent morality," wishing thereby to distinguish it from the "transcendent morality" characteristic of religion.[18] One is able to interpret this "immanent morality" as a secularized version of traditional Christian ethics; that is, as an extended commentary on the commandment "Thou shalt love they neighbor as thyself." Or, one can interpret Proudhon's view of morality as a nineteenth-century descendent of the focus on *moeurs* that was such a central part of the French tradition of republican thought.[19] What was important in his own mind was that there was a robust, secular, worldly morality that developed naturally, from reflection about human nature and human sociability. People should focus on the importance of respecting the integrity, rights, and equality of one's neighbors. Recognizing that others have rights and values equal to oneself provided the foundation of social morality, of what Proudhon termed "justice."[20]

On March 31, 1847, Proudhon wrote a series of passages in his notebook that expressed his particular understanding on humanity's abilities and potential failures. "[T]he passions of men cause perturbations, the drama

[18] The recommendation of "immanent justice" is the fundamental organizing theme of *De la Justice*, the work Proudhon considered his most important. P.-J. Proudhon, *De la Justice dans la Révolution et dans l'Église* [1858], ed. C. Bouglé and J.-L. Puech, 4 vol. (Paris: Rivière, 1930–1935).
[19] I discuss these traditions in *Pierre-Joseph Proudhon and the Rise of French Republican Socialism* (New York: Oxford University Press, 1984), esp. pp. 69–118.
[20] *De la Justice dans la Révolution et dans l'Église*, infra.

of history. One will know that society arrives at order, and above all at intelligence, when history ceases to be dramatic."[21] Proudhon's conviction of humanity's ability to reason correctly, recognize what is moral, and avoid the detrimental "drama of history" – that is, to move ahead in an ordered, rational, and just manner – was not uncommon during the middle of the nineteenth century. Like many of his contemporaries, Proudhon argued that social and moral laws could be discerned through a reasoned examination of human nature, human societies, and the larger universe, and that the recognition of these laws could be efficaciously translated into action. This common nineteenth-century optimism appears to many of us today as an exaggerated faith in the positive passions of mankind, and as an inflated belief in the efficacy of science. But there is little doubt that Proudhon shared this orientation. Just as Champollion had discovered the key that unlocked the mystery of the Egyptian hieroglyphs, Proudhon believed that he could discover the secrets of human behavior and social interaction, and that these would reveal scientific truths that would undergird inevitable progress. It speaks volumes that he could write in 1839 that "all that which is the material of legislation and of politics is an object of science, not opinion [. . .] Justice and legality are two things as independent of our assent as mathematical truth."[22] Four years later he made the entry of humanity into the epoch of science a major theme of his book *De la création de l'ordre dans l'humanité.* "The new science," he wrote, "must replace religion in everything."[23]

Proudhon nonetheless feared that the power of reason and science could be overwhelmed by strong human passions that led to selfish behavior. He understood that the drama of human history had revealed human actions informed by evil intentions. And, he recognized that history chronicled the emergence of institutions and social relations that were unjust.

Property Relations

One of the most widespread of these unjust social relations was the extant legal structure of property ownership. Proudhon became famous for his attacks on property inequities, especially for his argument in the 1840 book *Qu'est-ce que la propriété?* where he provocatively answered, "it is

---

[21] *Carnets de P.-J. Proudhon,* ed. P. Haubtmann, 4 vols. (Paris, 1960–1974), II, pp. 70–71.

[22] P.-J. Proudhon, *De la célébration du dimanche* [1839], ed. M. Augé-Laribé (Paris: Rivière, 1926), p. 45.

[23] P.-J. Proudhon, *De la création de l'ordre dans l'humanité ou principes d'organisation politique* [1843], ed. C. Bouglé and A. Cuvillier (Paris: Rivière, 1927), p. 63n.

theft."[24] He credited previous analysts like Rousseau with preparing the ground for his assault on property, though he argued that no one had gone far enough. In the election manifesto published in his paper *Le Peuple* in 1848, for example, Proudhon complimented his renowned predecessor, no doubt thinking of the argument Rousseau presented at the beginning of the second part of his *Discourse on Inequality*. "As we see it, the origin [of inequality] has been brought to light by a whole series of socialist criticisms, particularly since Jean-Jacques."[25]

Rousseau, of course, famously argued in this discourse that a second social revolution, corresponding with the discovery of metallurgy and agriculture, had led to the division of labor and establishment of property.[26] And, lamentably, these developments led to the emergence of the distinction between "mine" and "thine" that put individuals in permanent conflict. Even more disastrously, it led to the emergence of socioeconomic inequalities that henceforth would be inescapable elements of human interaction. According to Rousseau, as individuals attempted to become more prosperous and more powerful, inequalities, anxieties, and human conflicts grew. And, perhaps even more ruinously for society, individuals were no longer content to satisfy only their needs; they also sought abundance, superfluity, and ostentatious distinctions. This encouraged all of the negative attributes of human nature in modern society that Rousseau had enumerated in his *Discourse on the Arts and Sciences*: what he termed *amour propre* and the broader tendency of individuals to mask their true motives to satisfy "their hidden desire to achieve one's own profit at the expense of others."[27] These antisocial aspects of human action, this Hobbesian struggle of mutual enmity, Rousseau wrote, was "the first effect of property and of the inseparable attendant growth of inequality." They were not a part of mankind's original being; rather, they are defects introduced by the social state of modernity.

> The rich on their side, scarcely having achieved the pleasure of domination, soon disdain all others, use their ancient slaves to enslave others, and dream

[24] *Qu'est-ce que la propriété?* p. 131.

[25] Proudhon, "Election Manifesto of *Le Peuple*," in *Property is Theft! A Pierre-Joseph Proudhon Anthology*, ed. I. McKay, trans. P. Sharkey (Edinburgh: AK Press, 2011), p. 372.

[26] Rousseau gave a more benign account of property in *Discours sur l'économie politique*, where he argues that property is the foundation of civil society, and in *Émile*, where he suggests that property is the means by which one keeps in touch with the soil of one's country and the labor of one's ancestors. The focus here is on his argument in *Discours sur l'origine et les fondements de l'inégalité*. For a good secondary discussion of this, see A. Ryan, *Property and Political Theory* (New York: Basil Blackwell, 1984), pp. 49–72.

[27] *Discours sur l'inégalité*, PL III, p. 175.

only of subjugating and enslaving their neighbors; similar to hungry wolves that, having one time tasted human flesh, reject all other food, and no longer want anything but men to devour.

It is thus that the most powerful or the most miserable, making of their power or of their needs a kind of right to the possessions of others – equivalent, according to them, to the right of property – that equality is ruptured and the most frightful disorder followed: it is thus that the usurpations of the rich, the brigandage of the poor, the unbridled passions of all, stifle natural pity and the now feeble voice of justice, rendering mankind avaricious, ambitious, and cruel [...] Nascent society gave way to the most horrible state of war.[28]

The story that Rousseau goes on to tell in the *Second Discourse* recounts how the rich orchestrated the founding of a political association to protect their property. The rich were able to achieve this end by convincing the poor that all would be better off, but in essence this was a confidence trick the rich played on simple souls to protect their wealth and power. Property and inequality thereby became sanctioned by law.

All hastened to put on their chains believing to assure their liberty [...] Such was, or must have been, the origin of society and laws, which gave new fetters to the weak and new powers to the rich, irretrievably destroyed natural liberty, established forever the law of property and inequality, made a clever usurpation into an irrevocable right, and, for the benefit of a few ambitious individuals, henceforth subjugated the whole human race to labor, servitude, and misery.[29]

Proudhon shared many of Rousseau's misgivings about the connection between property and the wealthy class, but he did not frame his analysis as a quasi-anthropological historical account. Rather, he focused on the social, legal, and philosophical defenses of property provided by Grotius, Thomas Reid, and early nineteenth-century writers like Jean-Baptiste Say, Charles Comte, Destutt de Tracy, Joseph Droz, and Jérôme-Adolphe Blanqui. His major theme was the conflict between the poor and the rich, between *la misère* and its social opposite, *la propriété*. He argued that prosperity should be the reward for effort, rather than power, but that unfortunately modern societies generally did the opposite, rewarded power and punished effort. As was frequently the case with Proudhon's polemical style, however, his discussions of property and these wider issues blended abstract logic with agitated rhetoric, serious analysis with bitter social criticism.

---

[28] Ibid., pp. 175–176.   [29] Ibid., pp. 177–178.

Proudhon's attack on property was not as radical as his rhetorical blast – "property, it is theft" – at first might suggest. This is largely because of the narrow definition of property that he employed. It referred only to that type of ownership that produced an income without requiring any work: that is, income derived from the ownership of the means of production; or, income from the interest earned on lent money; or, income from rented lands or buildings. In a just society, all would work for their income. "Work is obligatory, property is usufruct," he wrote in his 1839 book *De la célébration du dimanche*.[30] Proudhon did not oppose the private possession of the land, dwelling, and tools that a worker needed to provide the day-do-day needs of himself and his family. He termed these "possessions," and he wished to protect these against the power of idle owners of property and against the power of the state. His famous 1840 book *Qu'est-ce que la propriété?* was informed by his desire to highlight the lack of justice in a society that was permeated by a grossly inequitable distribution of riches. He set out to condemn those types of ownership that unfairly benefited one class at the expense of another, or which enabled one individual or group of individuals to exploit others.

Most of Proudhon's essay on property was devoted to enumerating the ways in which the theories of the classical economists justified the abuses of ownership that Proudhon condemned. Proudhon turned the arguments they had employed in favor of property against it. He claimed that property was "impossible" because it would destroy itself, because it was logically contradictory, and above all because it was unjust.[31] And, more convincingly, he argued that the defenders of property were opposed to the positive values that should be protected. "Property is incompatible with political and civil equality," he argued; it "is the negation of equality."[32] The following year (1841), Proudhon summarized the message of his first essay on property: "Men equal in the dignity of their persons, equal before the law, ought to be equal in their conditions."[33]

This was closely related to the manner in which Proudhon defined what he called in 1839 his "program": "to find a state of social equality which is neither community, nor despotism, nor parceling out, nor anarchy, but liberty in order and independence in unity."[34] This program indicates that Proudhon wished to reconcile political liberty with social equality; that is,

---

[30] *De la célébration du dimanche*, p. 94.   [31] *Qu'est-ce que la propriété?* pp. 292, 293, 296.
[32] Ibid., pp. 286, 296.
[33] *Qu'est-ce que la propriété? Deuxième mémoire: lettre à M. Blanqui sur la propriété* [1841], ed. M. Augé-Laribé (Paris: Rivière, 1938), p. 22.
[34] *De la célébration du dimanche*, p. 61.

he insisted on radical and fundamental economic and social reform. He also emphasized that he did not wish this to be imposed from above. Social equality must be "neither community nor despotism"; that is, it must not be directed by the state. On the other hand, social equality must not lead to "anarchy." There is a telling contrast between this program and Rousseau's "program" as defined in the *Social Contract*: "To find a form of association which will defend and protects with the entire common force the person and goods of each associate, and by which each, unifying himself to all, obeys only himself, and remains as free as before."[35] Proudhon insisted on the social and economic contours of the society of his dreams; Rousseau focused on the political.

The Social Contract

Proudhon's focus on the socioeconomic dimension and his opposition to state power point to the most significant differences he had with the theories of Rousseau. When Rousseau turned to the issue of political organization, especially as articulated in his writings about the social contract, Proudhon argued that he had lost his way. In his mind, economic, and social reform must take priority.

Rousseau, as suggested above, was fearful of the possible dependence of one individual on another, but he believed that a positive form of politics was not only possible, but desirable. Such a positive politics was to be based on law and on having the particular wills of individuals replaced by the sovereignty of the general will. Such a political association, Rousseau reasoned, would avoid personal dependency. To clarify this distinction, Rousseau contrasted "dependence on things," which was natural and affected all humans equally (dependence on the law of gravity, for example), with "dependence on men," which was unnatural and harmful to freedom and morality.[36] Rousseau believed that the morally debilitating dependence of one human being on another could be avoided in a political system that relied on a morally benign dependency that paralleled the natural "dependence on things," rather than a system that was built upon the dependency of some individuals on others. He believed this could be achieved in a political system that located supreme political authority in the general will which reflected the interests of all members of the community.

---

[35] *Du Contrat social*, PL III, p. 360.
[36] Rousseau discusses these two types of dependence in *Émile*, PL IV, p. 311.

A detailed analysis of Rousseau's political thought is not possible here. Some of his writings focused on concrete constitutional issues; for example, his *Considérations sur le gouvernement de Pologne*.[37] His theoretical works, however, are more abstract, and they curiously lack some important institutional and procedural elements. Rousseau famously distinguished between the sovereign legislative will of the people, which was not to be delegated or "represented," and the executive power of government, which was to put laws in effect. This division meant that there was to be no representative body for the deliberation and passage of legislation, which was to emerge phoenix-like from the "general will." Furthermore, Rousseau insisted that legislative will and executive power be strictly separated, thereby reducing questions of "government" to functions we generally associate with the activities of the executive and judicial branches. It is perhaps not surprising that the popularity of this dimension of Rousseau's thought encouraged subsequent constitutional thinkers in France to insist on the unity of the "general will" and to focus on extreme versions of the separation of powers with no "checks and balances."[38] It also encouraged an insistence that sovereignty was indivisible and inalienable, implying that there must be absolute and irrevocable submission of every individual to a single unitary entity – that is, to the "general will." According to Rousseau, such dependence on the general will implied that particular and private interests expressed within and by smaller associations were to be discouraged. Such associations, Rousseau feared, would reinforce individuals' personal passions and would conflict with the struggle to attain virtue. Moreover, they would foster the kind of personal dependence of one individual on another for which Rousseau had so much distaste. True liberty would be threatened as a consequence. For Rousseau, the bonds between individuals should be deemphasized and replaced by a stronger bond between the individual and the whole.

Proudhon was more of a social pluralist, and was horrified by what he viewed to be the authoritarian implications of Rousseau's political theory. Like Rousseau, he was concerned about the dependence of one individual on another, but to counter this he emphasized the importance of contractual agreements between equals to avoid the dependency that could result from inequitable relations of power. Unlike Rousseau, Proudhon was a strong advocate of popular involvement in local organizations, especially

---

[37] J.-J. Rousseau, *Considérations sur le gouvernement de Pologne*, PL III, pp. 951–1041.
[38] I discuss this legacy of Rousseau's thought, and liberal reactions to it, in *Benjamin Constant and the Birth of French Liberalism* (New York: Palgrave-Macmillan, 2011), esp. pp. 170–190.

labor organizations and associations. Proudhon considered these to be important arenas for the blossoming of social harmony and the exercise of individual liberty. Rousseau was so worried about individuals gaining power over other individuals, and concerned that power might gain ascendency over right, that he counseled the avoidance of associative activity. Proudhon, to the contrary, worried about the same dependencies, but believed associative interaction to be essential for social and economic relations, and for the protection of individual liberty.

Proudhon also rejected Rousseau's drive to strengthen the bond between the individual and the whole. He rejected, in short, Rousseau's conception of sovereignty, insisting that sovereignty must be fractured, with power residing in local organizations and in the multiple sovereignties of workers' associations. Proudhon wished to avoid an excessive concentration of power, and he believed that this could be achieved through a process of peaceful negotiation among divergent interests. This negotiation would, he reasoned, lead to contracts that would balance the interests of the contracting parties, and thereby avoid empowering a central authority at the expense of all others.

It was this attachment to a specific notion of contract, and its oppositional relationship to Rousseau's theory of the "social contract," that informed Proudhon's strongest disagreement with Rousseau. Proudhon, in his own manner, was in favor of the "social contract," but for him this meant an agreement freely made between equals. Such a contract, he argued, provided "effective sovereignty," and was to be opposed to the "abstract sovereignty" that was provided by political contracts or by the "social contract" as envisaged by Rousseau. Such "political" contracts alienated an individual's liberty, while a true contract did not.

> That which characterizes the [true] contract [...] is the act by which two or several individuals agree to organize between or among themselves, to an extent and for a determined length of time, this industrial power that we call *exchange*; consequently obliging each toward the other, and reciprocally guaranteeing for all, a certain number of services, products, advantages, obligations, etc. ...
>
> Between contracting parties there is necessarily for each one a real and personal interest; it implies that a man drafts an agreement with the aim of reducing, at the same time, without possible compensation, his liberty and his revenue. Between governing and governed, on the contrary, no matter how the system of representation or of delegation of the governmental function is arranged, there is necessarily alienation of a part of the liberty and of the wealth of the citizen.[39]

---

[39] P.-J. Proudhon, *L'Idée générale de la révolution au XIXe siècle* [1851], ed. A. Berthod (Paris: Rivière, 1924), pp. 187–188.

Proudhon's attack of politics was a constant refrain, as was his attack of Rousseau as the most prominent theorist of things political. In his note-book of 1846, he wrote "Democrats, if you want to act effectively, [it is necessary] to transport the debate of politics onto to the terrain of political economy and to change principles. Rousseau is dead."[40]

Proudhon emphasized over and over again that the social contract that he favored was starkly different from Rousseau's social contract. In his 1851 book *L'Idée générale de la révolution au XIXe siècle*, he wrote the following:

> Rousseau, whose authority has ruled us for almost a century, understood nothing of the social contract. It is to him, above all, that it is necessary to ascribe the great deviation of '93, expiated already by fifty-seven years of fruitless disorder, and which certain minds more ardent than wise wish us still to regard as a sacred tradition [. . .]
>
> Is it necessary now to say that, out of the multitude of relations that the social pact is called upon to define and regulate, Rousseau saw only political relations; that is to say, he suppressed the fundamental points of the contract, and occupied himself only with those that are secondary? Is it necessary to say that Rousseau understood and respected not one of the essential, indispensable conditions, – the absolute liberty of each contracting party, the personal, direct part he plays, the signature each gives with full understanding of the issues, and the augmentation of liberty and prosperity which he should experience?
>
> For him [Rousseau], the social contract is neither a communal act, nor even an action of general society [. . .]
>
> Of the real, true contract, on whatsoever subject, there is no vestige in Rousseau's book. To give an exact idea of his theory, I cannot do better than compare it with a commercial agreement, in which the names of the parties, the nature and value of the goods, products and services involved, the conditions of quality, delivery, price, reimbursement, everything in fact which constitutes the material of contracts, is omitted, and nothing is specified but penalties and jurisdictions.
>
> Indeed, Citizen of Geneva, you talk well. But before having a conversation about sovereignty and the prince, about policemen and the judge, can you tell me a little about the nature of the negotiation?[41]

Proudhon argued that Rousseau's notion of the "social contract" was so focused on politics that it failed to encompass the socioeconomic dimen-sion that, for Proudhon, was critical. He also argued that Rousseau was so suspicious of social interactions that his theories only focused on the virtues of individuals, thereby missing considerations of sociability and of

---

[40] *Carnets de P.-J. Proudhon*, I, p. 280.
[41] P.-J. Proudhon, *L'Idée générale de la révolution au XIXe siècle*, pp. 187–190.

associational activity. Centrally, and in Proudhon's mind lamentably, Rousseau did not discuss economic relations.

> What does he give us? That which one calls today *direct government* [. . ..] But, there is not a word about work, nor of property, nor of industrial forces, those things which it is the object of a social contract to organize. Rousseau does not know what economics means. His program speaks exclusively of political rights; it does mention economic rights.[42]

***

Proudhon's objections to Rousseau's thought were numerous. He argued that it was based on a mistaken view of human nature; that it ignored the importance of dense social relationships; and, that it failed to consider the foundational nature of economic issues and, therefore, implicitly favored the rich at the expense of the poor. All of these criticisms are enumerated in the following passage, published in 1851:

> Rousseau is so far from desiring that any mention be made in the social contract of the principles and laws which rule the wealth of nations and of individuals, that he begins, in his demagogic program, as well as in his Treatise on education, with the false, thievish, murderous supposition that only the individual is good, that society depraves him, that man therefore should refrain as much as possible from all relations with his fellows; and that all we have to do in this world below, while remaining in complete isolation, is to form among ourselves a mutual insurance society, for the protection of our persons and property; that all the rest – that is to say economic issues, really the only issues of importance – should be left to the chance of birth or speculation, and submitted, in case of litigation, to the arbitration of elected officers, who should determine according to rules laid down by themselves, or by the light of natural equity. In a word, the social contract, according to Rousseau, is nothing but the offensive and defensive alliance of those who possess, against those who do not possess; and the only part played by the citizen is to pay the police, for which he is assessed in proportion to his fortune, and according to the risk to which pauperism exposes him.
>
> It is this contract of hatred, this monument of incurable misanthropy, this coalition of the barons of property, commerce and industry against the disinherited lower class, indeed this oath of social war, which Rousseau (with a presumptuousness that I would qualify as villainous if I believed in the genius of this man) calls *social contract*.[43]

***

---

[42] Ibid., p. 192.   [43] Ibid., pp. 191–192.

I'd like to close this short essay with an observation about the *political* dimension of the thought of both Rousseau and Proudhon, or rather the limited nature of their embrace of republican politics. Rousseau, of course, is a central figure of western political theory, and he wrote eloquently and influentially about liberty, sovereignty, and the separation of powers. As suggested above, however, there is a tendency in his writings to discount the deliberative nature of modern representative politics. He denigrated the messy confrontation, discussion, and hopefully compromise that make up the day-to-day actions of politicians in the plodding and ponderous process of negotiation among groups with different, even incommensurable, interests. He assumed that correct policy would emerge phoenix-like from the unified and infallible "general will."

Proudhon, in contrast, was a pluralist who recognized the importance of discussion and negotiation. He believed that correct policy would result from the associative interactions of workers, and from contracts drawn up through dialogue and compromise. Proudhon, of course, assailed what he called *political* dialogue and party politics because, he argued, it represented the interests of the rich and powerful, and because elections led to discord rather than to cooperation. This was in part driven by Proudhon's strident criticism of the "idle class." Only the workers who labored and created value, he reasoned, had the requisite moral strength and broad social vision to create a new consensus and a favorable development of altruism and "virtue." This led him to valorize the deliberations among workers in the context of their associations, assuming that from these deliberations "scientific" truths about social and economic issues would emerge. In essence, therefore, he advanced a truncated notion of "citizenship" (though did not use this term) that restricted power to those who accomplished productive tasks and created value. The effective consequence of this was a view of society that would exclude many from any active role in what we would term politics – namely, all those who did not fit the definition of a virtuous worker, including all women.[44]

Both Rousseau and Proudhon are justly famous for their mordant satires of the powerful and for their trenchant criticisms of the rich. Both believed that effort, not power, should be rewarded, and they were morally indignant that modern societies were structured in ways that prevented this from being the case. Both wrote popular works that ridiculed the hypocrisy of the wealthy who, they claimed, perverted liberty and justice in order to

---

[44] I discuss this dimension of Proudhon's thought at more length in "Pierre-Joseph Proudhon et son influence sur la pensée socialiste," *Corpus: revue de philosophie* 47 (2004): pp. 355–366.

protect their property, to pursue their personal enrichment, and to enhance their class privileges. Each advanced, though in markedly different ways, a vision of reform that they claimed would avoid these problems of modern society. Unfortunately, these visions entailed a renunciation of deliberative politics, or at best a cramped version of it. Rousseau, generally considered the more politically sophisticated of the two, wished to avoid entirely the unheroic interactions of discussion and compromise that make up deliberative politics. Proudhon, generally considered to have rejected politics entirely, wished to restrict these interactions to those who labored. Neither provided an attractive blueprint for a modern politics of dialogue and compromise.

CHAPTER 14

Rousseau and Marx: On Human Fulfillment

Jerrold Seigel

Of the various pairings discussed in this book, the one that joins Rousseau to Marx is at once one of the most obvious and one of the most significant. Each of them occupies an important place in the history of thinking about modern politics, history, and social relations, and both have close ties to the crucial modern phenomenon of revolution. I will have something to say about these topics, but I propose to approach them by way of a different and no less pertinent subject, namely the two thinkers' common positions as exemplary theorists of human fulfillment: each sought in his way to uncover what humanity might be if it lived up to its potential, to specify what stands in the way of our doing so, and to suggest how these impediments might be removed.

I will argue that, despite many differences, the two shared highly important ground in this regard, and that much of this closeness has to do with the fact that both were philosophical thinkers with a deep ambivalence toward philosophy. Each sought to realize philosophical ideals and aspirations, but in ways that set clear boundaries on the role that rational reflection and those who engage in it could play in bringing this realization to life. Neither was an enemy of reason to be sure, even if Rousseau sometimes spoke in ways that have made people think he was, but both sought to embed their hopes in nonrational elements of human existence, in feeling and affect in Rousseau's case, in material social relations in Marx's. But each one's program for doing this failed in some significant way, so that in the end both were fated to heighten the role of rational reflection in fulfilling human potential at the very points where they sought ways to diminish it.

To be sure, each thinker followed this pattern in his own manner, and I need to note at the start that the similarity between them coexisted with a sharp and pervasive contrast. Marx's vision of history and of revolution's role in it was powered by a fundamental optimism, despite his dark views about life in the present, whereas Rousseau, notwithstanding his often-expressed belief in the goodness of nature and human nature, was a pessimist, repeatedly driven to highlight the qualities of individual and social life that spoiled the recipes for repairing their ills he sought to provide. But the ways in which each one's thinking implicitly or explicitly restored to rational reflection the role both sought to assign to other dimensions of human existence transcended this contrast, making the opposition between the first's optimism and the second's pessimism only one side of a more complex relationship.

Because the patterns I want to highlight may be easier to identify in Marx than in Rousseau, I will begin with him, focusing on a place in his writings where they seem especially clear. This is the remarkable description of proletarian revolution he gave in the work that marked the emergence of Marxism in the form that would launch it into history, *The German Ideology* of 1845–46. It was here that Marx first theorized revolution in purely material terms, portraying it as the outcome of the sharpening and clarifying maturation of class conflict whose history he and Engels would later recount in *The Communist Manifesto*. Picturing working-class action in this way created a marked contrast with the image he projected two years before, in his earliest evocation of proletarian revolution. There he had made the uprising of workers dependent on their receiving an energizing bolt from outside, not from social conditions but from philosophy. The proletarians who both stood within civil society and suffered exclusion from it were potential rebels, but the weight of social oppression made them into a "passive element." They needed to be roused from outside, and the call to action would come from the critical philosophical vision that condemned life in the present in the name of what humanity and society should and could become. In his famous metaphor, when "the lightning of philosophy" struck "the rude soil of the people" then "the Germans will emancipate themselves and become men."[1]

It was precisely this scenario that *The German Ideology* set aside. Now "not criticism but revolution is the driving force of history," and it was class struggle that generated that force. The proletariat whose uprising would emancipate humanity was no less reduced to a passive state than before; indeed, Marx now said that the conditions of society deprived workers of any capacity for what he called self-activity (*Selbsttätigkeit*). What now turned them into agents of change, however, was their direct response to

---

[1] K. Marx, "Toward the Critique of Hegel's Philosophy of Law: Introduction," in *Writings of the Young Marx on Philosophy and Society*, trans. and ed. L. Easton and K. Guddat (New York: Anchor Books, 1967), pp. 263–264.

the social conditions that oppressed them; pushed by suffering and despair to rise up against an oppressive world, they would break the chains that bound them, generating a powerful energy out of themselves. It was this self-generated energy that would fill them with the wholeness of self-activity of which existing conditions robbed them. In this scenario, the proletariat's self-emancipation was still the vehicle for the realization of the potential lodged in humanity as a whole, but philosophical criticism lost the central role it had played before. Finding this outcome inherent in an oppressive material reality constitutes the aspect of Marx's thinking that has been described as "bootstrapping," the acrobatic miracle of rising to a higher level by reaching downward rather than up.[2]

Marx would not always insist that the path of entry into the world of the future had to pass through the portal of pure degradation. In the years when he worked to bring European workers together in the First International he emphasized the importance of communication, organization and discussion in preparing the proletariat for its role. But the bootstrapping vision of *The German Ideology* still remained somewhere in his mind, surfacing for instance in *The Eighteenth Brumaire of Louis Bonaparte*, where he proclaimed that proletarian revolutions could only succeed after experiencing a protracted series of defeats that gave overweening power to their adversaries, "until a situation has been created that makes all turning back impossible, and the conditions themselves cry out" for the leap into a new life. Marx liked to associate the moment when such conditions pushed people to action with the Latin motto "Hic Rhodus Hic Salta": come to such a pass, one must either demonstrate the ability to jump from one distant shore to the other or drown.[3]

It is of course easy to point out, but no less true for being so, that this was precisely what never happened. Instead the conditions of working-class life under capitalism, as the Bolshevik Lenin recognized along with the revisionist Edouard Bernstein, precisely robbed the proletariat of what Marxists took to be its revolutionary vocation, leaving it with a taste for the kind of self-improvement that capitalist society offered; this was the "trade-union" consciousness Bernstein valued and Lenin deplored, leading

[2] K. Marx and F. Engels, *The German Ideology*, trans. S. Ryazanskaya (London: Lawrence & Wishart, 1965 and Moscow: Progress Publishers, 1968), pp. 84–85. See my discussion in *Marx's Fate: The Shape of a Life* (Princeton: Princeton University Press, 1976), pp. 169–174. The notion of "bootstrapping" was suggested to me by L. Kolakowski, *Main Currents of Marxism*, Volume 1, trans. P. S. Falla (Oxford: Clarendon Press, 1978).

[3] Marx, "The Eighteenth Brumaire of Louis Bonaparte," in Marx and Engels, *Selected Works in One Volume* (New York: International Publishers, 1968), p. 100.

the first to abandon the Marxian vision of sudden revolutionary transformation and the second to seek a different way to preserve it.

In this situation, in contrast to the one that inspired Marx's expectation of revolution in the hungry 1840s, the path to radical transformation could only be kept open if it were entrusted to a vanguard party devoted to the vision workers could not generate by themselves. Its leaders were not exactly philosophers of the sort to whom Marx assigned a similarly active role in his early writings, but they too were fit to lead the masses because of their highly developed and theoretically honed consciousness. But the result, as radical socialists such as Rosa Luxembourg understood right away, was to impose an intellectual dictatorship over ordinary workers and eventually to set Russia on a historical course that issued in Stalinist terror and whose outcome would only become clear in 1989 and 1991. Marx never recommended precisely this sort of leadership by a vanguard infused with theory, but the many hours he spent struggling over *Das Kapital* in the last decades of his life returned him to the company of theoretical men from whom he had sought to separate his historical vision in the mid-century.[4]

Against this background, I now turn to Rousseau, approaching him first, as with Marx, through one particular work. The work in question is not one of his most famous, in fact it was a writing he never completed. But he attached great significance to it all the same and wrote about it in his *Confessions*. The idea behind it emerged around 1756 and its title was to be *Sensory Morality or the Wise Man's Materialism* (*La morale sensitive ou le matérialisme du sage*). The formula referred to a project whereby Rousseau proposed to cure himself of his vacillating, unsteady, and morally suspect nature not by engaging in moral reflection or self-education but by altering the conditions that determined his behavior. The fact that his actions were dictated by surrounding conditions was the materialist premise of the scheme; what made him and others morally unreliable and unable to set a clear course for themselves was that ideas, and the actions that stemmed from them, arose from the impressions made on our senses by external objects, and since the objects around us are always changing, so do our ideas and behavior. Rousseau here was operating on the basis of the Lockean empiricism that was so powerful an influence in his time; unlike Locke however, he did not believe that we have the capacity to delay and resist the impact impressions make on us, an ability Locke associated with the mind's ability to "examine, view and judge" what desire or impulse

---

[4] I consider various features of this turn in Marx's thinking in *Marx's Fate, passim.*

suggest, and which Locke saw as the basis of "the liberty of intellectual beings." In his *Confessions* Rousseau gave many illustrations of his own lack of such liberty and of the way its absence led him to be buffeted about by the various situations he encountered. In order to give his actions a more regular and more morally acceptable tenor, therefore, he proposed to control or manage his surrounding so as to "put or keep the mind in the state most conducive to virtue," and free it from the power of what he called "the brute functions" to dominate our thoughts and feelings.[5]

Interesting as this schema was, and typical of its author, there was something deeply problematic, even absurd about it. As Jean Starobinski has observed, Rousseau was here imagining that he could somehow give independent power over his person to situations he would have to create and control by himself, that he could both "orchestrate the mystery and to be duped by it." His aim was to arrange things in such a way that the directing power over his behavior possessed by external conditions would produce favorable results, obviating the need to rely on the weak and suspect faculties of reflection and self-command that contemporaries such as Adam Smith saw as essential for achieving both virtue and happiness. Smith, by the way, saw this self-command as developing out of reflection linked to human social interaction, just the ground where Rousseau repeatedly experienced his inability to develop it. In the overall schema of *La morale sensitive* however, this need to give rational reflection a role in moral formation and in recovering the human potential for happiness was not in fact denied, it was merely located as it were behind a screen. By putting it there Rousseau only made the inescapable role reflection had to play in his project stand out all the more clearly.[6]

Although the connection is not usually made, I think, this schema has much in common with Marx's vision of proletarians as being able to realize humanity's potential for self-liberation only when "the conditions cry out" for them to act in a certain way and with his image of workers being able to achieve genuine *Selbsttätigkeit* only in response to having lost the last shreds of it. It was just this absence of self-directing power that Rousseau located at the root of his moral debility. What Rousseau called the "wise man's materialism" had in common with the more famous historical materialism of Marx that it tied the possibility of realizing the human potential for freedom and virtue to actions determined wholly by the right sort of

---

[5] Rousseau, *Confessions*, trans J. Cohen (London: Penguin, 1953), pp. 380–381.
[6] J. Starobinski, *Jean-Jacques Rousseau: Transparency and Obstruction*, trans. A. Goldhammer (Chicago: University of Chicago Press, 1988), pp. 213–214.

material conditions, and in which the reflective capacity to stand at a distance from the desire and impulse Locke spoke about played no immediate role. Marx came to this understanding of history by turning against an earlier way of thinking that attributed the power to move humanity forward to the intellectual and cultural practices that generated what he called "the lightning of thought." Rousseau, similarly, arrived at the negative views of reason and reflection he expressed in both the First and Second Discourse through the famous moral crisis he described as taking place on the road to Vincennes in 1749, and which inspired his decision to answer the question posed by the Academy of Dijon about the effects of the arts and sciences on morality, in the terms that made him immediately famous.

Lest it seem that this comparison with Marx rests only on a single work of Rousseau, and that a piece of writing he never finished or published, let me point to the close connections between *La morale sensitive* and some of the Genevan's more famous books. The closest parallel is with *Julie ou la nouvelle Héloïse*. As Rousseau explained in his *Confessions*, the characters he created in this, his most popular work, were emanations of different sides of his own personality testifying, among other things, to his inability to unify them into a coherent character.[7] There are two main male figures in the book: first Saint-Preux, the idealistic young tutor whose love for Julie, and hers for him, both stimulated by their common love of virtue, leads the couple into the moral abyss of her pregnancy and his banishment; and second Wolmar, the older, steadier, less impulsive figure who becomes Julie's husband and establishes the prosperous and happy life of the estate Clarens, a system so well-ordered that it allows Saint-Preux to return, and enter into a wholly different relationship with Julie, one darkened by nostalgia for their earlier connection to be sure, but supportive of the virtuous life to which they aspired at the start and purified of the confusions that earlier led them astray. Saint-Preux and Wolmar, for all their differences, are both Rousseau, and their contrast corresponds quite closely to that between what we may call the two Rousseaus of *La morale sensitive*: the one who can never achieve the virtue to which he aspires because the power that shifting situations and impressions exercise over him deprive him of the steadiness and self-directedness that morality and happiness require; and the other who realizes the aspirations of the first by managing conditions so as to use the material inducements that direct the mind and the will in a way that furthers virtue instead of undermining it. There are

---

[7] *Confessions*, p. 399.

many testimonies to Wolmar's ability to affect such an order in the book, but the one of most import to the personal relations between Julie and Saint-Preux that stand at the center of the novel is the moment when he arranges for them to exchange a chaste kiss on the very spot where they first yielded to impulse and desire. The tranquility is not destined to be permanent, to be sure, and the story's tragic ending, Julie's death by drowning, reminds us that Rousseau had little faith in lasting solutions to deep human dilemmas. But until this point Wolmar does for Saint-Preux what Rousseau imagined he might do for himself in *La morale sensitive*, making clear first that no single person can be at once the subject who creates a morally regenerative order and the object who is directed by it, and second the essential role played by reflective consciousness in making such an order possible.

The role Wolmar fills in *La nouvelle Héloïse* is the very same one Rousseau assigns to the lawgiver in the *Social Contract*, effecting at once the recognition that social life must depend on subjection to laws based on fundamental and rational principles of social order, and the requirement Rousseau several times stated that laws in civil society have the same force, the same power to direct our actions, as the natural impulses to which we are subject in the state of nature. He assigned a similar part to the tutor in *Emile*, his famous book on education. There, and in spite of Rousseau's famous declarations about the goodness and innocence of unspoiled human nature, the young boy is recognized as so full of unreliable and potentially wicked impulses that the tutor who directs his progress must set up a whole series of scenarios in which the boy's behavior is controlled and directed by the circumstances the tutor creates, and in ways that are carefully hidden from the pupil. The result is not far from the direction Wolmar gives to Saint-Preux, or that Rousseau number one seeks to give to Rousseau number two in *La morale sensitive*.[8]

I think these references to Rousseau's more famous works, brief as they are, help to flesh out and substantiate the parallels with Marx I have suggested, and the perhaps surprising similarity in the two thinkers' programs for realizing the human potential that existing forms of life impede. Both thinkers, as I noted a moment ago, came to their reliance on material conditions of the right sort as giving direction to action by turning away from an earlier vision in which reason and reflection were assigned a more visible and positive role in promoting the progress of virtue and happiness. But the thinking both men produced in this way was led to

[8] See Rousseau, *Emile, ou de l'éducation*, ed. C. Wirz (Paris: Gallimard, 1969), pp. 202–204.

reinstate the role for reflective theorizing consciousness each sought in some way to cast off. Since Rousseau, for all his popularity and notoriety, did not inspire any movement comparable to the one that looked to Marx's thinking for direction, there was never any question of this reemergence of the need for intellectual direction issuing in a figure comparable to Lenin. But I think it not at all far-fetched to see two contrasting versions of Marxism as running parallel at once to the duality in both *La morale sensitive* and in *La nouvelle Héloïse*, as well as to the two contrasting programs of moral regeneration Mona Ozouf has identified in the cultural politics of the French Revolution in the 1790s. Of these, one looked to the everyday experience of Revolutionary conditions and activity to alter the consciousness and orientation of citizens. But the other, disappointed in the inability of the first to realize freedom and virtue, turned to the kind of insistent and dictatorial leadership attempted by the Robespierrist reign of terror.[9]

I recognize that the story I have tried to tell here might be read in a way that ends up being very critical of both these great thinkers. On some level that is the way I read it myself, but on another I think such a reading should be resisted. Marx was not Lenin, and in my view many central aspects of his thinking, including his revolutionary optimism itself, exhibit a desire to avoid precisely the kind of dictatorial conclusions Lenin drew from it. Similarly, Rousseau was not Robespierre and I think it is hard to imagine him as a participant in the reign of Terror, in part because of his pessimism about practical outcomes both personal and political. But both Marx and Rousseau infused material conditions with a quasi–utopian power whose unreality was demonstrated by the consequences of their own thinking. A similar danger lay in the attempts each made to seek realization of the potential for human fulfillment in a program that replaced the power of critical reflection with the force of what each hoped would be favorable circumstances.

---

[9] M. Ozouf, "Regeneration," in *A Critical Dictionary of the French Revolution*, ed. F. Furet and M. Ozouf, trans. A. Goldhammer (Cambridge, MA: Harvard University Press, 1989).

CHAPTER 15

Rousseau and Schmitt: Sovereigns and Dictators

David Bates

The emergence of Carl Schmitt as one of the acknowledged great thinkers of the twentieth century did not come uncontested. As Schmitt moved into the mainstream of debates in legal and political theory in the 1990s, there were many efforts to contain his influence. Noting in 1997 that there was a "remarkable lack of seriousness among those studying and promoting Schmitt today," Mark Lilla sought to discredit the "crown jurist" of the Third Reich by highlighting Schmitt's "peculiar theological vision," where existential politics and the critique of liberal democracy was inextricably bound up with cosmic, and often apocalyptic, views.[1] Schmitt's concerns were considered historically passé for theorists such as Jürgen Habermas, who emphasized the political importance of communication and deliberation. Yet in the wake of 9/11 (not to mention the Katrina catastrophe of 2005) Schmitt's work suddenly became acutely relevant again.

First, his Weimar-era writing on the nature of sovereignty, emergency power, and enmity, with his focus on the relation between norms and "exceptions," became critically important for those coming to grips with new constitutional crises concerning the nature and limits of executive power in its struggle with enemies of the state, especially in America. Second, Schmitt's lesser-known postwar work on the nature of international law offered insight into the new configurations of power that had emerged in the Cold War.[2] During the war, Schmitt had argued that the traditional locus political authority in the nation-state had been historically superseded by new "large space" groupings – what he called *Grossraume*.[3] After the war, these ideas were used to conceptualize the new

---

[1] M. Lilla, "The Enemy of Liberalism," *New York Review of Books* 44:8 (May 15, 1997): pp. 38–44.

[2] C. Schmitt, *The "Nomos" of the Earth in the International Law of the "Jus Publicum Europaem,"* trans. G. Ulmen (New York: Telos, 2003).

[3] Schmitt, "The *Großraum* Order of International Law with a Ban on Intervention for Spatially Foreign Powers: A Contribution to the Concept of *Reich* in International Law" (1939–1941), in *Writings on War*, trans. T. Nunan (Cambridge: Polity, 2011), pp. 75–124.

world order of the superpowers. In both of these contexts, domestic and international, Schmitt's ideas were often cited after 9/11 because he so clearly framed the very terms of the debate; whether one agreed with his conclusions or not, he offered a conceptual vocabulary attuned to the serious challenges democratic political and legal institutions faced, both new forms of globalized warfare (terrorism, drone assassinations, and the like) and emergency situations within liberal democratic nations.

One of the key issues after 9/11 was the relationship between democratic notions of popular sovereignty, liberal concepts of institutional order, and the need for sovereign decisions beyond the law in times of exceptional peril. One of Schmitt's main arguments in the Weimar period was that Rousseau, and later revolutionary thinkers such as Sieyes, had fused the metaphysical idea of the people with the structural figure of the sovereign, creating a dangerous hybrid – the constitutional dictator, above all law because it was the founder of law. The Rousseauist idea of the "general will" of the people threatened the stability of any institutional legal order, because those who could claim to speak for the people were justified in suspending the law that was valid only because the people had created it in the first place. Schmitt's conservative interest in defending institutional stability was in part a reaction to the Rousseauist tradition of democracy that emphasized the unitary will of the people. His conception of sovereignty hinged on the exception. Normal legal and political order did not require sovereignty. Decisions beyond the law were only legitimate if the very existence of the state was in question.

After the war, Schmitt focused on very different questions and Rousseau was at first glance hardly relevant to Schmitt's arguments. In the early 1960s, for example, Schmitt was grappling with the apparent "depoliticization" of the major political groupings of the Cold War era. Whether considering the Soviet bloc or the NATO states, it seemed one could point to the existence of relatively homogenous, administrative political-economic systems that avoided any serious existential conflict – either within the blocs, or between them. The serious nature of political life, defined as an agonistic or even violent struggle, had given way to mere "play." This was what Alexander Kojève called the "end of history."[4] In response, Schmitt tried to locate new zones where genuine political action was still possible.[5] For Schmitt, the

---

[4] A. Kojève, *Introduction to the Reading of Hegel*, trans. J. Nichols (Ithaca: Cornell University Press, 1980), pp. 159–160.
[5] On Schmitt's relationship with Kojève see J.-W. Müller, "Visions of Global Order: Schmitt, Aron, and the Civil Servant of the World Spirit," in *A Dangerous Mind: Carl Schmitt in Post-War European Thought* (New Haven: Yale University Press, 2003).

figure of the partisan fighter, or guerilla, represented such a possibility. While there was no doubt that partisans in the Cold War period were enmeshed in larger world-historical forces, because they resolutely defended their home territory, over and above any broader ideological goal, these figures resisted the inexorable evolution of pacified global history. The *telluric* nature of partisan action, along with the conservative desire to defend traditional values and institutions within the homeland, indicated for Schmitt the appearance of an authentic existential struggle at the center of world history. And yet, as Schmitt explained in his short book on the topic, *Theory of the Partisan*, published in 1963, the partisan was a somewhat paradoxical figure. Defined as an "irregular" fighter who was outside the large-space political units that determined any global order, and who actively resisted a new world order, the partisan was, at the same time, crucially dependent on what Schmitt called "interested third parties" for support and military armaments. The partisan therefore existed on the edge – legitimated and supported by dominant powers, but resistant to being swallowed up by them and transformed into their mere tool.[6] The irregular had to legitimate itself through the regular, without being reduced to it.

Here Schmitt returned, surprisingly, to Rousseau. These ideas on the partisan animated a short essay Schmitt published in 1962, on the occasion of Rousseau's two-hundred-and-fiftieth birthday, in the Swiss weekly newspaper the *Zürcher Woche*. In contrast to his earlier characterizations of Rousseau, during the Weimar Republic, where Schmitt castigated him repeatedly for dangerously conflating "ruler" and "ruled" with his democratic notion of popular sovereignty, Schmitt now saw him as a "serious" political thinker. But not because Schmitt had reconsidered Rousseau's legacy in the revolutionary tradition of popular sovereignty. Instead, Schmitt here commended Rousseau because of his importance for theorizing the political quality of the partisan. The "true" Jean-Jacques Rousseau – this is the title of the essay – is the one who resisted the overwhelming advance of industrialization and capitalism, the emergence of large administrative-military states, and, not least, global warfare. Just like the guerilla fighter, Rousseau the guerilla thinker is for Schmitt the "last man" (*Der letze Mensch*) to defend the space of authentic political action. As Schmitt explained, Rousseau saw modern civilization as a "great

---

[6] Schmitt, *Theory of the Partisan: Intermediate Remark on the Concept of the Political*, trans. G. Ulmen (New York: Telos, 2006). As Schmitt writes: "The powerful third party not only provides weapons and munitions, money, material assistance, and all types of medicine, he also creates the type of political recognition of that the irregular fighter needs in order not to be considered in the unpolitical sense of a thief or a pirate . . ." (p. 75).

disaster." Genuine freedom and equality would only be possible, Rousseau had argued, in "small, frugal, and homogeneous communities; everything else is illusion and deception." Rousseau could still inspire the partisans of the twentieth century, especially in the colonies, but ultimately his thinking was badly outdated and hardly relevant to the modern era.[7] In essence, it was only Rousseau's anachronism that made him a serious thinker in a new era of global conflict.

So it seems that for Schmitt, Rousseau was only ever an emblem of a certain historical moment in the history of political formation. Whichever was the true Rousseau – the revolutionary theorist of Jacobin terror, or the telluric defender of the small, homogeneous city-state – Rousseau's ideas were not central to contemporary world-historical developments, at least as Schmitt saw them. And yet Schmitt's own writing offers us a new way to look at Rousseau in the twenty-first century. Central to Schmitt's thinking was the concept of the political. The political was for him an independent category that transcended any historically contingent political entity. It was the concept of the political that allowed us to identify an organization or action *as* political. In a way, we can understand early modern natural law theory in a similar light. The goal of thinkers such as Grotius, Hobbes, Locke, and Montesquieu, for example, was to identify a foundational principle of political legitimacy that would ground a critique of existing states in the seventeenth and eighteenth centuries. While Schmitt usually scoffed at the efforts of Enlightenment *philosophes*, his own thinking on the political suggests that we read Rousseau, in particular, from this perspective. Was there an eighteenth-century concept of the political?

Schmitt on the Political and Its History

Schmitt subtitled his *Theory of the Partisan* "An intermediate commentary on the concept of the political," making a reference to his earlier, vastly influential book *The Concept of the Political*. Schmitt's initial conceptualization of the autonomous logic of the political was developed in the late Weimar republic, culminating in several editions of this much-cited work. One of Schmitt's goals in that text was to decouple the automatic association of the political with the modern nation-state, so that contemporary institutions and organizations could be criticized using a more foundational understanding of political association. Unlike other forms of human

---

[7] Schmitt, "Dem wahren Johann Jakob Rousseau," *Die Zürcher Woche* 26 (June 29, 1962).

groupings, such as economic or religious associations, a political grouping
had no essential content of its own, Schmitt argued. In other words, what
made a human collective political was not specific ideas, relations, or
interests common to the individuals making it up, but instead a peculiar
intensity of association.[8] The political was for Schmitt an existential
category. A particular form of association became political when individuals were willing to kill – and to die – to preserve this collective identity.
So any particular, historically contingent grouping could, in theory,
become political.[9] The criterion of the political was therefore making
a decision about the friend and enemy. This political logic was *independent*
of the qualities of the initial association, for Schmitt. The political decision
was concerned only with threats to the existence of the community. One
could not justify killing for economic or aesthetic reasons, only existential
ones. An implication of Schmitt's was the historical fact that the political
was not at all fixed in the modern state form. Indeed, the modern state, for
Schmitt, arose in the wake of the destructive religious wars of early modern
Europe as a counter to theological justifications of warfare. The state was
a "neutral" power that made the decision on friend and enemy based solely
on the interests of the political unity of the state and its continued
existence.[10]

Schmitt's critique of the modern parliamentary state rested on his theory
of the political logic of existence. Whatever the usefulness of interest-based
politics for the management of a society, Schmitt would argue that the
identification of a sovereign authority with the ability to make genuine
political decisions in times of extreme crisis was essential to the long-term
survival of any human community. These decisions beyond the law were
legitimated only by the preservation of the unity of the political
community.[11] Significantly, one of the most dangerous of these existential
crises was civil war, when different factions might compete for control of
the state's institutions. It was in relation to this problem that Schmitt
dismissed the revolutionary concept of popular sovereignty that he associated with Rousseau, and for two reasons. First, the idea that the people
were sovereign was a metaphysical delusion. If one defined sovereignty, like
Schmitt did, as "he who decides on the exception," then no collective of
concrete, historical individuals could ever act in such a strongly unified

---

[8] Schmitt, *The Concept of the Political*, trans. G. Schwab (Chicago, 1996), p. 38.   [9] Ibid., p. 44.
[10] See Schmitt, "The Age of Neutralizations and Depoliticizations," (1929) trans. J. McCormick, in
    Concept of the Political, pp. 80–96.
[11] See Schmitt, *Political Theology: Four Chapters on the Concept of Sovereignty*, trans. G. Schwab
    (Chicago: University of Chicago Press, 2005).

manner; it would demand complete homogeneity. This leads to the second reason: even if there was a foundational belief in the sovereignty of the people, this power could only be exercised by concrete political leaders. However, these figures would effectively have no *limit* to their authority, because they claimed to be a pure emanation of the people as a whole. This was indeed the logic of revolutionary terror, from France to the Soviet Union, according to Schmitt. And Rousseau was identified by Schmitt as a key theorist of this dangerous idea.[12] By identifying "ruler and ruled" in his political philosophy as the essence of democratic legitimacy, Rousseau opened up the possibility of Jacobin terror because no law, no institutional authority could ever oppose the true general will of the people as a whole – a will instantiated by any number of revolutionary leaders.[13] Schmitt himself advocated a modern form of sovereignty that would exist within the structure of liberal democratic constitutional regimes; this was the institution of *emergency power*.[14] Essential to his argument was the idea that emergency was always temporary and outside of all law, accountable only to the logic of political preservation. The emergency leader should never be legitimated by the "people," as Rousseau had envisioned them, for that would only lead to ever more brutal struggles as actual people fought to represent the people's will.

In the years leading up to the Second World War the opposition between dictatorial, fascistic regimes and constitutional states was often emphasized. However as these oppositions led to an exceptionally violent, and global, form of war and genocide, the idea of emergency authority was implemented by both constitutional and revolutionary states to justify the kind of "total war" necessary to survive extreme crisis.[15] By the end of the war, Schmitt saw (very concretely, in occupied Berlin) the emergence of new political configurations marked not by the boundaries of the original warring "states" but instead by the integration of states into fighting alliances that transcended traditional concepts of the friend/enemy distinction. The earlier Schmittian notion of decisive sovereignty became less and less relevant as a category of analysis. So, in his postwar work on the international forms of conflict, Schmitt supplemented his earlier account

---

[12] Schmitt, *The Crisis of Parliamentary Democracy*, trans. E. Kennedy (Cambridge, MA: MIT Press, 1988), pp. 26–27.

[13] Schmitt, *Constitutional Theory* (1928), trans. J. Seitzer (Durham: Duke University Press, 2008), p. 260.

[14] See especially the discussion of Article 48 of the Weimar constitution, in *Legality and Legitimacy*, trans. J. Seitzer (Durham: Duke University Press, 2004), particularly Part 2.

[15] See C. Rossiter, *Constitutional Dictatorship: Crisis Government in Modern Democracies* (Princeton: Princeton University Press, 1948).

of the political. He argued that the supposedly neutral states of Europe, the kind of absolutist sovereign states theorized by Thomas Hobbes, were not as autonomous as they first appeared. While these states showcased the kind of decisive sovereignty Schmitt championed in the Weimar period,[16] in the new environment of the Cold War, Schmitt emphasized the fact that the absolutist European states were, in fact, part of a larger grouping of states united by what he called a *Jus publicum europeam*. The security of the state entity was guaranteed in part by sovereign authority within the political community, but in practice these states avoided the kind of genuine existential conflict that marked the zone of authentic political action. War was limited and tactical. At least within Europe – for Schmitt pointed out that in the more open spaces of colonial appropriation, European states clashed repeatedly as they sought to dominate a complex political battleground that was now global in scale. At stake was not the particular existence of any one state but rather the secure organization of the European grouping of states as a whole.[17]

By identifying the political with existential conflict, Schmitt could show how the decisions of political security were not limited to state sovereign authorities. This was particularly evident in the postwar situation Schmitt was trying to conceptualize in the 1950s and 1960s. Clearly, the genuine political grouping consisted of the United States, and its allied western states, opposed by the Soviet Union, along with its own bloc of subjugated states. And yet the political character of this political opposition had been substantially weakened. Paradoxically, the extreme destruction made possible by nuclear weapons prevented the proper exercise of war in the postwar era because no particular decision to fight or defend one's own existential grouping could ever be justified when the very existence of the combatants was always in question. The total destruction of the enemy violated, in fact, the logic of the political, because killing was only justified when one's own existence was threatened. Any form of warfare between the superpower configurations would not doubt lead to massive destruction on the side of the loser as well as the "winner."

The importance of the partisan for Schmitt lay in this new global context, for in the Cold War there were no "open spaces" left in the world. And significantly, the new weaponry that dominated the air made any tactical decision immediately global in a way not possible in the time

---

[16] But not so clearly during the Nazi era. See D. Bates, "Political Theology and the Nazi State: Carl Schmitt's Concept of the Institution," *Modern Intellectual History* 3 (2006): pp. 415–452.

[17] Schmitt, *Nomos of the Earth*, Part 3.

before manned and unmanned flight. And yet, the two global blocs eventually found a new space for war *internal* to the global configuration. The existence of local conflicts, fought by deeply committed partisan figures who defended their historical and telluric forms of identity, became proxies for the global powers. By supporting partisan fighters unaffiliated with any global political form, the superpowers could indirectly test the political enemy in combat, without risking omnicidal nuclear war, for these local conflicts over control of territory were fought in a necessarily *limited* way.

With the end of the Cold War, we might say that the significance of Schmitt, who died in 1985, ends at the same time. But in fact it may be more important for us to take up the challenge of Schmitt's concept of the political in our new global age. For Schmitt, the political is not bound by any law, only the logic of existence. Where, today, does one locate the political if it cannot be automatically aligned with individual, sovereign state authorities, and how do we justify the legal state when political legitimacy has been displaced? Schmitt's celebration of Rousseau as a serious thinker in his 1962 essay was of course a rather backhanded compliment, since the partisan fighter existed only as an instrument of greater political powers operating on a global scale. But strangely perhaps, the shifting contours of our post 9/11 world seem to be especially suited to a Rousseauist perspective. The "war on terror" has caused a mutation again in configurations of the political that were already massively shaken by the dismantling of the Soviet bloc and the breakup of the Soviet Union itself. The defense of the "homeland" and the retrenchment of executive decision on the part of individual nation-states makes Rousseau's understanding of political community newly interesting.

Rousseau's Concept of the Political

A critical reading of Rousseau can elicit a political philosophy that has important implications for our current conceptions of the democratic legal state and the justification of decision and war within modern constitutional regimes. Yet the significance of Rousseau in this context will, I suggest, only be recognized if we adopt a Schmittian perspective on his work.[18] Like Schmitt, Rousseau was interested in identifying what I will call a pure concept of the political, as a way of critiquing existing regimes

---

[18] This section draws on "Rousseau's Cybernetic Political Body," chapter 5 of my book *States of War: Enlightenment Origins of the Political* (New York: Columbia University Press, 2012).

and institutions. In the process, Rousseau discovered an existential logic that mirrored Schmitt's in interesting ways. However, Rousseau developed his concept of an autonomous political sphere in such a way that it supported a radically *democratic* understanding of the legal state. Rousseau's thoughts on dictatorship and war in this context will point to the continuing relevance of both Schmitt and Rousseau for any contemporary understanding of the political.

Rousseau's *Second Discourse* on the origins of inequality denies that political and legal obligation can be easily justified, given that these "chains" are in fact always the product of asymmetric power relations that develop in any so-called civilized condition characterized by the total interdependence of individuals. Essentially, Rousseau argues in Part 2 that laws just confirm and reinforce preexisting social and economic domination. "Such was, or must have been, the origin of Society and of Laws, which gave the weak new fetters and the rich new forces ...."[19] The challenge was to conceive of these institutional restraints in a new way. Could justice, now just a perverse form of ideological deceit, ever be rehabilitated as a worthy goal? The *Second Discourse* fails to give much of an answer. At best, it suggests that the conjecture of a "natural" human being, described in Part 1, is at least a plausible fiction. And that individual was absolutely free and independent of any other human – but it was also cognitively, emotionally, and morally underdeveloped. Since a return to that (admittedly fictional) natural state was not at all possible, or even desirable, Rousseau suggested that we must find a way to rediscover that independence and freedom, within modern social and political organizations that were predicated on asymmetric interdependence and outright oppression. Was there any way that the law, currently a kind of poison that corroded human freedom and the dignity of individuals, could become a remedy that would ameliorate the depraved state of inequality and oppression marking modern life?

This was the problem taken up in the *Social Contract*, published a few years later. The relationship between these texts is important for understanding the nature of *political* organization for Rousseau, as opposed to any other kind of human grouping. In the earlier book, Rousseau had tracked the possible evolution of human history from a natural state of independence, through to a radically new form of social organization that was based purely on emotional attachment, and which preserved for the most part the natural independence of the individual. In other words, no

---

[19] J.-J. Rousseau, *Discourse on Inequality*, G1, p. 173.

matter what the pleasure and pain produced by inequalities in the primal social condition (made possible by new capacities for comparison and preference), these inequalities had no real effect on the *existential* condition of the individual, who still depended on no one else for material support. The fatal turn to civilization hinges on the turn away from this independence in society to a form of dependency that is the logical implication of any division of labor. What Rousseau underlines here in the *Second Discourse* is that the initial form of social organization preserved freedom and independence, even as it introduced new forms of inequality in the moral and psychological sphere. There was also no real political form of authority in nascent society, and no laws. The institutions of government and law emerged only later to protect the new and debilitating inequalities that were inherent in commercial exchange, where one is always forced to lie and deceive since every exchange is vital for one's own very survival.

So when we turn to the *Social Contract* to find out how law, those chains of oppression, could become a source of freedom, it is crucial to recognize that Rousseau is offering a wholly new conjectural narrative, one intended to elicit a form of organization that is not tracked in the *Second Discourse*, namely, a purely *political organization*. Significantly, Rousseau keeps the original individuals in their natural state of independence and freedom as he unfolds this political development. In other words, in this narrative, humans never enter into any genuine social relationship as they do in the earlier work, when sentiment is awakened with the building of the hut and the possibility of permanent association. The contingent moment of mutual attraction and the emergence of love simply do not happen here. Instead, individuals reach a moment where they realize that nature has become much too difficult for them to survive. The challenges that were met at the beginning of Part 2 of the *Second Discourse* ("difficulties soon presented themselves; it became necessary to learn to overcome them ...")[20] here become overwhelming. Without the *permanent* aid of other human beings, the individual knows he or she will inevitably perish – along with the whole human race perhaps. The challenge to cooperation is that each individual recognizes that other people are always a potential threat to their own individual liberty. One's need for another can easily (inevitably?) become an opportunity for someone to dominate in this relation.

Rousseau is carefully unfolding a logic of the political that is not at all contaminated by economic, social, or any existing authority relations.

[20] Ibid., p. 161.

Now, Schmitt argued that the political was an autonomous concept, with its own demands and its own criteria. This is, I think, what Rousseau is attempting. But according to Schmitt, a particular, historically contingent human grouping is suddenly transformed into a *political* association, that is, one with existential significance, when the form of association is intensified in a moment of crisis. This condition then produced new principles and new obligations, which are not at all derived from the initial association itself. Political legitimacy, then, stems from the existential quality of the association, and not the substantial relations inherent in that association. However, Rousseau offers a more radical approach to the political: he imagines an association of individuals that forms *prior* to any other human association. So unlike Schmitt, who argued that the essence of the political was the friend/enemy distinction (that is, decisions become political when they are made in light of existential threats to that particular human association), Rousseau suggests in the *Social Contract* that the political is a logic derived solely from the need to protect the security of individuals through association. This is protection against the forces of nature, but also, crucially, protection against the potential threat of any other individual within the association. This relation to other individuals cannot at all be a friend/enemy distinction, since one needs, Rousseau points out, the guarantee of *permanent* support from others. "How can he commit [his force and freedom] without harming himself, and without neglecting the care he owes himself?"[21]

This is why Rousseau characterizes the "social" contract itself not as an actual society defined by concrete ties and relations between individuals. The contract is in fact a giving up of one's force to the entire whole of the newly formed *political* group, whose sole function is the protection of the individual's existence and freedom. Every individual makes the same pledge. As Rousseau makes clear, the only goals of the new association are, first, the protection of every single one of the participants through the harnessing of everyone's powers, and second, the protection of this actual form of association – since, by definition, this association was created precisely because the individual could no longer defend his or her existence alone. The only thing that legitimates political organization here is the existential logic of defense. No prior community is threatened into political form, as Schmitt argued.

Rousseau claims that any concrete form of power or governance is, by definition, illegitimate if it does not provide for the equal protection of

---

[21] Rousseau, *Social Contract*, G2, p. 49.

every individual within the association. But what were its positive features? The political association is (as it was for Hobbes) an entirely *artificial* entity, and therefore it has no predetermined form or organization. But in contrast to Hobbes, who described this new being as a kind of machine, Rousseau calls it a body "whose life consists in the union of its members ...."[22] This is a key point, even though it has been under-developed in the literature on Rousseau. It is crucial, because Rousseau argues that political association begins with a pure logic of unity, but he also acknowledges that to act in concrete historical circumstances, the will of this political unity – the general will – must take into account the condition of every single member of the association. This requires first a method for gathering and synthesizing these individual perspectives, but it also requires an effective way to deploy the whole political body so that it maintains the security of all its members (and of itself). Since this political body is completely artificial, it must be constructed. In the earlier version of the *Social Contract* known as the Geneva manuscript, Rousseau noted that if such a political existence was in fact "natural" to human beings, then there would have to be some kind of "common sensorium" where all the perceptions of the body would be united, so that the general state of the organism would be intimately known. A political "nervous system" would also have to exist, as the channel for commanding the movement of the body.[23]

But as Rousseau emphasizes, the political body at its moment of origin is just a pure logic of possibility, a virtual body awaiting concretization. The construction of an actual political body is therefore a perpetual struggle. Structures have to be built that will allow for the constant participation of the individuals in the formation of the "general will," and for the effective use of individuals for any necessary political action. Rousseau repeatedly uses neurological metaphors to explain this process. In his *Discourse on Political Economy* Rousseau pointed to the brain as the center of law and command in the body.

> The body politic, taken individually, can be looked upon as an organized body, alive and similar to a man's. The sovereign power represents the head; the laws and customs are the brain, [which is] the origin of the nerves and the seat of understanding, of the will and of the senses, of which the judges and magistrates are the organs.[24]

---

[22] Ibid., p. 61.   [23] Rousseau, *Geneva Manuscript*, G2, p. 155.
[24] Rousseau, *Political Economy*, G2, p. 6.

Government, then, is a kind of artificial brain with an artificial *sensorium communis*. The life of the political body required a constant communication between the whole as foundational unity, and all of its parts. This was an especially difficult project because perfect identity of individual and whole (which characterizes genuine organic bodies) is, in an artificially created body, just an ideal. The neurological model provides a clear understanding of Rousseau's famous critique of political representation. Expressions of sovereignty are *performances*. In an organism, the brain does not "represent" varied interests and perceptions in the body. Rather, the brain is the space for the actual *synthesis* of every particular aspect of the organism. This is not some vague metaphysical claim on the part of Rousseau. In fact, it is just a logical consideration. In any organized body, the general interest can be precisely identified, because it is simply the continued existence of the living body. Even if the political body is absolutely artificial, it must also be driven by this unitary existential logic. The problem is that there is no natural political nervous system to integrate the different aspects of the body. The artificial form of that nervous system is the institutional forms of governance and law.

We can see then how Rousseau acknowledges that every concrete political regime is a work in progress. Yet the existential logic of the original political association remains clear in the midst of imperfection. This is the significance of Rousseau's concept of the political: the preeminent task of political institutions is to provide a shelter from the kinds of inequality and dependence that are likely when humans form concrete communities and social organizations. Only in the political form of association are we perfectly free (obeying only our natural inclination to protect our existence) and perfectly equal, since the political order makes absolutely no distinction between individuals within the association – at least in terms of their existential safety. This is a crucial point to remember. The political association has only one ultimate goal and one responsibility: the safety and security of the individual's life and goods.

Yet after its formation, the general will must confront concrete circumstances and decide what specific actions will best preserve the body politic and its members. In other words, the pure logic of the political must generate a concrete decision to act in certain ways. "By the social pact we have given the body politic existence and life: the task now is to give it motion and will by legislation. For the initial act by which this body assumes form and unity still leaves entirely undetermined what it must do to *preserve itself*."[25] This

---

[25] *Social Contract*, G2, p. 66.

was the function of law and the machinery of government. They are not themselves inherently political, for Rousseau. Rather, these are mechanisms that allow the general unified desire for security to be articulated in a specific manner. This helps explain the somewhat paradoxical figure of the Legislator, an outsider who brings to a newly formed political grouping a constitutional framework so that it can literally find its voice. The institutional structures of synthesis and decision are necessary if the general will is going to speak and act, yet these are completely absent at the origin of any pure political community. Concrete institutions provide both a space for integrating multiple perspectives and a kind of training ground where individuals can become accustomed to thinking beyond their own generality.

Of course, most historical states have not in fact benefitted from this kind of pseudo-divine intervention. And yet, the constitutive imperfection of any political body, understood here as a synthesizing power that integrates its parts into some form of unitary whole, does not at all compromise the foundational principle of the political – that is, the absolute commitment to the protection of the body and with it every member of the political community.

Exceptional Acts

The inevitable discrepancy between the pure logic of the political, and the concrete institutions that attempt to articulate it, necessitates and legitimates what Rousseau will describe as exceptional interventions in the life of the political body. For Rousseau, in contrast to Schmitt, these perilous moments of emergency will *not* be paradigmatic embodiments of sovereign decision beyond the law. They are instead what might be called *political pathologies*. For times of crisis, Rousseau will argue, the body sometimes needs an intervention from outside, analogous to the medical interventions that help a natural body to heal and return to its normal state.

In the *Social Contract*, Rousseau introduces two constitutional figures who can defend the integrity of the political body, but who are not a part of the normal functioning constitutional system. The first is the Tribune, modeled on the Roman institution. Rousseau sees that the balance between the various institutional organs of the people's unitary body may at times be disrupted. Rousseau proposes that a Tribune would be charged with restoring the true relations between organs, so as to avoid internal conflict or even paralysis. While he is not a "constitutive part of the City" (136) the Tribune nonetheless can intervene in order to protect, say, the sovereign people against their government, or, alternatively, perhaps save the properly functioning governing organs from the wayward desires of the people. The Tribune, according to Rousseau, is a limited figure: he has no positive power, only the power of the veto. The Tribune can do nothing, but prevent everything. The important point to make here is that the Tribune is not at all a Schmittian figure that voices, in an emergency, the sovereign will. The Tribune instead defends the given constitutional *order* within the state so that it can function properly, and continue to integrate the political body.

However, in moments of extreme crisis, what Schmitt would call true emergencies or states of exception, Rousseau agrees that the normal institutions may not always be up to the task of defending the body, even with the interventions of the Tribune. Hence the need for the second exceptional figure, the Dictator. As Rousseau puts it: "A thousand cases can arise for which the Lawgiver did not provide, and it is a very necessary foresight that one cannot foresee everything." If the political group faces dissolution in one of these moments, then a Dictator may be appointed. This is an extreme move. Rousseau explains that "one should never suspend the sacred power of the laws, except when the salvation of the Fatherland is at risk."[26] Again, we can see that the Dictator is not a purified expression of sovereignty, because genuine acts of the sovereign are, for Rousseau, identified with the acts of totalizing integration that take place within the body. Sovereignty therefore cannot bypass the complex institutional forms that make those integrations possible, because it comes into existence only with that act of integration. So what legitimates the Dictator, who functions outside the law?

As Schmitt pointed out in his book *Dictatorship*, Rousseau in fact offers two different variations on the dictator. The one is the classical Dictator who takes over "in the silence of the laws." The other form of dictatorship is when "the activity of the government . . . gets concentrated in one or two of its members."[27] Schmitt calls this last form "improper." Both are commissarial forms of dictatorship. The difference is that in the latter the laws remain in effect, only their administration is accelerated and concentrated. The "genuine" dictatorship, for Schmitt, is Rousseau's classic figure who operates in a space that the legislative authority has vacated altogether.[28] According to Schmitt, Rousseau fails here to define

---

[26] Ibid., p. 138.   [27] Ibid.
[28] Schmitt, *Dictatorship: From the Origin of the Modern Concept of Sovereignty to Proletarian Class Struggle*, trans. M. Hoelzl and G. Ward (Cambridge: Polity, 2014), p. 105.

the "legal foundation" that would institute this condition of lawlessness. The paradox, supposedly, lies in the problem of how the *volonté générale* could ever "suspend itself in a case of emergency," as Schmitt puts it. But Schmitt fails to understand Rousseau's argument here. Yes, the genuine Dictator is not a part of the body but an external power that is given the task of making decisions, but these decisions are perfectly congruent with the foundational logic of the political. For Rousseau, the general will becomes exceptionally clear in times of crisis when the life of the community is close to being extinguished (unlike more ambiguous and complex situations encountered in the normal course of affairs). As Rousseau writes, "it is obvious that the people's foremost intention is that the State not perish."[29] Whatever the Dictator does toward that goal is therefore *automatically* consistent with the general will. That is all the Dictator can do, legitimately: defend the life of the political body in all possible ways. It can do anything to achieve this goal, but it cannot transform the institutional forms of the State. During the crisis, we could say that the body politic becomes a kind of puppet, to be wielded by the Dictator, who is a foreign animating force. But the goal of a dictatorship is to return to the normal operation of the body as originally constituted. As Rousseau explains, referencing Roman history, as a political body first trains itself to operate as a unitary being early in its history, the need for these external interventions will be frequent. However, in its mature phase, the need for exceptional power will be limited to very rare cases of emergency. Thus the Dictator is not a paradigm of political unity, only a confirmation of the pure existential logic of the general will. In the normal (and artificial) life of a political being, the challenge is always to produce and maintain its own unity; it is a kind of self-enclosed system.

Still, Schmitt's question remains: who "decides" that the law must be abandoned and the Dictator summoned? Schmitt attempts to show that Rousseau's classic definition of dictatorship as a "commission," when fused with his idea of the general will of the people, "transforms the state into an arbitrary, revocable and unconditionally dependent commissarial operation."[30] But that interpretation relies on an overly metaphysical understanding of Rousseau's notion of the general will. If the general will is in fact a logical principle of unity, then we can see that in normal life the challenge is to make sure that institutions are founded to channel

---

[29] *Social Contract*, G2, p. 138.
[30] Ibid., 109. On Rousseau's place in the development of a modern notion of dictatorship, see P. Pasquino, "Between Machiavelli and Schmitt: Remarks on Rousseau's dictatorship," *Storia del pensiero politico* 1 (2013): pp. 145–154.

and integrate the citizens through law, and to execute that law in the particular conditions that the state finds itself in. The moment calling for dictatorship hinges on the patent *failure* of the laws to confront the extreme situation. That will simply be evident for the government, Rousseau is arguing. In this case, the general will remains in effect in a way – it is the will to survive. What is absent is only the knowledge of *what that will prescribes in these particular circumstances.*

Political Bodies and the State of War

We can see how Rousseau affirms Schmitt's notion that the political is an autonomous sphere of action, with its own logic and its own forms of legitimation. And like Schmitt, Rousseau identifies the foundation of political community as a primordial desire for security and survival. The social contract has a very simple form: to protect the individual from the obstacles of nature, but also to protect that individual from the oppression of any other member of the political body. The conjectural narrative of the political short-circuits any substantial forms of historical social life in order to show that political order is not dependent on any concrete relations between people in historical time. That much Schmitt would agree with. But Rousseau, unlike Schmitt, argued that the foundational moment of political existence is not at all predicated on enmity, and a willingness to kill and die. By locating the political before (and beyond) any historical organized community, Rousseau grounds the political not in enmity, but in law: every individual has an equal status in the political body, otherwise it would not be possible. So the Schmittian moment of security necessitates, for Rousseau, the foundation of the rule of law, because only law is general and concerns everyone equally.

But what about war? At the end of the *Social Contract* Rousseau notes that he still has to "buttress the State by its external relations," not that it has been founded on "true principles."[31] Inevitably, the existential demands of a political body will clash with those of another. As Rousseau notes in his manuscript fragment "The State of War," the emergence of civil states has made possible the most horrific violence. As Rousseau writes: "We shall see men united by artificial concord, assemble to slaughter one another, and all the horrors of war arise from the efforts made to prevent them."[32] There is no natural enmity between humans; such a relation exists only between artificial creatures, the political bodies.

[31] *Social Contract*, G2, p. 152.   [32] Rousseau, *The State of War*, G2, p. 167.

Yet why cannot these individual states recognize the mutual threat and enter into some kind of pact equivalent to the original social contract of individuals? The answer is simple: in the "state of nature" that individual political bodies find themselves, there is no natural equality and no natural independence. The state is an *artificial* body with no stability. Therefore they cannot be "equal" to one another – they are hardly ever equal to themselves in constantly changing conditions. If war is not at all *essential* to the formation of a political being, war does become a crucial space for decision and will. Indeed, Rousseau's depiction of the interstate condition is fundamentally Schmittian: the state must analyze opposing states and assess their threats, and decide by arms or make "fleeting treaties."[33] Yet the implication of Rousseau's understanding of these friend/enemy distinctions is decidedly not Schmittian. Since for Rousseau the political is an artificial body, the decision to destroy one's political enemy does not in fact entail the killing of other human beings at all. In a battle between states, the goal is to "reach the seat of life," in other words the general will that defines the political body. Once the integrating institutions of the state have been eliminated, there remains no general will and hence no enmity. "If the social pact could be severed with a single stroke, straightaway there would be no war; and with that single stroke the State would be killed, without a single man dying." Only if this surgical destruction of political identity is not possible can more concrete destruction of property and people be legitimated.[34] War, which is possible only between constituted political beings, can be justified only with respect to the life and death of those political bodies – and not the bodies of actual human beings. The only truly just war is, for Rousseau, a virtual war waged by virtual beings.

The main argument that we can take from Rousseau is this: we must defend the absolute autonomy of the political as a response to the threat of insecurity, while simultaneously defending the rule of law and the protection of individuals, since the political body is dependent on the legal articulation of the general will for self-preservation. Rousseau's insight was that only within a *political* community could individuals find shelter and security as individuals of modern societies – no matter if inequalities reigned in social and economic spheres. Schmitt derided Rousseau's belief that only homogeneous, frugal communities could have a genuine political existence, but if we understand Rousseau's argument, we can see that the extent of the political is always conditioned by the possibilities of

---

[33] Rousseau, *Extrait de projet de paix perpetuelle de Monsieur L'Abbé de Saint-Pierre*, OC III, p. 569.
[34] *State of War*, G2, pp. 176, 171.

communication and integration, which have changed dramatically since the eighteenth century. But this does not invalidate Rousseau's concept of the political. Our challenge today is to locate and defend new potential spaces of the political in changing global conditions. It is an open question, for example, whether human rights regimes should be understood as political organizations in this way. In any case, instead of seeking expressions of exceptional authority and decisions over life and death to identify the political (*pace* Schmitt), we need to look instead for communities in solidarity, linked by shared feelings of permanent insecurity, united by legal structures. There is no enmity at the heart of Rousseau's concept of the political, only the equality of law, though law must always be defended.

Bibliography

CHAPTER ONE

Bayle, P. "Machiavelli." In *Dictionnaire historique et critique*. 2nd ed. 3 vols. Rotterdam, 1702.

"Christianisme." In *Encylopédie ou Dictionnaire Raisonné des Sciences des Arts et de Métiers*. Fascimilie ed. 1751–1780. Stuttgart-Bad Cannstatt: Frommann, 1966.

Cicero. *De Officiis.*

Cottret, M. and B. Cottret. *Jean Jacques Rousseau en son temps*. Paris: Perri, 2005.

Gagnebin, B. "Le role du Législateur dans les conceptions politiques de Rousseau." In *Études sur le "Contrat social,"* pp. 277–290. Paris: Les Belles Lettres, 1964.

Gentili, A. *De Legationibus*. London, 1585.

Lübbers, A. *Alfieri, Foscolo und Manzoni als leser Machiavellis: Die Bedeutung der Literatur für das Risorgimento*. Würzburg: Königshausen u. Neumann, 2014.

"Machiavelisme." In *Encyclopédie*. Vol. 9. Neuchatel, 1765.

Machiavelli, Niccolò. *Discourses on Livy*. Translated by Harvey C. Mansfield and Nathan Tarcov. Chicago: University of Chicago Press, 1996.

—*Florentine Histories*. Translated by L. Banfield and H. Mansfield. Princeton: Princeton University Press, 1988.

—*Machiavelli and His Friends: Their Personal Correspondence*. Translated by J. Atkinson and D. Sices. Dekalb: Northern Illinois University Press, 1996.

—*Machiavelli: The Chief Works and Others*. Edited by A. Gilbert. Durham: Duke University Press, 1989.

—*Opere di Niccolò Machiavelli*. Edited by C. Vivanti. Turin: Einaudi, 1997.

—*The Literary Works of Machiavelli: With Selections from the Private Correspondence*. Translated by J. Hale. London: Oxford University Press, 1961.

—*The Prince*. Translated by P. Bondanella. Oxford: Oxford University Press, 2005.

Manent, P. *Naissance de la politique moderne: Machiavel / Hobbes / Rousseau*. Paris: Payot, 1977.

Monstesquieu, Charles Louis de Secondat, Baron de. *De l'espirit des lois*. In *Œuvres complètes*. Edited by R. Callois. Paris: Gallimard, 1951.

Nelson, E. *The Hebrew Republic: Jewish Sources and the Transformation of European Political Thought.* Cambridge, MA: Harvard University Press, 2010.
Ridolfi, R. *The Life of Niccolò Machiavelli.* Translated by C. Grayson. London: Routledge and Kegan Paul, 1963.
—*Vita di Niccolò Machiavelli.* Rome: A. Belardetti, 1954.
Rousseau, J.-J. *Correspondance complète de Jean Jacques Rousseau: Édition Critique.* Edited by R.A. Leigh. Publications de l'Institut et Musée Voltaire. 52 vols. Genève: Institut et musée Voltaire, 1965–1991.
—*Lettre à d'Alembert.* Edited by L. Brunel. Paris: Hachette, 1922.
—*The Collected Writings of Rousseau.* Edited by Christopher Kelly, Roger D. Masters, and Peter Stillman. Translated by Christopher Kelly. 13 vols. Hanover: Published for Dartmouth College by University Press of New England, 1990–2010.
Sasso, G. "Il celebrato sogno di Machiavelli." In *Machiavelli e gli antichi e altri saggi,* pp. 211–300. Milan: R. Ricciardi, 1988.
Shklar, J. *Men and Citizens: A Study of Rousseau's Social Theory.* Cambridge, MA: Harvard University Press, 1969.
Spinoza, B. *The Poetical Works.* Edited by A. Wernham. Oxford: Clarendon Press, 1958.
Viroli, M. *Jean-Jacques Rousseau and the "Well-Ordered Society."* Cambridge: Cambridge University Press, 1988.
—*Machiavelli's God.* Princeton: Princeton University Press, 2010.
—*Redeeming the Prince: The Meaning of Machiavelli's Masterpiece.* Princeton: Princeton University Press, 2013.
Voltaire. *Anti-Machiavel: Or, an examination of Machiavel's Prince. With notes historical and political. Published by Mr. de Voltaire. Translated from the French.* London, 1741.
—*Le docteur pansophe, ou lettre de Monseur de Voltaire.* London, 1766.

CHAPTER TWO

Cajot, J.-J. *Les Plagiats de M. J.J. R. de Genève sur l'éducation.* La Haye, 1766.
Dusaulx, J. *De mes rapport avec J.J. Rousseau.* Paris, 1798.
Montaigne, Michel de. *Les Essais.* Edited by P. Villey and V.-L. Saulnier. 3 vols. Paris: Presses Universitaires de France, 1965.
Plutarch. "The E at Delphi." In *Moralia.* Cambridge, MA: Harvard University Press, 2014.
Silber, E. "Rousseau and Montaigne: The Evolution of a Literary Relationship." PhD Dissertation: Columbia University, 1968.
Starobinski, J. *Montaigne in Motion.* Translated by A. Goldhammer. Chicago: University of Chicago Press, 1985.
—"Rousseau dans la marge de Montaigne: Cinq notes inédites." *Débat* 90 (1996): pp. 3–26.

CHAPTER THREE

Castel, Louis. *L'homme moral opposé à l'homme physique de Monsieur R***. Lettre philosophique ou l'on réfute le déisme du jour.* Toulouse, 1756.

Castillon, Jean de. *Discours sur l'origine de l'inegalité parmi les hommes.* Amsterdam, 1756.

Gerdil, Giacicinto Sigismondo. *Discours sur l'homme consideré relativement à l'état de nature, & l'état de société.* Turin, 1769.

Hobbes, T. *Behemoth, or the Long Parliament.* Edited by F. Tonnies. London, 1889.

—*Leviathan.* Edited by R. Tuck. Cambridge: Cambridge University Press, 1996.

—*On the Citizen.* Edited by R. Tuck and M. Silverthorne. Cambridge: Cambridge University Press, 1998.

—*The Elements of Law, Natural and Politic.* Edited by F. Tonnies. London: Frank Cass & Co., 1969.

Luzac, Eli. *Lettre d'un anonime à Monsieur Rousseau.* Paris, 1766.

Macintyre, A. *A Short History of Ethics.* London: Routledge, 1966.

Monstesquieu, Charles Louis de Secondat, Baron de. *The Spirit of the Laws.* Edited by A. Cohler et al. Cambridge: Cambridge University Press, 1989.

Pufendorf, S. *Of the Law of Nature and Nations.* Translated by B. Kennett. London, 1729.

Richter, M. *The Political Theory of Montesquieu.* Cambridge: Cambridge University Press, 1977.

Roosevelt, G. *Reading Rousseau in the Nuclear Age.* Philadelphia: Temple University Press, 1990.

Rousseau, J.-J. *Discourse on Inequality.* In *The Social Contract and Discourses.* Translated by G. Cole. Edited by J. Brumfitt and J. Hall. New York: Alfred A. Knopf, 1993.

—*Emile, or On Education.* Translated by A. Bloom. New York: Basic Books, 1979.

—*Lettre d'un citoyen de Genève à un autre citoyen.* Geneva, 1768.

Sieyès, E. *Political Writings.* Edited by M. Sonenscher. Indianapolis: Hackett Pub. Co., 2003.

Tuck, R. "Hobbes's Moral Philosophy." In *The Cambridge Companion to Hobbes,* edited by T. Sorell, pp. 175–207. Cambridge: Cambridge University Press, 1996.

Wokler, R. "The Influence of Diderot on the Political Theory of Rousseau: Two Aspects of a Relationship." *Studies on Voltaire and the Eighteenth Century* 132 (1975): pp. 55–111.

CHAPTER FOUR

Adam, A. "De quelques sources de Rousseau dans la littérature philosophique (1700–1750)." In *Jean-Jacques Rousseau et son oeuvre: problèmes et recherches.* Paris: Librairie C. Klincksieck, 1964.

Althusser, L. *Ecrits philosophiques et politiques.* Paris: Stock, 1994.

—*Montesquieu, Rousseau, Marx.* Translated by B. Brewster. London: Verso, 1972.

—*Politique et histoire, de Machiavel à Marx.* Edited by F. Matheron. Paris: Éditions du Seuil, 2006.

Berman, M. *The Politics of Authenticity: Radical Individualism and the Emergence of Modern Society.* London: Atheneum, 2009.

Brooke, C. *Philosophic Pride: Stoicism and Political Thought from Lipsius to Rousseau.* Princeton: Princeton University Press, 2012.

Derathé, R. *Jean-Jacques Rousseau et la science politique de son temps.* Paris: J. Vrin, 1970.

Ehrard, J. "Le fils coupable." In *L'esprit des mots: Montesquieu en lui-même et parmi les siens.* Geneva: Droz, 1998.

Grace, E. and C. Kelly. *The Challenge of Rousseau.* Cambridge: Cambridge University Press, 2013.

Hampson, N. *Will and Circumstance: Montesquieu, Rousseau, and the French Revolution.* Norman: University of Oklahoma Press, 1983.

Launay, M. *Jean-Jacques Rousseau et son temps.* Paris: A.G. Nizet, 1969.

Manin, B. "Montesquieu." In *A Critical Dictionary of the French Revolution*, edited by F. Furet and M. Ozouf, translated by A. Goldhammer, pp. 728–741. Cambridge, MA: Harvard University Press, 1989.

McCormick, J. *Machiavellian Democracy.* Cambridge: Cambridge University Press, 2011.

Monstesquieu, Charles Louis de Secondat, Baron de. *De l'esprit des lois.* In *Œuvres complètes de Montesquieu.* vol II Edited by A. Masson. Paris: Nagel, 1955.

—*Persian Letters.* Translated by C.J. Betts. Baltimore: Penguin Books, 1973.

—*The Spirit of the Laws.* Edited by A. Cohler et al. Cambridge: Cambridge University Press, 1989.

Nelson, E. *The Greek Tradition in Republican Thought.* Cambridge: Cambridge University Press, 2004.

—*The Hebrew Republic: Jewish Sources and he Transformation of European Political Thought.* Cambridge, MA: Harvard University Press, 2010.

Ohji, K. "Nécessité/Contingence: Rousseau et les Lumières selon Louis Althusser." *Lumières* 15 (2010): pp. 89–112.

Rahe, P. *Against Throne and Altar: Machiavelli and Political Theory under the English Republic.* Cambridge: Cambridge University Press, 2008.

—*Montesquieu and the Logic of Liberty: War, Religion, Commerce, Climate, Terrain, Technology, Uneasiness of Mind, the Spirit of Political Vigilance, and the Foundations of the Modern Republic.* New Haven: Yale University Press, 2010.

—*Soft Despotism, Democracy's Drift.* New Haven: Yale University Press, 2009.

Radica, G. "De Montesquieu à Rousseau: les Anglais sont-ils libres?" *Revue française des Idées Politiques* 35 (2012): pp. 159–169.

—"Rousseau, Jean-Jacques." On-line Dictionnaire Montesquieu, under the direction of C. Volpilhac-Auger, ENS de Lyon, septembre 2013. URL: http://dictionnaire-montesquieu.ens-lyon.fr/fr/article/1377669928/fr.

Rosenblatt, H. *Jean-Jacques Rousseau and Geneva: From the First Discourse to the Social Contract, 1749–1762.* Cambridge: Cambridge University Press, 1997.

Rousseau, J.-J. *Confessions*. Translated by A. Scholar. Oxford: Oxford University Press, 2000.

—*Correspondance complète de Jean Jacques Rousseau: Édition Critique*. Edited by R.A. Leigh. Publications de l'Institut et Musée Voltaire. 52 vols. Genève: Institut et musée Voltaire, 1965–1991.

—*Emile, or On Education*. Translated by A. Bloom. New York: Basic Books, 1979.

—*Reveries of the Solitary Walker*. Translated by R. Goulbourne. Oxford: Oxford Univeristy Press, 2011.

Roza, S. and P. Crétois. *Le républicanisme social: une exception française?* Paris: Publications de la Sorbonne, 2014.

Sénéchal, A. "Jean-Jacques Rousseau, secrétaire de Madame Dupin d'après des documents inédits avec un inventaire des papiers Dupin dispersés en 1957 et 1958." *Annales des la Société Jean-Jacques Rousseau* 36 (1963–65): pp. 173–288.

Sonenscher, M. *Before the Deluge: Public Debt, Inequality, and the Intellectual Origins of the French Revolution*. Princeton: Princeton University Press, 2007.

—*Sans-Culottes: An Eighteenth-Century Emblem in the French Revolution*. Princeton: Princeton University Press, 2008.

Spector, C. *Au Prisme de Rousseau: usages politiques contemporains*. Oxford: Voltaire Foundation, 2011.

Spitz, J.-F. *La liberté politique: Essai de généalogie conceptuelle*. Paris: Presses Universitaires de France, 1995.

Strauss, L. *What Is Political Philosophy?* Chicago: University of Chicago Press, 1959. pg. 45

Terrel, J. *Les Théories du pacte social: Droit natural, souveraineté et contrat de Bodin à Rousseau*. Paris: Éditions due Seuil, 2001.

Whatmore, R. *Against War and Empire: Geneva, Britain, and France in the Eighteenth Century*. New Haven: Yale University Press, 2012.

Wootton, D. "Introduction." In *The Basic Political Writings* by J.-J. Rousseau. Translated by D. Cress. Indianapolis: Hackett Pub. Co., 2011.

Yack, B. *The Longing for Total Revolution: Philosophic Sources of Social Discontent from Rousseau to Marx and Nietzsche*. Berkeley: University of California Press, 1992.

CHAPTER FIVE

Altmann, A. *Moses Mendelssohn: A Biographical Study*. Tuscaloosa: University of Alabama Press, 1973.

Arkush, A. *Moses Mendelssohn and the Enlightenment*. Albany: State University of New York Press, 1994.

Bachmann, H.-M. *Die naturrechtliche Staatslehre Christian Wolffs*. Berlin: Duncker und Humblot, 1977.

Beiser, F. *Diotima's Children: German Aesthetic Rationalism from Leibniz to Lessing*. Oxford: Oxford University Press, 2009.

Berghahn, K. "On Friendship: The Beginnings of a Christian-Jewish Dialogue in the 18th Century." In *The German-Jewish Dialogue Reconsidered:*

A Symposium in Honor of George L. Mosse, edited by K. Berghahn, New York: Peter Lang, 1996.

Blum, C. *Rousseau and the Republic of Virtue: The Language of Politics in the French Revolution*. Ithaca: Cornell University Press, 1986.

Bourel, D. *La naissance du judaïsme moderne*. Paris: Gallimard, 2004.

—"Les Réserves de Mendelssohn: Rousseau, Voltaire et les Juif de Berlin." *Revue Internationale de Philosophie* 32 (1978): pp. 309–326.

Cassirer, E. *Rousseau, Kant and Goethe*. New York: Harper, 1963.

Erlin, M. *Berlin's Forgotten Future: City, History and Enlightenment in Eighteenth-Century Germany*. Chapel Hill: University of North Carolina Press, 2004.

—"Reluctant Modernism: Moses Mendelssohn's Philosophy of History." *Journal of the History of Ideas* 63:1 (2002): pp. 83–104.

Freudenthal, G. *No Religion Without Idolatry: Mendelssohn's Jewish Enlightenment*. Notre Dame: University of Notre Dame Press, 2012.

Gottlieb, M. *Faith and Freedom: Moses Mendelssohn's Theological Political Thought*. New York: Oxford University Press, 2011.

—*Moses Mendelssohn: Writings on Judaism, Christianity and the Bible*. Waltham: Brandeis University Press, 2011.

Hamann, J.G. *Abaelardi Virbii Chimärische Einfälle über den zehnten Theil der Briefe die Neuste Literatur betreffend*. Königsberg, 1761.

Hornig, G. "Perfektibilität: Eine Untersuchung zur Geschichte und Bedeutung dieses Begriffs in der deutschsprachigen Literatur." *Archiv für Begriffsgeschichte* 24 (1980): pp. 221–273.

Jaumann, H., ed. *Rousseau in Deutschland: Neue Beiträge zur Erforschung seiner Rezeption*. Berlin: Walter de Gruyter, 1995.

Kayserling, M. *Moses Mendelssohn: Sein Leben und seine Werke*. Leipzig, 1862.

Kors. A., ed. *Encyclopedia of the Enlightenment*, 4 vols. New York: Oxford University Press, 2003.

Liebeschütz, H. "Mendelssohn und Lessing in ihrer Stellung zur Geschichte." In *Studies in Jewish Religious and Intellectual History*, edited by S. Stein and R. Loewe, pp. 167–182. University: University of Alabama Press, 1979.

Litvak, O. *Haskalah: The Romantic Movement in Judaism*. New Brunswick: Rutgers University Press, 2012.

Marks, J. "Rousseau's Use of the Jewish Example." *The Review of Politics* 72 (2010): pp. 463–481.

Mendelssohn, Moses. *Gesammelte Schriften. Jubiläumsausgabe*. 27 vols. Stuttgart: Frommann, 1972-.

—*Biur Milot Ha-Higayon*. 1760.

—*Jerusalem* (1783).

—*Kohelet Musar* (1758?).

Meyer, M., ed. *German-Jewish History in Modern Times*, 4 vols. New York: Columbia University Press, 1996.

Rapp, F. and H.-W. Schuett, eds. *Philosophie und Wissenschaft in Preussen*. Berlin: Universitätsbibliothek, 1982.

Rosenblatt, H. "Luxury." In *Encyclopedia of the Enlightenment*, edited by A. Kors, 4 vols, vol. II, pp. 440–445. New York: Oxford University Press, 2003.

—*Rousseau and Geneva: From the First Discourse to the Social Contract, 1749–1762*. Cambridge: Cambridge University Press, 1997.

Rotenstreich, N. "On Mendelssohn's Political Philosophy." *Leo Baeck Institute Yearbook* 11 (1966), pp. 28–41.

Rousseau, J.-J., *Rousseau patriotische Vorstellungen gegen die Einführung eine Schaubühne in Genf.* Zurich, 1761.

Schmidt, J., ed. *What Is Enlightenment? Eighteenth-Century Answers and Twentieth-Century Questions*. Berkeley: University of California Press, 1996.

Sorkin, D. *Moses Mendelssohn and the Religious Enlightenment*. Berkeley: University of California Press, 1996.

Tubach, F. "Perfectibilité: der zweite Diskurs Rousseau und die deutsche Aufklärung." *Etudes Germaniques* 15 (1960): pp. 155–151.

Wiedemann, C., ed. *Rom-Paris-London: Erfahrung und Selbsterfahrung deutscher Schriftsteller und Künstler in den fremden Metropolen*. Stuttgart: Metzler, 1988.

CHAPTER SIX

Berry, C. "Smith under Strain." *European Journal of Political Theory* 3 (2004): pp. 455–463.

Delatour, A. *Adam Smith, sa vie, ses travaux, ses doctrines*. Paris: Guillaumin, 1886.

Dent, N. *Rousseau: An Introduction to his Psychological, Social and Political Theory*. Oxford: Blackwell, 1988.

Faccarello, G. "A Tale of Two Traditions: Pierre Force's Self-Interest before Adam Smith." *European Journal of the History of Economic Thought* 12:4 (2005): pp. 701–712.

Force, P. "Putting Categorizations in Context." *The Adam Smith Review* 3 (2007): pp. 211–214.

—*Self-Interest before Adam Smith. A Genealogy of Economic Science*. Cambridge: Cambridge University Press, 2003.

—"Self-Love, Identification, and the Origin of Political Economy." *Yale French Studies* 92 (1997): pp. 46–64.

Goldschmidt, V. *Anthropologie et politique. Les principes du système de Rousseau*. Paris: J. Vrin, 1974.

Hont, I. *Politics in Commercial Society: Jean-Jacques Rousseau and Adam Smith*. Cambridge, MA: Harvard University Press, 2015.

Hont, I. and M. Ignatieff. "Needs and Justice in the Wealth of Nations." In *Jealousy of Trade: International Competition and the Nation-State in Historical Perspective*, edited by I. Hont, pp. 389–443. Cambridge, MA: Harvard University Press, 2006.

Hundert, E. *The Enlightenment's Fable: Bernard Mandeville and the Discovery of Society*. Cambridge: Cambridge University Press, 1994.

Hurtado, J. "Pity, Sympathy and Self-Interest: Review of Pierre Force's Self-Interest before Adam Smith." *European Journal of the History of Economic Thought* 12:4 (2005): pp. 713–721.

Ignatieff, M. *The Needs of Strangers*. London: Chatto & Windus, 1984.

—"Smith, Rousseau and the Republic of Needs." In *Scotland and Europe 1200–1850*, edited by T. Smout, pp. 187–206. Edinburgh: John Donald, 1986.

Larrère, C. "Adam Smith et Jean-Jacques Rousseau: sympathie et pitié." *Kairos. Revue de Philosophie* 20 (2002): pp. 73–94.

Macfie, A. *The Individual and Society: Papers on Adam Smith*. London: George Allen & Unwin, 1967.

Marshall, D. *The Figure of Theater: Shaftesbury, Defoe, Adam Smith, and George Eliot*. New York: Columbia University Press, 1988.

Meek, R. *Social Science and the Ignoble Savage*. Cambridge: Cambridge University Press, 1976.

Morrow, R. *The Ethical and Economic Theories of Adam Smith: A Study in the Social Philosophy of the Eighteenth Century*. New York: Longmans, Green, and Co., 1923.

Pack, S. *Review of Self-Interest before Adam Smith. Journal of the History of Economic Thought* 27:4 (2005): pp. 465–467.

—"The Rousseau-Smith Connection: Towards an Understanding of Professor West's 'Splenetic Smith.'" *History of Economic Ideas* 8:3 (2000): pp. 35–62.

Raphael, D. *Adam Smith*. Oxford: Oxford University Press, 1985.

Rousseau, J.-J. *The Collected Writings of Rousseau*. Edited by Christopher Kelly, Roger D. Masters, and Peter Stillman. Translated by Christopher Kelly. 13 vols. Hanover: Published for Dartmouth College by University Press of New England, 1990–2010.

Schliesser, E. Review of Pierre Force, *Self-Interest before Adam Smith*. *The Adam Smith Review* 3 (2007): pp. 203–211.

Sewall, R. "Rousseau's Second Discourse in England from 1755 to 1762." *Philological Quarterly* 17:2 (1938): pp. 97–114.

Smith, A. *The Glasgow Edition of the Works and Correspondence of Adam Smith*. 6 Vols. Oxford: Oxford University Press, 1976–1983.

Tribe, K. Review of P. Force, *Self-Interest before Adam Smith*. *History of Economic Ideas* 12:3 (2004): pp. 123–125.

Vivenza, G. Review of *Self-Interest before Adam Smith: A Genealogy of Economic Science*. EH.NET, September 2004: http://eh.net/book_reviews/self-interest-before-adam-smith-a-genealogy-of-economic-science/ (Accessed September 16, 2014).

Winch, D. *Riches and Poverty. An Intellectual History of Political Economy in Britain*. Cambridge: Cambridge University Press, 1996.

CHAPTER SEVEN

Alembert, Jean Le Rond d'. *Oeuvres complètes de d'Alembert*. 5 Vols. Paris, 1822.

Badinter, E., ed. *Qu'est-ce une femme?* Paris: P.O.L., 1989.

Bonnet, J.-C. *Naissance du Panthéon: Essai sur la culte des grands hommes*. Paris: Fayard, 1998.

Boon, S. *The Life of Madame Necker: Sin, Redemption, and the Parisian Salon*. London: Pickering & Chatto, 2011.

Brown, G. *A Field of Honor: Writers, Court Culture and Public Theater in French Literary Life from Racine to the Revolution*. New York: Columbia University Press, 2005.

Craveri, B. *The Age of Conversation*. Translated by T. Waugh. New York: New York Review Books, 2005.

Darnton, R. "The High Enlightenment and the Low-Life of Literature." In *The Literary Underground of the Old Regime*, pp. 1–40. Cambridge, MA: Harvard University Press, 1982.

Daston, L. "The Naturalized Female Intellect." *Science in Context* 5 (1992): pp. 209–235.

De Bellegarde, M. *Réflexions sur le ridicule*. Paris, 1696.

Delille, J. *Oeuvres avec les notes de Parcerval*. Paris, 1836.

Dubeau, C. "L'Epreuve du salon ou Le Monde comme performance dans les Mélanges et les Nouveaux Mélanges de Suzanne Necker." *Cahiers staëliens* 57 (2006): pp. 201–225.

—*La lettre et la mère: Roman familial et écriture de la passion chez Suzanne Necker et Germaine de Staël*. Quebec: Presses De L'Université Laval, 2013.

Goldsmith, E. and D. Goodman, eds. *Going Public: Women and Publishing in Early Modern France*. Ithaca: Cornell University Press, 1995.

Goodman, D. *The Republic of Letters: A Cultural History of the French Enlightenment*. Ithaca: Cornell University Press, 1994.

—"Suzanne Necker's Mélanges: Gender, Writing, and Publicity." In *Going Public: Women and Publishing in Early Modern France*, edited by E. Goldsmith and D. Goodman, pp. 210–223. Ithaca: Cornell University Press, 1995.

Henriet, M. *L'académicien Thomas (1732–1785) d'après des correspondances inédits*. Paris: H. Leclerc, 1918.

Hepp, N. "La belle et la bête, ou la femme et le pédant dans l'universe romanesque du XVIIe Siècle." *Revue d'Histoire littéraire de la France* 77:3/4 (1977): pp. 564–577.

Klein, L. and A. La Vopa, eds. *Enthusiasm and Enlightenment in Europe, 1650–1850*. San Marino: Huntington Library, 1998.

Lilti, A. *Figures publiques: L'invention de la célébrité*. Paris: Fayard, 2014.

McMahon, D. *Divine Fury: A History of Genius*. New York: Basic Books, 2013.

Micard, E. *Un écrivain académique au XVIIIe siècle, Antoine-Léonard Thomas (1732–1785)*. Paris: E. Champion, 1924.

Necker, S. *Mélanges extraits des manuscrits de Mme. Necker*. Paris, 1798.

—*Nouveaux Mélanges extraits des manuscrits de Mme. Necker*. Paris, 1801.

Pocock, J. *Barbarism and Religion. Volume I: The Enlightenments of Edward Gibbon, 1737–1764*. Cambridge: Cambridge University Press, 1999.

Rosenblatt, H. *Rousseau and Geneva from the First Discourse to the Social Contract, 1749–1762.* Cambridge: Cambridge University Press, 1997.

Russo, E. *Styles of Enlightenment: Taste, Politics, and Authorship in Eighteenth-Century France.* Baltimore: Johns Hopkins University Press, 2007.

Thomas, A.L. *Essai sur le caractère, les moeurs et l'espirit des femmes dans les différents siècles.* 1772.

—*Essai sur les éloges, ou histoire de la littérature et de l'éloquence.* 1773. Reprint, Paris, 1812.

—*Oeuvres.* 4 Vols. Paris, 1792.

Villa, A. *Enlightenment and Pathology: Sensibility in the Literature and Medicine of Eighteenth-Century France.* Baltimore: Johns Hopkins University Press, 1998.

La Vopa, A. "Sexless Minds at Work and at Play: Poullain de la Barre and the Origins of Early Modern Feminism." *Representations* 109 (2010): pp. 57–94.

Waquet, F. *Latin or the Empire of the Sign.* Translated by J. Howe. London: Verso, 2001.

CHAPTER EIGHT

L'Aminot, T. "D'Holbach et Rousseau ou la relation déplaisante." *Corpus: Revue de philosophie* no. 22/23 (1993): pp. 117–128.

—ed. *Politique et révolution chez Jean-Jacques Rousseau.* Oxford: Voltaire Foundation, 1994.

Archives Parlementaires. Series 1 (1787–1794). Edited by M.J. Mavidal et al. 102 Vols. Paris, 1879–2005.

Badinet, E, ed. *Correspondance inédite de Condorcet et Mme Suard, M. Suard, et Garat (1771–1791).* Paris: Fayard, 1988.

Bonnerot, O.-H. "Louis-Sebastian Mercier: lecteur et éditeur de Jean-Jacques Rousseau." In *Rousseau, l'Émile et la Révolution*, edited by Robert Thiery, pp. 415–423. Paris: Universitas, 1992.

Carra, J.-L. *Annales patriotiques et littéraires de la France.*

Cérruti, J. *Supplément au Journal de Paris* 336 (2 December 1789): pp. 1567–1568.

Cohen, J. *Rousseau: A Free Community of Equals.* Oxford: Oxford University Press, 2010.

Crow, T. *Emulation: David, Drouais, and Girodet in the Art of Revolutionary France.* New Haven: Yale University Press, 2006.

Culoma, M. *La Religion civile de Rousseau à Robespierre.* Paris: Harmattan, 2010.

Curran, M. *Atheism, Religion and Enlightenment in pre-Revolutionary Europe.* Woodbridge: Boydell Press, 2012.

Cushing, M. "Baron d'Holbach: A Study of Eighteenth Century Radicalism in France." PhD Dissertation: Columbia University, 1914.

Damrosch, L. *Jean-Jacques Rousseau.* Boston: Houghton Mifflin, 2005.

De Bolla, P. *The Architecture of Concepts: The Historical Formation of Human Rights.* New York: Fordham University Press, 2013.

[Feller, F.] *Journal historique* (Maastricht, 15 January 1793).

Gagnebin, B. "L'Influence de Rousseau sur la Déclaration des droits de l'Homme et du citoyen." In *Reappraisals of Rousseau: Studies in Honour of R. A. Leigh*, edited by S. Harvey et al., pp. 75–89. Manchester: Manchester University Press, 1980.

Garrard, G. *Rousseau's Counter-Enlightenment: A Republican Critique of the Philosophes*. Albany: State University of New York Press, 2003.

Ginguené, P.-L. *Lettres sur les Confessions de J.J. Rousseau*. Paris, 1791.

D'Holbach, P.H.T., Baron. *La Morale universalle, ou Les Devoirs de l'homme fondés sur sa nature*. 3 vols. Amsterdam, 1776.

—Baron. *La Politique naturelle*. Amsterdam, 1773.

—Baron. *Le Bon-Sens du cé J. Meslier suivi de son testament*. Londres [Amsterdam], 1772.

Hulliung, M. *The Autocritique of Enlightenment: Rousseau and the Philosophes*. Cambridge, MA: Harvard University Press, 1994.

Hunt, L. "Louis XVI wasn't killed by Ideas. This is what happens when you ignore the role of Politics in Intellectual History." *New Republic*, 27 June 2014.

Israel, J. *Democratic Enlightenment: Philosophy, Revolution and Human Rights 1750–1790*. Oxford: Oxford University Press, 2011.

—*Revolutionary Ideas: An Intellectual History of the French Revolution from the Rights of Man to Robespierre*. Princeton: Princeton University Press, 2014.

Jayne, A. *Jefferson's Declaration of Independence: Origins, Philosophy and Theology*. Lexington: University Press of Kentucky, 1998.

Lemay, E. "Le Part d'Émile dans la « regéneration » de 1789." In *Rousseau, l'Émile et la Révolution*, edited by R. Thiery, pp. 375–383. Paris: Universitas, 1992.

Lemny, S. *Jean-Louis Carra (1742–1793): parcours d'un révolutionniare*. Paris: Harmattan, 2000.

Loft, L. *Passion, Politics and Philosophie: Rediscovering J.P. Brissot*. Westport: Greenwood Press, 2002.

McPhee, P. *Robespierre: A Revolutionary Life*. New Haven: Yale University Press, 2012.

Mercier, L. *De J.J. Rousseau considéré comme l'un des premiers auteurs de la Révolution*. Paris, 1791.

Müller, L. "Marie-Therèse Lavasseur." In *Dictionnaire de Jean-Jacques Rousseau*, edited by R. Trousson and F. Eigeldinger, pp. 539–544. Paris: H. Champion, 2006.

Naigeon, J. "Lettres sur la mort de M. Le baron d'Holbach." *Journal de Paris* 40 (9 February 1789): pp. 176–177.

Naville, P. *Paul Thiry d'Holbach et la philosophie scientifique au XVIIIe siècle*. Paris: Gallimard, 1943.

Raynal, T. G. *T.G. Raynal démasqué, ou Lettres sur la vie et les ouvrages de cet écrivain*. Paris, 1791.

Riley, P. *The General Will before Rousseau: The Transformation of the Divine into the Civic*. Princeton: Princeton University Press, 1986.

Robespierre, M. *Le Défenseur*.

Rousseau, J.-J. *The Confessions.* In *The Collected Writings of Rousseau.* Edited by Christopher Kelly, Roger D. Masters, and Peter Stillman. Translated by Christopher Kelly. Vol. 5. Hanover: Published for Dartmouth College by University Press of New England, 1995.

Scurr, R. *Fatal Purity: Robespierre and the French Revolution.* London: Vintage, 2006.

Staum, M. *Cabanis: Enlightenment and Medical Philosophy in the French Revolution.* Princeton: Princeton University Press, 1980.

Swenson, J. *On Jean-Jacques Rousseau Considered as One of the First Authors of the Revolution.* Stanford: Stanford University Press, 2000.

Trousson, R. *Jean-Jacques Rousseau.* Paris: Tallandier, 2003.

Urbinati, N. *Representative Democracy: Principles and Genealogy.* Chicago: University of Chicago Press, 2006.

Valsania, M. *The Limits of Optimism: Thomas Jefferson's Dualistic Enlightenment.* Charlottesville: University of Virginia Press, 2011.

Vercruysse, J. *Bibliographie descriptive des écrits du Baron d'Holbach.* Paris: Minard, 1971.

Villaverde, M. "Rousseau, lecteur de Spinoza." *Studies on Voltaire and the Eighteenth Century* 369 (1999): pp. 107–139.

—"Spinoza, Rousseau: dos concepciones de democracia." *Revista de estudios políticos* 116 (2002): pp. 85–106.

Williams, D. "Spinoza and the General Will." *The Journal of Politics* 72 (2010): pp. 341–356.

Wokler, R. *Rousseau, the Age of Enlightenment and Their Legacies.* Princeton: Princeton University Press, 2012.

—*The Social Thought of J.J. Rousseau.* New York: Garland, 1987.

CHAPTER NINE

Ballstadt, K. *Diderot: Natural Philosopher.* Oxford: Voltaire Foundation, 2008.

Citton, Y. "Retour sur la misérable querelle Rousseau-Diderot: Position, conséquence, spectacle et sphère publique." *Recherches sur Diderot et sur l'Encyclopédie* 36 (2004): http://rde.revues.org/index282.html.

Diderot, D. *Oeuvres complètes.* Edited by H. Dieckmann et al. 28 vols. Paris: Hermann, 1975-.

Fabre, J. "Frères ennemis: Diderot et Jean-Jacques." *Diderot Studies* 3 (1961): pp. 155–213.

Gatefin, E. *Diderot, Sénèque et Jean-Jacques: Un dialogue à trois voix.* Amsterdam: Rodopi, 2007.

Israel, J. *Democratic Enlightenment: Philosophy, Revolution, and Human Rights 1750–1790.* Oxford: Oxford University Press, 2011.

—*Enlightenment Contested: Philosophy, Modernity, and the Emancipation of Man 1670–1752.* Oxford: Oxford University Press, 2006.

Melzer, A. *The Natural Goodness of Man: On the System of Rousseau's Thought.* Chicago: University of Chicago Press, 1990.

Rousseau, J.-J. *Oeuvres complètes.* 5 vols. Paris: Gallimard, Bibliothèqu de la Pléiade, 1959–1969.

Russo, E. "Slander and Glory in the Republic of Letters: Diderot and Seneca Confront Rousseau." *Republics of Letters: A Journal for the Study of Knowledge, Politics, and the Arts* 1:1 (2009): http://rofl.stanford.edu/node/40.

Shea, L. *The Cynic Enlightenment: Diogenes in the Salon.* Baltimore: Johns Hopkins University Press, 2009.

Stalnaker, J. "Diderot's Brain." In *Philosophical Turns: Eighteenth-Century Literature, Thought, and Aesthetics,* edited by A. Conway and M.H. McMurran. Forthcoming.

CHAPTER TEN

Guyer, P. "Freedom as the Foundation of Morality: Kant's Early Efforts." In *Kant's 'Observations' and 'Remarks': A Critical Guide,* edited by S. Shell and R. Velkley, pp. 77–98. Cambridge: Cambridge University Press, 2012.

Kant, I. *Anthropology, History, and Education.* Edited by Günther Zöller. Cambridge: Cambridge University Press, 2007.

—*Bemerkungen zu den Beobachtungen über das Gefühl des Schönen und Erhabenen.* Edited by M. Rischmüller. Hamburg: F. Meiner Verlag, 1991.

—*Kant's gessamelte Schriften.* 29 vols. Berlin: G. Reimer, 1902-.

—*Observations on the Feeling of the Beautiful and Sublime and Other Writings.* Edited by P. Frierson and P. Guyer. Cambridge: Cambridge University Press, 2011.

Rousseau, J.-J. *Oeuvres complètes.* 5 vols. Paris: Gallimard, Bibliothèqu de la Pléiade, 1959–1969.

CHAPTER ELEVEN

Austen, J. *Pride and Prejudice, The Complete Novels.* London: Penguin, 2006.

Backscheider, P. *Eighteenth-Century Women Poets and Their Poetry.* Baltimore: Johns Hopkins University Press, 2005.

Bending, S. *Green Retreats: Women, Gardens and Eighteenth-Century Culture.* Cambridge: Cambridge University Press, 2013.

Berman, M. *The Politics of Authenticity: Radical Individualism and the Emergence of Modern Society.* New York: Atheneum, 1970.

Burke, E. *A Philosophical Enquiry into the Origins of Our Ideas of the Sublime and the Beautiful.* 1759.

Carter, P. *Men and the Emergence of Polite Society: Britain, 1660–1800.* London: Longman, 2001.

Chandler, J., ed. *The Cambridge History of English Romantic Literature.* Cambridge: Cambridge University Press, 2009.

Damrosch, L. *Jean-Jacques Rousseau: Restless Genius.* New York: Houghton Mifflin, 2005.

Duffy, E. *Rousseau in England: The Context for Shelley's Critique of the Enlightenment*. Berkeley: University of California Press, 1979.

Ferguson, A. *An Essay on the History of Civil Society*. 1767.

Furbank, P. *Diderot: A Critical Biography*. London: Minerva, 1993.

Haggerty, G. *Men in Love: Masculinity and Sexuality in the Eighteenth Century*. New York: Columbia University Press, 1999.

Havens, R. "Solitude and the Neoclassicists." *English Literary History* 21:4 (1954): pp. 251–273.

Hill, B. "A Refuge from Men: The Idea of a Protestant Nunnery." *Past and Present* 117 (1987): pp. 107–130.

Holmes, Richard. "Introduction." In *A Short Residence in Sweden and Memoirs of the Author of a 'Vindication of the Rights of Woman'* by Mary Wollstonecraft and William Godwin, pp. 36–42. Harmondsworth: Penguin, 1987.

Johnson, S. *The History of Rasselas: Prince of Abissinia*. 1759.

Koch, P. *Solitude: A Philosophical Encounter*. Chicago: Open Court, 1994.

Laqueur, T. *Solitary Sex: A Cultural History of Masturbation*. New York: Zone Books, 2003.

Leigh, R.A. "Boswell and Rousseau." *The Modern Language Review* 47:3 (1952): pp. 290–318.

Mossner, E. *The Life of David Hume*. Oxford: Oxford University Press, 1980.

Mullan, J. *Sentiment and Sociability: the Language of Feeling in the Eighteenth Century*. Oxford: Oxford University Press, 1988.

Neidleman, J. "Rousseau and the Desire for Communion." *Eighteenth-Century Studies* 47:1 (2013): pp. 53–67.

Noyes, W. "The Insanity of Jean-Jacques Rousseau." *The American Journal of Psychology*. 3:3 (1890): pp. 406–429.

Pearson, J. *Women's Reading in Britain, 1750–1835: A Dangerous Recreation*. Cambridge: Cambridge University Press, 1999.

Porter, R. *Enlightenment: Britain and the Creation of the Modern World*. London: Penguin, 2000.

Rousseau, J.-J. *Emile, or On Education*. Translated by A. Bloom. London: Penguin, 1991.

—*Letter to D'Alembert on the Theatre*. In *Politics and the Arts*. Translated by A. Bloom. Ithica: Cornell University Press, 1991.

—*Rêveries of the Solitary Walker*. Translated by P. France. London: Penguin, 1979.

—*The Collected Writings of Rousseau*. Edited by Christopher Kelly, Roger D. Masters, and Peter Stillman. Translated by Christopher Kelly. 13 vols. Hanover: Published for Dartmouth College by University Press of New England, 1990–2010.

—*The Confessions*. Translated by J. Cohen. London: Penguin, 1973.

—*The Discourses and Other Early Political Writings*. Edited and translated by Victor Gourevitch. Cambridge: Cambridge University Press, 1997.

—*The Social Contract and Other Later Political Writings*. Edited and translated by Victor Gourevitch. Cambridge: Cambridge University Press, 1997.

Sayre, R. *Solitude in Society: A Sociological Study of French Literature*. Cambridge, MA: Harvard University Press, 1978.

Schwartz, J. *The Sexual Politics of Jean-Jacques Rousseau.* Chicago: University of Chicago Press, 1984.

Seigel, J. *The Idea of the Self.* Cambridge: Cambridge University Press, 2005.

Shea, L. *The Cynic Enlightenment: Diogenes in the Salon.* Baltimore: Johns Hopkins University Press, 2010.

Smith, A. *The Theory of Moral Sentiments. 1759. Reprint,* Cambridge: Cambridge University Press, 2002.

Spacks, P. *Privacy: Concealing the Eighteenth-Century Self.* Chicago: University of Chicago Press, 2003.

Starobinski, J. *Transparency and Obstruction.* Chicago: University of Chicago Press, 1988.

Taylor, B. *Mary Wollstonecraft and the Feminist Imagination.* Cambridge: Cambridge University Press, 2003.

—"Separations of Soul: Solitude, Biography, History." *American Historical Review* 114:3 (2009): pp. 640–651.

Todd, J. *The Sign of Angelica: Women, Writing and Fiction, 1660–1800.* London: Virago Press, 1989.

Todorov, T. *Imperfect Garden: The Legacy of Humanism.* Princeton: Princeton University Press, 2002.

Wollstonecraft, M. *Collected Letters of Mary Wollstonecraft.* Edited by R. Wardle. Ithica: Cornell University Press, 1979.

—*The Works of Mary Wollstonecraft.* 7 vols. Edited by J. Todd and M. Butler. London: Pickering, 1989.

CHAPTER TWELVE

Annales Benjamin Constant. 8–9: Le Groupe de Coppet et la Révolution francaise. Lausanne & Paris: Institut Benjamin Constant & Jean Touzot, 1988.

Berman, M. *The Politics of Authenticity: Radical Individualism and the Emergence of Modern Society.* Second edition. London: Verso, 2009.

Constant, B. *Oeuvres Complètes, vol. IV. Discours au Tribunat. De la possibilité d'une constitution républicaine dans un grand pays (1799–1803).* Edited by M. Sánchez-Mejia and K. Klooke. Tübingen: Niemeyer Verlag, 2005.

Craiutu, A. "Flirting with Republicanism: Madame de Staël's Writings from the 1790s." *History of European Ideas* 36:3 (2010): pp. 343–346.

—"Moderation and the Group of Coppet." In *Germaine de Staël's Politics of Mediation: Challenges to History and Culture,* edited by K. Szmurlo, pp. 109–124. Oxford: Voltaire Foundation, 2011.

—A Tale of Two Moderates." *History of European Ideas* 39:1 (2013): pp. 141–150.

—*A Virtue for Courageous Minds: Moderation in French Political Thought, 1748–1830.* Princeton: Princeton University Press, 2012.

De Diesbach, G. *Madame de Staël.* Paris: Perrin, 1983.

De Staël, G. *Considerations on the Principal Events of the French Revolution.* Edited by A. Craiutu. Indianapolis: Liberty Fun, 2008.

—*Des circonstances actuelles qui peuvent terminer la Révolution et des principes qui doivent fonder la république en France.* Edited by L. Omacini. Geneva: Slatkine, 1979.

—*Lettres sur les écrits et le caractère de J.J. Rousseau.* In *Oeuvres Complètes de Madame la Barone de Staël publiées par son fils.* Vol. 1. Paris: Treuttel and Würtz, 1821.

—*Oeuvres Complètes, Série III: Oeuvres historiques, Tome I, Des circonstanceos actuelles et autres essais politiques sous la Révolution.* Edited by L. Omacini. Paris: Honoré Champion, 2009.

Furet, F. and M. Ozouf, eds. *A Critical Dictionary of the French Revolution.* Cambridge, MA: Harvard University Press, 1989.

Gengembre, G. and J. Goldzink. "Une femme révolutionnée: le Thermidor de Mme de Staël," *Annals Benjamin Constant* 8–9. Lausanne & Paris: Institute Benjamin Constant & Jean Touzot, 1988, p. 275.

Grange, H. *Les idées de Necker.* Paris: Klinksieck, 1974.

Gwynne, G. *Madame de Staël et la Révolution française.* Paris: A.G. Nizet, 1969.

Jaume, L. *L'Individu effacé ou le paradoxe du libéralisme français.* Paris: Fayard, 1997.

—ed. *Coppet, creuset de l'esprit libéral: les idées politiques et constitutionnelles du group de Madame de Staël.* Marseille & Paris: Presses Universitaires d'Aix-Marseille & Economica, 2000.

Lottérie, F. and G. Poisson, eds. *Jean-Jacques Rousseau devant Coppet.* Geneva: Slatkine, 2012.

Marso, L. *(Un)Manly Citizens: Jean-Jacques Rousseau's and Germaine de Staël's Subversive Women.* Baltimore: Johns Hopkins University Press, 2001.

Mortier, R. "Comment terminer la Révolution et fonder le République," *Annales Benjamin Constant* 8–9. Laussane & Paris: Institute Benjamin Constant & Jean Touzot, 1988, pp. 293–307.

Munteano, B. *Les idées politiques de Madame de Staël et la Constitution de l'an III.* Paris: Les Belles Lettres, 1931.

Orwin, C. and N. Tarcov, eds. *The Legacy of Rousseau.* Chicago: University of Chicago Press, 1997.

Paulet-Grandguillot, E. *Libéralisme et démocratie. De Sismondi à Constant, à partir du Contrat social (1801–1806).* Geneva: Slatkine, 2010.

Roussel, J. *Jean-Jacques Rousseau en France après la Révolution, 1795–1830.* Paris: Armand Colin, 1972.

Sismondi, J. *Recherches sur les constitutions des peuples libres.* Edited by Marco Minerbi. Geneva: Droz, 1965.

—*Libertà e scienza del governo in Sismondi, vol. II: Essais sur les constitutions des peoples libres.* Edited by R. di Reda. Rome: Jouvence, 1988.

Tilkin, F., ed. *Le groupe de Coppet et le monde moderne: conceptions-images-débats.* Geneva: Droz, 1998.

CHAPTER THIRTEEN

Grimsley, R. *The Philosophy of Rousseau.* Oxford: Oxford University Press, 1973.

Haubtmann, P., ed. *Carnets de P.-J. Proudhon.* 4 vols. Paris, 1960–1974.

—*Pierre-Joseph Proudhon: sa vie et sa pensée (1809–1849)*. Paris: Beauchesne, 1982.

Proudhon, P.-J. *Correspondance de P.-J. Proudhon*. Edited by J.-A. Langlois. Vol. 1. Paris: Lacroix, 1875.

—*De la célébration du dimanche*. 1839. Edited by M. Augé-Laribé. Paris: Rivière, 1926.

—*De la création de l'ordre dans l'humanité ou principes d'organisation politique*. 1843. Edited by C. Bougle and A. Cuvillier. Paris: Rivière, 1926.

—*De la Justice dans la Révolution et dans l'Église*. 1858. Edited by C. Bouglé and J-L. Puech, 4 vols. Paris: Rivière, 1930–1935.

—*Deuxième mémoire sur la propriété*. 1841. Edited by M. Augé-Laribé. Paris: Rivière, 1938.

—*L'Idée générale de la révolution au XIXe siècle*. 1851. Edited by A. Berthod. Paris: Rivière, 1924.

—*Property Is Theft! A Pierre-Joseph Proudhon Anthology*. Edited by I. McKay. Translated by P. Sharkey. Edinburgh: AK Press, 2011.

—*Qu'est-ce que la propriété?* 1840. Edited by M. Augé-Laribé. Paris: Rivière, 1926.

—*Qu'est-ce que la propriété? Deuxième mémoire: lettre à M. Blanqui sur la propriété*. 1841. Edited by M. Augé-Laribé. Paris: Rivière, 1938.

Proudhon, P.-J. *Système des contradictions économiques ou philosophie de la misère*. 1846. Edited by R. Picard. Paris: Rivière, 1923.

—*What Is Property?* Edited by D. Kelley and B. Smith. Cambridge: Cambridge University Press, 1994.

Rousseau, J.-J. *Oeuvres complètes*. 5 vols. Paris: Gallimard, Bibliothèqu de la Pléiade, 1959–1969.

Ryan, A. *Property and Political Theory*. New York: Basil Blackwell, 1984.

Starobinski, J. *J.-J. Rousseau, la transparence et l'obstacle, suivi de sept essais sur Rousseau*. Paris: Gallimard, 1948.

Vincent, K.S. *Benjamin Constant and the Birth of French Liberalism*. New York: Palgrave-Macmillan, 2011.

—*Pierre-Joseph Proudhon and the Rise of French Republican Socialism*. New York: Oxford University Press, 1984.

—"Pierre-Joseph Proudhon et son influence sur la pensée socialiste." *Corpus: revue de philosophie* 47 (2004): pp. 355–366.

CHAPTER FOURTEEN

Furet, F. and M. Ozouf. *A Critical Dictionary of the French Revolution*. Translated by A. Goldhammer. Cambridge, MA: Harvard University Press, 1989.

Kolakowski, L. *Main Currents of Marxism*. Translated by P. S. Falla. Volume 1. Oxford: Clarendon Press, 1978.

Marx, K. "Toward the Critique of Hegel's Philosophy of Law: Introduction." In *Writings of Young Marx on Philosophy and Society*. Translated and edited by L. Easton and K. Guddat. New York: Anchor Books, 1967.

—"The Eighteenth Brumaire of Louis Bonaparte." In Marx and Engels, *Selected Works in One Volume*. New York: International Publishers, 1968.

Marx, K. and F. Engels. *The German Ideology.* Translated by S. Ryazanskaya. London: Lawrence and Wishart, 1965.

Rousseau, J.-J. *Confessions.* Translated by J. Cohen. London: Penguin, 1953.

—*Emile, ou de l'éducation.* Translated by C. Wirz. Paris: Gallimard, 1969.

Seigel, J. *Marx's Fate: The Shape of a Life.* Princeton: Princeton University Press, 1976.

Starobinski, J. *Jean-Jacques Rousseau: Transparency and Obstruction.* Translated by A. Goldhammer. Chicago: University of Chicago Press, 1988.

CHAPTER FIFTEEN

Bates, D. "Political Theology and the Nazi State: Carl Schmitt's Concept of the Institution." *Modern Intellectual History* 3 (2006): pp. 415–452.

—*States of War: Enlightenment Origins of the Political.* New York: Columbia University Press, 2012.

Kojève, A. *Introduction to the Reading of Hegel.* Translated by J. Nichols. Ithica: Cornell University Press, 1980.

Lilla, M. "The Enemy of Liberalism." *New York Review of Books* 44:8 (May 15, 1997): pp. 38–44.

Müller, J.-W. "Visions of Global Order: Schmitt, Aron, and the Civil Servant of the World Spirit." In *A Dangerous Mind: Carl Schmitt in Post-War European Thought.* New Haven: Yale University Press, 2003.

Pasquino, P. "Between Machiavelli and Schmitt: Remarks on Rousseau's Dictatorship." *Storia del pensiero politico* 1 (2013): pp. 145–154.

Rossiter, C. *Constitutional Dictatorship: Crisis Government in Modern Democracies.* Princeton: Princeton University Press, 1948.

Rousseau, J.-J. *Extrait de projet de paix perperuelle de Monsieur L'Abbe de Saint-Pierre.* In *Oeuvres complètes.* Vol. 3. Paris: Gallimard, 1959.

—*The Discourses and Other Early Political Writings.* Edited and translated by Victor Gourevitch. Cambridge: Cambridge University Press, 1997.

—*The Social Contract and Other Later Political Writings.* Edited and translated by Victor Gourevitch. Cambridge: Cambridge University Press, 1997.

Schmitt, C. *Constitutional Theory.* Translated by J. Seitzer. Durham: Duke University Press, 2008.

—"Dem wahren Von Johann Jakob Rousseau." *Die Zürcher Woche* 26 (June 29, 1962).

—*Dictatorship: From the Origin of the Modern Concept of Sovereignty to Proletarian Class Struggle.* Translated by M. Hoelzl and G. Ward. Cambridge: Polity, 2014.

—*Legality and Legitimacy.* Translated by J. Seitzer. Durham: Duke University Press, 2004.

—*Political Theology: Four Chapters on the Concept of Sovereignty.* Translated by G. Schwab. Chicago: University of Chicago Press, 2005.

—"The Age of Neutralizations and Depoliticizations." In *Concept of the Political,* Translated by J. McCormick, 1929.

—*The Crisis of Parliamentary Democracy.* Translated by E. Kennedy. Cambridge, MA: MIT Press, 1988.

—*The Concept of the Political.* Translated by G. Schwab. Chicago, 1996.

—"The *Großraum* Order of International Law with a Ban on Intervention for Spatially Foreign Powers: A Contribution to the Concept of *Reich* in International Law." In *Writings on War.* Translated by T. Nunan. Cambridge: Polity, 2011.

—*The "Nomos" of the Earth in the International Law of the "Jus Publicum Europaem."* Translated by G. Ulmen. New York: Telos, 2003.

—*Theory of the Partisan: Intermediate Remark on the Concept of the Political.* Translated by G. Ulmen. New York: Telos, 2006.

Index

Feuillant movement, 161–162, 163–166
Florentine Histories (Machiavelli)
  law and authority in, 10
  redeemer figure in, 20–21
  republicanism in, 17–22
  Rousseau's discussion of, 7–13
Force, Pierre, 3, 115–131
Foscolo, Ugo, 9
founder, Machiavelli's political theory and role of, 19
Fragments d'un ouvrage abandonné sur la possibilité d'une constitution républicaine dans un grand pays (Constant), 242–244
France, cult of Greco-Roman antiquity in, 84–86
Franklin, Benjamin, 161–162
Frederik II King of Prussia, 22–28
freedom, reason and self-correction and, 198–202
French Revolution
  cult of Greco-Roman antiquity and, 84–86
  de Staël's reflections on, 247–249
  educational reform during, 170–171
  Enlightenment ideologies and, 149–174
  general will *vs.* rights in, 159–161
  d'Holbach and, 156–157
  Rousseau and, 4, 74–75
Friedländer Lectures on Anthropology, 204–207
friendship, Mendelssohn's discussion of, 98–99
Furet, François, 249–251

Gauffecourt, Vincent Capperonnier de, 65–66
gender
  eighteenth-century ideology concerning, 221–223
  in *Émile*, 225
  Kant's discussion of, 202–207
  in *La Nouvelle Héloïse*, 221–223, 226–230
  Rousseau's discussion of, 202–207
  Thomas and Necker on, 144–148
general will *(volonté générale)*
  d'Holbach and Rousseau on, 157–161, 163–166, 168
  Kant's focus on, 196–198
  Schmitt's theory and Rousseau's concept of, 277
Geneva Manuscript (Rousseau), 13–17
genius, Necker's and Thomas's discussion of, 140–148
Gentili, Alberico, 8
Georgics (Virgil), 135–136
Gerdil, Hyacinth, 42
The German Ideology (Marx), 269–271
Germany
  Machiavelli's discussion of, 10–13
  Rousseau's influence in, 3, 92–114
Ginguiné, Pierre Louis, 161–162, 163–167, 173–174

Godwin, William, 216–219, 230–234
*Gorsas, 151–153, 163
Gournay circle, 77–78
government
  private property and rise of, Smith's views on, 116–118
  sovereignty *vs.*, 56–58
Greco-Roman antiquity, French cult of, 84–86
The Greek Tradition in Republican Thought (Nelson), 78–81, 83–84
Grimm, Melchior, 63, 132–148, 153–155, 165–166, 213–216
Grossraume, Schmitt's theory of, 276–279
Grotius, Hugo, 63, 68–69, 86–87, 259
Guerci, Luciano, 84–86
*Guibert, 168
Guicciardini, Francesco, 23–28
Guyer, Paul, 201–202

Habermas, Jürgen, 276
Hampson, Norman, 73–74
*Hayek, 73–74
*Hébert, 166–167, 173–174
The Hebrew Republic (Nelson), 84
Hegel, G. F. W., 20–21, 84–86
Helvétius, Claude-Adrien, 4, 77–78, 157–159, 171–172, 173–174, 175–177
  Diderot and, 180–182, 183–184
*Hénault, 65–66
Herder, Johann, 193–196
hidden human nature, Kant's concept of, 193–196
hidden law, Kant's concept of, 193–196
Hisoria Critica Philosophiae (Brucker), 43–45
Histoire Naturelle de l'homme (Buffon), 177–185
Histoire Philosophique des Deux Indes ("Raynal"), 150–151, 168
history
  Kant's discussion of, 196–198
  Schmitt on politics and, 279–283
Hobbes, Thomas
  double contract theory and attack on, 54–56
  Mendelssohn and, 92–94
  on natural rights, 86–87, 196–198
  on partial associations, 52–54
  on representation, 58–59
  Rousseau and, 2, 37–62
  on sovereignty, 59–62, 281
  Strauss's critique of, 74–75
d'Holbach (Baron), 4, 38–39
  on equality, 168–169
  French Revolution and influence of, 156–157
  on "general will," 157–161, 163–166, 168
  Naigeon *and*, 153–155
  pantheonization movement and, 165–166
  Rousseau and, 149–174

For EU product safety concerns, contact us at Calle de José Abascal, 56–1°,
28003 Madrid, Spain or eugpsr@cambridge.org.

www.ingramcontent.com/pod-product-compliance
Ingram Content Group UK Ltd.
Pitfield, Milton Keynes, MK11 3LW, UK
UKHW020454240426
470322UK00016B/350